MW00423527

Detlef Lienau
(1818-1887)

The Domestic Architecture of Detlef Lienau, A Conservative Victorian

Ellen Weill Kramer
Edited by Dale Chodorow
Foreword by Mimi Findlay

ISBN 0-7414-2778-8

Cover design and book design by Dale Chodorow

Cover photographs: Bottom—Lockwood-Mathews Mansion Museum, Norwalk, Connecticut; Inset—Detlef Lienau (Paris, 1864)

Published by:

INFINITY
PUBLISHING.COM

1094 New DeHaven Street, Suite 100
West Conshohocken, PA 19428-2713
Info@buybooksontheweb.com
www.buybooksontheweb.com
Toll-free (877) BUY BOOK
Local Phone (610) 941-9999
Fax (610) 941-9959

Printed in the United States of America

Printed on Recycled Paper

Published March 2006

Table of Contents.

Part V. Appendices and Bibliography

List of Illustrations.

*Denotes building still standing (October 1957)

16. (76) *Blesch & Eidlitz. St. George's Church, Stuyvesant Square, New York, 1846-1848. From Meeks, "Romanesque before Richardson," *Art Bulletin*, Vol. XXXV (1953), Fig. 2.

17. (77) *Alexander Saeltzer. Astor Library, Astor Place, New York, 1849-1854. From *Putnam's Monthly Magazine*, Vol. II (1853), p. 13.

18. (78) Wall Street, 1850. Deroy lithograph from August Köllner painting. Eno Collection, No. 251, New York Public Library.

19. (--) Wall Street, corner of Water Street, 1849. From *New-York Pictorial and Business Directory of Wall-st., 1850*, plate VIII. Eno Collection, No. 230, New York Public Library. (Not found in dissertation.)

20. (82) Detlef Lienau. Michael Lienau Cottage, Jersey City, NJ. Study, c.1849. Portfolio I, No. 1, Lienau Collection.

21. (84) _____. Working drawing.

22. (87) *_____. Grace Church (Van Vorst), Erie Avenue and Second Street, Jersey City, NJ, 1850-1853. Old photo from *Grace Church Messenger*, 1915, p. 12, Lienau Collection.

23. (88) _____. Architect's rendering as originally planned. From *Grace Church Messenger*, 1915, p. 8, Lienau Collection.

24. (89) _____. Contract drawing, plan. Portfolio III, No. 3, Lienau Collection.

25. (90) _____. Interior. Old photo from *Grace Church Messenger*, 1915, p. 8, Lienau Collection.

26. (92) Lienau & Marcotte. Study for a church on Fifth Avenue, c.1852-1854. In folder, "Church Projects, Unexecuted," Portfolio III, Lienau Collection.

27. (99) Detlef Lienau. Shiff House, Fifth Avenue at 10th Street, New York, 1850-1852. Old photo, Lienau Collection.

28. (103) _____. Elevation drawing. Portfolio II, No. 3, Lienau Collection.

29. (103) John B. Snook. Haight House, Fifth Avenue at 15th Street, New York, c.1849. From *Putnam's Monthly Magazine*, Vol. III (1854), p. 240.

30. (108) Detlef Lienau. Shiff House. First floor plan.

31. (108) _____. Second floor plan.

32. (115) *_____. Cottenet Villa, Dobbs Ferry, NY, 1852. Architect's sketch, courtesy Mr. and Mrs. J. Fearon Brown.

33. (116) *Thomas R. Jackson. Stevens Castle, Hoboken, NJ, c.1852. Photo taken 1957, courtesy Mrs. Kathryn C. Waid, Stevens Institute of Technology.

34. (117) Detlef Lienau. Cottenet Villa. Old photo showing extension of c.1858-1859. From Lienau Collection.

35. (120) _____. Enlarged plan (additions of c.1858-1859 shaded). From *Villas on the Hudson*, 1860.

36. (121) _____. Drawing for the extension. Portfolio IV, No. 6, Lienau Collection.

37. (122) _____. Miller House, Jersey City, NJ, 1852. Elevation drawing. Portfolio VI, No. 10, Lienau Collection.

38. (123) _____. Mayo House, Elizabeth, NJ, c.1855-1856. Elevation drawing. Portfolio VI, No. 6, Lienau Collection.
39. (124) _____. First floor plan.
40. (125) _____. Toler House, Newark, NJ, c.1859. Watercolor rendering. Portfolio VI, No. 11, Lienau Collection.
41. (126) _____. First floor plan. Portfolio VI, No. 11.
42. (127) _____. "Beach Cliffe," Kane Villa, Newport, RI, 1852. Façade. Old photo, Lienau Collection.
43. (137) _____. Seaward view. Old photo, Lienau Collection.
44. (139) _____. Plan. Portfolio IV, No. 5, Lienau Collection.
45a, b, c. (131) *Downing & Vaux. Parish Villa, Newport, RI, 1852, 1855. From Downing and Scully, *Architectural Heritage of Newport*, plate 167.
46. (133) *Chateau-sur-mer, Newport, RI, 1852. Old photo from Downing and Scully, plate 165 top.
47. (140) *Leopold Eidlitz. The Chalet, Newport, RI, c.1854. Photo from Downing and Scully, plate 169 bottom.
48. (143) Renwick & Sands. Booth's Theater, Sixth Avenue at 23rd Street, 1868-1869. From *Building News*, Vol. XVI (1869), p. 290.
49. (144) Napoleon Le Brun. Masonic Hall, Sixth Avenue at 23rd Street, New York, 1870-1875. Competition drawing. From *American Architect and Builders' Monthly*, Vol. I (1870), between pp. 92-93.
50. (148) Detlef Lienau. William C. Schermerhorn House, 49 West 23rd Street, New York, c.1858-1859. Old photo from *Old Buildings of New York*, 1907, p.114.
51. (149) _____. Front elevation, working drawing. Portfolio V, No. 7, Lienau Collection.
52. (149) Thomas & Son. Union Club House, Fifth Avenue at 15th Street, New York, 1855. From *Ballou's*, Vol. IX (September 8, 1855), p. 45.
53. (150) Richard Morris Hunt. Rossiter House, East 36th Street, New York, 1855 ff. Old photo from *American Architect*, Vol. III (June 22, 1878), p. 216.
54. (151) Frederick Diaper. Daniel Parish House, 2 East 16th Street, New York, c.1854-1855. J.P. Newell lithograph, courtesy New-York Historical Society.
55. (152) Residence of John Jacob Astor II, Fifth Avenue at 33rd Street, New York, c.1859. Old photo of 1887, courtesy New-York Historical Society.
56. (153) Detlef Lienau. William C. Schermerhorn House. First floor plan, working drawing. Portfolio V, No. 7, Lienau Collection.
57. (153) _____. Second floor plan, working drawing.
58. (154) _____. Edmund Schermerhorn House, 45-47 West 23rd Street, New York, c.1867-1869. Front elevation, working drawing. Portfolio V, No. 8, Lienau Collection.
59. (155) _____. First story plan, working drawing.
60. (156) _____. Study for an unidentified house. Lienau Collection.

61. (157) John Kellum. A.T. Stewart's "Marble Palace," Fifth Avenue at 34th Street, New York, c.1867. Old photo from Brown, *Fifth Avenue*, p. 78.

62. (158) Detlef Lienau. Colford Jones Block, Fifth Avenue, 55th to 56th Streets, New York, 1868-1870. Old photograph, Lienau Collection.

63. (159) Robert Mook. Mary Mason Jones Block ("Marble Row"), Fifth Avenue, 57th to 58th Streets, New York, 1867-1869. Old photo from *King's Handbook of New York City*, 2nd edition, 1893, p. 747.

64. (161) Detlef Lienau. Colford Jones Block. Study. Portfolio VIII, No. 15, Lienau Collection.

65. (162) _____. Study.

66. (163) _____. Presentation drawing.

67. (163) _____. Study, first floor plan.

68. (164) _____. Working drawing, first floor plan.

69. (168) *Lewis M. Rutherfurd Row, 139-147 East 15th Street, New York, c.1852-1854. Photo, April 1957, courtesy Alfred Frazer.

70. (171) H.H. Holly. "The Terrace." From *Holly's Country Seats*, 1863, Design No. 30.

71. (169) A.J. Davis. "House of Mansions," Fifth Avenue, 41st to 42nd Streets, New York, 1856. From Eno Collection, No. 341, New York Public Library.

72. (174) *Detlef Lienau. LeGrand Lockwood Mansion, Norwalk, CT, c.1864-1868. Photo courtesy Lockwood-Mathews Mansion Museum.

73. (178) _____. Working drawing, front elevation. Portfolio IX, No. 16, Lienau Collection.

74. (180) _____. Detail from south. Photo courtesy Lockwood-Mathews Mansion Museum.

75a, b, c. (181, 182, 183) _____. First story plan as built. Courtesy City Planning Commission, Norwalk, CT.

76. (184) _____. Rotunda. Old photo, Lienau Collection.

77. (185) _____. Grand staircase. Old photo, Lienau Collection.

78. (186) _____. Music room. Old photo, Lienau Collection.

79. (187) _____. Drawing room. Old photo, Lienau Collection.

80. (191) *_____. "Düneck," Michael Lienau Villa, Ütersen, Germany, c.1872-1873. Old photo, Lienau Collection.

81. (191) _____. Elevation drawing. Portfolio XIV, No. 25, Lienau Collection.

82. (191) _____. First floor plan, working drawing.

83. (194) _____. Booraem Block, Second Street, Jersey City, NJ, 1871. Working drawing, elevation, right side only.

84. (198) *_____. Schermerhorn Apartments, 2131-2137 Third Avenue, New York, 1870-1871. Working drawing, front elevation. Portfolio XVI, No. 30, Lienau Collection.

85. (199) _____. Second story plans, working drawings.

86. (203) _____. Grosvenor House, Fifth Avenue at 10th Street, New York, 1871-1872. Old photo, Lienau Collection.

87. (204) H.H. Holly. Family Hotel (Trinity College), Hartford, CT. From *American Architect and Builders' Monthly*, Vol. I (1870), opposite p. 49.

88. (206) Detlef Lienau. American Jockey Club, Madison Avenue at 27th Street, New York, 1871. Old photo, courtesy Brown Brothers, photographers.

89. (208) _____. Working drawing, side elevation. Portfolio X, No. 18, Lienau Collection.

90. (214) _____. Bech Villa, Poughkeepsie, NY, c.1875. Study. Portfolio XXI, No. 40a, Lienau Collection.

91. (217) _____ or J. August Lienau. Study for unidentified house, c. 1880s. Lienau Collection.

92. (218) *_____. "Anglesea," Lewis Cottage, Newport, RI, c.1880. View from southeast. Old photo, Lienau Collection.

93. (220) _____. North elevation, contract drawing. Portfolio XXI, No. 41, Lienau Collection

94. (221) _____. First floor plan, contract drawing.

95. (222) _____. Detail of shingling. Photo by the author, 1953.

96. (222) _____. View from northeast. Photo by the author, 1953.

97. (224) *_____. Cruickston Park, Blair, ON, Canada. View of original building and Lienau extension, 1872-1873. Old photo, courtesy Miss Keefer.

98. (225) _____. First floor plan, working drawing. Portfolio XI, No. 19, Lienau Collection.

99. (226) _____ and J. August Lienau. Williams Cottage, New Brunswick, NJ, 1883. View of exterior. Old photo, courtesy the Misses Mary M. and Catherine Lienau.

100. (227) _____ and J. August Lienau. Interior, view of living hall. Old photo, courtesy the Misses Mary M. and Catherine Lienau.

101. (228) _____. Mosle House, 5 West 51st Street, New York, 1878-1879. Contract drawing, front elevation. Portfolio XXII, No. 42, Lienau Collection.

102. (229) _____. Howland House, 10 West 18th Street, New York, 1881-1882. Working drawing, front elevation. Portfolio XIX, No. 36, Lienau Collection.

103. (230) _____. First floor plan, working drawing.

104. (235) _____. Williams Row, 37-47 West 82nd Street, New York, 1883-1884.

105. (236) *_____. Lienau-Williams Row, 48-54 West 82nd Street, New York, 1886-1887. Contract drawing, front elevation. Portfolio XXIII, No. 45, Lienau Collection.

106. (238) _____. First floor plans, working drawings.

107. (247) *_____. Loft building for Kane estate, 676 Broadway, New York, 1873-1874. Contract drawing, front elevation. Portfolio XV, No. 28, Lienau Collection.

108. (248) Clinton & Pirsson. Queens Insurance Company Building, Wall Street, New York, 1877. From *American Architect*, Vol. II (September 29, 1877), No. 92.
109. (249) McKim, Mead & White. John Innes Kane House, Fifth Avenue, New York, 1907. Old photo, courtesy Picture Collection, New York Public Library.

Foreword.

The publication of Ellen Kramer's research on the 19th century architect Detlef Lienau comes almost a half a century after it was written. During these intervening years, we have witnessed a new appreciation of Victorian architecture, the flowering of the historic preservation movement, the acceptance of the study of interior design history, and the recognition that wealthy 19th century businessmen were not all Robber Barons. These four elements coalesce around Lienau's most significant extant structure, now called the Lockwood-Mathews Mansion Museum in Norwalk, Connecticut, designed in 1864.

Detlef Lienau's importance to mid-19th century American architecture was his ability to present a restrained, classical design in contrast to the picturesque, romantic house styles of the period. He introduced the French mansard style to New York's urban landscape in 1851, swinging residential design away from Greek Revival and Italianate designs, which were so popular in England. But his greatest contribution to American architecture was his ability to incorporate his rigorous classical European training with new America ideas, such as the attempt to minimize the impact of the outer walls of the house by including verandas, conservatories, and large, low walk-through windows. At the same time, he used the most advanced technologies in designing systems for the comfort of his patrons: systems for plumbing, heating, ventilation, and security.

All these design concepts and technological innovations may be found in the Lockwood-Mathews Mansion. It is Lienau's most significant extant structure and introduced the *chateauesque* style of the country house to the American public. In recognition of this fact, the U.S. Department of the Interior declared the Mansion a National Historic Landmark in 1971. Ellen Kramer's pioneering work on this major architect, whose *oeuvre* launched the architectural style of America's Gilded Age mansions, was accomplished long before appreciation of this decorative style and building type was generally accepted.

In fact, the Mansion, left derelict and unloved, was nearly demolished by the City of Norwalk in 1963. Its present existence represents another momentous change in public opinion—the concept of the preservation of 19th century high-style buildings, significant for their architecture, but not necessarily for the people who lived in them. In addition, the Mansion was saved by a small grassroots group of concerned citizens, who fought valiantly, and wisely, against their city fathers, bringing architectural experts to tour the structure and give public pronouncements, while collecting period photographs and documents about the Mansion. Following a citywide referendum and a lawsuit at the state level, they won the battle and established a precedent for such a case. It was not until Congress passed the National Historic Preservation Act in 1966 that the historic preservation movement gained helpful legal tools for such efforts.

Furthermore, the study of the history of interior design was in its infancy. In the 1950s, I was fortunate to have taken one of the rare courses given on the subject in college. As a result, 10 years later, I was able immediately to appreciate the remarkable designs seen in the 1868 photos of the Mansion's interiors. By 1970, Marilyn Johnson, curator of American Decorative Art with the Metropolitan Museum of Art, had identified the Mansion's major interior designer as the firm of Herter Brothers. It took another quarter century for this New York City design-cabinetmaking-decorating firm to receive a traveling multi-museum exhibition entitled "Herter Brothers: Furniture and Interiors for a Gilded Age". The Mansion's original interior is remarkably intact, with its elaborately inlaid and carved woodwork and marble fireplaces. Its walls and ceilings are sumptuously decorated with stenciled borders, *grisaille* subject matter, and oil-painted canvases by the pre-eminent French decorator Pierre-Victor Galland.

Finally, recent rethinking of the roles of our early capitalists has salvaged many reputations from the early 20th century muckraking image of the Robber Barons. A more accurate portrayal of many of these brilliant entrepreneurs would describe them as cultured, affectionate, religious family men, and public-spirited citizens. LeGrand Lockwood was a superb example. His incredible wealth enabled him to build his highly visible palace on the most prominent residential street of his hometown, which was also the path of the horse car railroad. His carefully landscaped lawn was filled with marble sculpture for public enjoyment, noted as a "gift to the city" by the local press. A true Renaissance man, Lockwood, with his wife, was intimately involved in designing, decorating, and furnishing his Mansion, and especially in selecting all its works of art in New York City and during their many trips abroad. Paintings from his noted art collection had been viewed in various cities to raise funds during the Civil War. Lockwood, as a sponsor of artist William Bradford, also underwrote Bradford's 1869 expedition to Labrador with a crew that included a scientific explorer, photographer, and his teen-age son, Henry Lockwood.

The tragic events of Black Friday, September 24, 1869, seriously strained Lockwood's financial and railroad companies. When he died of pneumonia only three years later at the age of 52, his Lockwood & Company had been one of the few companies ruined in the crash by attempting to repay its business debts. In order to do so, he sold $10-million worth of stock in the Lake Shore & Michigan Railroad to Commodore Vanderbilt and then mortgaged his Norwalk mansion. His widow sold his art collection, then the Mansion's furnishings, through a New York City auction house. But the Depression of 1873 deepened, low prices resulted, and Mrs. Lockwood was unable to provide the final payment on the mortgage, which had passed to the Lake Shore & Michigan Railroad under Vanderbilt's control.

Along with only a handful of other early millionaires at the end of the Civil War, Lockwood had set the style of the self-made businessman and patron of the arts by surrounding his family and his collection with the greatest architecture available. It would be another generation before other country homes of this scale and elegance, such as those in Newport, would be built. Detlef Lienau was the right person at the right moment to establish this *chateauesque* style of the Gilded Age.

It is astonishing that so much of the original fabric of the building is still able to be enjoyed, but in its first 100 years it had only three owners: the Lockwood family, the Mathews family, and the City of Norwalk. The Lockwood-Mathews Mansion Museum was incorporated in 1966 to preserve and restore the Mansion and to create educational programming that is based on the material and artistic culture of the Victorian period.

As a member of the Junior League of Stamford-Norwalk (CT) in 1965, I volunteered to write a booklet about this enormous Victorian building in Norwalk that the League had just offered to help preserve. Within weeks, I found myself meeting with Dr. Kramer, listening to her slide lectures on Lienau, and being generously offered copies of her dissertation for my use in this endeavor. The following year, the Lockwood-Mathews Mansion Museum was incorporated with a mission to preserve and restore the Mansion and to create educational programming based on the material and artistic culture of the Victorian period.

Ellen Kramer visited the Mansion regularly to speak to groups about the building and its architect. She would be pleased that her doctoral dissertation has finally been published and that its architect is finally getting the public recognition he deserves. All of us at the Lockwood-Mathews Mansion Museum are honored to be included in this important project.

Mary (Mimi) Findlay, Trustee
Lockwood-Mathews Mansion Museum
Norwalk, Connecticut

Editor's Prologue.

This biography of Detlef Lienau is the only one in America or elsewhere ever written about him. This tribute is long overdue.

Until 1957, Detlef Lienau's name appeared in books and articles on history and architecture pretty much in passing reference: "European-born architect," "studied at L'Ecole des Beaux-Arts," "one of the founders of the American Institute of Architects," "designed homes and cottages for wealthy patrons in New York and Newport," "introduced the mansard roof and the Second Empire style," etc. In brief, the details of his career were largely unknown.

That year, after more than a decade of tedious research and writing, Ellen Kramer put the finishing touches on her dissertation about Lienau and submitted it to the Institute of Fine Arts at New York University, where it was accepted for her doctoral degree in 1958. After that, Kramer's biography of Lienau remained largely unappreciated, although it was cited in a few journal articles and in Paul R. Baker's biography on Richard Morris Hunt (Cambridge, MA: The MIT Press, 1980).

Ellen Weill Kramer has performed an inestimable service to the written record of social and architectural history in America and Europe. It was in the mid-1940s, inspired by the work of Dr. Talbot F. Hamlin at Columbia University, that she took on the almost-impossible task of documenting and writing about the life and works of Detlef Lienau.

Lienau was a European-trained architect, who in the mid-1800s introduced the "French style" to American building construction, notably the mansard roof and all its decorative flourishes. It was a time when public, commercial and residential building was in a state of flux, and architects were searching for a new direction. As the French style caught on, it spurred the development of several retrospective interpretations and design elements that forever defined Victorian architecture. His particular professional contributions lasted for about forty years, yet his influence has never waned. With multiple talents based on numerous associations in the formative years of his professional life, Lienau practiced his crafts in the middle phase of the Victorian period in American history, which reached its pinnacle in the mid-1890s and didn't begin to fade until the outbreak of World War I.

Some have likened the Victorian period to America's Golden Age. While many still wonder what the Victorian period was all about, many are now actively rediscovering, talking about, and restoring its best philosophies, social ideas, decorative arts and architecture. Why was it so important in our history? There are many answers, and Kramer's narrative of the life of Detlef Lienau will help to explain much of this mystery, at least as it relates to the world of architectural design and construction, and the fascinating world in the 19th century of the industrial and merchant classes, especially the wealthy patrons and other clients with whom he worked.

"Facts by themselves are all but meaningless," said Henry Steele Commager in his Introduction to *The Timetables of American History* (New York: Simon & Schuster; 1981). It is "the inescapable duty of every historian to select out of the myriad facts... those that are of interest to more than a single individual and those that have contributed in some fashion to society, economy, law, culture, and morals: those, in short, that appear to be *significant*," he said. "Facts... take on a meaning only in connection with a hundred or a thousand other facts. By themselves, they are like bricks, lying about in hopeless disarray; it is only when the historian fits them together in some formal design that they build a harmonious structure."

In this regard, Kramer has done a masterful job, for within her original 429 pages, she was able to paint not only a comprehensive and lively portrait of Lienau, but also of the many colleagues he worked with (and among) and, more broadly, the exciting period in which he lived. Despite the dearth of information about this illustrious, multinational personality, she was able to unearth the most obscure facts and comments by sifting through correspondence, family mementoes and voluminous public records, not only in the United States, but also in France and Germany. This exercise, to which she dedicated nearly two decades of her life, gave her the additional opportunity to explore the Victorian period, both here and abroad, which she loved (as I do). As you read through the text and consult the hundreds of footnotes and references, you will be in awe of the facts and commentary and minutiae she was able to discover, and relate.

Frederich Nietzsche said that "Nobody knows what news is important until a hundred years afterward". It is now more than a hundred years ago that Detlef Lienau provided new definitions, technical expertise and vitality to the practice of architecture in America. In short, he is important for many more reasons than the mere passage of time.

Despite the fact that Lienau performed most of his work in New York—actually Manhattan before the consolidation of the five boroughs in 1898—his work is largely (if not completely) ignored, uncredited or credited to others. (Prince Albert, Consort to Queen Victoria, is similarly ignored in the history books, despite the fact that he conceived, located and designed the Crystal Palace of 1851 in London's Hyde Park and oversaw its innovative construction.)

In the third edition of *Lost New York* (New York: Mariner Books, 2000), Nathan Silver illustrates a block of row houses on Fifth Avenue between 55th and 56th Streets by "distinguished architect, the Danish-American, Detlef Lienau". And, though there may be extant structures elsewhere in New York City that were designed by Lienau, the third edition of the *Guide to Historic Landmarks of New York* (New York: John Wiley & Sons, 2004) fails to mention Lienau's name, either in the text or in the index. Ironically, while serving as Deputy Director of Research with the New York City Landmarks Preservation Commission in the mid-1960s, Ellen Kramer was largely responsible for conducting the research and compiling the data on which the first edition of the guide was based.

This book should correct some of those oversights.

How This Book Came to be Published

I discovered Kramer's dissertation in the spring of 2003 after many years of frustrating efforts to find definitive biographic information on Lienau. After reading only the first few pages of the dissertation, however, I knew (based on my years of news writing and public relations) that this was a story that had to be told to a wider audience. I felt the next logical step was to see that it got published so that history and architectural scholars and other interested readers like me could enjoy this comprehensive and meticulously documented exposition. Luckily, I had enough experience in publishing at least to initiate the project. Through a series of "finds" on the Internet and some basic correlations, I was able to locate Felix Kramer, one of Ellen Kramer's two sons, who himself had written a book on desktop publishing in 1990 and had experience in the field as well. After a brief conversation, we both decided that we should have the book published. You too will understand why when you read it.

About the Transcription

I transcribed the typescript for this book from a photocopy of the original doctoral dissertation, which had been typed in the late 1950s on what looked like a typical Underwood-style manual typewriter. As a result, the manuscript was sometimes difficult to read through the fabric-ribbon images of the individual characters she typed. I did the best I could with it. As editor, I also made what I felt were some minor changes, such as spelling out most abbreviations (for those of us who always wonder what some of them mean), adding and deleting some punctuation to aid in the cadence of certain sentences, and making other minor structural changes, which again I felt would better aid you, the reader, in comprehending and finding information within the body of the text and in the endnotes.

In the original dissertation, all of the footnotes weren't endnotes, as presented here, but rather footnotes at the bottoms of the running text pages. Anyone who has typed such a document before "the computer age" will appreciate how difficult this is. In any case, some of her minor footnotes were deleted. In every case, this is indicated by the brief phrase, "Refers to page in the original manuscript" (which I felt wasn't relevant here). I did this instead of trying to reorder the full endnote sequence, which might have introduced some new errors.

Despite some factual changes that obviously have taken place in the past 50 years, I have made few editorial changes to the text, unless there was a glaring error, oversight or misspelling of particular names. In other words, I have tried to be as faithful to the original manuscript as is humanly possible. I will leave it to others to update any information about individuals and structures mentioned in the text. And later, I hope to be able to conduct some of this research myself, which might lead to the publication of a revised and updated edition. If any items were misinterpreted in any way by me or the author, I apologize for both of us. Further, if any readers know of any information that ought to be added, changed or deleted, I would be more than happy to receive it for incorporation into a revised edition.

Finally, the original dissertation appears on the following pages between the Author's Dedication and the Bibliography, and the other original sections are the Table of Contents and the List of Illustrations. For purposes of greater elucidation for you, the reader or scholar, Felix and I added a detailed Index to the Text Pages, as well as brief biographic sketches of the author and editor.

Now, at last, let's get on with meeting Mr. Lienau...

Dale Chodorow
Chapel Hill, North Carolina

Author's Dedication.

To the memory of Talbot Hamlin

"Quand on sait voir, on retrouve l'esprit d'un siècle."
—Victor Hugo
(When one knows to see, one rediscovers the spirit of a century.)

Author's Preface.

A study of the work of Detlef Lienau as a dissertation topic was suggested to me in 1950 by the late Talbot Hamlin of Columbia University, who knew of my interest in mid-19th century American architecture in general and in the New York scene in particular. Though he himself was more concerned with other phases of architecture, Professor Hamlin was eager to see justice done to a period of architectural history that had too long been neglected. Seven years ago, the Victorian period was still treated like the proverbial family skeleton in the architectural historian's closet; the less said about it, the better. To be sure, one or two architects, like Richard Upjohn or Henry Hobson Richardson, were considered interesting, but exceptional—and this tended to throw the work of their lesser known colleagues even deeper into the shadow of oblivion.

Today, Victorian is the rage. In *The Gingerbread Age: a View of Victorian America* (1957), John Maas, the most recent writer to jump on the bandwagon, traces the vicarious fortunes of Victorian furniture most amusingly from parlor to attic, from attic to junkshop, and now back to the living room by way of the "Antique Shoppe" (p. 176). The faint traces of a Victorian Revival observed in 1954 by Henry-Russell Hitchcock in the preface to his *Early Victorian Architecture in Britain* have burgeoned forth into a really full-fledged renaissance on the popular level. Pevsner, in a review of Carroll L.V. Meeks's *The Railroad Station* in the current issue of *Victorian Studies* (Vol. I, No. 1, p. 78), notes that the uncritical hostility of past decades has now been replaced by an equally uncritical nostalgia for things Victorian. Florid examples of wrought iron garden furniture, far more flamboyant than any dreamed up by our Victorian great-grandfathers, awaits the eager new homeowner along the roads of suburbia. The sharp, clean-cut, straight-lined aesthetic of the late 1940s is still beating a steady retreat before the onslaught of the curve and the bulge on all fronts: furniture, "free form" swimming pools, women's fashions, and even in the current crop of cinema stars.

This revival of Victoriana in architecture and the decorative arts is only part of a general change in cultural climate, a desire for stability and tradition, the formulation of a new conservatism. Within the last few years, an increasing number of scholars and social historians have concerned themselves with a reappraisal of the contributions of the great Victorians to literature, public life, business, and science. Indeed, the launching in September 1957 of a new revue entitled *Victorian Studies* is in itself significant. In the field of architecture, the contributions of the period have been made transparently clear by scholars such as Turpin Bannister, Sigfried Giedion, Henry-Russell Hitchcock, Carroll Meeks, Nicolaus Pevsner, Vincent Scully, Everard Upjohn, and Winston Weisman, to name only a few. But there is still much to be done, particularly at the local level.

When this study was begun, the history of New York architecture between 1850 and 1880, with the exception of a few buildings mentioned in any general account of American architecture, was almost literally a complete blank. Yet, as Lewis Mumford pointed out almost thirty years ago in *The Brown Decades* (pp. 54-55),

> when the shallow fashion of debunking comes to an end, here is obviously a whole gallery of interesting personalities to work upon—if only the necessary material is available... There is a danger that both the works and days of the principal figures of this period will vanish before either have been properly evaluated or fully assimilated.

Detlef Lienau was one New York architect whose work could be studied at first hand. Over the course of nearly forty years of practice in this country, he designed almost every kind of building: simple cottages and great mansions, town houses, early apartment and tenement houses, commercial structures of every description, banks, stores, offices, warehouses, and factories, as well as schools, libraries, and even a museum.

The restriction in the scope of this study to Lienau's residential architecture is deliberate. The choice lay between presenting a very general outline of his work or in giving a detailed account of one phase of his practice, relating it to the general background of the period and to the work of some of his contemporaries. I have chosen the latter presentation as the more fruitful. While Lienau's work in other spheres is also interesting, his houses provide the most coherent picture of both his own architectural development and of the eddying tides of taste in the Victorian period. Then, too, houses are fascinating social documents, showing us exactly how people of all sorts, rich and poor, lived a hundred years ago. In order to round out this rather specialized picture of Lienau's activities, the reader may refer to the list of Lienau's work in Appendix II and to my article, "Detlef Lienau, an Architect of the Brown Decades" in the *Journal of the Society of Architectural Historians* (March 1955).

As Mumford had prophesized, many of Lienau's buildings have long since been demolished. A reconstruction of his work was made possible by the existence of the Lienau Collection at Columbia University's Avery Library. Consisting of between 700 and 800 drawings, photographs of his executed work, and original documents, this material was acquired by the library in 1935 by Avery Librarian Talbot Hamlin from Detlef Lienau's last surviving son, J. Henry Lienau. He died on November 21, 1957, at the age of eighty-six [see Epilogue]. In 1942, J. Henry Lienau had presented the library with a short biographical sketch of his father and copies of a number of documents of a personal nature, bound together in one volume: "Detlef Lienau, Architect, 1818-1887; Biography, Memorabilia". This has been my primary source of information.

The collection of Lienau drawings includes over 170 examples of his student work and early commissions in Europe (discussed in Chapter 1) and architectural drawings for over forty projects, which include studies, working drawings, and working details. The importance of these drawings as examples of changing methods of architectural practice and of building techniques cannot be overly stressed. In his "Report of the Librarian" (1936), Hamlin pointed out that they are not merely fine illustrations of the exquisite perfection of linear drawing, which characterized the period in which Lienau was brought up, but also show how, over the course of four decades of work in New York, "mechanical equipment of buildings developed in complexity and perfection, how structural metal became more and more important, and how, with the complication and specialization of the building industry, drawings became more and more instruments of technical information and less works of art in themselves". Except for an exhibition in January 1936 of items from the collection, organized by Talbot Hamlin, this material had received no publicity and was completely unpublished. For this and other reasons, I (as a native New Yorker with a natural interest in the field of art) began work in 1951 with the hope of stimulating additional research into this little known field.

In addition to the buildings *in situ* and the material in the Lienau Collection, I have drawn upon greatly diversified sources of information. Contemporary newspapers, popular illustrated weeklies, periodicals, and other publications proved of incalculable value. *The New York Times*, the *Tribune*, the *World*, and the *Evening Post* were among the New York newspapers that provided much interesting data, as did magazines such as *Harper's, Harper's Weekly, Putnam's,* the *New York Weekly Review, Frank Leslie's Illustrated News,* etc. Among the art and architectural journals, *The Crayon,* the *Architects' and Mechanics' Journal,* the *American Architect and Builder's Monthly,* the *American Builder and Journal of Art,* the *New-York Sketch-Book of Architecture,* the *American Architect and Building News,* the *Architectural Record,* the *Architectural Review* (Boston), and the *Proceedings of the Annual Conventions of the AIA* were all prime sources, as were for comparative purposes the various British and continental publications such as the *Builder,* the *Building News,* and the *Journal of the BIBA,* the *Review générale de l'architecture, the Moniteur des architects,* and the *Encyclopédie d'architecture,* the *Allgemeine Bauzeitung, Architektonisches Skizzenbuch,* and *Zeitschrift für Beuwesen.*

Official records, though often difficult to use, are veritable mines of information. For New York, the State Census of 1855 is particularly valuable for biographical data otherwise unobtainable. Tax assessment records are immensely helpful in dating buildings erected before 1866; thereafter, the records of the Department of Buildings may be consulted. For example, in the volumes in which are recorded the plans for new buildings (New Building Dockets) filed with the Department, I found a number of Lienau works previously unknown. Listings in the various New York City directories, when checked against other sources, are also directly useful in dating new buildings.

In addition to the dozens of builder's guides and plan books of the period, several rare 19th century publications dealing with New York architecture in particular deserve special mention, since they contain data not available elsewhere: *Illustrations of Iron Architecture* (1865), John Kennion's *Architects' and Builders' Guide* (1868), the *History of Real Estate, Building and Architecture in New York City* (1898), all at the Avery Library, the two-volume *History of Architecture and the Building Trades of Greater New York* (1899) at the New York Public Library, and last, but fortunately more generally available, the voluminous writings of Montgomery Schuyler.

The numerous guide books of New York, such as *Appleton's New York Illustrated,* often contain excellent views of buildings not found in more ambitious modern publications like Stokes's six monumental volumes, *The Iconography of Manhattan Island* (1915-1929) and Kouvenhoven's *Columbia Historical Portrait of New York* (1953). The print and photographic collections of the New York Public Library, the New-York Historical Society, the Metropolitan Museum of Art, the Museum of the City of New York, and the files of Brown

Brothers, photographers, are all fine sources for illustrative material. The hundreds of descriptions of New York by both American and European travelers and the diaries of the period make fascinating reading and often contain unexpectedly astute comments on architecture. Excerpts from such a journal, the four-volume *Diary of George Templeton Strong* (1952), are contained in my typescript, "George Templeton Strong: Architectural Historian" (1953), copies of which are on deposit at the Avery Library and the New-York Historical Society. The literature of the period in general also reveals much of interest: Passing references will be made, for example, to Walt Whitman, Mark Twain, Harriet Beecher Stowe, William Dean Howells, Henry James, and to Edith Wharton's reminiscences of the era.

Acknowledgments

To list all the people who have helped bring this study to completion is obviously impossible here; in many cases, a footnote reference must suffice. My thanks first go to the members of the Lienau family, both here and abroad, who so willingly furnished me with the biographical details concerning Detlef Lienau, most particularly Mr. J. Henry Lienau, his son, and his [Detlef's] granddaughters, the Misses Mary M. and Catherine Lienau, all of New York. It would be exceedingly ungracious to pass over without special mention the staff of the Avery [Architectural and Fine Arts] Library, Columbia University, to whose cordial hospitality and incredible patience I owe more than I can express. To James G. Van Derpool, Avery Librarian, who did everything in his power to facilitate my research, and A.K. Placzek, Assistant Librarian, I am immeasurably indebted for expert guidance and countless fruitful suggestions. M. Halsey Thomas, Curator of Columbiana and co-editor with Allen Kevins of the *Strong Diary*, kindly permitted me to examine the original folio volumes of the "Journal" in search of material that had been deleted from the published text; I called upon his vast fund of knowledge of the period on numerous occasions. My thanks also go to the staff of the New York Public Library, including members of its Newspaper Division, Municipal Archives Center, the Municipal Reference Library. At Forty-second Street, Rosalie Bailey and Gunther Pohl, Local History and Genealogy Room, and Wilson Duprey, Print Room, were especially helpful, as were Grace Mayer and Betty Ezequielle in the Print Room respectively of the Museum of the City of New York and the New-York Historical Society. The records of the American Institute of Architects proved extremely useful: At the local headquarters, I was permitted access to the "Minutes" of the meetings of the Board of Trustees and of the New York Chapter; special thanks go to Henry A. Saylor at national headquarters in Washington. I found the staff of New York's Department of Buildings and of the County Clerk's Office, where census records and wills are preserved, helpful in spite of the constant pressure of their more immediately urgent work.

Everywhere, both in this country and abroad, I found the same generous spirit of cooperation. The following is a list of officials of various organizations and institutions who very kindly responded to my requests for information: in Newport, Rhode Island, Gladys Bolhouse, Executive Secretary, the Newport Historical Society, and Kenneth Stein, Tax Collector's Office; Irving C. Freese and George R. Brunjes, respectively the former and present mayors of Norwalk, Connecticut; Elizabeth Meed, Art Department, Vassar College; Harry A. Roberts, formerly Secretary to the Chairman of the Board, American Sugar Refining Company, New York; James A. Kelly, Deputy Clerk and Brooklyn Borough Historian, Brooklyn, New York; in New Jersey, Julia Sabine, Chief Librarian, Music and Art Department, Newark Public Library, who was always on the look-out for Lienau material in her neighborhood, Maud H. Greene, Corresponding Secretary, New Jersey Historical Society, Newark, M.R. Whaley, Director, Free Public Library of Elizabeth, Florence Lukens Newbold, formerly Headmistress, St. Mary's Hall, Burlington, the late Dr. William H.S. Demarest, President Emeritus, General Theological Seminary, New Brunswick, and Margaret Wilson, Librarian of the Sage Library at the same institution, Richard J. Scheibner, First National Bank, Jersey City; N. Neil Franklin, Chief, General Reference Section, National Archives, Washington, D.C.; Lilla M. Hawes, Director, Georgia Historical Society, and Raiford J. Wood, Telfair Academy of the Arts and Sciences, both in Savannah, Georgia; Frances Bryson Moore, Acting Executive Director, Louisiana State Museum, New Orleans; James C. Palmes, Librarian, Royal Institute of British Architects, London; Jean Vallery-Radot, Curator of Prints, Bibliothèque Mazarine, Madame Bouleau-Rabaud, Curator, Bibliothèque de L'Ecole des Beaux-Arts, Paris; and J. Gierlinger, Municipal Archives, Hamburg.

My greatest debt, however, is to my advisors, who have patiently read and re-read this manuscript and shared with me without reserve their knowledge of the field. To the late Talbot Hamlin (1889-1956), one of America's truly great architectural historians, I owe to him far more than the assignment of a topic: His gentle yet just criticism and the memory of his boundless enthusiasm, as well as each new small fact that he discovered, were a great source of comfort to me on the many occasions when I felt discouraged. My faculty advisor at New York University, Richard Krautheimer, the devoted scholar and inspired teacher, who many years ago first aroused my interest in the history of architecture, has been a source of never-failing encouragement over the years. It is impossible to adequately acknowledge the infinite amount of time and effort most generously granted to me by Henry-Russell Hitchcock, without whose valuable criticism and counsel at every stage of progress this study could never have been completed. My warm thanks likewise go to Carroll L.V. Meeks of Yale University, whose specialized corpus of information proved of great value in his correction of the final draft.

Others who have helped me by their perceptive criticism are Vincent Scully of Yale University, who read the first five chapters; Agnes Addison Gilchrist, A.K. Placzek, Alan Burnham, and Winston Weisman have been good enough to give me their thoughts on individual chapters. In addition, I wish to acknowledge the kindly interest shown by Leopold Arnaud, Dean of the School of Architecture, James Marston Fitch, and Everard M. Upjohn, all of Columbia University, Paul Zucker of Cooper Union and the New School for Social Research, Clay Lancaster, Walter Knight Sturges, formerly on the staff of the Avery Library, and Wayne Andrews, for many years Curator of Manuscripts at the New-York Historical Society. Lisa Basch, Photographic Services, Columbia University, who did such a splendid job in photographing the difficult Lienau drawings, is to be credited with most of the accompanying illustrations.

Last, but certainly not least, my thanks go to my mother, Elsa Weill, and to my husband, George Kramer. Without their moral support, interest, and cooperation, this study could never have been undertaken, much less brought to completion.

Ellen W. Kramer
New York, New York
November 1, 1957

Author's Introduction.

The following pages attempt to restore the memory of one of the forgotten architects of the 19th century: Detlef Lienau (1818-1887), FAIA[1]. A German-Dane by birth, he was one of thousands swept onto these shores by the rising tide of revolution in 1848. Lienau arrived in New York on December 26, just a few months after the discovery of gold in California. The time was ripe. The land was opening up. But skilled artisans, competent builders, and professionally trained architects were in short supply here. Experience, vision, and a sense of moral responsibility were needed to cope with a multitude of new problems resulting from mass shifts of population and a constantly changing and expanding economy in the decades following. Lienau's thorough training in trade schools and architectural schools in Hamburg, Berlin, and Munich, his years of study in the *atelier* of Henri Labrouste in Paris, and his work in the architectural office of the Paris-Lyons Railroad equipped him well to meet the challenge of the new age of progress.

Lienau made his way quickly here. By 1850, he was already listed as a practicing architect in the New York City directories. The mansard-roofed Shiff house of 1850 on Fifth Avenue immediately established his reputation as an architect of high ability. From this time on until his death in 1887, he enjoyed a fairly large and varied practice. Though many of Lienau's buildings have been razed, a number are still standing in metropolitan New York, New Jersey, Connecticut, Georgia, and in Ontario, Canada. Even the demolition of some of these structures has a positive aspect: It mirrors faithfully the changing patterns of urban growth, sky-rocketing land values, and the development of more modern methods of construction. Indeed, one of the most fascinating aspects of the study of Victorian architecture is the evidence it provides of rapidly changing social and economic conditions, well illustrated by the various types of residential buildings that Lienau was called upon to build, and in the shift from domestic to commercial and industrial character in the design of business structures.

Although perhaps of lesser importance in his day than Richard Upjohn, James Renwick, or Richard Morris Hunt, Lienau was nonetheless recognized by clients and colleagues alike as one of the most able architects of the third quarter of the 19th century in

America. Among his clients, he counted such prominent figures in the social and business world of the period as August Belmont, the Schermerhorns, the Joneses, the Langdons, and DeLancey Kane, the latter a member of the Astor clan. The active role played by Lienau within the American Institute of Architects, of which he was a founder, and the faithful patronage of his clients, imply that Lienau was one of the few professional architects available here in the decades before the establishment of architectural schools in this country. Most of the well known architects active in New York in the middle of the century, with such exceptions as Alexander Jackson Davis, James Renwick, and R.G. Hatfield, were foreigners like Lienau. Among the fifty-three foreign architects in the city listed in the New York State Census of 1855, by far the largest number came from England and Germany, in both cases nineteen[2]. The English coterie was headed from the 1840s on by Richard Upjohn; a close second in authority was a man whose name is all but forgotten today—Frederick Diaper. Others were Thomas Thomas and his son Griffith, Joseph A. Wells, and Frank Wills[3]; later arrivals in the early '50s were Calvert Vaux, Henry Dudley[4], and Jacob Wrey Mould. Among the Germans and the East Europeans, the most important were Leopold Eidlitz and Alexander Saeltzer, both established here since the early 1840s. Frederick A. Petersen[5], the architect of Cooper Union, arrived here as a political refugee a few years after Lienau.

Lienau was, then, one of a relatively small group of trained architects, of whom the majority were fairly recent arrivals from Great Britain and the continent. All brought with them to the New World the traditions of the Old. But Lienau differed in one important respect from his colleagues: Molded by his early Danish and North German environment, and by years of study in various German art centers and in Paris, Lienau's point of view was more international than theirs—a rarity in an age of ardent nationalism. Thus, fusion of traditions enabled him to adapt quickly to life in America and to deal successfully with the demands of an increasingly eclectic age. One more point should be stressed at the outset, since it has long been ignored: Lienau, and not Hunt, was the first to bring to the United States a mind and a hand that was shaped, through contact with Labrouste, by the French Beaux-Arts tradition. His career provides a dramatic illustration of the contributions made by the professionally trained European architect to American architecture at a critical period in its development—the years immediately preceding the Civil War and those that followed it, so aptly called by Lewis Mumford, "the Brown Decades".

Part I. Background

Chapter I.
Lienau's Background and Education

Lienau's Early Years

Detlef Lienau, the son of Jacob and Lucia Lienau, was born on February 17, 1818, in Ütersen, a small town some thirty-five miles north of Hamburg in the Duchy of Holstein. Today a part of Germany, Holstein at that time was still nominally a Danish holding, though locally allied with the German Confederation. While one can only speculate as to the political sympathies of the Lienaus on the Schleswig-Holstein question, it seems reasonable to assume that they were pro-German rather than pro-Danish, since the young Detlef, in spite of his Danish name, was educated largely in Germany.

As for the name Lienau, originally Slavic in origin, it apparently was derived from the Linan[1], whose inhabitants are believed to have migrated to Holstein in the 14th century from a region east of the Elbe[2]. A surgeon by the name of Jacob Lienau is known to have lived in Ütersen in 1699. Detlef's father, also called Jacob (1781-1827) was a wine merchant, a man of some substance and influence in public affairs.

Schooling and Years of Apprenticeship

Very little is definitely known about Detlef Lienau's youth and early education. His son, Mr. J. Henry Lienau, believes that he attended elementary and technical schools in Stettin. Three notebooks[3], written in fine German script, have proven extremely useful in providing a clue to the type of education he received. Their subject matter—(1) organic and inorganic chemistry, (2) physics, and (3) *Technologie*, a detailed anthology of the textile industry from raw material to finished product—is far too advanced and specialized to assume that these were notes taken in a *Realschule*, or even in a *Real-Gymnasium*[4]. Two of the notebooks were based upon lectures given by a certain Herr Direktor Klöden. Since the subject matter was typical of technical or trade (*Gewerbe*) schools, it is almost certain that these notes were based on courses given at the municipal trade school (*Städtische Gewerbeschule*) in the city of Berlin, which had been founded by Dr. Klöden in 1824[5]. The professed aims of Dr. Klöden's school—to give the necessary scientific training to young men who expected to establish themselves independently or in a managerial capacity in trade or industry—and its curriculum (with special emphasis upon the natural sciences, physics, and chemistry) are reflected in the Lienau notebooks.

On the basis of what we know of German education in the early 19th century, and on the evidence provided by the notebooks themselves, one must agree with English commentators[6] about German education of the 1830s and '40s that German students of the period, even when judged by 20th century standards, were extremely well grounded in the fundamental branches of learning and could avail themselves of a good deal of specialized training in the basic sciences. This could not fail to aid Lienau later in the development of a sound approach to technical problems of construction.

In 1837, after the completion of his course at the municipal trade school, Lienau began a three-year apprenticeship under master carpenters (*Zimmerleute*) in Berlin, followed by several months of similar training in Hamburg[7]. One can assume that, by 1837, at the age of nineteen, he decided upon an architectural career, a statement that may seem strange to those unfamiliar with the course of instruction given the carpenter's apprentice, as outlined, for example, in Schinkel's *Grundlage der praktischen Baukunst*[8], and the meaning of the word *Zimmerman*. The German language makes a much sharper distinction than does the English between the carpenter who does cabinet work (*Tischler*) and the carpenter responsible for rough work, including timbering (*Zimmerman*)[9]. Many years later, Lienau himself dated the beginning of his career as an architect back to the year 1837[10], an indication that he considered this phase of his education to be an integral part of his architectural training.

Of much greater value than the notebooks in attempting a reconstruction of Lienau's early training is the remarkable series of student drawings in the Lienau Collection at the Avery Library. These drawings, dating between 1836 and 1847, provide us with valuable data on architectural training in Germany and France during this period, and enable us to trace the development of a young schoolboy's nascent interest in architecture to its full development in his work of the 1840s. This group of 177 student drawings is probably unique for its period among architectural collections in the United States, both quantitatively and qualitatively. Executed partly in the fine-line rendering characteristic of the Classical Revival manner and partly in watercolor, these drawings really deserve a special study. My typescript, "Detlef Lienau: Catalog of Student Drawings and Early European Commissions, 1836-1847" (1954), on deposit at the Avery Library, is a revision of an earlier catalog I made under the supervision of Talbot Hamlin. For a résumé of its contents, the reader is referred to Appendix I.

Probably the earliest drawings (Series I) are five careful tracings of details of Greek ornament, evidently directly copied from Lewis Vulliamy's *Examples of Ornamental Sculpture in Architecture* (London, 1824)[11]. Dating from 1836 to 1838, these drawings should in all likelihood be associated with Lienau's trade school training in Berlin. Another set (Series II) provides further evidence of the type of training received by Lienau in these years. All of these drawings are on mounted tracing paper; considerable emphasis must have been placed upon tracing from books or model drawings[12]. Most of them deal with architectural details in stone or wood, rather than with buildings as a whole. Romanesque and early Gothic capitals, moldings, and details of church furniture from the great cathedrals of Germany were studied with care, reflecting the tremendous revival of interest in national origins so characteristic of the Romantic period. In Germany, this brought forth, particularly from the second decade of the 19th century on, an avalanche of superb publications of German architectural monuments. Of primary importance was Georg Moller's *Denkmaler der deutschen Baukunst*; though the Lienau drawings were clearly derived from a different source, much of the subject matter is the same[13]. Publications dealing with the medieval period and individual buildings delineated in the Lienau sketches are legion. Only the most prominent monographs can be mentioned here, such as the fine publications dealing with Mainz, Speyer, Trier, Cologne, Gelnhausen, and Strassburg[14]. Joseph von Egle's *Munster zu Ulm* is later, but offers interesting points of comparison with some of Lienau's drawings[15].

It is worth noting that Lienau must have had some access to English publications. In addition to his tracings from Vulliamy, he made use of two of Augustus Pugin's books, an indication of the wide influence of the elder Pugin on the continent, as well as in England. Pugin's *Ornamental Timber Gables* furnished the subjects of three Lienau drawings, one of which is illustrated here (Fig. 1)[16]. It must have been a kind of Bible for *Zimmerleute*. Sheets of ornament, an important part of education in drawing at this time, appear again and again in the Lienau drawings, based probably upon one or another of the many books on ornament published in these decades.

The best known example today is Karl Heideloff's series, *Ornamentik des Mittelatters*[17].

Figure 1. Architectural detail by Detlef Lienau.

Perhaps the most interesting of Lienau's early drawings are twelve sheets illustrating chalets (Series II, Nos. 38 and 48-58). They are undated; therefore, it is impossible to assign them with certainty to the period of Lienau's carpentry training in Berlin or Hamburg. They may have been kept by Lienau as souvenirs of his days in Munich, where we know he studied at the Konigliche Baugewerksschule from November 2, 1841, to March 26, 1842[18]. Here, Lienau must have received for the first time what we think of as a specifically "architectural" education.

The usual curriculum at schools of this type, intended primarily for the training of master builders and contractors, included general subjects such as German, mathematics, and the natural sciences, as well as courses in building construction, materials, estimating, architectural drawing, and designing[19]. One example of these drawings of wooden houses is illustrated here (Fig. 2): They all show careful study of the bracketed type of construction known in Germany as "Tirolerhauschen" and elsewhere as the "Swiss" chalets. This style became popular in Germany quite early in the 19th century as a natural result of romantic associations and the strong nationalistic tendencies of the period, for the Swiss style was native to the mountainous regions of southern Germany and Austria, as well as to Switzerland proper. In the 1830s, it was encouraged even in Berlin[20], the stronghold of the classical tradition.

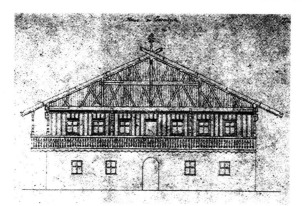

Figure 2. Student drawing by Detlef Lienau.

By the middle of the century, Germany was swamped with Swiss chalets adapted to every conceivable use[21]. Lienau could have traveled in southern Germany, but these drawings are on tracing paper and were undoubtedly school assignments and not travel sketches. Landscape elements, so charming an adjunct of earlier and contemporary publications of chalets, are conspicuously lacking; one must conclude that Lienau's drawings were copied from model sketches or from a German manual of the type later published by Gladbach[22]. Related to these studies are two sheets of drawings showing wooden-truss bridge construction[23].

Only one drawing can be assigned with certainty to Lienau's short stay in Munich, a project for a municipal hospital (Fig. 3)[24]. The drawing, scaled in Bavarian feet and signed "D. Lienau 42," will be discussed at greater length in another connection[25]. Undoubtedly, there must have been many such projects among the Lienau drawings that have disappeared. This one survived, because it probably was for this that he received the prize mentioned in his certificate from the Konigliche Baugewerksschule[26]. In any case, it is an important drawing. We find Lienau, now an accomplished student, putting to use the lessons he learned over the previous years. Here, he was called upon to create something new, rather than to copy something old. The result "has a good deal of the best functional spirit of the '30s in Prussia and Bavaria[27].

German Architectural Background:
Berlin, Hamburg, Munich

It is singularly disappointing (though of some interest) that, among all the drawings of 1837 to 1842 preserved in the Lienau

Collection, so few appear to have been modeled on existing buildings or historical examples, which he might have seen. They were school exercises, and nothing more. Nowhere is there a reflection of Lienau's particular interests or of contemporary work. We look in vain for a fragment or a sketch that might give us a clue to the buildings that might have impressed Lienau in all the years he spent in Berlin—the triumphal Berlin of Schinkel—or during the months in the new Munich created by Ludwig I of Bavaria.

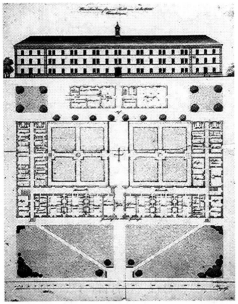

Figure 3. Study for a hospital by Detlef Lienau.

Both these great German cities had been completely transformed in a matter of decades by the genius of two generations of architects whose true creativity is often disregarded by architectural historians outside of Germany[28]. To be sure, we all know the important names: Erdmannsdorf, the elder Langhans, the two Gillys, Schinkel, and Persius in Berlin; Fischer, Klenze, and Gartner in Munich. The mere mention of their names conjures a vision of severely classical buildings erected at the behest of two lines of art-minded rulers: Frederick William II (1786-1797) of Prussia, followed by his son (1797-1840), and even more enthusiastic grandson (1840-1861), and Maximilian I (1806-1825) and Ludwig I (1825-1848) of Bavaria. While these monuments evoked the glories of the past, they also expressed the aspirations of a nation on the march. The new style was also making inroads into the medieval brick tradition of the old Hansa town of Hamburg and its environs, which Lienau knew so well, especially in the work of the great Danish neo-classicist, C.F. Hansen, and later of Wimmel & Forsmann, Semper, Klees-Wulbern, and de Chateauneuf.

Germany was building, but what was it building? It is easy to dismiss the work of these men as archeological pastiches and to point out their various sources: Greek, Roman, Early Christian, Romanesque, Gothic, and Italian Renaissance. It is more difficult to try to understand their struggle to adapt to new needs the old forms, with all their symbolic, associative meanings[29]. It is important to recognize that there was another side to the work of many of these architects[30]. In their unofficial commissions, in unexecuted projects, and in architectural theory, they showed an awareness of the need for a simple, functional type of architecture, which was often amazingly prophetic of the future. This was particularly true of Schinkel. Pevsner, in a short but brilliant analysis of this period of European architecture, calls him the best architect of his generation[31]. Karl Friedrich Schinkel (1781-1841) stood head and shoulders above the rest, not only in his truly original achievements within the cadre of traditional styles[32], but also as an architect who could create buildings with simple design, direct and functional planning, and expressive use of materials that were unparalleled in Europe at this time.

To believe that Lienau might have remained untouched by Schinkel's achievements would be fantastic. His early impressions in Berlin, as well as his later Neo-Grec training in France instilled in him a love of the classical vocabulary and those ideals of clarity, restraint, balance, and harmony, which stayed with him all his life.

Lienau's ideas must have been influenced not only by the classical monuments of Berlin, but also by the extraordinarily rational and unprecedented use of brick[33] in such buildings as Schinkel's Feilnerhaus and Bauakademie (1831-1835), completed precisely during the time when Lienau was studying there. The way Lienau later used brick in many of his buildings shows that he never forgot the examples of Schinkel and his own North German and Danish heritage[34]. A copy of Schinkel's *Grundlage der praktischen Baukunst* was in Lienau's library[35]. He could hardly have been acquainted, however, with Schinkel's architectural theories, except via the students' grapevine, since these were expressed chiefly in private correspondence, and not published until later[36]. But Lienau's own theories, to which he gave expression in later years, undoubtedly owed something to Schinkel's emphasis on function as the determining factor in building and the necessity of creating new forms to meet the needs of one's own age[37].

Leinau's understanding of contemporary adaptations of the Italian Renaissance style, with which he must have been acquainted through Schinkel's and Persius's work in Berlin and its environs[38], was probably deepened in Hamburg by the work of Wimmel & Forsmann. The Johanneum (1837-1840), strongly influenced by early Florentine palaces, had just been completed[39]. Work on the new Stock Exchange, in high Renaissance style, proceeded apace. The real transformation of the city of Hamburg took place, however, in the years following Lienau's stay there. The catastrophic fire of May 5 to 8, 1842, which reduced one third of the city to ashes, made necessary a vast amount of rebuilding[40]. From a modern point of view, probably the most interesting work in Hamburg in the 1840s was done by Alexis de Chateauneuf (1799-1853); turning his back on the Renaissance style with which he had started, he created some of the most beautifully designed unadorned brick buildings of the period. Lienau must have been familiar with his work, if not at first hand, then through the fine illustrations in the *Allgemaine Bauzeitung*[41].

Surely, the fame of the new Ludwigstrasse, as well as superb educational facilities in Munich, drew Lienau to that city at the end of 1841. Described by a contemporary English writer as the "Athens of Germany[42]," Munich was one of the greatest literary, educational, and artistic centers in Europe at this time. Nowhere in Europe, we might even say, was there so much new building on such a grandiose scale concentrated in so small an area. And as for styles, there was something for everybody: Devotees of Greek and Renaissance architecture admired Klenze's work, and those who preferred earlier

Italian modes were impressed by the new Library and State Archives building completed by Gartner in 1840, as fine an example of the Italianate *Rundbogenstil* as anything produced in Europe at this time. The new *Rundbogenstil*[43] was coming into its own, and many architects all over Germany were following the lead established by Gartner in the new Ludwigskirche, begun in 1829 and still under construction when Lienau was in Munich. As we shall see later, Lienau must have absorbed some of this interest by Munich architects in round-arched architecture[44]. Of the drawings of this period, however, only a few can definitely be associated with his stay there; one of these illustrates the plan and details of furniture for the Munich Synagogue[45].

Paris: Atelier of Henri Labrouste, 1842-c.1846

Lienau stayed only a few months in Munich. By May 1842, he was already in Paris. We may only hazard a guess as to why Lienau left Munich so soon. Possibly, he was confused by the very richness and variety of the architectural scene. Or the choice between the classic and medieval camps was one which he, as a young man of twenty-two, was not yet prepared to make. Since it was to Paris that he turned, he probably felt the need for a strong tradition and broader training in architectural planning.

Architectural Climate of the 1830s and '40s

A whole new world of experience awaited him there. It is quite unlikely that he would have agreed with Kugler's unflattering description of Parisian architecture: chaotic and full of futile allegory on the one hand, raw and coldly reasoned on the other[46]. To be sure, the dominant trend in official architecture was classical, a classicism much dryer and certainly less creative than Schinkel's. The Beaux-Arts training of French architects encouraged adherence to time-honored traditions[47]. Interest in the restoration of French national monuments of the Renaissance, and the conservative taste of Napoleon, Charles X, and later of Louis Philippe and the middle classes, had strengthened the hold of the classical tradition on French architecture[48]. But it is significant that Lienau did not turn to a traditionalist for training; he headed straight for the *atelier* of Henri Labrouste, acknowledged leader of the opposition.

Already, the voice of authority was being questioned, resulting in a bitter struggle between the academicians and the rationalists[49].

Quietly, amidst the general uproar, a small group of architects banded together during the 1830s, men more interested in finding the answers to problems of planning, design, and construction posed by contemporary needs, and in experimenting with new materials, than in designing projects according to the rigid precepts of the Academie des Beaux-Arts. Particularly important in the little group were Felix Duben (1797-1870), Henri Labrouste (1801-1875), Joseph Duc (1802-1879), and Léon Vaudoyer (1803-1872); all had been prize students at the Beaux-Arts and the French Academy in Rome. Their classical training and background are reflected in the term so often used to describe their work—Neo-Grec[50]—a somewhat misleading name[51]. True, their forms were often Greek in derivation, but they were not used for the sake of imitation, or revival, but because the great simplicity, clarity, and directions of Greek classical art appealed to these men. Though the term Neo-Grec may describe the style they handled as a means to an end, it is far more expressive of their aims and basic principles to call theirs the Ecole Rationaliste, as the French prefer[52]. In 1840, with Cesar Daly as their editor, the group began to publish the *Revue générale de l'architecture et des travaux publics* in order to disseminate their point of view. The subtitle of the magazine, *Journal des architectes, des ingenieurs, des archeologues, des industriels, et des proprietaires*, suggests the broad synthesis they wished to achieve. Their motto was: *Respect pour le passé; Liberté dans le present; Foi dans l'avenir* [Respect for the past; Freedom in the present; Faith in the future]. If one wishes to understand the architectural climate of this period in France, nothing is more instructive than to leaf through the issues of *Revue générale*. Constantly agitating for reform in the education of architects, editor and contributors alike repeatedly took to task L'Ecole des Beaux-Arts for its completely one-sided classical outlook[53] and the total lack of rapport between its teaching of architecture as design, and architecture as construction[54].

The acknowledged leader of this group of progressive architects was Henri Labrouste. Until the early 1840s, Labrouste had had no important commissions, because he was blacklisted by L'Ecole and had done no writing. His status, therefore, requires some explanation. A winner of the Prix de Rome in 1824, he had stirred up a controversy that rocked the Academy: In 1829, he sent back to Paris from Rome his restoration of the Greek temples at Paestum. His drawings completely undermined the traditional notions of the academicians as to the original appearance and construction of Greek temples. The new evidence Labrouste submitted, particularly with regard to Greek polychromy, was based upon exhaustive study and examination at first hand. It was finally accepted only after a battle royal between Horace Vernet, Director of the French Academy in Rome, who sided with Labrouste, and Quatremere de Quincy, Secretary of L'Ecole des Beaux-Arts[55]. When Labrouste returned to Paris in 1830, his was a *cause célèbre*. He became the recognized spokesman for those who believed architecture should be based upon truth and reason, rather than upon sterile conventions and outworn traditions. Undaunted by opposition from official sources, he immediately opened an *atelier* in Paris to which eager young men from all over France flocked to learn the gospel of the new *rationalisme*[56]. Accepting nothing at face value, Labrouste taught his students to proceed only after thorough study of all aspects of a problem. As in science, this method often results in the reversal of accepted ideas and principles.

Young Lienau came to Labrouste's *atelier* in the spring of 1842[57]. Five years later, he proudly signed his name, "Lienau, archte"[58].

Labrouste's stinging denunciation of "paper" architectural training, which completely divorced architectural design from construction, appeared in the very first issue of *Revue générale de l'architecture*[59]. "The projects of an architect," he was fond of saying, "can only be regarded as finished when they have been built."[60] His own teaching aims are very clearly stated in a letter to his brother Theodore, written shortly after he had opened his *atelier*.

20 novembre 1830
Mon cher Theodore,
   Je travaille enormement, et ce qui est plus difficile, je fais travailler mes élèves.
   J'ai redigé quelques programmes pour exercer utilement les debutants, je veux leur apprendre a composer avec des moyens très simples. Il faut d'abord qu'ils voient clairement la destination de leur oeuvre, qu'ils en disposent les parties selon l'importance qu'il est raisonnable de leur donner. Puis je leur explique que la solidité depend plus de la combinaison des materiaux que de leur massé et, des qu'ils connaissent les premiers principes de construction, je leur dis qu'ils doivent tirer de la construction elle-même ornementation raisonnée, expressive.
   Je leur répété souvent que les arts ont le pouvoir d'embellir toute chose; mais j'insiste pour qu'ils comprennent que *la forme, en architecture, doit toujours être appropriée à la fonction qu'on lui destine.* [emphasis added]

Enfin, je suis heureux de me trouver au milieu de ces
jeunes camarades, attentifs, pleins de bonne volonte et resolus
à suivre la toute que nous allons parcourir ensemble.

Ton frère,

Henri Labrouste[61]

This letter is extremely interesting as a statement of Labrouste's
aims, and prophetic of modern attitudes. More, it gives us an insight
into Labrouste's personality: He was so completely devoted to his
ideas and to his teaching, there was hardly time for a personal touch.
While he appeared to some reserved and cold, he won the respect of
all his colleagues, and the admiration—one might say veneration—of
his students for his single-minded dedication to the cause of
architecture[62]. In spite of his inflexible basic principles, he allowed
his students considerable latitude in the development of personal
taste and inclination. Lessus (1807-1857), one of the outstanding
medieval revivalists of the century, came from the *ateliers* of
Vaudoyer and Labrouste. He dedicated his *Album de Villard de
Honnecourt* to Labrouste as a public expression of the sincere
affection of his students[63].

Lienau came to the *atelier* at a crucial time. In 1843, work began
on Henri Labrouste's first important commission, the Bibliothèque
Sainte-Genéviève. The building was not completed until 1850, when
Lienau was already in the United States, but he must have shared his
master's excitement at this first victory over the conservative wing of
French architects. There is no need to discuss the library at any great
length here. The Bibliothèque Sainte-Genéviève has long been
recognized as an epochal monument in the history of architecture
and engineering[64]. But in its day, the daring use of wrought- and cast-
iron construction from foundation to roof and the logical design of
the building aroused considerable debate[65]. Fruit of long years of
study, the Bibliothèque Sainte-Genéviève was the first concrete
embodiment of Labrouste's contention that *form must be appropriate to
function* [editor's emphasis; see Epilogue] and subordinated to the
materials of construction. The building must have made an indelible
impression on his students. Two drawings in the Lienau Collection
bear witness to Lienau's interest in the work of his *patron*[66]. Other
drawings of iron construction and wrought-iron decoration[67] indicate
that Labrouste had been demonstrating to his students the
possibilities of the new material, which he himself had treated in
such an appropriate and novel way in the arch trusses of the reading
room of the library[68].

Lienau's Student Drawings, 1842-1846

At this point, you may question how, on the basis of such slim evidence, we can be sure that Lienau studied with Labrouste for any length of time. Statements that he had been trained by Labrouste needed substantiation[69]. For a clarification of Lienau's relation to Labrouste, the student drawings in the Lienau Collection proved of immense value.

The clue to certainty was provided by one of twenty-two large, carefully measured ink and wash studies done to scale of the orders of Roman and Italian monuments, a type later made familiar to architectural students by Esquie. These drawings (Series III in the "Catalog of Student Drawings") are obviously derived from a single source. While they are similar in style to all the early 19th century French publications from Percier and Fontaine down to Letarouilly[70], and obviously reflected careful study of Italian antiquities and Renaissance buildings so typical of Beaux-Arts training, there is no exact correspondence between the Lienau drawings and those in any of these books. Finally, one drawing of Lienau, a plan of the Temple of Concord at Paestum, was traced to its source—a plate in *Les temples de Paestum. Restauration executée en 1829 par Labrouste*[71], published only in 1877, when all doubt as to the authenticity of Labrouste's restoration had been dispelled.

The sixty-two exquisite watercolors on Whatman paper (Series IV), watermarked for the most part between 1842 and 1846, posed an even more difficult problem. Most of the subjects were Italian, ranging in period from Etruscan times through the Renaissance. Several of the drawings were signed "D. Lienau" and/or dated in the 1840s[72]. A logical assumption that these were Lienau's travel sketches, as Talbot Hamlin believed at first, was quickly proven false by a comparison of the presumed itinerary with the dates. How, for example, could Lienau have been in Paris in May 1842 and in Corneto on May 9 of the same year[73]? Obviously, these had to be copies of someone else's travel sketches and drawings. Since Labrouste had been a winner of the Prix de Rome in 1824 and had lived in Italy from 1825 to 1830, it seemed logical to assume that the Lienau watercolors were copies of Labrouste drawings worked up from the latter's travel sketches. Delaborde and Millet both referred to the fact that Labrouste had made hundreds of drawings in Italy; according to Millet, a magnificent portfolio of drawings was always at the disposal of Labrouste's students[74]. Other references to his drawings of Etruscan monuments, discovered precisely during the years when he was in Italy, suggested a possible source for the Etruscan subjects in the Lienau drawings[75]. Finally, something really concrete turned up: the illustrations of San Miniato in Florence in Jules Gailhabaud's *Monuments anciens et modernes*, illustrations the author acknowledged had been furnished to him by Henri Labrouste, which agreed in almost every detail with three Lienau drawings, two signed "D. Lienau" and two dated June 23 and June 26, 1842[76].

In 1952, an exhibition of Labrouste drawings and other memorabilia was held at the Bibliothèque Nationale[77] to celebrate a gift of 757 Italian drawings to the Library from the Labrouste family. A catalog of this exhibition, *Labrouste, architecte de la Bibliothèque Nationale de 1854 à 1875*[78], drawn up by R.-A.Weigert, made it easy to check the Lienau drawings against the work of Labrouste. Two of the illustrations agreed exactly with the corresponding drawings by Lienau[79], one of which is reproduced here (Fig. 4), and in many other cases titles were so exactly worded as to preclude any mistake. Though I personally have not seen the Labrouste originals, I feel confident that they are the source not only for the drawings in Series IV and some in Series III, but also for all of the drawings done to scale in Series II—a total of between seventy-five and eighty Lienau drawings[80].

Figure 4. Student drawing by Detlef Lienau of fresco.

The quality of the watercolors of Lienau's Series IV is superb. Minutely detailed in execution and exquisitely tinted as they are, it is difficult to conceive that the originals could be more beautiful. The medieval miniaturist lavished no more loving care on his work than did Lienau on rendering a section of the nave mosaics of the Cathedral of Monréale (Fig. 5)[81]. Surely, these drawings were for him not only a souvenir of his days in the *atelier* Labrouste, but also an evidence of his own technical skill. He may have intended someday to bind them together in a book (as Talbot Hamlin once suggested to me in the course of conversation).

In any case, the drawings prove conclusively that Lienau studied with Labrouste from May 1842 until some time in 1846[82]. The documentary value of the Lienau student drawings, over and beyond their importance as Lienau drawings *per se*, is considerable. Their archeological value was noted with interest by Professor Luisa Banti of the University of Florence: They show us the appearance of buildings and monuments in Italy in the 1820s, which in some cases have deteriorated sadly since. They also furnish us with additional examples of Labrouste drawings, now lost, as reflected in the Lienau copies[83]. Their final value, however, lies not in their reflection of the travels and methods of teaching by Labrouste, but in their own intrinsically high quality of draftsmanship. They are proof that the talented carpenter's apprentice of Berlin, Hamburg, and Munich was a man transformed by the delicate taste and stimulating presence of Henri Labrouste, leader of the rationalist school of French architectural thought in the second quarter of the 19th century.

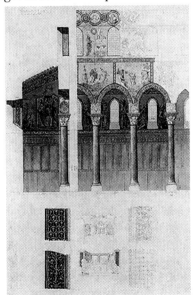

Figure 5. Student drawing by Detlef Lienau of cathedral mosaics.

It is somewhat surprising to learn through the Lienau drawings that Labrouste relied to such a large extent on the copying of model examples to teach the principles of architectural construction and the history of architecture. If the method was traditional—one must remember that the most revolutionary Frenchman always retains a certain respect for tradition[84]—then the subjects were not. As noted previously, the history of architecture in Italy was represented by examples ranging in time from the 6th century B.C. through the 16th century A.D. One should realize, of course, that the Lienau drawings show us but one side of Labrouste's training methods. Copying drawings of the patron was only part of the program. Even newly arrived students were given contemporary projects to work on at the same time. Labrouste focused on the future, rather than on the past. He preferred to deal with what must be done, rather than what was already accomplished[85], an attitude best expressed in his own words:

> Nous desirons encourager les études faites sur les oeuvres du passé, les *rélevés* des monuments antiques ou les restaurations des édifices de notre pays; mais nous devons surtout, selon moi, faire une part plus grande aux projets d'un intérêt general, aux inspirations du moment, aux propositions de l'avenir. C'est un regret pour moi de voir les architectes... après de fortes études, se resigner à emprunter des formes qui one été inventées, avec raison, à d'autres epoques; au lieu de chercher eux-mêmes les expressions qui reponderaient actuellement à nos besoins, à nos moeurs, à nôtre sentiment artistique...[86]

As Viollet-le-Duc recalled later[87], those were the days when architecture was really learned in *ateliers*. He describes the ferment of intellectual activity and the heated discussions stirred up among the students by heads of the various *ateliers*, whose principles were so often opposed to each other. The succeeding generations of architects in France, as a result, were men of great independence of thought and often striking originality.

Interesting in themselves and as an additional proof of Lienau's study in Labrouste's *atelier* are six sketches (Series VI), given to Lienau by friends, three of them dated May 1847. In every case where it was possible to verify the signatures (Adam, C. Patouelle, P. Saybothes, and Langlais), the men who signed them are listed in E. Delaire's *Les architectes élèves de L'Ecole des Beaux-Arts* as having come to L'Ecole from the *atelier* Labrouste[88]. The same is true of a certain "George," from whom Lienau copied two drawings[89], and of Mimey, as well as of the same George and of Vanginot, whose drawings for the Beaux-Arts competitions were copied by Lienau[90]. For many years, Lienau kept in touch with at least one of these men, Mimey, as may be surmised from two letters of 1865 from Henry Van Brunt to Lienau, in which he asked Lienau to forward a letter to Mimey for him[91]. Van Brunt hoped, through the kind offices of Lienau and Mimey, to secure Viollet-le-Duc's approval of his long cherished project, a translation of the latter's *Entretiens sur l'architecture*. Lienau's efforts to reach Viollet-le-Duc through Mimey must have been successful: Van Brunt's translation appeared in 1875.

It is entirely possible that Lienau may have supplemented his work at the *atelier* Labrouste with courses elsewhere. Several small drawings[92] may stem from special courses such as those on ornamental composition given by Ruprich-Robert at L'Ecole Impériale et Spéciale de Dessin. (This probably corresponds with L'Ecole Royale et Spéciale de Dessin et de Mathématiques, appliqués aux Arts Industriels, described by Kugler[93].) A state-supported school with an enrollment of 2,000 students, its most distinguished graduate had been Percier. According to Engler's descriptions of the curriculum, strong emphasis was placed on industrial application of the arts. Drawings of plants and ornaments were made after models and pattern books. In other words, it was a normal school like the trade schools Lienau had attended in Germany, though on a much larger scale.

By the end of 1846 at the latest, Lienau was judged ready to be on his own. His *Lehr und Wanderjahre*, years of apprenticeship, travel, and study were at an end. But his work and statements in later years show that he did not forget the lessons in straightforward designing and functional planning he learned during his early years of training in Germany and France. The principles of Schinkel and Labrouste remained with him all his life, a sturdy bulkhead against the tide of shoddy construction practices and poor design that was threatening to engulf American architecture in the third quarter of the 19th century. According to J. Henry Lienau, a picture of Labrouste[94] hung over his father's desk in his New York office for many years, a constant reminder that the practice of architecture was a public trust.

First Job and Early European Commissions

Draftsman for the Paris-Lyons Railroad, c.1847

Toward the end of January 1847, Lienau received official notification of his appointment as a draftsman at 1,800 francs a year in the architectural office of the Chemin de Fer de Paris à Lyon. Two letters attesting to this, both dated January 2, 1847, are preserved among the Lienau memorabilia. One is signed by Ad[olphe] Jullien, Ingénieur des Ponts et des Chaussées, the Chief Engineer of the railway; the second is a corroborating letter from A. Cendrier, Chief Architect of the company[95], whose career is discussed briefly below. Interesting too is a list of thirty-eight employees of the railroad who took part in its first annual banquet at the famous Restaurant Véfour on January 1, 1847[96]. At ten francs a head, it offered a fine dinner and *vin à discretion*. Along with two of his friends from the *atelier* Labrouste, Langlais and Queyron[97], Lienau is listed among the five draftsmen employed in the office of the chief architect, indicating that he may have worked there for some time, perhaps on a trial basis. Langlais continued in the employ of the railroads for many years.

It is hardly surprising that Lienau, and others from Labrouste's *atelier*, went directly from Labrouste to Cendrier's office to work. The fact that Lienau should have gotten his first job in what was then a new field—railroad architecture—is significant. It reveals not only the direction of Lienau's interests, channeled by Labrouste, but also the general situation confronting young men of the time embarking on an architectural career. The railroads, less fettered by tradition than official architecture of the period, were proving receptive to new ideas and making full use of the new materials at their disposal[98]. Some years later, J.I. Hittorf (1792-1867), one of Labrouste's intimates, and the engineer Leonce Reynaud (1803-1880), demonstrated this dramatically in their magnificent use of iron and glass in the second Gare du Nord (1861-1865) in Paris[99]. But this station was a relatively late example in the development of Parisian railroad architecture. At the time, when Lienau was studying with Labrouste, Reynaud was building Gare du Nord I (1845-1847), the first important station of the "head" plan with a *salle des pas perdus*. In 1847, construction was begun by the architect François Duquesney (1800-1849) on the Gare de l'Est, notable for its new concept of interior space and for the successful integration of the shed (revealed by the glazed lunette) with the otherwise quite traditional monumental façade[100]. To these early stations, we should add the Gare de Lyon I (1847-1852), built at exactly the same time as the Gare de l'Est, on which Lienau worked as an employee in Cendrier's office.

The career of François Alexis Cendrier (1803-1892), one of these pioneer railroad architects, centered largely around the development of the French railroads[101]. Cendrier had studied under elder Vaudoyer and le Bas and, like his contemporary Labrouste, had spent several years in Italy as a young man. Associated first with the Paris-Orleans line, Cendrier then became chief architect of the Paris-Lyons Railroad, more familiarly known today as the PLM. After the Paris station had been completed, he built the Gare de Perrache (1855-

1857) in Lyons; these terminal stations were soon followed by many others along the line, including the present one at Dijon.

Since the terminal stations of the Paris-Orleans line show a rather timid, unimaginative approach to the problem of adapting Roman traditions of design to railroad architecture, we may probably take Blouet's word that Callet, and not Cendrier, was in charge[102]. Cendrier's work for the PLM was that of an architect of vision, of a man who knew how to organize on a grand scale. Since he was prepared by his Beaux-Arts training to handle large-scale projects competently, the Paris station[103] was not just a brilliant design on paper: the plan really worked! The relationships between waiting room and shed, departing and incoming passengers and baggage, all were handled efficiently, with great understanding of the problems involved, by the two-sided plan. The Paris station of the PLM was characterized as the most successful one of its day by no less an authority than Chabat[104]. The simple, yet effective, treatment of the main façade, entered through three huge glazed arches under low gables, strongly suggests that Cendrier had not forgotten his early impressions of the great Baths of Caracalla and Diocletian in Rome.

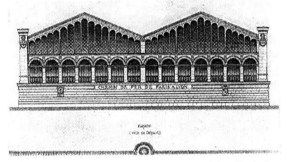

Figure 6. Paris-Lyons Railroad Station by Cendrier. End elevation.

Far more original, however, was the design of the shed end of the station, which faced the Place Mazas (Fig. 6). Here, in what was surely one of the most striking designs of the period, Cendrier deliberately played up the contrast between traditional heavy masonry construction in the base and the grace and delicacy of the new materials of the age—iron and glass—in the beautifully designed upper section, which clearly expressed the character of the shed behind it. Cendrier's later Gare de Perrache[105] is an interesting example of Labrouste's influence: The glazed arches of the second story are used to light the waiting room below in much the same way as Labrouste had used them in the Bibliothèque Sainte-Geneviève. The decorative details of Cendrier's work, like those of Labrouste, are decidedly Neo-Grec. However, the similarities in the work of the two men go far deeper than such superficialities. Cendrier shares with Labrouste his interest both in the Roman past and in exploring the possibilities of metal construction.

Other Work

Exactly how long Lienau worked for Cendrier and the PLM is not known. By the spring of 1847, he was already taking on outside jobs, such as the installation of new machinery for the Chemical Works of Conrad & Waldmann at St.-Denis near Paris[106]. The gay design for a bathing establishment may also date from this period (Fig. 7)[107]. Approached by a narrow bridge and built on a floating platform, it combined a swimming pool with all kinds of facilities. Here, one could spend a pleasant day and swim, get a haircut and shave, replenish one's stock of tobacco, and have a light lunch and liquid refreshment in the café overlooking the pool. The structure, built of wood in bracketed style, was screened from public view by large pieces of canvas stretched between masts appropriately shaped in the form of Neptune's triton. Possibly, this was a design for a public pool in the Seine; many were built later as part of the public works program sponsored by Louis Napoleon as President, and subsequently as Emperor, of France[108].

Altona Hospital Competition, 1847

More important proof of Lienau's early success in architecture is a study for a new municipal hospital for the city of Altona, near Hamburg[109]. Announcement of a competition, open to architects from all over Germany, Austria, and Denmark, was made in the *Altonaer Mercur* on July 10, 1847; applications were posted in bookstores in Berlin, Dresden, Hannover, Karlaruhe, Stuttgart, Copenhagen, and Vienna[110]. The designs were submitted in November 1847. Lienau's plan, published in the *Altonaer Nachrichten* on April 17, 1855, won first prize (Fig. 8).

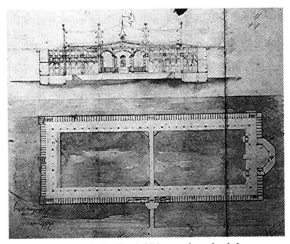

Figure 7. Study by Detlef Lienau for a bath house.

Lienau had given some thought to the problems of hospital planning before this. The drawing for a hospital mentioned in connection with his training at the Konigliche Baugewerksschule in Munich, was an elevation and plan for an institution to serve a town of 10,000 to 12,000 inhabitants[111]. Extremely simple in design, yet avoiding excessive monotony in the handling of the elevation (which may perhaps owe something to the Florentine *palazzo* style popularized in Munich by Gartner), the plan conformed to the contemporary German ideal of hospital construction.

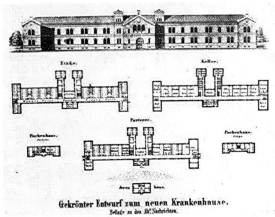

Figure 8. Prize-winning drawing by Detlef Lienau for a hospital.

The Lienau building was conceived as a U-shaped block around a court and garden. It was of the usual German "corridor" type; that is, a long hall, running along one side of the building and serving as a promenade for ambulatory patients, providing continuous access to all the rooms and wards that opened on to it. The chief disadvantage of the arrangement was its lack of adequate ventilation and light, for the wards were open only on one side. Almost all the German hospitals of the period were built upon variations of this block-corridor type[112]. At the rear of the court, entirely separate from the main building, were the laundry, morgue, and dissection room. The left of the building was to be for men, the right side, for women; each side was provided with unusually generous bathing and sanitary facilities, at least when judged by mid-19th century standards.

In the 1847 plan of the hospital for Altona, Lienau evidently tried to combine the German corridor type with the newer "pavilion" plan being developed in France, where the hospital was thought of as a series of separate units, or pavilions, loosely linked by communicating corridors. The chief advantages of the pavilion plan, which dominated hospital planning in England, France[113], and the United States for the next several decades, were that it introduced a greater amount of light and air into the wards, which were open on two sides, and that one unit might be isolated from the next, reducing the possibility of the spread of contagious diseases from one ward to another. The H-shaped plan of the central section of the design for the Altona municipal hospital undoubtedly owed something to Lienau's familiarity with the newest developments in French planning. Gauthier's Lariboisiere, the great new hospital on the outskirts of Paris, considered by most writers as the archetype of the pavilion plan, was already under construction at the time[114]. But the wards along the corridor at Altona, with ten beds to a room, were to be lighted by only two windows, as was customary in Germany. When the hospital finally was built, the progressive features of Lienau's plan were discarded completely in favor of the old German corridor system.

Other points worthy of notice in the plan of the competition drawings are the central placing of the small operating room, the number and sensible location of the baths and water closets, and the isolation of the buildings for smallpox patients and the insane. The non-violent insane were to be confined in cells in the basement of the main building—hardly in keeping with modern methods of psychiatric treatment!

The elevation of the Altona competition drawing, in contrast to the plan, owes far more to German than to French sources. It is strongly reminiscent of Theodor Stein's design for the new Bethanien Hospital in Berlin (1843-1847), which was already famous and for many years thereafter considered a model hospital[115]. The general relation of one story to the next, the use of stair towers (so strangely underscaled) flanking a central section with a triple arcade, the alternation of similarly spaced single and double round-headed windows in the towers, the position of the clock, the working of a cruciform design into the corners of the central gable—all these features seem too similar to have been fortuitous. Stein's design in the Italian-Gothic tradition has, however, a certain thinness and linear quality quite different from that of Lienau, who conceived his in terms of projecting and receding masses entirely in keeping with its simplified Italian Romanesque design.

What happened between 1847, the date of the competition, and 1859, when construction actually began, is extremely vague. The hospital project apparently was shelved as a result of the revolution of 1848; the subject did not come up again until the end of 1854. In December 1855, the City Council decided to go ahead with construction but, again, there was a delay. The hospital finally was erected from 1859 to 1861 and has remained substantially unaltered, with the exception of an extension built in 1888-1889. A photograph of the building taken in 1900 (Fig. 9) and the ground plan indicate that Lienau's original design was changed considerably by the new architect in charge of construction, O. Winkler, municipal architect of the city of Altona[116].

Figure 9. Municipal Hospital by Winkler in Altona.

Although it had been recommended by the City Council that as much as possible of the Lienau plan be retained, a strong Victorian Gothic feeling, typical of Winkler's work, completely altered the broadly treated Italian Romanesque conception of the competition drawing. The increase in height of the building from two to three stories, the steeper pitch of the gables, the introduction of a decidedly Gothic porch and the gothicization of the brickwork design under the eaves, bear witness to the passage of the years and the swift change in taste. Whether Lienau was consulted regarding these changes, I do not know, but it seems unlikely. He was in America by this time.

The municipal hospital in Altona survived the devastating bombings of the Hamburg area during World War II and is still in use today (1957).

Lienau Comes to America

We have no reliable information regarding Lienau's activities from the early part of 1847, when we know he was working in Paris, until late autumn 1848, when he embarked for New York from Amsterdam. He appears to have left Paris in May 1847, if we take as evidence the six drawings given to him by his French friends[117]. These sketches must surely have been meant as souvenirs and *bon voyage* gifts. According to Elie Brault, Lienau returned to Germany and practiced there for two years before coming to the United States[118]. That he must have spent at least the summer of 1847 in Germany is attested by his participation in the Altona hospital competition. Unfortunately, we are completely in the dark regarding his whereabouts from the end of 1847 until the following fall. J. Henry Lienau believes that he spent some time in England before coming to the United States[119]. This trip must have been made some time late in 1847 or early in 1848. No substantiating evidence in the form of visas, documents, letters, or drawings has survived.

Reasons for Lienau's decision to emigrate to the United States are not hard to find. We can assume that, like thousands of others[120], he was disturbed by the unsettled political and economic conditions in Europe as a result of the crop failures of the middle '40s and the revolutions of 1848. Conditioned also by long years of association with Labrouste to look forward rather than backward, he must have found the vision of a relatively undeveloped country too hard to resist. Many of the German guidebooks on the United States, which appeared in great quantity from the mid-'40s on, mentioned the excellent opportunities for an educated architect in America[121]. Finally, the fact that Lienau's older brother Michael was established here and doing well certainly must have helped him make the decision to leave the Old World behind.

Shortly after October 24, 1848, when the police of the city of Amsterdam gave him permission to leave for the United States[122], Lienau set sail on one of the small barks plying between Amsterdam and New York. These boats carried cargo and a limited number of passengers. It is strange that he sailed on a vessel of this kind, instead of taking advantage of the much more highly recommended service offered by the lines operating between Le Havre, Bremen, Hamburg, Liverpool, and New York[123]. He could well have afforded first-class accommodations on a clipper ship or on one of the new, fast steamboats that negotiated the transatlantic crossing in ten and a half to twelve days[124]. Moreover, the winter months, with the risk of high winds and heavy seas, were hardly the ideal time for an ocean voyage. The reason for his choice of port and time of departure is made clear by a small note in the *New York Evening Post* of December 26, 1848:

> Arrived this forenoon. Bark Edinburgh, Conway [skipper], 44 ds fm Amsterdam, with mdze to Adams, Lienau & Co. 20 passengers[125]

Lienau sailed from Amsterdam on November 12 on a ship chartered by his brother Michael, a commission merchant and importer of wines and liquors. Detlef had apparently been asked to keep an eye on the cargo!

During the unusually long voyage, Lienau is supposed to have made the acquaintance of another young architect by the name of Léon Marcotte[126]. This Léon may have been referred to him by a member of the Marcotte family, who studied with Lienau in Labrouste's *atelier*, one Léon-Florentin Marcotte[127]. We shall see that, a few years later, Léon Marcotte and Lienau formed a short-lived partnership, and they remained life-long friends.

Leinau was fortunate. While many "Forty-eighters" arrived here penniless without a trade and without friends, he was sure of a hearty welcome from his brother Michael, who had been established in the States since 1839 and was willing and able to give Detlef, now a mature man of thirty, a good start.

Chapter II.
New York in Mid-Century

Lienau's Arrival in New York

As his ship slipped quietly into the harbor early on that morning so long ago, Detlef Lienau, like so many immigrants before and since, scanned the horizon for his first glimpse of New York. Dozens of steamers, ships, schooners, sloops, and ferryboats dotted the icy waters. Beyond lay New York, a city of a half million inhabitants, clouded over by a great roll of smoke from the chimneys of countless steamboats, houses, and factories[1]. The many church spires, dominated by Trinity, provided welcome vertical accents to a city still predominantly horizontal (Fig. 10). When Lienau's ship docked at one of the many wharves along the East River, the din and confusion of the waterfront and muffled hum of the busy city beyond would have sounded strange after the long ocean voyage. He must have been glad to see his brother Michael, who quickly whisked him past the disreputable characters who haunted the docks in the hope of fleecing new arrivals. City streets were full of slush, remains of a pre-Christmas nor'easter, which had blanketed New York with snow. On the ferry to Jersey City, where Michael lived, Lienau got a closer look at New York[2], the city he would come to know so well and to whose architectural development he himself would contribute so much in the next four decades.

Figure 10. New York from the steeple of St. Paul's Church (1848).

Almost at once, there set in a most rewarding give-and-take between Lienau and his new environment. Lienau warmly responded to and wholeheartedly adopted—and adapted to—current American architectural practices, while at the same time New York profited from the background, taste, and extensive training the young architect brought to it from Europe. Thus, he was able to discipline the manner and definitely raise the standards of New York architecture. Lienau and the city of New York needed each other; on that December morning of 1848, they entered into a long and fruitful collaboration.

Michael Lienau, the Boorӕms, and Van Vorsts

Detlef owed most of his early commissions, as well as some of the most important undertakings of his later years, to his older brother Michael (1816-1893)[3]. Michael Lienau had been trained in Frankfurt, Germany, by an uncle who, like his own father, was in the wine business. At the age of twenty, he went to work for a well known firm of French wine exporters, on whose behalf he traveled to North Africa and South America. As their agent, he made his first trip to the United States in 1838, an abortive expedition, for the vessel was wrecked off the coast of New Jersey. There were few survivors. Michael Lienau's heroic rescue of the ship's mate was recalled many years later. After several trips to France, and back again, Michael decided to make his home in the United States.

In 1841, he established the firm of Diedrichs & Linau [*sic*], importers of wines and liquors, at 54 Broadway. After the death in 1844 of his partner, Francis Diedrichs—whose widow Detlef later married[4]—Michael decided to try his luck as a cotton broker. This enterprise, under the firm name of Bell, Adams & Linau at 87-89 Wall Street, lasted for only two years (1845-1847), after which it was continued by Adams alone. For the next few years, Michael Linau was listed as a commission merchant in the New York City directories[5]; he dealt chiefly in wines and liquors[6]. From 1847 on, the listing "Lienau" replaced "Linau". Eventually, as the head of the firm M. Lienau & Company, incorporated in the early 1850s, Michael built a considerable reputation and amassed a good-size fortune[7]. According to his obituary, he was a Free Mason and "highly esteemed by everyone who knew him... in the wine and spirit trade, he was venerated as a merchant of the old school, whose word could always be trusted without question." In later years, his activities took him into other fields: He served as the first president of the German

Savings Bank, and as a director of several New York fire insurance companies. In his official capacity on the Board of Directors of the Matthiessen-Weichers Sugar Refining Company and president of the First National Bank of Jersey City, he was able to swing at least two important commissions for new buildings for his brother[8]. Michael Lienau is an excellent example of the German immigrants of the last century, whose foresight, venturesome spirit, and hard work laid the foundation for many of our present-day industries and commercial enterprises[9].

Michael's social contacts were also extremely important for Detlef from both a professional and personal standpoint. When Detlef arrived in the United States, Michael had just moved to Jersey City, having first lived in New York City and then in New Brighton. Through Michael's family connections, Detlef Lienau made the acquaintance of some of New Jersey's leading citizens. Michael married twice, both times into prominent New York and New Jersey families. Sarah Adeline (1823-1847), his first wife, was a daughter of Henry (Hendrik) Booræm (1784-1834), a very successful New York importer and a director of several New York banks. The Booræm family was descended from one of the earliest settlers in New Amsterdam. Hendrik himself was described by Scoville, the author of a chatty but informative work in several volumes, *The Old Merchants of New York*, as "a very elegant man in his manners, and very rich"[10]. Michael Lienau must have met the Booræms through the Diedrichs family: Francis's brother had been a business associate of Henry Booræm. Henry A. Booræm (1815-1889), Sarah Adeline's brother and also a well known figure in the New York business world and in the political and social life of Jersey City, later became an important client of Detlef[11].

Michael's second wife, whom he married in 1859, was Sarah Francis Van Vorst, a widow. She and her sister Cornelia, the wife of Henry A. Booræm, both were daughters of Johannis Van Vorst, a sixth generation descendant of one of the oldest and wealthiest families of New Jersey. The Van Vorsts had acquired large land holdings since the first of the name had settled in New Jersey in 1636. Part of this tract was known as Van Vorst Township, until it merged with the township of Jersey City. The Van Vorst mansion, a fine example of Greek Revival style[12], was famous for its lovely garden. In it was preserved the base of the statue of George III, which had stood in Bowling Green in New York until its demolition by overzealous patriots during the Revolutionary War. A Van Vorst had run the first ferry from New York to Jersey City in 1764, with a landing at Powles Hook. The family continued to figure prominently in the affairs of New Jersey throughout the 19th century.

These were the people with whom Detlef was associated most intimately in his first years in this country. Now let us take a look at the town in which he found himself.

New York in 1849

During his first year in New York, naturally enough, Lienau did little architectural work. Foreseeing that it might take some time for his brother to establish a practice as an architect, Michael put Detlef into business as a commission merchant at 55 Broadway[13]. One can assume that Detlef took advantage of the normal activities connected with his business to familiarize himself with the language, customs, and architecture of his new surroundings.

Figure 11. Broadway at Exchange Place (1848).

Language difficulties must have been negligible; in addition to the English commonly taught in German schools, Detlef presumably had had some time to speak it in England. Moreover, a great many French people and a large number of Germans lived in New York in the 1840s, with whom Lienau certainly had a common bond. They established their own newspapers, built their own houses of worship, and founded numerous clubs and societies that took a benevolent interest in new arrivals to this country[14]. Directly across from Lienau's office (Fig. 11)[15] was the Hotel Français-Espagnol; Delmonico's, the favorite eating place of the French and German merchants, was but two blocks away; and farther uptown was the Café de la Republique.

First Impressions

But these must have seemed like green oases in a desert waste; there was little else in the New York of 1849 to remind Lienau of Berlin, Munich, or Paris. Indeed, New York must have seemed decidedly small-town and rather raw to him, despite its half million inhabitants[16]. Old timers like Philip Hone and James Fenimore Cooper could still remember the town of 1800 with some 60,000 souls. With its population adding refugees from the Irish potato famine of 1845 and also by forty-eighters like himself, Lienau saw that New York was growing by leaps and bounds[17]. [Population figures for Manhattan rose from 371,223 in 1845 to a figure variously reported as 515,394 and 515,547 in 1850.]

Most of the prints of the period are misleading. Almost without exception, they give to the city a mistaken appearance of genteel dignity and quiet repose, as though they had been sketched on a Sunday with both the houses and the people freshly scrubbed and on their best behavior[18]. To get the real "feel" of the New York of 1849, we must go to literature, to the diarists of the period like Philip Hone and George Templeton Strong, to the impressions of travelers from abroad, and to writers such as James Fenimore Cooper and Walt Whitman. John C. Myers's vivid and still timely description of "the greatest emporium of the western hemisphere" will serve as our introduction to New York, which he characterized as

> a dusty, busy, great and animating emporium. In this mighty metropolis, the stranger from abroad may see its fine buildings, its long streets and handsome places; its dense throngs of inhabitants, the immense shipping and its enormous trade. He may observe on the one hand, the princely dwelling, the costly equipage and the splendid appearance; and on the other hand, the squalid hut of poverty, the filth of extreme misery and degradation. He may perceive the edifying throngs gathering and whirling, scattering and hurrying hither and thither, in the activity of commercial pursuits. He may here become confused by the never-ending turbulence and commotion, with the hundreds of mingled notes and noises which are ever rising from the multifarious trades and occupations of its thousands of inhabitants. And among its mingled crowds, he may get Frenchmen, Spaniards, Italians, Austrians, Swiss, Germans, Russians, Chinese, Jews, Turks, Africans, Portuguese, English, Southrons and Yankees; all co-mingling in the same hour, in the same street, in the same scene... He here sees

that nothing is fixed, nothing is permanently settled—all is moving and removing, organizing and disorganizing, building up and tearing down; the ever active spirit of change seems to pervade all bodies, all things in this mighty metropolis[19].

The constant search for something new, the driving desire for change, the purely provisional quality that still characterizes New York today, fascinated American writers and European visitors alike[20].

What most impressed foreign visitors to these shores was the noise, the confusion, the dirt, and the traffic problem. What a familiar ring this has! The crowded omnibuses and particularly the horse cars running on rails were a constant source of surprise to Europeans[21]. All agreed that it was quicker to walk than to ride, and that to cross Broadway at the noon hour was to take your life in your own hands[22]. An elevated railroad had already been proposed as a solution to the constantly recurring question of "what to do with Broadway"[23]. A few years later, Genin, the enterprising hatter, put up his famous bridge across Broadway, from his store to St. Paul's Chapel, to take care of the terrific crush just below City Hall and P.T. Barnum's American Museum (Fig. 12)[24].

Figure 12. View of Broadway (1850).

Broadway, so different from anything Lienau knew, was the most famous street in America. To Walt Whitman, Broadway epitomized the life of the city[25]. Already over two miles long, it extended from the Battery to Union Square[26]. Only a few years earlier, Grace Church had been built at the "head" of the street, for at that time it was assumed that Broadway would not extend much beyond Tenth Street. Now, Grace Church was finished and looked down upon a city rushing far beyond it, reaching out into places where, in Philip Hone's words, only "a few years since cattle grazed, and orchards dropped their ripened fruits"[27]. Hone, a former mayor of New York, and George Templeton Strong, whose *Diary* provides us with such a wonderful picture of the development of New York between 1835 and 1875, remembered the days when the Battery and lower Broadway had been a quiet residential district[28], lined with neat two- and three-story red-brick houses[29]—New York's favorite promenade. The Battery, with its fine weeping willows, was still a favorite promenade for moonlight strolls; on a Sunday, it was crowded with children, sailors, and new arrivals to this country, all enjoying the fresh sea breezes and magnificent view of the harbor[30]. By the time Lienau arrived here, the character of lower Broadway had changed completely. As far uptown as Bleecker Street, it had become a street of shops, warehouses, and hotels[31]. That this transformation was far from orderly is attested to by all the writers of the period, one of whom aptly compares Broadway to a boy "who grows so fast that he can't stop to tie up his shoes"[32]. Every visitor to the city commented on the disgraceful condition of the streets. Lady Wortley, who visited the United States in 1849, found our thoroughfares littered with "piles of lumber, mounds of brick, pyramids of stones, and stacks of goods," which made the sidewalks practically impassable. Of New York itself, she wrote it "certainly is handsome... yet, there is something about it which gives the impression of a half-finished city"[33]. Every visitor was impressed by the "go-ahead" Yankee spirit[34] of New Yorkers, who then as now were in such a hurry that they hardly allowed time to complete what they had already begun. "American minutes," wrote the Scottish publisher William Chambers, "would seem almost to be worth English days!"[35]

New York Architecture

The building boom of the mid-'30s in New York, stemmed for a time by the panic of 1837, resumed in the '40s. By 1845, it had assumed such proportions that it was commented upon time and again in the press[36]. At first, the old downtown residences, such as the one in which Lienau kept his office in 1849, were left unaltered on the exterior, But, as time went on, a glass front with granite piers on the street level was substituted for the regulation classical entrance portico, which had been raised a half story above the street. The effect of such alterations and rebuilding of whole blocks, particularly after the fire of 1845, may be seen in prints of the east side of Broadway between Bowling Green and Exchange Place (Fig. 11). This kind of building alteration was modeled after the store type originated in 1829 by Ithiel Town in his design for Tappan's store on

Pearl Street. The effect of this revolutionary design on commercial architecture in New York—particularly after the fire of 1835 that destroyed so much of the older section of the city—and its rapid spread to other cities in the United States has been discussed fully elsewhere[37]. By 1849, however, the Town formula, so well adapted to the needs of the '30s, was outmoded. Larger, more monumental buildings were needed[38], expressive of the ever-increasing importance of New York as a commercial center.

Figure 13. Broadway from Chambers Street, looking north (1850).

In 1845, A.T. Stewart, quick to sense the temper of the times, purchased the land on which had stood McComb's Washington Hall, with the intention of erecting a dry goods store. When it was opened a year later, Stewart's "marble palace" (Fig. 13) was acclaimed as "magnificent beyond anything of its kind in the New World, or in the Old"[39]. Certainly to contemporaries, of all the buildings on Broadway, this seemed best to symbolize the spirit of the new commercial age. Today, we pass by the building on the northeast corner of Chambers Street and Broadway without, perhaps, giving it a second glance, though it is still a handsome edifice. But its unusual height, the use of gleaming marble, and its well organized, if much simplified, Italian high Renaissance design, made it one of the real turning points in the history of New York's commercial architecture[40] (for its period comparable in importance to Lever House). Let us read a description of it a few years later by the editor of the "Easy Chair Chats" in *Harper's*:

> A few year ago, when a man returned from Europe, his eye being full of the lofty buildings of the continent, our cities seemed

insignificant and mean... But the moment Stewart's fine building was erected, the difficulty appeared. That tyrannized over the rest of the street—that was a keynote, a model. There had been other high buildings, but none so stately and simple. And even now, there is, in its way, no finer street effect than the view of Stewart's building on a clear, blue, brilliant day, from a point as low on Broadway as... Trinity Church, it rises out of the sea of green foliage in the Park, a white marble cliff, sharply drawn against the sky.

He concludes the article with a sigh of relief that the Greek temple epoch of architecture has passed, and

as we totter up to our Easy Chair, and look up to the beautiful buildings in the Broadway, [we] will not long for Italy and Italian beauty, but [will] be gratefully contented for what we see[41].

Of Ottoviano Gori, the Italian marble cutter who is generally credited with the design of the Stewart building[42], little is known beyond the fact that he had superintended the erection of the eight marble pillars in Isaiah Rogers's Merchants' Exchange in the late '40s. By 1855, according to the State Census of that year[43], his marble manufactory at 895 Broadway was doing a thriving business. He grossed $80,000 annually and employed fifty-six in help. As Winston Weisman points out in his discussion of the Stewart store, one would imagine that A.T. Stewart would have sought out a well known architect, rather than a marble cutter, to design such a large structure[44]. P.B. Wight's attribution to Gori only of the design of the exterior marble work and to Snook of the architectural superintendence of the structure would be worth investigating, particularly since the Stewart store is rather closely related stylistically to the Metropolitan Hotel, known to have been designed by John B. Snook (1815-1901)[45].

Lienau certainly must have admired the store: This was one of the few buildings in New York that, though lacking the finesse of a great master, nonetheless achieved a monumental effect with the simplest of means. Years later, Anthony Trollope, the English novelist and author of the finest description of America of the early '60s, called Stewart's the handsomest building in the city[46]. It was undoubtedly the first building in New York to use the popular Barryesque Italian *palazzo* mode[47] on a large scale. Following the enthusiastic advocacy of the style by Arthur Gilman (1821-1882) in the *North American Review* (1844)[48], the Barryesque mode was introduced simultaneously in this country by John Notman (1810-1865) in the Philadelphia Athenæum (1845-1847)[49], often referred to as the first exemplar of the type here, and in the Stewart store in New York. In the case of Stewart's, the early application of the clubhouse mode to commercial architecture is quite understandable if one takes into account the national origins of Gori and Snook (Italian and English respectively) and, more important perhaps, the character of that astute Scotch-Irishman, Alexander T. Stewart himself (1803-1876). As Henry-Russell Hitchcock points out, Barry's club style "early came to be accepted as an expression of urban wealth and power"[50], a fact that would have been lost on the man who, in the course of the next several decades, did his best to immortalize himself in architectural monuments[51].

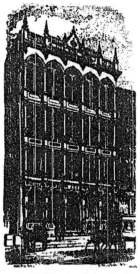

Figure 14. Bowen-McNamee Store by Joseph A. Wells.

Of almost equal importance in contemporary descriptions of New York's commercial architecture was Joseph C. Wells's store for the silk merchants Bowen & McNamee at 112-114 Broadway, opposite Trinity Church, built in 1849-1850 (Fig. 14)[52]. This firm, interestingly enough, had begun as an offshoot of Arthur Tappen & Company, which had made architectural history twenty years earlier. Built of white marble, the Bowen & McNamee building was described as an "Elizabethan palace," presenting "the most showy and elegant front on Broadway"[53]—quite a contrast to the sober Roman *palazzo* style of Stewart. In this building, Wells introduced New Yorkers to that other variant on the palace theme, the gay and picturesque Venetian type[54], here cleverly combined with Tudor reminiscences. Wells (c.1819-1860) was an English architect, established here since the mid-'30s, and a founder of the American Institute of Architects[55]; he should not be confused with Joseph Morrell Wells (1853-1890) of the firm of McKim, Mead & White. The Bowen-McNamee store created quite a stir. The extensive use of iron for interior supports was unusual; the open design and picturesque verticality of the façade displeased some critics. The anonymous author of that most interesting and well illustrated series of articles on New York architecture, "New York Daguerreotyped," published in *Putnam's Monthly Magazine*, objected strenuously to this perpendicularization[56]. Later, this feature was emphasized further by the addition of an extra story and, still later, by a mansard roof. Other less ornate specimens of definitely commercial architecture were beginning to appear on Broadway. The Moffat Building (1847-1848) and the Arcade Building (1848-1849)[57], the latter a large brownstone edifice given architectural distinction by rounding the corner of the building, a favorite device of English architects of the '40s[58], were but two of several constructed between 1847 and 1849 for strictly commercial use.

Figure 15. Metropolitan Hotel by Trench & Snook.

The hotels of Broadway greatly impressed visitors from abroad. Walking up Broadway, one noted that they ranged in size from modest boarding houses, lodged in former private residences, to large handsome buildings such as Delmonico's at the corner of Morris Street, designed by Frederick Diaper, or the older City Hotel built by John McComb and soon to be taken down. Finally, one reached the most splendid establishment of all just below City Hall— the Astor House. Built between 1832 and 1836 by the Boston architect Isaiah Rogers, it was one of the finest specimens of the Classical Revival in New York (Fig. 12)[59]. It was, indeed, the "Palais Royal" of New York[60]: All the bigwigs of the city gathered here to discuss the affairs of the day. But its position was soon to be challenged. Within a year or two of Lienau's arrival, larger and far more splendid hotels were built: the Metropolitan (1851-1852) by John B. Snook[61] (Fig. 15) and the St. Nicholas, attributed to both Snook and to Thomas & Son[62]. Both establishments catered to the ever-increasing demand for luxurious accommodations in this most cosmopolitan center of the United States. Indeed, the so-called "hotel-mania" was the subject of many an angry and sarcastic article in the journals of the time[63].

About the churches, while other visitors to New York had good words to say of the city's two grandest and newest houses of worship—Richard Upjohn's Trinity Church (1839-1846) and James Renwick's Grace Church (1843-1848)—I suspect that Lienau, his memories of the Old World still fresh in his mind, might have agreed with Horatio Greenough's characterization of Trinity as "an elephant dwindled to the size of a dog[64], and with Whitman's and Strong's condemnation of Grace Church as an inexcusably "showy" piece of architecture"[65]. Even the ladies found much to criticize in the latter, according to Philip Hone[66]. Strong was undoubtedly influenced by the thinking of the ecclesiologists. Both the English Ecclesiological Society[67] and the American one[68] vigorously attacked tendencies toward display in church architecture and criticized the current disregard for what they called "reality" in architecture. To these men, reality meant adherence to the principle of truth to the nature of the material, an idea expounded here by Andrew Jackson Downing and later by Ruskin[69], and subservience to structural necessity—then, as now, a fundamental yardstick of architectural criticism. Any deviation therefrom, as in the case of Grace Church's "nasty" wooden steeple[70] or its "pipe-cleaners of columns"[71] supporting the clearstory and plaster vault, was considered anathema from a moral, as well as an aesthetic and structural, point of view[72]. Certainly, Lienau, as a disciple of Schinkel and Labrouste, would have been aware of Renwick's striving for effects that lay beyond his grasp. As one writer so aptly put it, Grace Church provided proof positive that "all that flams is not flamboyant"[73].

More likely, Blesch & Eidlitz's newly opened St. George's Church (1846-1848) at Stuyvesant Square, deeply under the influence of the *Rundbogenstil,* would have struck a responsive chord in Lienau (Fig. 16). *Putnam's* correspondent called this "the most sincerely built church in New York—we are not afraid to say in the United States..."[74]. George Templeton Strong also found the massiveness and solidity of St. George's to be consoling after Renwick's "pasteboard abominations"[75]. Of course, one must remember that Strong's criticisms of Renwick's architecture were always colored by his intense personal dislike of the man[76]. James Renwick, Jr. (1818-1892), one of the most successful architects of the period (whose work deserves a full-length study), seems to have been extremely unpopular[77]. His building for the Free Academy (later named the College of the City of New York), which opened on January 27, 1849, at Twenty-third Street and Fourth [Lexington] Avenue, was likewise severely criticized[78].

Figure 16. St. George's Church by Blesch & Eidlitz, with spires (left) until 1892 and after their removal (right).

If in this discussion of New York architecture of the mid-century, I have given special emphasis to the creation of the commercial palace, it is because these buildings represented the "last word" in architectural fashion. This is not surprising: The dry-goods industry, accounting for more than half of New York City's trade, enjoyed a unique position within the city's economy. As one writer expressed it, "calico is omnipotent, and whole streets melt away at her approach"[79]. Winston Weisman has very rightly called the commercial palace "the architectural symbol of the merchant prince"[80]. He notes that the showy aristocratic façades of the commercial palaces, which far exceeded their English prototypes in splendor[81], faithfully reflected the reaction in taste of the new "calico aristocracy" against the simpler ideals of the previous decades. This is a subject to which we shall return in discussing the private residences of the period, which have been deliberately omitted from this introductory section. One extremely important point was made by Weisman, namely that the flexibility and economy of the *palazzo* formula, whereby additional units could be added at little cost without destroying its visual effect, contributed in no small measure to its continued popularity throughout the next decades[82].

Figure 17. Astor Library by Saelzer.

It should not be forgotten that these buildings also represented the work of the younger generation of architects, Lienau's contemporaries, in whose work he would naturally be interested. Another outstanding *palazzo* of the time—this one closer to Venetian early Quattrocento palaces than to Roman examples, but described by its architect as "Byzantine"[83]—was Saeltzer's Astor Library (Fig. 17) on Lafayette Street, still is use today after extensive enlargements and alterations as the headquarters of the Hebrew Immigrant Aid Society (HIAS). In a competition held in the spring of 1849[84], Alexander Saeltzer (born c.1814)[85], a German architect who had established himself here in the early '40s, won first prize, and James Renwick, second prize. It would be interesting to know if Lienau was among the thirty architects who submitted designs; unfortunately, the records pertaining to the competition are lost[86]. In both the Astor Library and the Bowen-McNamee store, the early use of iron[87], including interior supports of columns, beams, and girders, is of considerable importance from a structural point of view, doubtless attributable to James Bogardus's experiments of 1848 and 1849[88]. We can assume that Lienau, fresh from Cendrier's office and indoctrinated by Labrouste, must have followed with great interest the erection of the Laing stores on Washington and Murray Streets and of Bogardus's own factory at the corner of Murray and Duane.

Until now, no mention has been made of the obviously important public and semi-public buildings of New York, which were fully described in every guidebook of New York and by every visitor to the city. The buildings of which New Yorkers were proudest—the City Hall, the "Tombs," the Custom House, the new Merchants' Exchange—were all products of stylistic tendencies of the previous decades[89]. Monumental though they were, to Lienau they must have seemed somewhat *retardataire* and provincial[90]. The French Renaissance flavor of New York's City Hall, however, as well as its charming setting, probably appealed to him. Like other visitors to New York, he must have been impressed by the tremendous amount of engineering knowledge that was poured into the construction of the Croton Water Works, with its great distributing reservoir (1842) at Fifth Avenue and Forty-second Street, on which Renwick had worked.

Figure 18. Wall Street (1850).

Walking back and forth between his own and his brother's place of business, Lienau must have come to know Wall Street and its architecture very well. With the exception of a few notable buildings (all products of New York's Classical Revival of the 1830s), the general aspect of Wall Street in 1849 (Fig. 18) belied its reputation, well established by this time, as the financial capital of the United States—the center of worship of the God Mammon and the "Almighty Dollar"[91]. As a matter of fact, with the exception of the Custom House and the Merchants' Exchange, which dwarfed the other buildings, Wall Street still retained much of its original quiet residential character. It is interesting to note that both the Custom House and the Merchants' Exchange, completed only a few years before Lienau's arrival here, were considered passé and impractical by the more advanced architectural critics of the period, less than a dozen years after their completion[92]. To Lienau, the lack of correspondence between the exterior and interior of the Custom House must have been disturbing, however fine each might be in itself. Perhaps, the Merchants' Exchange recalled to his mind Schinkel's use of a similar colonnade on a much more grandiose scale in his (Schinkel's) Altes Museum in Berlin. He must have been interested in the fireproof construction of the building and in the introduction of ironwork in the balconies.

But in Wall Street, indeed in all of New York (with the exception of City Hall Park), where were the great vistas, those magnificent avenues of approach that architects in Europe had exploited so dramatically for centuries[93]? Our illustration (Fig. 18) is misleading: The artist has made Wall Street appear much wider than it actually was. Even the more important banks, such as Isaiah Rogers's Bank of America on the north side of Wall Street between the Custom House and William Street, elbowed one another uncomfortably. They were, moreover, relatively small structures, two to three stories in height, their Classical Revival pretensions to architectural beauty no longer valid by the early 1850s. *Putnam's* description of these banks of the *ancien regime* reveals the change in taste:

> Doubtless, in their day, these tough granite dowagers bloomed with grace in the eyes of the young men who now look down regretfully upon their beards, gray as the structures they once admired. Yet to our eyes, these grim temples... are matters only for lamentation.

Concluding his description, the writer likens "these forsaken specimens of pseudo-Greek remains... to a crowd of... ballet dancers, who stand shivering and unregarded after the play and its applauses are over[94]."

The rest of the business concerns on the street operated from high-stooped converted residences[95] or from three- to four-story buildings of the Ithiel Town type, such as Jones Court (1829-1830), of which 87-89 Wall Street, Michael Lienau's headquarters [Fig. 19, not found in dissertation], was also a good example. But a new age was approaching. During the summer of 1849, the century-old stables at 37-43 Wall Street were replaced by Jauncey Court, a group of seven brick office buildings[96]. Unpretentious and utilitarian in style, they nonetheless were prophetic of the trend that ultimately produced the office building as we know it.

Nor was the new Barryesque *palazzo* formula long in making its appearance on Wall Street. The Bank of Manhattan was built in 1847-1848 in the old, rather undistinguished, residential style[97]. Other banks, demolished in the course of the next few years, were replaced by buildings more closely related to progressive stylistic trends. The razing of the old Bank of the Republic was reported without regret by *Putnam's* correspondent. Of the new bank (1851-1852), built by the firm of Burry & Rogers, he said: "In architecture, as in history, Greece has fallen a victim to Italy."[98] There can be no doubt that the English Barryesque tradition for banks and assurance offices, well established as the dominant mode in Britain by 1850, furnished the inspiration for this and many other buildings of the period in New York[99]. Yet, one should note a persistent emphasis on vertical elements in the organization of the façades, as mentioned previously in connection with the Bowen-McNamee store. This stylism sharply differentiates the early examples of commercial architecture both in New York and Philadelphia from their British prototypes, a fact that is not without significance for the future.

Summary

The New York of 1849 that Lienau saw upon his arrival in this country was a busy, bustling city. The streets were not lined with gold, as many an ignorant immigrant had been lead to expect, but there was still room for an energetic young fellow who was not afraid to work hard and adapt himself to new ways. As Benjamin Franklin said years before of new arrivals to this country, "if he has any useful art, he is welcome..."[100] New ideas were eagerly taken up, in architecture as in business, Everyone agreed that it was "time for a change". The Classical Revival was spent. Reacting against the old ideas of red brick and white trim, the city was beginning to clothe itself in brownstone and marble. New Yorkers prided themselves on the fact that Broadway, at least in their eyes, had begun to rival the great thoroughfares of Europe. The commercial palaces and mansions of our great merchant princes were unhesitatingly equated with the palaces of the Italian grandees. Such, then, was the architectural climate that Lienau found upon his arrival here.

Now, let us see how quickly Lienau adapted himself to dominant architectural trends in this country, and indicate his specific contributions to the development of domestic architecture here. With the fine training he received during years of study abroad, he was far better equipped to deal with the manifold problems of design and construction than most of his colleagues. With few exceptions, even the best of them, men such as Richard Upjohn and Leopold Eidlitz, could not boast of such thorough professional training. Lienau initiated his career in this country with a small suburban cottage for his brother Michael. This will serve as a good introduction to the work of Lienau, for it provides a perfect illustration of the ease with which this immigrant adapted himself to American ways in architecture.

Chapter III.
First Commissions

Cottage for Michael Lienau, Jersey City, c.1849

Two sheets of drawings in the Lienau Collection[1], one a preliminary rendering and the other a working drawing, are all that remain of the cottage in Jersey City that was designed by Detlef for his brother shortly after the former's arrival here. It is quite evident that Lienau, anxious to show Michael what he could do, lavished considerable love and care on the beautifully rendered preliminary watercolor he executed in pale tan, blue, pink, and green wash (Fig. 20). The simple five-bay façade gains a certain distinction through its very concise articulation: The central section is clearly set off from the side bays; horizontally, the three stories are differentiated from each other by the studied alternation of vertical and horizontal planking. The contrast is subtly worked out between flat lighted wall surfaces and shadows cast by projecting eaves, canopies, and porches, by the deep reveals of windows, and by the delicate openwork patterns of porch and balcony railings and the verge board.

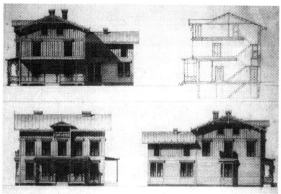

Figure 20. Michael Lienau cottage by brother Detlef.

The chief interest of the sketch lies in its clever amalgamation of old and new world traditions, and the fusion of the Swiss chalet type with the "American cottage style"[2]. The Swiss mode, as already noted[3], was extremely popular in the 1840s in Europe, particularly in France and Germany, because the chalet carried with it associations that irresistibly endeared it to a generation brought up on the works of Goethe, Schiller, and Chateaubriand. Both the chalet style on the continent and the cottage mode here and in England are interesting, moreover, as an architectural expression of the endeavor of the middle and working classes—fleeing from overcrowded cities created by the Industrial Revolution—to re-create for themselves in the new suburban areas[4] ways of life known to their parents and grandparents. In the United States, Downing's promotion of an American cottage style, which was meant to provide a simple yet tasteful home for even the plain workingman, translated into architectural terms the principles of Jacksonian democracy. His ready-made plans were the architectural parallels to the popular prints of Currier & Ives and the sculptural groups of John Rogers. In matters of taste, Andrew Jackson Downing (1815-1852) was the acknowledged dictator of the mid-century[5].

This, then, was the general background of the Lienau cottage in Jersey City. Its immediate architectural antecedents are provided by Lienau's student drawings of Tyrolean architecture and by the type of Swiss chalet popularized by Victor Petit, whose popular plan book, *Habitations champêtres* (1848), displays as frontispiece a cottage in the Swiss style[6]. The jagged outline of the Swiss farmhouse was characteristically compressed into a rigidly formal pattern in its transfer from the Alps to a suburban French environment. This type of French-Swiss villa, rather than its original prototype, provided the background for the Lienau cottage, greatly facilitating a fusion with the traditional American five-bay symmetrical house façade and plan. The plan of the house, with narrow center hall flanked by a pair of rooms to each side and rear service ell, is purely American[7]. So are the porches, three in number, and the parlor with its polygonal bay window. These features were already typical of the American cottage at this time, thanks to their enthusiastic promotion by Downing.

The early appearance of Swiss elements is of considerable interest, since the chalet style was just beginning to make its appearance in the United States. After Downing briefly mentioned it as a possibility for the American cottage type in *Cottage Residences* (1842)[8], its earliest advocate, at least in print, seems to have been William Ranlett, who included several Swiss designs in *The Architect* when it first appeared in book form in 1847[9]. The New York *Evening Post* of August 22, 1849, made special note of the sudden popularity of the Swiss style in rural areas of Brooklyn[10]. Leopold Eidlitz did much to promote this new idiom[11]. But the Swiss mode never became quite as ubiquitous in the United States as in Europe; English cottage and Italian villa traditions were too strong in this country. M. Field, British-born architect whose *Rural Architecture* was one of the most widely read plan books of the 1850s, somewhat condescendingly characterized the "German villa" style of Staten Island as a cross between the Swiss and the Italian, having the faults of both and the virtues of neither. "To adopted citizens from Germany, we should be far from denying the pleasure of reviving home associations, but to all others we cannot recommend the style for any aesthetic qualities."[12]

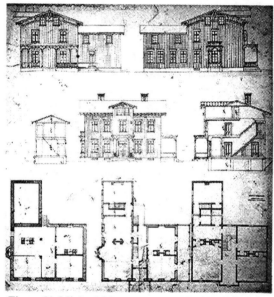

Figure 21. Michael Lienau cottage. Working drawing.

Apparently, Lienau's early attempt to introduce the style here was not a success, for in the working drawings for the house (Fig. 21), he abandoned many of the refinements (which makes the sketch so charming), perhaps for reasons of economy, or because Michael wanted something more "American". Particularly drastic was a substitution of vertical board and batten construction throughout for the much more sophisticated contrast of vertical and horizontal planking of the sketch, a reduction in the width of the porch, and the elimination of the balcony in the front elevation. The result was a house differing very little from hundreds of simple bracketed cottages of the period. This, of course, had its positive side as well: It demonstrated how quickly Lienau adapted himself to American taste, methods of designing, and construction practices. Perhaps, he felt that a Swiss cottage, eminently suitable for a wild mountain retreat, would be out of place on a suburban street, a point made by many writers of the period, such as Cleaveland and Backus in *Village and Farm Cottages*[13]. The substitution of board and batten construction, which Downing advocated for its greater truth in expressing the essentially vertical skeleton of the frame house[14], may simply have been grounded here in the desire to economize.

As for the construction of the house, it is interesting to note that "furring-off" of the walls to prevent dampness was a practice more usual in brick and stone houses in America than in frame structures[15]. French casement windows and doors opening onto the side porch were features that were gaining in popularity[16]. Lack of built-in plumbing is typical of the middle-class house of the period, while on the other hand the amount of closet and storage space is above average. The house must have served Michael Lienau well: He lived in it for almost twenty years.

Description of Jersey City

It seems incredible that a cottage of this type could have been built in the middle of Jersey City a little over a hundred years ago. But Jersey City in 1849 was a very different place from what it is today. The woodlands opposite New York—in what is now Jersey City and Hoboken—were still a favorite picnic ground for New Yorkers on a Sunday ramble[17]. By the end of the 1830s, the area began to change. George Templeton Strong, whose *Diary* provides us with such a wonderful picture of the development of metropolitan New York, foresaw that the section was destined to become a future metropolis. He described dreary and desolate vacant lots, "neither city nor country, but a detestable approximation of both"[18]. The strategic location of Jersey City, on the point of land called Powles Hook directly opposite New York City (to which it was early linked by ferry service) and the fact that from the late 1830s on it was the terminus of the Morris Canal and of the present Pennsylvania and Erie railroad systems, made it certain that the town would develop into an important distribution and industrial center.

When it acquired a city charter in 1838, Jersey City entered a new epoch. A year later, the city was described as having two hundred and fifty buildings, one bank, four churches, and a glass factory[19]. The decade of the '40s witnessed great commercial and industrial development. Foundries, additional railroad terminals, and the

Cunard wharves[20], were built, old concerns were expanded (*e.g.* the Colgate soap factory and the Lorillard Snuff and Tobacco Manufactory), and new industries were established. As a result, Jersey City drew to its side of the Hudson River many new settlers, among them Michael Lienau, joined a few years later by Detlef, who maintained residence there until just a few months before his death in 1887. By 1850, according to the census of that year, the combined townships of Jersey City and Van Vorst (separately incorporated in 1841 and named after the Van Vorst family) had a population of almost 12,000[21]. The completion of the water works in 1854 gave additional stimulus; by 1855, there were approximately 22,000 people living there, and residences of the wealthier citizens (who had established themselves in business or commuted to New York by ferry[22]) were compared to those of Fifth Avenue[23]. Michael had come to Jersey City at the beginning of the boom, hence the modest countrified appearance of his suburban cottage.

The later history of Jersey City, its expansion into one of the great industrial centers of the United States, need not concern us here; the problems of 1849 and 1850 were of a different order.

Grace Church (Van Vorst), Jersey City, 1850-1853

Figure 22. Grace Church (Van Vorst) by Detlef Lienau.

One of the most pressing of these problems among Lienau's relatives and friends in Jersey City revolved around building a suitable place of worship for the small Episcopalian congregation that was officially organized in 1847 at a meeting held at Henry A. Booræm's home[24]. Services were first held in the Baptist meeting place; then, a small temporary chapel was built according to plans by Robert C. Bacot, a well known civil engineer, originally from Charleston, who for many years figured prominently in the development of Jersey City[25]. Late in 1848, the parish began to give serious consideration to the project of building a church, made possible by a gift from the Van Vorst family[26] of three lots of land at the corner of Erie Avenue and South Seventh (now Second) Street. Since Michael Lienau was an active member of the congregation and Henry A. Booræm's brother-in-law, the choice of Detlef Lienau as the architect for the new building was a natural one. Plans were drawn up and accepted by the vestry on May 7, 1850. The original contract drawings, as well as many other drawings connected with the church (known as Grace Church [Van Vorst]) are preserved in the Lienau Collection[27].

Figure 23. Grace Church (Van Vorst). Architect's rendering.

Illustrated here (Figs. 22-25) is a photograph of the building, which still stands today, the architect's rendering of the elevation as originally planned, the plan, and a view of the interior. Though this building really falls outside the scope of this paper, its inclusion here is a natural one: It was one of Lienau's first important commissions and helped establish his reputation as a serious architect among his neighbors in Jersey City.

The cornerstone of Grace Church was laid on December 6, 1850, but the church was not opened until the spring of 1853. Mrs. Van Vorst, the moving spirit of the parish, died early in 1851; then, money ran low and work progressed very slowly. The church stood without a roof all through the winter of 1851 to 1852 "for the storms to beat upon, and the spotless snow, apt symbol of grace, descended from heaven and so became the first occupant of the sanctuary"[28]. Building was again resumed in the spring of 1852 and by summer the building was under roof and the first stage of the tower completed. The latter remained unfinished until 1912 when the present tower was built. The church was first opened, appropriately enough, for a special service on May 11, 1853, to celebrate the marriage of the architect, Detlef Lienau, to Catherine Van Giesen (1819-1861), the widow of Francis Diedrichs, Michael Lienau's former partner, and Henry A. Booræm's younger sister. A week later, on May 18, the first general service was held, followed by a luncheon for the whole parish at John Van Vorst's home. It can readily be seen that the building of Van Vorst church was strictly a family affair, sponsored and carried out by the Van Vorsts and the Booræms.

Grace Church, which recently celebrated its hundredth anniversary[29], is an unpretentious, but extremely pleasant, little church, built of warm, orange-tinted brownstone from nearby quarries in Belleville, New Jersey. At first glance (Figs. 22 and 23), the church seems typical of the English parish churches of the period.

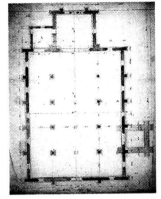

Figure 24. Grace Church (Van Vorst). Plan.

The plan (Fig. 24), not only in general proportions and shape, but also in the use of the rectangular chancel, is obviously derived from English sources, more probably from Frank Wills's popular book, *Ancient English Ecclesiastical Architecture*, published in New York in 1850, than from A.W.N. Pugin's churches of the 1840s. At Donington, for example, the usual south porch is replaced by a tower, as at Grace Church[30]. Wills, an English architect, mentioned previously in connection with Henry Dudley, was to all intents and purposes the spokesman for the ecclesiologists in the United States. His book, published early in 1850, was based upon a series of papers he had read before the New York Ecclesiological Society in previous years[31]. Any Episcopal congregation contemplating building a church in the metropolitan area would have been familiar with his point of view. Wills's special fondness for Early English Gothic may also have influenced the choice of style for Van Vorst church. (Ecclesiologists preferred to call this style "First Pointed," for which Wills was criticized by orthodox ecclesiologists[32], who preferred the Decorated or "Second Pointed" phase of Gothic.) The heavy wall construction of the church, faced with small irregular local stone (in this case, brownstone) laid in random courses, is of the type usually recommended for English parish churches. The broach spire in the architect's original rendering (Fig. 23) also is typical.

Figure 25. Grace Church (Van Vorst). Interior (1915).

On the other hand, it is important to note that elements quite foreign to the English parish church tradition entered into both the design and construction of the building, in contrast to, say, Richard Upjohn's Grace Church (1847-1848) in Newark, with which Lienau was doubtless familiar[33]. The use of buttresses in combination with a corbel frieze and the round clearstory windows (oculi) certainly are based more upon Romanesque traditions. These elements are found again and again in German and Italian churches of the 12th and 13th centuries. Grace Church thus takes its place among the early examples of Romanesque Revival churches in this country, recently investigated by Carroll Meeks[34]. Inside (Fig. 25), the small church was divided into a nave and two aisles by eight monolithic columns and covered with an open timber roof, reinforced with "scissor" beams at the juncture of nave and chancel. Such a roof was rather rare in England, though used occasionally by A.W.N. Pugin; it occurred far more frequently in Germany, where this form of construction was considered standard practice[35].

Grace Church is, therefore, a very early example of what Meeks has called a "synthetic eclectic" approach to architecture[36], combining in a single edifice motifs from various sources, in this instance early English Gothic and Italo-German stylistic elements, together with German traditions of timber construction. These Lienau must have learned during his years of training as a carpenter's apprentice in Berlin and Hamburg. As may be seen from the illustrations, the result is a simple but harmonious design, achieved by a fine balancing against each other of the main masses of the building. The deep cutting of the windows into the wall surface and the sparse use of decorative elements produce an effective play of light and shade. The use of irregularly shaped stones of various sizes and tints of brown, tan, and orange gives an interesting texture and coloration to the building, which are lacking in the later additions to the church[37].

Except for the fresco job on the interior in 1872, the church itself remained unchanged until 1912, when a donation by Mrs. Mary Ann King permitted the completion of the tower over the Baptistry. As is very apparent even in the photograph (Fig. 22), the square battlemented tower in the tradition of some of Upjohn's famous churches[38] gives a stunted appearance to the entire edifice and is completely out of keeping with the original intention of the architect (Fig. 23).

Today, Grace Church, built as a parish church for a small, select community, serves an overcrowded slum area. It is run by a three-priest team[39], which in a determined effort to curb juvenile delinquency has dedicated itself to working toward bettering race relations in a mixed neighborhood, improving housing conditions, and providing a youth program for the entire community.

Unexecuted Church Projects

Before considering Lienau's other important commissions of the early 1850s, mention should be made of several unidentified, undated drawings[40], which evidently belong to this period. A pencil sketch for a small church with a tall tower to the left of the entrance is notable as the only purely Gothic architectural project in the entire Lienau Collection. It is surely significant that Lienau used only the earlier phases of Gothic, in contrast to Renwick and Upjohn: A constant element in his work is the love of simple forms and the retention of the solid wall surface.

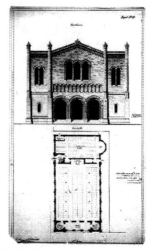

Figure 26. Study for a church by Lienau & Marcotte.

Other drawings provide evidence of the strength of the
Romanesque Revival of the middle of the 19th century. Alternate
designs for a church on Fifth Avenue, of which one is illustrated
here (Fig. 26), are interesting chiefly because they provide the sole
evidence among all the drawings in the Lienau Collection of Lienau's
partnership with Léon Marcotte, a topic to which we shall return.
Both drawings are signed in Lienau's hand, "D. Lienau & L.
Marcotte, archts". According to the New York City directories, the
firm of Marcotte and Lienau existed for only two years, from 1852 to
1854[42]. We may therefore safely assign this date to the drawings,
which were probably competition drawings for one of several
churches built on Fifth Avenue in those years[43]. The plans of both
projects are basically the same. A porch, flanked by a staircase
leading to the gallery, gives access to a hall in which the space is
barely divided into nave and aisles by slender columns. The pulpit is
separated from the main body of the church only by a railing in the
one drawing and by a low flight of steps in the other, a concept
familiar to American churchgoers of the Low Church tradition.
Opposite the entrance and at right angles to the hall was the lecture
room, with a Sunday school on the second floor. As for the design
of the façade, one drawing is definitely in the Romanesque mode, the
other closer to early Gothic principles of organization, though the
vocabulary is still Romanesque. It is, of course, possible that Lienau
and Marcotte may have drawn upon recollections of European
churches or prints thereof[43], but it seems more likely that they were
influenced by recent churches in New York by Eidlitz, Renwick, and

Upjohn[44]. It is important to note that both projects are strictly symmetrical and eschew the picturesque effect to be gained by the use of dissimilar towers, a common practice in this period.

Though neither of these projects is particularly happy from an aesthetic point of view, they are worth mentioning if only to round out the picture we have now—thanks to Carroll Meeks—of the pre-Richardsonian Romanesque Revival of the second and third quarters of the 19th century in America. Note, however, that Romanesque designs by Lienau have little in common with the style as Richardson later developed it. Richardson emphasized mass, plasticity, and surface texture. The style of the Lienau drawings is much closer in spirit to the *Rundbogenstil* of the 1840s, even to the Neo-Grec. One point deserves particular emphasis: The elements, though not themselves classical, are used in a classical, not a romantic or picturesque, manner. Symmetry, balance, and the surface plane are always maintained, and the designs themselves are presented sharply and crisply as tinted pen and ink drawings.

Chapter IV.
Lienau and the Origins of the Second Empire Style in the United States

Lienau & Marcotte, c.1852-1854

The two drawings for a Fifth Avenue church mentioned in the previous chapter are our only proof of the existence of a working partnership between Lienau and Marcotte. Nothing else is known about their relationship or about Marcotte himself at this period. The two men, as mentioned previously, are supposed to have met on the boat on the voyage to this country. This is quite possible, since the earliest listing for both occurs in *Doggett's New York City Directory of 1849/1850*[1]. Marcotte's name does not appear in the directories of 1850/1851, but he is again listed in *Doggett's Street Directory of 1851*, this time as a member of the firm of Runguet, Leprince & Marcotte, architects[2]. By the middle of 1852 (until 1855, the directories appeared in July), Detlef Lienau and Léon Marcotte had evidently formed a partnership: The firm of Marcotte & Lienau at 654 Broadway is listed in the directories of 1852/1853 and 1853/1854. The following years, Detlef is listed alone as an architect at 341 Fourth Street, and Marcotte, furniture-maker, at 347 Fourth. As early as 1852, the latter had a separate listing in *Doggett's Business Directory* under "furniture". It is evident that Marcotte gradually became more interested in designing furniture than in architectural work, even though at this time he was still officially Lienau's partner. But Marcotte must have retained some interest in architectural matters: He was an honorary lifetime member of the New York Chapter of the American Institute of Architects[3].

Léon Marcotte is supposed to have come to this country from France, very highly recommended and with good contacts, so he may have been instrumental in getting Lienau some of his early commissions. It is impossible to know whether or not, in the two years of their association, he took part in the design of any of Lienau's projects, with the exception of the drawing for the Fifth Avenue church discussed previously. While the firm name according to the directories was "Marcotte & Lienau," it may be of some significance that the church projects were signed "Lienau & Marcotte". This might indicate that in architectural matters, Lienau was the boss; he was Marcotte's senior by seven years. In any case, the two men remained on friendly terms throughout the years. J. Henry Lienau recalls that, when he was a young boy, Marcotte often came to his house for Sunday dinner[4]. Lienau later built Marcotte's shops and warehouses[5].

Léon Marcotte: Furniture Designer and Decorator

Marcotte soon developed into a power to be reckoned with. He became one of the top-notch furniture designers of the day, specializing in the elegant and expensive French styles that wealthy Americans loved to display in their Fifth Avenue mansions and Newport "cottages". While popular interest in France had been evident earlier[6], the revolution of 1848 (followed by the *coup d'état* of 1852), the establishment of the Second Empire, and the marriage of Louis-Napoleon to the beautiful and charming Eugénie undoubtedly were a tremendous impetus in this country to adopt a taste for all things French[7]. Men like Lienau and Marcotte, trained in France, profited by this turn of events. They rode to success on the crest of a tidal wave of French influence, which by the 1860s had engulfed the entire upper *bourgeoisie* of the eastern seaboard.

By 1857, according to the city directories, Marcotte had assumed the more glamorous title of "interior decorator". In the decades following, his firm catered particularly to people of exquisite taste— provided, *ça va sans dire*, their taste was matched by their pocketbooks. Reporting on the American furniture exhibits at the Centennial of 1876 in Philadelphia, the correspondent of the *American Architect and Building News* devoted most of his discussion to the exhibits of Marcotte, whose rooms drew hordes of admiring people.

> The Renaissance work of L. Marcotte & Co., of New York, and the Pottier & Stymus Manufg. Co., has been brought up to the highest degree of refinement and luxury... With the former house, this style has been the life study of the eminent artist at its head, and we have every reason to expect remarkable results from the labors of such a master. His work shows an entire familiarity with all the resources of decorative art, and he is able to bring out the strongest points of his favorite style, and make a strong bid for the favor of the art-loving people.

After a few critical remarks, interesting for their rationalist point of view, the writer concluded that the exhibit of Marcotte & Co. was on the whole a splendid illustration of the latest phases of decorative art as employed by the French in the adornment of house interiors. It was the best effort of this kind in the American department[8].

One of the most influential critics of the time, Clarence Cook, had nothing but praise for the work of Marcotte, whom he mentioned a number of times in his best seller, *The House Beautiful* (1878). An allusion to Marcotte's "Eastlake" style, as much better than most examples of that mode[9], demonstrates that the firm had kept up with the times. By the late '70s and early '80s, what was most inaccurately known in America as "Eastlake," was all the rage[10], particularly among "young marrieds," who wanted something "simple" and "honest" after the deluge of French Renaissance that had engulfed their parents[11]. Léon Marcotte appears to have retired from active participation in the business by the early 1880s, when he returned to France. The firm of L. Marcotte & Company, later at 298 Fifth Avenue, continued in existence for a number of years after the death of its founder around 1886-1887[12].

The Development of "French Taste"

To return to the early '50s. "Louis" furniture was but one facet of almost complete French domination of the taste of the educated upper classes and of the self-made man, who might acquire the outward look of refinement through the services of a man such as Marcotte or Roux (Downing's favorite French furniture designer[13]). For the next two decades, until the overthrow of Napoleon III in 1870, Americans turned to France for inspiration in all fields. In the early 1860s, the visiting English novelist, Anthony Trollope, described the phenomenon in these rather sarcastic words:

> The taste of America is becoming French in its conversation, French in its comforts and French in its discomforts, French in its eating, and French in its dress, French in its manners, and will become French in its art[14].

French influence was all-pervasive. Even tombstones were French in style[15]! But, to borrow a phrase from the cabinetmaker, it was a surface glaze or veneer, rather than a penetrating stain, for its appeal, generally speaking, was limited to the upper stratum of society.

In wealthy private homes, as well as in hotels, the plain substantial fare of the earlier days gave way to "artistic" multi-course dinners under the supervision of a French chef[16]. It became the fashion to give *soirées musicales* at one's home, to invite a hundred people to an "informal" party, and to give amateur theatrical performances, as had been the fashion in France for many years[17]. From the descriptions of the social life of the '50s and early '60s, one derives a distinct impression of preciosity, which Moliere had satirized some two hundred years earlier. The *bal costume* took Society by storm: The most memorable event of the social season of 1854 was the *bal costume, style Louis XV* given by the Schermerhorns[18] in their family home on Park Place, a few years before they moved uptown to their new house on Twenty-third Street, designed for them by Lienau. At this ball, New York Society was introduced to the German cotillion, only a few short months after it was initiated by Eugénie at the Tuileries. As time went on, these soirées and dinners became more and more elaborate, until it required the services of Ward McAllister to manage an evening's entertainment. And as for professional performers, the period of the '50s and '60s was the heyday of the *opera bouffe* and the French theatre. Rachel and her troupe visited here in 1856[19]. On Twenty-third Street, Franconi's Hippodrome, an institution of French origin[20], packed them in for three years until the building burned in 1856.

It is hardly necessary to remind the reader that the tyrannical hold of the French *couturier* over American women, which continued until the 1930s, began in the middle of the last century. In the old days, it would have been considered vulgar to dress in the newest fashion, but now ladies were "beginning to flaunt abroad their Paris dresses as soon as they were out of the Custom House"[21]. The very idea of extravagance in dress as not only permissible, but highly desirable, a social asset, is a legacy of the Second Empire[22]. A glance through any of the magazines of the period, such as *Harper's* or, better yet, *Godey's Lady's Book*, will serve to demonstrate that fashions introduced in Paris were made available here almost immediately. Products of a courtly environment, they nonetheless profoundly influenced American middle-class habits of dress.

A case in point was the quick adoption of the crinoline in the late 1850s. A style designed exclusively for display (to sit down or pass through a narrow doorway became a major operation!), it is paralleled by dominant trends in furniture design and interior decoration and by general architectural tendencies of the period. One might cite the vogue for large ponderous pieces of furniture, gorgeous but uncomfortable; the number of pieces of furniture and bric-a-brac designed solely for show; and the absolute necessity, even in middle-class homes, of having a "front parlor," seldom used, yet expensively furnished and thickly curtained lest the sun fade the precious carpet[23]. In architecture, we may mention the emphasis on the façade, the general lack of concern for practical considerations in domestic planning, and particularly in iron architecture the masking or camouflaging of structural elements by an overlay of decoration. Critics and writers who attacked these tendencies in architecture were legion, but to discuss them would lead far beyond the scope of this study.

Returning to women's fashions, it is interesting to note that even the language used to describe women's wear changed radically. Certain words, for example, like bias, corsage, gilet, and trousseau, whose meaning had to be explained to *Godey's* readers in 1849[24], have long since become an accepted part of the English language. Walt Whitman championed the incorporation of foreign—particularly French—words into the American vernacular in an article in *Life Illustrated*, April 12, 1856[25], the same year that saw the publication of two large French-English dictionaries here. Not only were French terms used constantly, but also, even more significantly, one often tended to substitute French words where English would have done as well or better: *jupe* for skirt, *ruches* for ruffles, *noeuds* of ribbons, instead of bows, *bijouterie* for jewelry, *coiffure*, and so on[26]. The famous ditty, "Nothing to Wear," the great literary success of 1857, illustrates in no uncertain terms the hold that Paris had over the "smart set" of New York. It begins:

> And yet, though scarce three months have passed since the day,
> This merchandise went, on twelve carts, up Broadway.
> This same Miss M'Flimsey, of Madison Square,
> At last time we met was in utter despair,
> Because she had nothing whatever to wear![27]

Less good-humored were descriptions of the society of the period that came from the pens of Charles Astor Bristed, a grandson of John Jacob Astor[28], and George William Curtis, author and journalist, the two sharpest critics of the New York social scene. There can be no doubt that Curtis was referring to men like Léon Marcotte in one of his chapters in *The Potiphar Papers*, which deals with the plight of the husband who has been nagged by his wife into building a fancy and expensive house "after the latest Parisian models" and then forced to deliver it "into the hands of a certain eminent upholsterer to be furnished, as we send Frederic to the tailors to be clothed"[29]. A hint of rebellion can even be detected in Strong's confidences to his diary. Though he saw no sense in the splendors of Louis XIV chairs, *ormolu*, rosewood, brocateele, and tapestry carpets[30], nonetheless he availed himself of Marcotte's services when he redecorated the boudoir of his *palazzo* on Twenty-first Street[31]. He was only one of the elite of New York who patronized L. Marcotte & Company[32].

The foregoing discussion of the work of Léon Marcotte and his role in the development of the so-called "French taste" of wealthy New Yorkers will serve as an introduction to Lienau's other important commission of 1850, the Shiff House, in all likelihood the first monument of the Second Empire mode in this country.

The Shiff House, New York, 1850-c.1852

The Client: Hart M. Shiff

Figure 27. Shiff House by Detlef Lienau.

Lienau's first New York job of consequence was a townhouse on the southwest corner of Fifth Avenue and Tenth Street for Hart M. Shiff, a French merchant and banker, commissioned in 1850. This residence, formerly at 32 Fifth Avenue, was demolished in 1923 to make way for an apartment building. It is, therefore, fortunate that an old photograph (Fig. 27), numerous drawings, and the original carpenter's and mason's specifications for the house are preserved in the Lienau Collection[33]. Mr. Shiff had arrived only recently in New York and, awaiting the construction of his house, lived at 5 Depau Row on Bleecker Street[34], then one of the most exclusive residential neighborhoods in the city. Depau Row, demolished in 1867 to make way for Vanderbilt's railroad depot, had been built by Francis Depau, founder of the first line of Havre packets to New York. His wife, Silvie, Mr. Shiff's neighbor, was a daughter of Admiral de Grasse.

Hart M. Shiff, born in France in 1772, had come to New Orleans years before on business[35]. There, he married Marguerite Basilice de Chesse, the daughter of a French nobleman who had narrowly escaped the guillotine. Their children are supposed to have been educated in France, a not unlikely assumption, since a "Shiff, *rentier*," is listed in the *Almanac de Paris* of 1840[36]. Just why Shiff chose to settle in New York in 1850, rather than return to New Orleans where other members of the Shiff family were established, is a matter for conjecture, perhaps attributable to the disastrous floods and extremely serious cholera epidemic of the previous year[37].

The Cadre: Fifth Avenue

Mr. Shiff, in deciding to build at Fifth Avenue and Tenth Street, had chosen his lot and his neighbors well. In 1850, Tenth Street was, of course, considered far "uptown". Fifth Avenue itself had only been in existence since 1837; above Twenty-third Street, it was still unpaved and almost rural in character[38]. But, beginning with the 1840s, we find references to the shifting of the fashionable residential district from Astor Place to University Place and lower Fifth Avenue. In 1845, it was already predicted that Fifth Avenue "will be one of the finest streets on the continent"[39]. Houses, each more "magnificent" than the next, according to the diarist Philip Hone[40], were one by one filling up the vacant lots on the Avenue. The *Evening Post* of May 21, 1850, commenting on the unusual amount of building activity since the first of the month, particularly noted the number of stately and magnificent mansions being built uptown[41]. By the early 1850s, Fifth Avenue was known as the home of the "Upper Ten"[42] and the "Belgravia"[43] of New York. Along with the fine houses came the fashionable churches. The Church of the Ascension by Upjohn, which had begun the uptown trend in 1840, was on the northwest corner of Tenth Street, just opposite the Shiff lot; a block away on the northeast corner of Eleventh Street stood Joseph C. Wells's First Presbyterian Church (1844-1846). Grace Church, the most exclusive of New York's "Courts of Heaven"[44] was nearby. St. George's Church, which gave architectural distinction to the Stuyvesant Square area farther uptown, has already been mentioned.

Diagonally across from the Shiff lot was the residence of Francis Cottenet, a well known French merchant, who later became one of Lienau's clients. The Brevoort mansion by Alexander Jackson Davis[45] at Ninth Street, next to the Shiff lot and the scene of many a gay party, had just been purchased from the Brevoort estate for $57,000 by Henry de Rham, a wealthy importer and the Swiss consul-general in New York. Robert Minturn, James Lenox, and August Belmont, to mention only a few of the great figures in the commercial and financial circles of the day, all lived on the Avenue between Twelfth and Fourteenth Streets. The Grinnell mansion (later taken over by Delmonico's), which stood at the corner of Fifth Avenue and Fourteenth Street, marked the end of the line. Beyond this point, the Avenue was still largely undeveloped in 1850[46].

Such was "The Cadre". To Lienau fell the task of designing a townhouse that would reflect his client's social prestige, wealth, and cultural inheritance, a residence that would not pale in comparison with its neighbors. There is no doubt that the upper middle class in America was becoming increasingly conscious of the fact that one's home, in the absence of other marks of special distinction in a republican society, was regarded as a true index of one's social position and economic status[47]. The creation of a state of mind favorable to what Veblen later called "conspicuous consumption" was already an established fact, expressed in no uncertain terms by a Southern visitor to New York in 1852:

> These people no longer live for themselves... but to show their neighbors how very elegantly they can live. There is but one genuine, sincere, and earnest wish throughout the city: Its divinity is the goddess, Caliconia—its scribe, Fashion—King, Mammon—its high priest, Stewart[48].

These tendencies toward equating show with beauty, and cost with value—recognized already some years earlier by the writer

Edgar Allan Poe in a remarkable little article entitled "The Philosophy of Furniture"[49]—met with severe criticism from some quarters[50], but were stoutly defended in others[51]. Weisman's statement regarding commercial palaces—that it mattered little whether a building was labeled Italian, French, or English in style so long as it was showy, rich, and aristocratic in appearance[52]—is equally applicable to the domestic architecture of the later 1840s and the years following. Although the Shiff house was far more restrained in design than many other houses along the Avenue, it is an excellent example of the efforts by the wealthy merchant class in America to emulate the residences of the European aristocracy[53].

Stylistic Innovations

The Greek, the Gothic, and the Italian—these were the stylistic alternatives before the Shiff house was built. In 1850, there was no one truly dominant mode in residential architecture[54]. In contrast to the Grecian designs of Davis (*e.g.*, the Breevoort House and "Stevens's Palace" at College Place), to his castellated mode (*e.g.*, Waddell villa at Thirty-seventh Street)[55], and the newer Anglo-Italian *palazzo* style of Snook's Haight House (Fig. 28)[56], which had become increasingly popular for residences as well as for commercial architecture, Lienau proposed to base his design on French Renaissance and Neo-Grec sources. Studies were made, plans drawn up, and finally the contract drawings and specifications were signed early in May 1850[57].

Figure 28. Shiff House. Front elevation.

For a preliminary study that was strongly influenced by Labrouste[58], Lienau substituted a much simpler design in the presentation of sketches and the contract drawings for the house, signed May 4, 1850. Less *recherché* but bolder in general concept, this design (Fig. 29) was given a certain distinction by the superposition of a giant order over the pilasters of the lower story—a favorite French Second Empire motif[59]. But the most startling innovation was the treatment of the attic story as a low mansard roof with prominent dormer windows, the likes of which had never been seen in New York. Singled out again and again for comment, the house was unhesitatingly described by contemporaries as a "French *chateau*" and praised as "an agreeable departure from the uniformity of our city residences..."[60].

Figure 29. Haight House by John B. Snook.

Let us read the description of the Shiff house that appeared in *Putnam's* in 1854, accompanied by a charming illustration:

> At the corner of Tenth-street and Fifth Avenue stands a large, quaint, old-fashioned single house of red brick and brown stone, with a steep slated roof, and conspicuously ornamented dormer windows; which, when time shall have destroyed its freshness, and mellowed its tone, may appear to some stranger... a relic of ante-revolutionary times. This is the residence of a French gentleman; which may account for the owner's adoption of a style of building which would remind him of the courtly formality, and solid gentility of the olden time in his native country. The style of this building is a mixture of French and Italian, with a remnant of the Gothic principle in the kneed architraves over the third story windows. Its general good effect will be found to arise from the string-courses in every floor, which seem to bind it together, and form agreeable subdivisions of the whole mass. The railings and entrance steps are very rich and effective. A conservatory may be seen in the rear; there is also an entrance to the courtyard beyond, not delineated in our cut[61].

In the interesting but little-known article, "The Modern Architecture of New-York," published in the *New-York Quarterly* of 1855, the anonymous author—who may have been Clarence Cook—singled out three houses for extensive description, of which the Shiff house was one, the Haight house another:

> In the same avenue, on the west side, near Washington Square, is a house, built something after the fashion of an old French chateau on a small scale. We like it, but prefer it for a country rather than a city house. Its roof and window-dormers are picturesque, and the combination of brown stone with the brick-work very pleasing. The great difficulty in designing buildings where one order of architecture is placed over another is this: the cornice must almost of necessity be feeble; if proportioned to the whole building, it would crush the columns or pilasters to which it belongs, and be a positive eye-sore; if designed with reference to them, the result must be as above. Consequently, this house has the characteristic tameness of the style to which it belongs; otherwise, both as a whole and in detail, it will bear close inspection, and come well up to the mark[62].

The emphasis on the mansard roof in these and other descriptions of the house leads one to suspect that this type of roof was indeed a radical innovation in this country, a supposition borne out by Lienau's one careful description of the roof construction on the first page of the "Carpenter's Specifications" for the house: "The roof to be a roof 'à la mansard' [*sic*]" (note the quotation marks, indicating the carpenter's probable unfamiliarity with the term). Lienau then continued with an exact description of the framing, for which he also provided a careful sectional drawing on the sheet with the plan for the attic story.

The sources of this type of very low mansard roof with steep sides are not too difficult to find. As Henry-Russell Hitchcock has pointed out, the 17th-century mansard roof actually never completely disappeared in France[63]. As a matter of fact, it appears to have staged quite a comeback in the second quarter of the 19th century[64], particularly in residential architecture. This may easily be verified by checking Normand's *Paris moderne* and Victor Petit's *Habitations champêtres* (1848). The first two volumes in *Paris moderne* are an excellent source of information concerning residential architecture built in the new suburban sections of Paris in the 1820s, '30s, and very early '40s. House after house makes use of the mansard[65], sometimes of the low type of the Shiff residence, often considerably higher, and occasionally of the very tall, two-story type, the last particularly useful for providing ample servants' quarters in the large apartment houses of the period. An example of the low mansard of the Shiff type is one of the houses built c.1821 by the architect Constantin[66] in the rue de la Tour des Dames, immediately after this new section of Paris was laid out. Other examples illustrated in Normand date mostly in the '30s, while Petit enables us to trace the development well into the '40s[67].

While the mansard was used chiefly in residential architecture in this period, it also appeared in isolated instances in the semi-public architecture of Paris, as for example in Visconti's projects of the 1830s and '40s for libraries, Vaudoyer's Conservatoire des Arts et des Metiers (1838) and A.H. de Gisots' Ecole Normale Superieure (1841-1847)[68]. An interesting case in point was its use by the brothers Labrouste in two buildings in the Bibliothèque Sainte-Geneviève complex, in Theodore's College Sainte-Barbe, and in Henri's administration building[69], the last two built when Lienau was studying in the latter's *atelier*. This vernacular tradition, in combination with the official interest in the French heritage of the 16th and 17th centuries (evidenced by the publication in the mid-'40s of Victor Calliat's magnificent monograph on the Hotel de Ville)[70], provides us with the immediate background for the unprecedented appearance of the mansard in the Shiff house in New York. In the United States and also in Austria[71], isolated examples of earlier mansard roofs may be found as, for example, the French architect L'Enfant's much earlier house for Robert Morris in Philadelphia[72].

The late Fiske Kimball, basing himself on a reference in Justin Winsor's *Memorial History of Boston* (1880-1881), credited an obscure French architect, Jean Lemoulnier, with the introduction of the style to Boston in the 1850s, an assumption that can hardly be taken seriously on the basis of such scanty evidence[73].

Contemporary descriptions of the Shiff house and A.J. Bloor's remarks some years later—when he recalled that the mansard roof had made its first appearance in this house[74]—indicate beyond all reasonable doubt that this was indeed the first building in the Second Empire mode in America[75]. The house has been discussed recently by Mrs. McKenna in her study of Renwick's work[76] and by Henry-Russell Hitchcock in an article devoted to the genesis of the Second Empire style in England, "Second Empire 'avant la lettre,'" reprinted in his *Early Victorian Architecture in Britain*[77]. While there can be no doubt that many architects—Calvert Vaux[78], James Renwick, and a host of others—later contributed to the development of the Second Empire style in the United States, it is important to note that Lienau's Shiff house does, in point of fact, mark a beginning. In the past, Hunt has usually been given credit for the introduction of the French influence here after his return from Paris in 1855[79]. That he played an extremely important role from that time on no one can deny, but he was hardly in a position to play any role at all before his return to the United States in 1855, unlike various other architects already settled here[80].

We have seen that the architectural atmosphere of 1850 was far from stable. Architects used now one, and now another, style. The time was right and the scene wide open for a new architectural language. In the cultural atmosphere of the 1850s, so overtly receptive to anything and everything French, the Second Empire architectural ideal easily took root; it ultimately spread all over the country. The really developed Second Empire style of the 1860s, with its rich orders, corner pavilions, and deliberate reflections of the New Louvre, does not interest us at the moment. We are concerned here with the simple fact of the appearance of the mansard roof in America in 1850. This is important, since the French curb roof, more than any other single feature of the Second Empire style, became the hallmark of architecture all over the country from the latter part of the 1850s to the early '70s when, in Kennion's words, "no building, great or small, would be a building without its 'French roof'; even when the building is itself so low that another treatment would be obviously better"[81].

The fall of the Second Empire in 1870, the subsequent cultural re-orientation of the United States toward England and, even more important, the disastrous fires of 1871 and 1872 in Chicago and Boston, whose rampant spread was largely blamed on the tall wood mansard, dealt the mansard its death blow. In spite of later abuse and indiscriminate use[82], the mansard roof performed a valuable service to American architecture of the third quarter of the century. It was of course valued for its provision of adequate attic space at minimal cost. But, like the contemporary Victorian Gothic style, it was cherished particularly for its heavy sculptural quality and its highly picturesque silhouette[83]. Symbolic and powerfully evocative, the mansard roof also answered the psychological and sociological craving for aristocratic distinction. In view of the pre-eminent position of France in the 1850s in matters of style, and the social snobbism of New York's "Avenoodles" (as the smart set was jokingly called), it would be foreseen that the new look of the Shiff house would prove a *success fou* and establish, in one bold stroke, the reputation of both the client and the architect.

Description of the House

The plan of the house (Fig. 30), set upon a double (fifty-foot) lot, also represents a radical departure from the simpler twenty-five foot house plans of the previous decades in New York. While it may be argued with good reason that the Shiff house lacks the imaginative planning of some of the other large mansions of the period (*e.g.*, Davis's earlier "Stevens's Palace" and R.G. Hatfield's [1815-1879] Henry Parish House at Union Square)[84], it nonetheless was an attempt to introduce a more expansive plan into New York architecture. The space was handled effectively, except for the oddly planned front section with small flanking rooms and an extremely cramped entrance hall. The drawing room, back parlor, and dining room could be opened up into one continuous area for gala affairs, such as the party given by the Shiffs in 1855. (George Templeton Strong wrote: "Friday night, it was rumored that a Socialist mob was sacking the Schiff [*sic*] mansion in the Fifth Avenue, where there was a great ball and mass-meeting of the Aristocracy."[85])

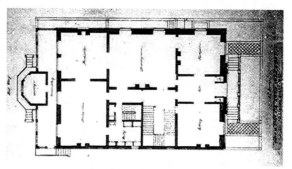

Figure 30. Shiff House. Plan of first floor.

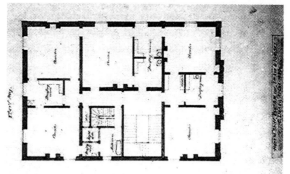

Figure 31. Shiff House. Plan of second floor.

Certain details, such as the designation of a specific locale for the gentlemen's smoking room and the location of the parlor floor water closet, a rarity in American houses of this period, bring up the question of the amalgam of French-American features that are evident in this house[86]. The U-shaped staircase, with a landing between the floors, and the casement windows are French. The sliding doors between the main rooms, a survival of Greek Revival practices, and the high stoop are American. While parallels to the raised monumentalized entrance may of course be found in French country houses[87], the stoop was most closely identified with the Dutch in this country, and became an indissoluble part of the brownstone house tradition in New York. Many small details made life more pleasant for the owners of the house and their numerous servants, features not generally used in French houses of the period—running hot and cold water on all the main floors, speaking tubes to all the rooms, central heating from a hot-air furnace in the basement, and dressing rooms with built-in drawers and wardrobes (Fig. 31). On his visit here in 1861, Prince Jerome-Napoleon, like all

Europeans, was particularly impressed by the marvels of plumbing in our houses[88].

Regarding the materials used in the construction of the house, the early combination of brick and brownstone, singled out for comment by Cook in 1855, is rarely found before the 1850s in New York[89]. Brick, so beautifully expressive of the clear-cut simplicity of the Greek Revival house, is combined here with the popular rough-textured Connecticut freestone. Considered early in the century as good enough only for the back of the City Hall, from 1840 on it found its way into the façades of the proud houses it adorned[90]. Richard Upjohn was one of the first architects to make extensive use of the new material. Within a few years, in spite of its known susceptibility to flaking, brownstone became the rage. Its warm tone and rough texture appealed to a generation that was sick to death of the everlasting red brick and the pristine whiteness of the Classical Revival house[91]. In the Shiff house, brownstone was used very sparingly to give relief and surface interest to certain architectural features: the stoop, the pilasters, corner quoins, moldings, and cornices. Within the decade, the "brownstone front" became a synonym throughout the United States for all that was respectable and solid in domestic architecture[92]. But by the late '60s, as we shall see, a reaction against brownstone set in. It is to Edith Wharton (1862-1937) and the generation which grew up in the 1870s that we owe the gloomy picture of a New York covered with "chocolate sauce"[93].

As for the construction of the Shiff house, its specifications called for everything to be of the best quality material and workmanship,

> subject at all times to the inspection of the superintendents of the building, who shall have the power to reject any work or materials that do not in their opinion, conform to the spirit of the specifications and plans[94].

Lienau, unlike other architects of the period[95], never sacrificed quality for the sake of cheap effects, even when economy was the order of the day. Mr. Shiff could afford the best—and the best is what he got. Even the smallest details were thought through with utmost care. The "Mason's Specifications" (p. 14) included instructions for the flagging of the yard leading to the stable at the rear of the lot; it was to have "crossing lines cut into the surface, at least 1/4 of an inch, for affording hold to the horses on it". Interestingly enough, this stable, of which only one elevation drawing remains[96], is conceived in a completely different style from the main house. It has a typically German look. The simply treated brickwork with segmented arches over all the openings is reminiscent of the work of the Schinkelschule in Berlin. The wooden balcony and decorated verge board, with the owner's initial worked into the design, gives a vaguely Swiss look to the building, again probably more in keeping with German than French tendencies of the mid-century[97].

The juxtaposition of a chalet-type stable and a predominantly French type of house leads us back to an issue already mentioned briefly in connection with Grace Church and the Michael Lienau cottage, namely the combination of elements drawn from various styles and periods, occurring so often in architecture from this period on. The house itself, as is apparent from the photograph (Fig. 27), was far from a consistent example of French Renaissance style, as was noted by *Putnam's* correspondent[98], who pointed also to Gothic elements. Reminiscences of the period of Francois 1er are even clearer in a small pencil "doodle" on the elevation contract drawing, which interestingly enough also recalls a *chateau* of 1845 in this style published in *Paris moderne*[99]. Even more important to the general impression is the strong Neo-Grec spirit evident everywhere. Stripped, planar, and linear in conception, even the two-story pilasters framing the central bay project very little. Carved ornament in the capitals and around the mansard windows is reduced to a minimum, flattened into forms of utmost simplicity, in which the details are incised rather than carved. The type of eclecticism apparent here was not only thought quite respectable in the mid-19th century[100], but also considered by most architects, even those most anxious to find an "American" style, a perfect answer to the problem of adapting European traditions to American requirements. Much still remains to be written on the subject of eclecticism, although Professors Hitchcock, Hamlin, and Meeks have shed interesting light on the problem, to which we shall return in the concluding chapter[101].

As for the interior of the Shiff house, we can assume that it was decorated in the French [*sic*] style, an assumption based on general descriptive sources and on certain items mentioned in the "Carpenter's Specifications". The fancy black walnut staircase, the elaborate wainscoting of white pine throughout the parlor floor, and many other items mentioned by Lienau were built according to drawings "to be given". Such working drawings are repeatedly mentioned in both the carpenter's and mason's specifications.

Unfortunately, only one has survived, a careful study of the paneled entrance door. Lienau, with his background in carpentry training and Teutonic thoroughness, evidently considered such details of interior decoration extremely important[102], as modern architects do today. The appearance of the house upon its completion must have corresponded closely with the wonderful descriptions of houses on Fifth Avenue supplied to us by Mrs. Bishop, Eugene Jouve, and William Chambers, whose book, *Things as They Are in America* (1854) provides an excellent picture of the period.

> Advancing northwards from the more busy parts of town, the elegance... of the houses becomes more conspicuous, and at last we find ourselves in the quietude and splendour of a Belgravia. Here, the edifices are entirely of brownstone, and of a richly decorated style of street architecture; all the windows are of plate-glass; and the door-handles, plates, and bell pulls silvered... The furnishings and interior ornaments of these dwellings, particularly those of Fifth Avenue, are of a superb kind; no expense being apparently saved as regards either comfort or elegance[103].

The appearance of the interior of the Shiff mansion—its high ceilinged rooms, shuttered French casement windows of the best French plate glass with hand-made silver-plated *espagnolettes*, heavy draperies under elaborately gilded mirrors, and crystal chandeliers— can be reconstructed with the help of the prints of the period[104]. Since the Shiff residence was credited to Lienau *and* Marcotte by Bloor, it is very likely that Marcotte was responsible for the furnishing and interior decoration of the house, particularly since the partnership was formed at just about the time the house was finished[105]. According to Mrs. W. Kennedy Cromwell[106], a great-granddaughter of Mr. Shiff, one of the family's proudest possessions was a clock in the form of an equestrian statue of Napoleon Bonaparte, reportedly stolen from the Tuileries during the Revolution of 1848, which is now in the Walters Gallery in Baltimore.

Unfortunately, Mr. Shiff never lived long enough to see his house finished, much less to occupy it, for he died of pneumonia on February 26, 1851. He was buried in Greenwood Cemetery, Brooklyn, the most beautiful, fashionable, and expensive cemetery in the United States at that time. The vault, for which two studies are preserved in the Lienau Collection, was designed by Lienau[107].

As for the house itself, according to the terms of the contract, it was to have been ready for occupancy by August 1, 1851. Although the Shiff family was not listed at 32 Fifth Avenue until 1853, the house must have been completed before the middle of 1852 when tax assessments jumped[108], the house appeared in the Dripps Map[109], and the carpentry contractor left the job[110]. The house was occupied by Mrs. Shiff and her family only through 1859 or so[111]. After 1860, the firm of Shiff Brothers, importers, disappears from the New York directories. With the threat of Civil War, the Shiff family scattered; some members returned South to Louisiana; others, like Mrs. Shiff herself, took refuge in France, where she died[112]. From 1860 to 1867, the house was occupied by Paul Forbes, a former Bostonian who had made his fortune in the China trade, and a Francophile; next, it passed to Dr. Josiah H. Gautier (1818-1895)[113], a pioneer manufacturer of steel whose plant was located in Jersey City. Gautier, who probably knew the Lienaus, came from a family long prominent in the Huguenot community of New York; he may have felt that the Shiff house suited his background. After his death, the house was purchased by Amos F. Eno (1834-1915)[114], son of the builder of the Fifth Avenue Hotel. Historians and lovers of fine prints remember him as the collector of the magnificent collection, later acquired by the New York Public Library, which bears his name and to which reference has been made here repeatedly. Memories of the old house provided the late Arthur Train with the architectural setting for his novel, *His Children's Children*[115], which was published in 1923, the year the house was torn down. (Train was a well known lawyer, writer, and man-about-town, famous for his *Tut, Tut, Mr. Tutt* stories.)

Summary

The Shiff house, then, was the architectural expression of a given period in time and of peculiarly personal circumstances. The general factors have been noted—the overall prosperity of the early '50s reflected in the erection of imposing private residences and of commercial "palaces," the basic orientation of fashionable Society toward France, and the lack of a single dominant stylistic idiom. The specific factor was the fortuitous meeting, either through Marcotte or Michael Lienau, between a wealthy French client and Detlef Lienau. Lienau's French training and continental background made him perhaps the only architect in the East who could give full expression both to his client's native preferences and to latent stylistic tendencies of the period. As we have seen, contemporaries were fully aware of the importance of the house. The Second Empire style had indeed become a reality. The reputation of Lienau as an architect of taste, distinction, and sound principles of construction was established beyond all doubt.

Soon, Detlef Lienau received other important commissions: a Newport "cottage" for DeLancey Kane, married to an Astor granddaughter; a villa in Dobbs Ferry for the French merchant, Francis Cottenet, and several suburban houses in the metropolitan area. These will be discussed in the next chapter, devoted to suburban and resort architecture of the early 1850s.

Chapter V.
Early Suburban and Resort Houses

Introduction

The rise of the city, the concentration of industry, the urbanization of culture, all natural results of the Industrial Revolution, are facts of paramount importance for the understanding of the architecture of the mid-19th century and the decades following. Concentration of wealth in the hands of the great merchants expressed itself, as we have seen, in the erection of imposing semi-public buildings such as the Merchants' Exchange in New York, in the creation of the commercial "palace," and in a series of sumptuous private residences that sprang up in the fashionable quarters of town, of which the Shiff house was a fine example. Almost equally important in any discussion of the modes of living of the 1840s and '50s was the beginning of a "flight to the country," a phenomenon that, with the parallel process of decentralization of industry in our own times, has finally trickled down to all sections of the population. If the origins of suburban living are rooted in the mid-19th century, so too were the beginnings, among the wealthier class of Society, of "cottage life". These facts provide us with a point of departure for a discussion of Lienau's suburban houses of the 1850s and resort architecture in Newport, Rhode Island.

The Cottenet Villa, Dobbs Ferry, New York, 1852

Francis Cottenet, a Frenchman, lived opposite the Shiffs on the northeast corner of Fifth Avenue and Tenth Street. His house at 35-37 Fifth Avenue was described by George Templeton Strong as elegant and costly, without, however, being showy, for these were "nice people"[1]. Perhaps, Mr. Cottenet was a friend of the Shiffs; at any rate, he must have liked his neighbor's house, for when he began to give serious thought to retiring from business, he called on Lienau to design a suburban villa for him.

Francis [François] Cottenet (1790-1884) was a native of Burgundy, who had come to New York in the 1830s[2]. He had built up a substantial business as an importer, dealing chiefly in silks and fancy goods. The disastrous fires of 1835 and 1839 in New York had wiped him out, but by 1845 he was described by Moses Beach (a gentleman who knew everything there was to know about anyone with an income over $100,000 a year) as "one of the most respectable and prominent of our French importers". Beach added that Cottenet's marriage to the daughter of General Edward Laight was "one of the few instances of the alliance of respectable French and American families"[3]. In 1854, Cottenet retired and from that time on spent much time in his charming residence in Dobbs Ferry, which was designed in 1852 by Detlef Lienau (Fig. 32). Some years later, this was described by the eminent historian Benson J. Lossing as the most elegant villa on the banks of the Hudson River[4].

Figure 32. Cottenet Villa by Detlef Lienau. Architect's sketch.

Dobbs Ferry, some twenty miles from New York, was rapidly becoming a favorite place of residence for wealthy New York merchants. The trains of the Hudson River Division ran several times daily; a steamboat also plied back and forth daily from the foot of Chambers Street. This new suburb provided an ideal retreat for a gentleman like Mr. Cottenet, who had accumulated sufficient wealth to enjoy his hard-won leisure. From his property on the banks of the Hudson, which he purchased in 1852[5], he enjoyed a magnificent view of the river and of the Palisades. The estate was a large one reaching from Broadway to the river; over the years, it has been parceled into smaller lots, so the present acreage represents only a fraction of its original site.

As planned by Lienau in 1852, the house was not a big one; within a few years of its construction, however, it was enlarged by a rear extension (Fig. 34). Drawings for the house in its original state and for alterations, as well as an old photograph, are in the Lienau Collection[6]. Happily, in this case we need not rely solely on such documents, for the house today is in an excellent state of preservation, thanks to the care of its present owners, Mr. and Mrs.

J. Fearon Brown[7]. A small pencil sketch of the house, signed by the architect and dated 1852, still hangs in their library (Fig. 32).

Figure 33. Stevens's Castle by Thomas R. Jackson.

Benson Lossing described the Cottenet villa as French[8], evidently confusing the style of the house with the nationality of the owner. The Cottenet house is unmistakably an Italian villa, indeed one of the finest examples of its period in this style. Again, as in the house for Michael Lienau and the design of Grace Church, we find Lienau accommodating himself to the prevailing stylistic tendencies of the time. In the *Model Architect*, published the same year the Cottenet villa was designed, Samuel Sloan (1815-1884) wrote that

> country residences in the Italian style are becoming more and more popular, both here and in the old world. Its great simplicity of design, its facile adaptation to our wants and habits, together with its finished, elegant, and picturesque appearance, gives it predominance over every other. It speaks of the inhabitant as a man of wealth, who wishes in a quiet way to enjoy his wealth. It speaks of him as a man of educated and refined tastes... who, accustomed to all the ease and luxury of city life, is now enjoying the pure and elevating pleasures of the country[9].

A more perfect description of the specific requirements of Mr. Cottenet would be hard to find! Elsewhere in the same volume, Sloan, echoing Downing, describes the Italian mode as a style with little real rural feeling, and thus particularly well suited to areas near the city[10], or what we would now call the suburbs.

The Italian style had still other features to recommend it. Combining picturesque elements of design with classical associations, to Downing it represented a compromise between the classical style preferred by the man of reason and the Gothic, which attracted the man of sentiment[11]. From a psychological point of view, he felt that the Italian villa bespoke the owner as a man of imagination and energy[12]. An interesting study might be made of the symbolic associative values of the various architectural modes of the mid-19th century ("Gothic," "Tudor," "Elizabethan," "Italian," "Romanesque," "Swiss," etc.) with the aesthetic, economic, moral, and psychological points of view[13]. Indeed, the importance of these various stylistic designations in the builders' guides of the time, even if incorrectly applied according to modern architectural standards, is so characteristic of the period that it seems a great pity simply to brush aside this terminology, as is too often done, in favor of 20th-century criteria and personal methods of architectural criticism.

Figure 34. Cottenet Villa with extension (1858-1859).

If we compare the design of the Cottenet house with the better known Italian villas of the period, we find that it achieved a monumentality and classical repose unusual within the Italian villa tradition. More regular in design, with considerable emphasis on the block from which the wings and the three-story tower detach themselves far less than usual[14], this house lacks the irregular, picturesque qualities of the best of Notman's, Upjohn's, and Austin's Italian villas of the 1840s[15], or of Davis's designs of the '50s. From Davis's work, it is clear that his aim, whether he used a castellated Gothic or an Italian villa vocabulary, was primarily the creation of a highly picturesque mass to which even the characteristic tower element of the Italian type became subordinated[16].

The Cottenet residence is certainly very different from the best publicized Italian villa of the 1840s, Richard Upjohn's King house of 1845-1847 in Newport, Rhode Island, now the People's Library (which was published in Downing's *Country Houses* of 1850)[17]. In the King house, the two dissimilar tower-like masses at each end of the façade are linked by a two-story triple arcade reminiscent of the Italian *loggia*. The detailing is noticeably coarse. In plan, the house is considerably less logical than Lienau's. The Newport villa also suffers from Upjohn's chronic disregard for any principle of coherence in the design of his openings[18]. Note that Lienau also introduced three distinct types of fenestration in his design: plain square-headed windows, a double- and triple-round arched Florentine type, and a third type surmounted by a hood molding of Gothic and *cottage orné* origin. The result is a pleasant variety without disharmony, in contrast to Upjohn's hodge-podge. These remarks may also in large part be applied to Castle Stevens, now the Alumni House of the Stevens Institute of Technology in Hoboken, New Jersey. Designed in c.1852 by T.R. Jackson[19], it is justly famed for its magnificent interiors, particularly its beautiful spiral staircase. The stuccoed exterior, however, is marked by a complete lack of unity in design, especially on the entrance façade. The river façade (Fig. 33), designed with a fine feeling for broad effects, is somewhat marred by its ornament. In contrast to the structural treatment being given decorative features, here the ornament appears to have been stuck on as an afterthought. Had not Schinkel and Labrouste always insisted that architectural ornamentation grow naturally out of the materials and processes of construction? Lienau's design may slightly recall Sloan's Italian villa published in *Model Architect*[20]; here again, comparison only serves to point out the difference in quality between the design of Sloan, who suddenly breaks the line of the porch to introduce an incongruous-looking pediment, and the design of the educated architect.

Closest in spirit to the Cottenet house is John Notman's Prospect House (1849) in Princeton, New Jersey, which still serves as the home of the president of the university. It is perhaps the finest example of the Italian villa style in this country[21]. Here, as in Lienau's design, the *campanile* is the central dominant feature, behind which the house takes shape. Like Notman, and unlike Austin and Upjohn, Lienau left exposed the fine Caen stone of which the house was built. No stucco was used. In his later villas, Upjohn also turned to a more centralized, regular, less picturesque type of design, as in his E.B. Litchfield house in Brooklyn, New York, of the mid-'50s[22]. Many more examples might be cited, but they would add little to our analysis. The fine qualities of the Cottenet villa stem from its classic design, the logic with which the various elements are organized, the unusual refinement in the handling of details, and the excellence of its construction.

The villa was built of Caen stone shipped to this country from Normandy. It was laid so carefully that to this day one cannot get a pen-knife blade between the joints[23]. If the study mentioned previously[24] for an Italian-type villa in stone with brick trim was really meant for the Cottenet house, the brick might have been discarded as too citified in appearance, although a number of Italian villas of the 1850s were built of this material[25]. Caen stone, it might be noted, was mentioned a few years later by Calvert Vaux as having been "lately" introduced in New York[26]. Although he conceded it to be a beautiful material, delicate in color, he did note that unless specially imported by well known firms, its quality was apt to be uneven. In the Cottenet house, the stone has weathered extremely well, in spite of its exposed location. Vaux questioned the desirability of importing stone to this country, where already there is such an abundance of good material. In the case of the Cottenet villa, Caen stone might well have been used for the associative values it had for its French owner. The sharply cut pattern of grapevines ornamenting the sunken panels under the soffit of the arched entrance to the house was undoubtedly meant as a reminiscence of Cottenet's birthplace. He called the house "Nuits," quit possibly after Nuits-St.-Georges in the heart of the Burgundian wine-growing district whence he came.

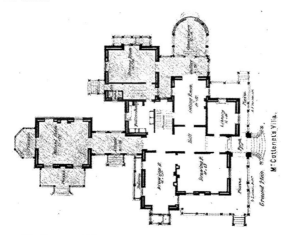

Figure 35. Cottenet Villa. Plan with 1858-1859 additions (shaded).

If the design of the house was almost classic in its restraint and regularity, its original plan (Fig. 35)[27] was considerably freer than most of the Italian villas of the 1840s and early '50s[28]. Note, however, that within this irregular, picturesque framework, all openings and architectural features (windows, doors, mantels, etc.)

were carefully studied to achieve symmetry within each room unit. A broad transverse central hall with a separate stair well separated the drawing and dining rooms on the left from the library, billiard room, and butler's pantry on the right; upstairs were five large bedrooms, each with its own dressing room, one bathroom, and ample built-in storage space. In the attic were four additional bedrooms, as well as a "look-out" in the tower. Excellent provision was made in the basement for all the services and a large wine cellar. A dumbwaiter (a relatively recent innovation)[29] connected the kitchen with the butler's pantry upstairs.

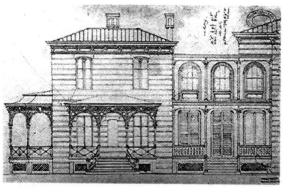

Figure 36. Cottenet Villa. Elevation drawing of addition.

Some time in the late '50s, probably between 1858 and 1859[30], the house was enlarged by the addition of a new dining-room wing, a conservatory, and a rear extension connected to the house by a two-story arcade (Fig. 36). This extension housed a large billiard room, a ubiquitous feature of villas in France, which was rapidly "becoming an indispensability in every elegant home"[31] in this country as well, and additional bedrooms above. At least three sets of plans were prepared by Lienau for this extension. Two of the studies were strictly in keeping with the original design of the house. The working drawings introduced a completely new note, perhaps at the owner's special request: The two porches of the extension were made of wrought iron, twisted into fancy spiral columns with the spandrels given a light openwork treatment, as in Upjohn's E.B. Litchfield house. This supplied Mr. Cottenet's Italian villa with just the proper "rustic" touch, according to the taste of the later '50s and '60s[32]. The house apparently remained unchanged until it was altered in 1918 by a local contractor, John Hunter & Sons of Irvington[33], which relocated the kitchen from the basement to the dining room wing, moved the main staircase inside the house, added a set of windows on the third floor to each side of the tower, and made several other minor changes.

After foreclosure by the Mutual Life Insurance Company against a mortgage of $250,000 just a few months after Francis Cottenet's death, the property was owned successively by Cyrus W. Field, promoter of the first Atlantic Cable, by John Jacob Astor II in 1887, and by Manhattan College in the 1890s. It has been in the hands of the Brown family since 1926; it is used as a summer residence and weekend place the year round.

Suburban Houses in New Jersey, 1852-1859

Before turning to Lienau's other important commission of 1852, the Kane House in Newport, Rhode Island, drawings for three suburban houses of the 1850s in New Jersey should be mentioned.

Miller House, Jersey City, 1852

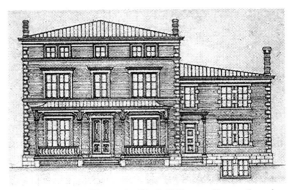

Figure 37. Miller House by Detlef Lienau. Front elevation.

The earliest in date was probably a house for J. Dickinson Miller (1804-1867), a prominent and wealthy lawyer of Jersey City[34]. He served for several years as an alderman of that city and was married to Ann Eliza Van Vorst. Michael Lienau married her younger sister at the end of the '50s. In any case, Mr. Miller must have been acquainted with the Lienaus for some time; Jersey City Society and the Grace Church (Van Vorst) group were small and closely knit. Original drawings for the Miller house, located at Henderson and Second (later Seventh) Streets, are preserved at the Avery Library[35]. The style of the architectural drawing, dated 1852, is clearly related to the delicate and exact pen-and-ink drawings of the Shiff house, the brick study of an Italian villa, and to the Kane villa. The house itself (Fig. 37), sturdy and foursquare, is a respectable example of a comfortable suburban brick house of the period, providing for a large parlor, dining room, library, and U-shaped staircase with its own stair hall, plus servants' stairs in the kitchen-laundry wing to the right of the house. Upstairs were four master bedrooms, three of them with access to dressing rooms and closets, a bathroom, and two servants' rooms over the kitchen wing. The low attic space above, for which plans are no longer extant, must have provided for additional storage space and extra rooms.

The elevation of the house, carried out in brick with stone trim, is remarkably neat and precise. It is characterized by a strong emphasis on regularity and the precise demarcation of each zone, vertically by corner rustication and terminal chimneys, and horizontally by the use of prominent string courses between each story. In general proportion and feeling, it seems closer to French types than to local sources, with the possible exception of Tefft's Tully Bowen house in Providence of 1852-1853[36]. Despite its two bracketed porches covered with typical "pagoda"-type roofs, the house has a citified look, emphasized strongly in the kitchen wing by its studied quoining around doors and windows, a detail we find again in the Kane villa (Fig. 41). The small square third-story windows were of a type commonly used both here and abroad to illuminate a low attic. The pitch of the roof is very low, carrying out the general horizontality of the design.

Mayo House, Elizabeth, c.1855-1856

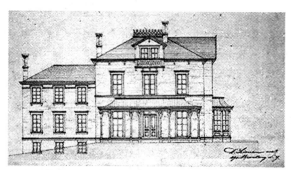

Figure 38. Mayo House by Detlef Lienau.

Another house of the period was built for a Mrs. Mayo in Elizabethtown, today known as Elizabeth, New Jersey. Elizabethtown, the oldest English community in New Jersey, was a pleasant community favored as a place of residence by commuters to New York or nearby Newark[37]. In all probability, this Mrs. Mayo was Adeline Mayo, listed in *Boyd's Directory of 1869* at 138 West Jersey Street[38]. The Mayos were one of the town's leading families: The wife of General Winfield Scott, the great military hero, was a Mayo. Drawings for the house[39], two of which are signed "D. Lienau, archt, 490 Broadway," must have been made between 1855 and 1856, as this was the only year Lienau was listed at that address in the New York directories.

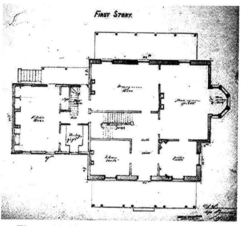

Figure 39. Mayo House. Plan of first floor.

The house Lienau designed for Mrs. Mayo (Fig. 38), in spite of its essentially simple character, exhibits Lienau's usual careful planning and attention to detail. Built of wood, it featured a bracketed porch with "pagoda" roof, a Swiss balcony that recalls the study for Michael Lienau's house, and a hipped roof and deck finished off with an iron railing in a *fleur de lys* design. On the side elevation, there appear two features used in the Cottenet villa, an Italian triplet window and a polygonal bay window. The house thus becomes an example of the "Swiss-Italian" villa type censured so vehemently by Field a year later[40]. As a matter of fact, the Italian touch does seem rather unnecessary. Otherwise, the house possesses considerable charm, particularly when compared to some of the examples of suburban houses issuing from Upjohn's office[41]. The plan (Fig. 39), with the usual kitchen ell, is similar to that of the Miller house; its regular outline is broken only by the projection of the bay window of the drawing room. The stairs again are placed in a separate hallway, in contrast to the usual center-hall American type.

Toler House, Newark, c.1859

Figure 40. Toler House by Detlef Lienau. Watercolor rendering.

Very different in spirit from both the Miller and Mayo houses was a picturesque residence built in Newark, New Jersey, for Hugh A. Toler and his bride, Mary Pennington, the daughter of a former governor of the state[42]. They were married in April 1859; according to tradition, the house was a wedding present to them from the bride's father. It was later described as an "imposing brownstone edifice... a sightly place with the river at its feet"[43] and was built on Belleville Road on part of the Sanford family grounds near Mount Pleasant Cemetery. Hugh Toler lived in the house only until about 1862[44], which may be attributed to his young wife's death late in 1861. In later years, the house was known as the Gibbs house; it was demolished in 1924[45].

Preserved in the Lienau Collection are seven sheets of drawings for this house[46]. A charmingly rendered watercolor perspective view of the house (Fig. 40) emphasizes its irregular, picturesque quality. Built of brownstone of varied sizes laid in random courses, three sides of the house were encircled by a bracketed porch. Enhancing its picturesque character were a number of canopied balconies and two polygonal bay windows, one a feature of the dining room, the other occupying the entire end wall of the parlor[47]. The latter type of bay window, of full room width, was much favored by Upjohn in his work of the middle 1850s[48]. The rather loose type of plan (Fig. 41), in which each room seems to push out from the center, had become very popular by the late '50s, if one can judge by the number of plans of this type in *Holly's Country Seats*[49].

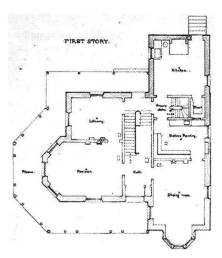

Figure 41. Toler House. Plan of first floor.

The Toler house, both in plan and in elevation, appears closer to the work of architects adhering to Anglo-American and German traditions of picturesque design than to French or Italian sources. It was unusual in Lienau's work of this time; gone were the classical canons of symmetry, regularity, and balance. Although definitely not a *cottage orné*, it is the closest that Lienau ever came to the spirit animating the cozy houses in this mode of Upjohn, Davis, Holly, and Eidlitz—a very successful example of a picturesque villa of the period. No doubt, Lienau found Italian and French styles more congenial. The Cottenet house was a fine example of the former; the Kane house in Newport, to which we shall turn now, is an excellent example of the latter.

The Kane Villa (1852) and the Beginnings of "Cottage Life" in Newport, Rhode Island

"Beach Cliffe" (Fig. 42), designed by Lienau in 1852 for DeLancey Kane of New York, was one of the earliest of Newport's "cottages". The subject of American resort architecture was first touched on by Roger Newton, whose interest was stimulated by the pioneer exhibition at the Avery Library, which was organized in 1940 by Talbot Hamlin[50]. The subject also recently has been explored by Vincent Scully in several publications. The most recent one, as well as the best, is his *Shingle Style*[51]; Scully's analysis in his earlier essay, "Nineteenth Century Resort Architecture," in *The Architectural*

Heritage of Newport, Rhode Island (1952), is extremely provocative, though admittedly biased in its point of view. My own interest in the subject was sparked by discussions with Talbot Hamlin and by the lectures of Henry-Russell Hitchcock at the Institute of Fine Arts, New York University, in the summer of 1951, both of whom called attention to the necessity of further research into the period of the 1870s and '80s, particularly of the work of architects such as William Ralph Emerson and Arthur Little of Boston, John C. Stevens of Portland, Lamb & Rich and Bruce Price in New York, and Wilson Eyre of Philadelphia[52]. The following pages on the history of Newport and the place of Lienau's Kane house within the stylistic development, written after a visit I made there in 1953, are intended to round out the picture of the origins of resort architecture.

Figure 42. Kane Villa (Beach Cliffe) by Detlef Lienau.

Development of Newport as a Resort

The development of resort architecture in Newport was a direct result of peculiar historical circumstances. Newport's transformation from a busy shipping center in Colonial times to a world-famous resort and the "social capital"[53] of the United States is an interesting story, of which no more than a brief outline can be given here.

Already in the 18th and early 19th centuries, Newport was enjoying considerable popularity as a summer resort, particularly among Southerners[54]. The War of 1812, however, cut Newport off from the South. With shipping crippled by the depression of the post-war years, Newport's wharves and beaches lay deserted until the 1830s[55]. Then, one by one, boarding houses and small hotels began to open once more. Slowly, the magic of sea, sky, and clouds, of the heavy surf breaking upon Newport's rocky shore, began to work upon a generation steeped in the literature of Romanticism. Painters, following in the footsteps of Gilbert Stuart and Washington Allston, as well as writers and intellectuals, came to Newport to find grateful solace from the noise, heat, dirt, and crowds of Boston, New York, and Philadelphia. So completely is Newport associated in the popular imagination with the fabulously wealthy, one tends to forget that, in the mid-19th century, it was an important cultural center[56]. Here, as Henry James so aptly phrased it, one could "find a solution to the insoluble problem—to combine an abundance of society with an abundance of solitude"[57]. James gives us a clue to the real meaning of Newport to painters like William Morris Hunt and John La Farge, and to intellectuals like himself, when he describes Newport as "the barren isle of our return from Europe"[58]. To such men, Newport became a refuge from the growing materialism of the later 19th century, an ivory tower where it was physically and psychologically possible to devote oneself to leisure and the arts[59].

The renascence of Newport in the 1840s should not, however, simply be construed as a spontaneous development of romantic Pantheism in the second quarter of the 19th century. Hotel keepers began to plan ahead and, in 1844, two large hotels, the Atlantic House and the Ocean House, opened for business. Another hotel, the Brinley, was enlarged, and its name was changed to the Bellevue. The really decisive move, however, was made in the mid-'40s, when several astute gentlemen bought up some three hundred acres of farm land south and east of Touro Street, on which they realized a handsome profit within the next few years as the demand for property increased. Of this group of pioneers in Newport real estate[60], the most important were Alfred Smith (who, as the years passed, came to have virtual monopoly over sales of property in Newport), Joseph Bailey, after whom Bailey's Beach is named, and Robert Johnson, owner of the old Easton Farm[61], a portion of which later became the DeLancey Kane estate. By the end of the '40s, creation of a second or "suburban" town on the fringes of the old seaport was well on its way.

Within a couple of years, the hotels, patronized by well-to-do Society people, were bursting at the rafters: 500 at Ocean House, 275 at Atlantic House, and more coming every day[62]. In August 1852, the editor of *Harper's* "Easy Chair" wrote that "the hundreds who peopled the uptown walks with silks and plumes are gone to the beach at Newport, or the shady verandas of the 'United States' [Saratoga's great hotel]"[63]. City streets were deserted. An excellent analysis of this revolution in the summer habits of upper-class

Northerners was made in 1856 by the writer of "The World of New York," a feature in *Putnam's*. After noting that the practice of "emptying" the town was a modern phenomenon, a quite natural consequence of the increased transportation facilities in the new "Age of Steam," he continued:

> A few years ago, you might have counted upon your fingers the families who habitually "went into the country" every summer... even the most respectable and flourishing citizens of Boston and Philadelphia, New York, and Baltimore kept themselves as cool as they could in their city houses... Now all this has been changed, and everyone goes off to Saratoga and Newport, Sharon and Rockaway, New Hampshire, Quebec, and Virginia Springs[64].

It is evident that, by the early 1850s, Newport had become *the* great summer resort in the United States. Saratoga's days of splendor were numbered[65]. More importantly, the people who used to stay at hotels were beginning to build. According to George Champlin Mason's account of 1854, so charmed were these people with Newport's climate and scenery, that "a desire to build becomes irresistible, and the result is a lot with a commanding view is purchased, a neat cottage is erected"[66]. George William Curtis, in a little book enticingly called *Lotus-eating* (1852), gives us an unforgettable picture of the beginnings of "cottage life" in Newport:

> The glory utterly gone from that huge, yellow pagoda factory, the Ocean House... For fashion dwells in cottages now, and the hotel season is brief and not brilliant. The cottagers will come, indeed, and hear the Germania play, and hop in the parlor; but they come as from private palaces to a public hall, and disappear again into the magnificent mystery of "cottage life"[67].

In 1853, the arrival in Newport of Ward McAllister, who was to become unquestioned arbiter of New York Society in the ensuing decades, marked the beginning of the transformation of Newport's social life[68]. Just as the simple picnics of the early days became elaborate *fêtes champêtres*, so cottages became increasingly large and elaborate, an evolution that reached its climax in the 1890s with the *chateaux* built by Hunt for the Vanderbilts. The beginning of this trend, however, is clearly discernible in houses erected in the early 1850s: Curtis, as is apparent from the quotation above, already sensed the incongruity of the term "cottage" to describe what was being built in Newport in this period[69]. While Mr. Russell's Oaklawn, as originally planned by Upjohn in 1852, and Mr. Willoughby's Chalet of 1854 by Eidlitz still may be defined as "cottages," the implication of rustic simplicity (with which the term was originally endowed) is conspicuous by its absence in Lienau's house for DeLancey Kane, Mr. Wetmore's Chateau-sur-Mer (Fig. 46), and in Downing & Vaux's villa for Daniel Parish (Figs. 45a, b, c), all built between 1852 and 1853. One example will illustrate the extent to which "conspicuous consumption" had engulfed Society in Newport, as well as in New York by the mid-'60s: Ellen Strong, wife of the diarist, brought up in an atmosphere of quiet luxury, was so revolted by Mrs. Paran Stevens's ostentatious display of her wealth and the fourteen servants with which her Newport cottage was staffed, that she vowed never again to visit her[70]. By 1870, "cottage life" at Newport had become a highly organized ritual[71], involving social customs and obligations undreamed of by the original cottagers like DeLancey Kane. Indeed, to quote a contemporary description, this was "the best place for people who know how, to do nothing"[72]—a sanctuary of America's new leisure class.

(*Figs. 43-44, see pp.137, 139.*)
Figure 45a. Parish Villa by Downing & Vaux.

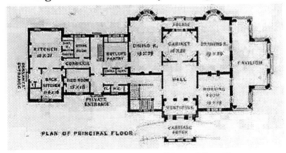

Figure 45b. Parish Villa. Plan of first floor.

FRONT FACING THE SEA.

Figure 45c. Parish Villa. Architect's drawing.

DeLancey Kane and the Astors

Before discussing the house itself, let me introduce DeLancey Kane, who has been credited with a major share in the development of Newport as "a select resort and community of fine houses"[73]. The Kanes had been active in the commercial and social life of New York since the middle of the 18th century, when John Kane (O'Kane), DeLancey's grandfather, had migrated to this country from Ireland. Members of the following generations had married into the Codwise, Hone, Brevoort, and Morris families of New York and Philadelphia. DeLancey Kane (c.1816-1874) himself was the son of Oliver Kane[74] and Ann Eliza Clark, daughter of a former governor of Rhode Island. Like so many sons of prosperous merchants, he turned to the law[75]; he was listed as a practicing attorney in *Longworth's City Directory of 1841*, the year he eloped with Louisa Dorothea Langdon. She was a daughter of Walter Langdon, of the Langdons of New Hampshire[76], and, on her mother's side, a granddaughter of John Jacob Astor, the richest man in the United States. As a result of her elopement, Louisa was read out of the family by her father, and Mr. Astor changed his will. In due course, however, all was forgiven and her grandfather presented the Kanes with a townhouse at 676 Broadway[77]. (In 1873, this was replaced by a store and loft building, designed by Lienau for the Kane estate, which still stands today.) While Mrs. Kane's share in the Astor estate was less than those of others in her family[78], the prestige attached to the Langdon name and financial backing from the Astor estate helped establish Mr. and Mrs. DeLancey Kane among the leaders of New York and Newport Society, a position which was retained by their children.

The eight Kane children, for whom Lienau provided a large nursery in the attic of Beach Cliffe, were well known in social and sporting circles of the '70s and married into the Iselin, Jay, and Schermerhorn families. Of the eight, two are of special importance and will be mentioned again. Colonel DeLancey Astor Kane, who married Eleanor Iselin, was a leader of the "horsey set" of the '70s, with headquarters at the Hotel Brunswick in New York[79]. A founder of the Coaching Club, he was famous as the owner of the Tally-ho (preserved at the Museum of the City of New York), which he had imported from England, and whose name became generic of the coach-and-four. Kane introduced the practice—in imitation of the Marquis of Blanford—of taking paying passengers on regularly scheduled runs between the Hotel Brunswick and the Westchester Country Club. His country house in New Rochelle was designed by Gilman. A reliable index to their social standing is the inclusion of Mr. Kane in that select group of twenty-five gentlemen known as the Patriarchs, organized in 1872 by Ward McAllister ("Mr. Make-a-Lister"). An invitation to one of the Patriarch's cotillion balls at Delmonico's was the open sesame to high Society. Other members of this distinguished coterie were Walter Langdon, Theodore Roosevelt, and two gentlemen whose names we shall encounter again later, Louis Colford Jones and William Colford Schermerhorn.

Figure 46. Chateau-sur-mer, Newport, RI (1852).

As is clearly apparent from even so brief a biographical sketch, the Kanes were eminently well suited to their role as leaders in the development of Newport. Grandson of a governor of Rhode Island, DeLancey Kane had been a visitor to Newport for many years before he decided to build there; one of his sons, DeLancey Astor Kane, was born in Newport in 1844. The records show that, in 1846, Kane began buying property on Bath Road (now Memorial Boulevard)[80]. The first lot was purchased from Robert J. Johnson, the son of the Robert Johnson mentioned previously. Over a period of years, DeLancey gradually acquired more land until, by 1852, he had accumulated a large tract bounded by Bath Road, Cliff Avenue, and Merton and Annandale Roads. This property had originally been part of Robert Easton's farm, known familiarly as "the Old Easton Farm" or simply "Beach Farm"[81]. The main building on the property was an old farmhouse that in 1776 had served as the headquarters of Lord Percy, commander of British troops in Newport during the Revolutionary War. This was moved to another site by the Kanes and replaced by a small frame house. The needs of a growing family, however, made it necessary to build a more spacious and comfortable residence, and one more in keeping with their social standing. The choice of Lienau as the architect may have been influenced by Mr. and Mrs. Kane's favorable impression of European architecture, which they had seen on a trip to the continent two years earlier[82]. For it is quite evident, as we shall see, that DeLancey Kane was not interested in building an ordinary bracketed cottage.

Architectural Background of the 1840s

Mention should first be made of the three most important houses built in Newport during the 1840s: Kingscote and the King house, both by Richard Upjohn, and A.J. Davis's Malbone. Then, we will be in a better position to understand the distinctive values that were brought to Newport architecture by Beach Cliffe and two other houses built at the same time: Chateau-sur-mer and the Parish villa.

J. Prescott Hall's Malbone[83], built by A.J. Davis in 1848-1849 for that wealthy New York barrister and friend of Daniel Webster, was, without a doubt, one of the period's most picturesque and impressive country houses in the Gothic mode. But it represents the end, rather than the beginning, of a tradition: By the end of the 1840s, the feudal architecture of the "Robber Barons" had few advocates[84]. Much simpler was Kingscote, built in 1841 by Richard Upjohn for Noble Jones, a summer resident from Savannah. One of the most charming examples in this country of the *cottage orné* type, Kingscote must be seen to be appreciated[85]. Surrounded by trees and shrubs that screen it from the street, the house seems literally to "nestle in, or grow out of, the soil"[86]. This sense of oneness with nature, so integral a part of the romantic philosophy and one of Downing's first principles[87], is artfully brought about by the studied informality of the plan and design, by the play of light and shadow, and the conscious effort to relate exterior and interior space[88]—

which we naively claim as a special achievement of 20th century architecture. In contrast to Kingscote, the Edward King house of 1845-1847—Newport's first Italian villa—seems aggressively large, crude in detail, and heavy in design. From this line, with its insistence on massive monumentality, rather than from the light and informal trend represented by Kingscote[89], stem Beach Cliffe and the two other houses.

Beach Cliffe and Other Early "Cottages"

According to an old print in the Museum of the City of New York[90], Beach Cliffe, now demolished, was beautifully situated with a fine view over gently sloping ground down toward the ocean and Easton's beach. In bygone days, Easton's Beach had been a favorite retreat for Bishop Berkeley and the painters Allston and Malbone. When it was built in 1852, Beach Cliffe stood almost alone in this region; Bath Road marked the end of Bellevue Avenue. The area beyond was undeveloped farmland. With the exception of Chateau-sur-mer and the Parish villa, the other houses of the 1840s and early '50s were all nearer to the center of town. Much farther out was William Beach Lawrence's estate, Ochre Point, which covered many acres, including the site now occupied by The Breakers and Anglesea (the latter, a Lienau cottage built in 1880).

Unhappily for the architectural historian, the Kane house was torn down in 1939 when the property was purchased by its present owner and divided into small lots[91]. Only the gate lodge, a small section of the enclosure wall, and a stable converted into apartments remain. However, drawings and photographs in the Lienau Collection[92], together with Champlin Mason's photograph and description of Red Cross, as the house was later called[93], enable one to visualize a villa that, indeed, must have represented the last word in architectural fashion.

> The house cannot be seen from the road, nor indeed till one is almost upon it, as he approaches through the avenue from the highway, under overarching trees. It is built of brownstone and brick, after a French design, and reminds one of some of the best specimens of French domestic architecture. The string courses, corbels, quoins, and other prominent features, all show careful treatment... At a glance, one sees that it was built alike with reference to durability, finish, and architectural proportions. The same attention has been bestowed on the interior: the broad hall, with its polished oak and marquetry,

spacious rooms, chastely designed mantels, and other features, add to its attractions, and make it worthy of observation.

At the entrance gate... there is a lodge built wholly of brownstone, happily conceived, and in perfect keeping with the place. On the right, at some distance within the grounds, one sees the long line of graperies and the conservatory[94].

Mason's emphasis upon the French character of the design, and the lack of available information regarding the architect and the date of the erection of the house, led Scully, who reproduces the Mason photograph in *The Architectural Heritage of Newport, Rhode Island*, to assign a date of "about 1872" to Red Cross and to compare it with the George R. Fearing house of the early '70s. Scully wrote:

> Comparable to it in its static academicism was Red Cross, the C.J. Peterson house, built at about the same time. This was a brick block with symmetrically disposed porches and heavy manneristic detail. Like the Fearing house, it was academic and dead in plan and, while its roots were certainly archeological, it seems most similar to the medium-sized chateaux published in the French architectural books of the mid-century. If academic, these "chateaux" are at least not overblown, but they express a new and disturbing point of view after the originality and willingness to experiment of the American mid-century development... The looting of European manorial farms which they represent... was eventually to exert a pernicious effect upon American architectural invention[95].

Had Red Cross, *i.e.* Beach Cliffe, been built in 1872, it would indeed represent an academic point of view. Its actual date of 1852, however, makes it with Chateau-sur-mer[96] the earliest example of Second Empire style in Newport—avant-garde, not reactionary. In pointing out the similarity of the design to the small chateaux of the mid-century, Scully undoubtedly had in mind the several publications of Victor Petit, which do, as a matter of fact, offer some points of comparison[97]. But it is difficult to understand why he called the plan, which he did not know, "dead and academic," for as we shall see very shortly, this was far from the case (Fig. 44).

To modern eyes, Beach Cliffe may seem extremely formal for a seaside cottage or villa (Fig. 42). The intention of the architect was, unmistakably, to create a setting for the Kanes where their manifold social activities could be displayed to advantage. The wide, symmetrical, three-bay façade is given a monumental air by the projection of the central bay, flanked at ground level by banded rusticated columns[98], at second-story height by flat pilasters, both motifs decidedly French in flavor, the whole surmounted by a somewhat overscaled dormer window. The use of brick with brownstone trim gives the house a definitely citified look[99], quite unaffected by the addition to either side of that distinctly American vernacular element so highly prized by Downing, the bracketed porch[100]. From the rear view (Fig. 43), the *piazza* seems to "belong," but from the front the porches give the impression of having been tacked on as an afterthought. That they were an integral part of the architect's original intention is, however, obvious from a study of the plans for the house. Indeed, this strange combination of European and vernacular elements and of city and country architecture gives the house its special character, a certain ambiguity and tension not wholly agreeable.

Figure 43. Kane Villa. View toward sea.

The straining after monumental effect, noticeable here, is even more apparent in the cottages of Messrs. Wetmore and Parish. In establishing summer residences in Newport, these gentlemen evidently were endeavoring vicariously to acquire some of the prestige enjoyed for centuries by the landed gentry in Europe. It is not surprising then to find echoes of the *chateaux* of France and the *palazzi* of Italy in these Newport cottages; the actual comparisons are of course rather with the smaller *seigneuries*, villas and manors. Thus, the use of the "French" order on the façade of Beach Cliffe was undoubtedly meant to impart to it, by association, some of the glory of the Tuileries. Precisely contemporary and extremely apropos are George William Curtis's remarks regarding the *nouveaux riches* of Newport, who he said value money and possessions for themselves, rather than as a means to an end. He commented on their exaggerated taste, or lack of it, and—most interesting from our point of view—their competitive spirit in architecture, in which each one endeavored to outdo the other. He concluded with these words:

> We are still peasants and parvenus, although we call each other princes and build palaces. Before we are three centuries old, we are endeavoring to surpass, by imitating, the results of all art and civilization and social genius beyond the sea. By elevating the standard of expense, we hope to secure select society[101].

The Parish villa (Figs. 45a, b, c), long pointed out as the most beautiful cottage in Newport[102], introduced still another variant on the cottage theme, this time inspired in part by the Venetian palaces of the *Cinquecento*. By employing Downing and Vaux, Daniel Parish, one of New York's leading dry goods merchants and later one of Lienau's clients[103], made clear his desire to have as fine a house as possible. The monumental Bellevue Avenue façade, with its pedimented gable, round-headed windows, heavy string courses, and impressive *porte-cochère*, is quite close in feeling to the Renaissance mode popularized in this country by Ammi B. Young[104]. The rear, or seaward elevation, with its bay windows, two-storied *loggia* and end pavilion replacing the traditional American porch, is far more interesting. A little playful, definitely picturesque, here we meet for the first time in Newport the influence of the Venetian rather than the Tuscan villa type. Downing recently had returned from a trip abroad, where he had met Vaux. Perhaps, Vaux had been to Italy; in any case, the star of Venice was in its ascendancy[105]. In general conception, the design is quite similar to several of the North Italian villas published by Victor Petit in his *Habitations cosmopolites*[106]. Less far afield, one might also point to the use of the two-storied *loggia* in at least one of Sloan's designs of 1852[107]. Judged by the standards of its own day, the Parish house was an extremely successful design that combined monumentality with a touch of the picturesque and the exotic. Broadly treated, it has none of the rather unfortunate fussiness of Beach Cliffe.

In plan (Fig. 44), Beach Cliffe was quite different from the formal regularity of the Downing-Vaux design, a fact partly accounted for by the natural slope of the land. In contrast to the rigid symmetry of its façade, Beach Cliffe's plan was a relatively loose one, with a pleasant variety, not only in the size, but also in the shape, of the rooms. There appears to have been considerable feeling for the flow of space through the wide transverse hall, and through openings into the rooms leading from it.

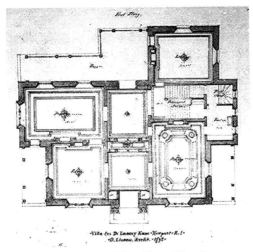

Figure 44. Kane Villa. Plan of first floor.

The deliberate introduction of an irregular element, the library, jutting out beyond the T-shaped plan, is noteworthy. Easy access to the outdoors was provided by French doors opening onto the porches from the hall, library, and drawing room; conversely, each room (but not the hall) was equipped with a fireplace as protection from the chilling late-summer fog, which can be so thoroughly unpleasant in a seaside cottage. It is quite possible that the Kanes spent a large part of the year here, since they are not listed in the New York directories between 1853 and 1873. It would be interesting to compare the original plan of Chateau-sur-mer with Beach Cliffe. Scully describes it as departing only slightly from the academic type, with a central hall on axis and symmetrically disposed rooms to each side[108].

Summary

If Beach Cliffe, Chateau-sur-mer, and the Parish villa share with one another, to a greater or lesser degree, a general air of pompousness in the design of the exterior, the Kane house seems to have been the least rigid in plan. Most important was the early appearance of a French influence, a distinction it shares with the Wetmore "cottage".

Figure 47. The Chalet by Leopold Eidlitz.

In contrast to all these houses was the Chalet (Fig. 47) by Leopold Eidlitz for Hugh Willoughby on Halidon Hill on the other side of Newport and published in Bullock's *American Cottage Builder* in 1854[109]. The Swiss style, which gave the house its name, was eminently well suited to the picturesque wooded slope on which the house was built. Eidlitz, who was extremely fond of the Swiss mode for residential architecture[110], comes far closer in this house to modern notions of seaside architecture[111]. Here was a perfect adjustment of house to site, an informal and open plan, interpenetration of exterior and interior space, and bold handling of the wood material. If Eidlitz's Chalet was prophetic of progressive trends in Newport's architecture, which reached their climax in the 1870s and early '80s, then Beach Cliffe, Chateau-sur-mer, and the Parish villa marked the beginning of stylistic tendencies and psychological attitudes developed to their logical conclusion by Hunt in The Breakers—the architectural symbol of Newport's "Golden Age". Men of the 1850s like DeLancey Kane were blissfully unaware that a time would come in America when one could not maintain even a relatively modest cottage such as Beach Cliffe. Death and taxes have taken their toll; the future of Beach Cliffe, like that of many old Newport estates, now lies in the hands of the speculative builder.

Chapter VI.
Town and Country Houses

Introduction

The next two chapters, dealing with eight of Lienau's commissions from the late 1850s through the early '70s in metropolitan New York, will serve to demonstrate his importance in shaping the course of architectural development in the United States during the years immediately preceding and following the Civil War. The two Schermerhorn residences on Twenty-third Street, the Jones Row on Fifth Avenue, and the Lockwood Mansion in Norwalk, Connecticut, were his most important commissions of these years and his finest creations in the field of domestic architecture. The interest of these works lies not only in their stylistic features—they provide excellent examples of the developed Second Empire style in this country—but also in the insight they provide into modes of living of the period. Moreover, when considered in relation to companion works discussed in the next chapter—the suburban row built for Henry A. Booræm in Jersey City, the Schermerhorn apartments in uptown New York, the Grosvenor apartment hotel on Fifth Avenue, and the clubhouse erected on Madison Avenue for the American Jockey Club—these commissions provide one with a fairly comprehensive picture of the housing problems of those days on nearly all economic levels, and show how a creative architect met their challenge.

Detailed analysis of Lienau's domestic architecture will end with these commissions of the early '70s, since the disastrous years 1872 and 1873 brought to an abrupt end the stylistic trends that have been traced here from their beginnings in the Shiff house of 1850. French influence virtually ceased as an important factor in architecture, as in politics, after the Franco-Prussian War and the overthrow of Napoleon III (1870). The fires of 1871 in Chicago and 1872 in Boston sounded the death knell of the mansard roof and the Second Empire style in this country; the depression of 1873 all but put an end to serious building for several years. When building resumed at the end of the '70s, a new era began. Lienau's houses of the '70s and early '80s will be dealt with more summarily than his earlier work,

since they were less important to the general development of
American architecture. The outstanding New York architects of the
last quarter of the century, with the exception of Richard Morris
Hunt (1828-1895), all were much younger than Lienau. The up-and-
coming firm of McKim, Mead & White, acknowledged dictator of
taste and pacesetter in the next decades, came to represent the new
generation. Yet, as we shall see, Lienau's work was not without its
lessons for the younger men, particularly for architects like
Hardenbergh and Pelz, who trained in Detlef's office.

The Schermerhorn Houses, West Twenty-third Street, New York

For the two houses designed by Lienau for the Schermerhorn
brothers, William and Edmund, members of the one of New York's
oldest and most respected Knickerbocker families, we return once
again to New York City. Following the expansion of the city
northward, we find ourselves at Twenty-third Street, which at the
end of the '50s was just beginning to acquire a city look. William
Colford Schermerhorn, the younger brother, was the first to move
from the family mansion at Lafayette Place to the newly fashionable
Madison Square area at Twenty-third Street. We shall see that the
transformation of Twenty-third Street—first into a distinguished
residential district and later into a busy commercial thoroughfare—is
extremely well illustrated by the history of the Schermerhorn
holdings. Stylistically, the two houses clearly illustrate the
development of the Second Empire style in New York between the
late '50s and the end of the '60s. A number of outstanding examples
of this style by architects other than Lienau were concentrated
precisely in the Twenty-third Street district.

Description of Twenty-third Street

The development of Twenty-third Street[1], still a semi-rural area
in the early '50s, was begun by Amos R. Eno, father of the last
occupant of the Shiff house. In 1856, when news leaked out that he
planned the erection of a mammoth hotel on the northwest corner
of Fifth Avenue and Twenty-third Street, the project was popularly
dubbed "Eno's Folly". But the Schermerhorns evidently shared his
faith in the future of the neighborhood: They began buying property
on West Twenty-third Street the following year[2]. The story of the
fabulous success of the Fifth Avenue Hotel (1859-1908)[3], usually

credited to the architect William Washburn of Boston, but probably actually designed by Thomas & Son[4], is too well known to be recounted in great detail here. Suffice it to say, within a few years it replaced the Astor House as the finest hotel in town. It quickly became the political center of the city, indeed of the entire country. Here, the bigwigs of the Republican Party gathered to discuss the affairs of the nation in the dark days of civil war. And so, Twenty-third Street and Madison Square became not only the political, but also the social, hub of the city, amply justifying "Eno's Folly" and real estate speculations of men like the Schermerhorns. Here lived the men (many of them intimates of the Schermerhorns) who shaped the course of history in those days: Secretary [of State William H.] Seward, Samuel J. Tilden, James G. Blaine, Cyrus Field, Peter Cooper, Russell Sage, Commodore Vanderbilt, Leonard Jerome, and last but not least the notorious Jay Gould and Jim Fisk, who operated from the Grand Opera House on Twenty-third Street and Eighth Avenue.

Figure 48. Booth's Theater by Renwick & Sands.

The Grand Opera House, originally called Pike's Opera House, was built in 1864-1868 by Griffith Thomas and is still standing. It was only one of several large public buildings erected during the post-war boom that transformed Twenty-third Street into the cultural and entertainment center of the city. Until the building of the Fifth Avenue Hotel, Renwick's Free Academy at Fourth (Lexington) Avenue had been the only large building in the area. Built in 1863-1865, Peter B. Wight's National Academy of Design, New York's best known example of Ruskinian Gothic[5], stood on the northwest corner of Fourth Avenue. The Young Men's Christian Association building was erected directly opposite on the southwest corner a few years later (1868-1869). This and Booth's Theater (Fig. 48) on the southeast corner of Sixth Avenue, both built at the same time, were by the architectural firm of Renwick & Sands[6]. The last of this series of important public buildings in the area was Masonic Hall (1870-1875; demolished in 1911), designed by Napoleon Le Brun (Fig. 49), one of New York's most successful architects in the last decades of the century[7].

Figure 49. Masonic Hall by Napoleon Le Brun.

All of these buildings, with the exception of the National Academy, were excellent examples of New York's fully developed Second Empire style. They imparted an air of elegance to the neighborhood, echoed by private dwellings in the street, of which the most outstanding example was unquestionably Edmund Schermerhorn's mansion, and provided a particularly appropriate setting for the social activities of the Schermerhorns.

The Schermerhorns

Sons of Peter Schermerhorn "the Younger" (1781-1852) and Sarah Jones, the Schermerhorn brothers had inherited a large fortune that enabled them to devote themselves to public service, charitable causes, and the development of New York's cultural life[8]. This fortune, originally based upon ship chandlery and New York's flourishing coastal trade, had been greatly expanded by Peter the Younger through banking interests and shrewd investments in East Side Manhattan real estate. Peter had been one of the pillars of Grace Church and a member of the building committee that supervised its erection. He died in 1852, his constitution undermined, it was said, by that "chronic disease—enlargement of the bank account"[9]. Of the two brothers, William Colford Schermerhorn (1820-1903) was by far the more active in New York's economic, social, and intellectual life. A graduate of Columbia College and a lawyer, William spent much of his time managing the family estate, quite a considerable undertaking, since the Schermerhorns were among the richest landowners in the city. But, like his good friend, George Templeton Strong, he was a man of many outside interests to which he unstintingly devoted both time and money. "A tower of strength to Columbia[10]," he served for forty-three years as a member and later as Chairman of the Board of Trustees, and contributed substantially to the support of the college. He was the donor of Schermerhorn Hall, erected by McKim, Mead & White in 1898, and a half million dollar endowment fund for religion, given by his daughter, Annie (Mrs. John Innes Kane), likewise perpetuates his name.

For a more intimate picture of the life of the Schermerhorns—important because it helps to explain the kind of house that Lienau designed for them—we are again indebted to Strong's *Diary*, as well as to other writers of the period. Many are the accounts of the delightful musicales and theatricales that were held at William's *palazzo* on Twenty-third Street[11]. The costume balls given by the Schermerhorns were always notable events of the season. Mention has already been made of the first of these memorable balls held in 1854 at the family residence at 6 Great Jones Street[12]. The guests had been commanded by Mrs. Schermerhorn to appear in French court costume of the period of Louis XV—a direct reflection of Eugénie's special predilection for this type of retrospective diversion. This ball was remembered for years thereafter, not only for its unprecedented magnificence and grandiose scale—six hundred guests, the elite of New York Society, had been invited—but also because the gentlemen were forced to sacrifice their carefully cultivated mustaches and *impériales* to the interests of historical accuracy! The Schermerhorns needed plenty of room for these affairs. Edith Wharton, William's cousin, remembered the house on Twenty-third Street as one out of possibly four houses in New York (the others being owned by the Astors, Belmonts, and Mortons) that boasted a real ballroom[13]. All of these gatherings were presided over by Mrs. Schermerhorn, who was noted for her beauty, personal charm, and gracious hospitality. Née Ann Elliott Huger Laight (1825-1907), she was the daughter of Francis Cottenet. Lienau was the logical choice of architect: He was building the extension to the Cottenet house in

Dobbs Ferry[14] at just about the time the Schermerhorns might have been planning to build on Twenty-third Street. William Schermerhorn proved to be one of Lienau's most faithful clients. In later years, Lienau erected a number of structures for him, including commercial buildings and a block of apartment houses on Third Avenue. The latter, an early example of the "French flat," or apartment house plan, will be discussed in the next chapter.

Edmund Schermerhorn (1815-1891), in contrast to William, led a rather retiring life on income largely derived from his real estate investments[15]. His only known position, probably more honorary than otherwise, was an appointment in 1856 as Engineer-in-Chief of the New York State Militia. He was a bachelor. According to Strong, his one great and abiding love was music. Active in several musical organizations, in the '70s he served as president of the New York Philharmonic Society. The large house Lienau built for him was obviously planned as a suitable setting for his fortnightly musicales. Commenting regretfully on their termination at the end of the season of 1873, Strong wrote that "few entertainments so refined, so civilizing, and so pleasant have ever been given in New York"[16]. Some years later, Edmund retired to a life of complete seclusion. In his declining years, he had the reputation of being extremely eccentric. His mansion, described after his death in 1891 in an article in the New York *Herald* captioned "Home of the Dead Hermit[17]," was, as we shall shortly see, an architectural curiosity in more ways than one.

Following Edmund's death, William Schermerhorn had his brother's mansion razed. In its place, he erected a loft building designed by Henry J. Hardenbergh[18] who, in Detlef's later years and after his death, earned many of the Schermerhorn commissions. Edmund Schermerhorn's house was thus the first of the two houses to disappear beneath the rising tide of trade. William was quick to recognize that times had changed. Facing the Schermerhorn houses on the south side of Twenty-third Street was Stern's, which began the "uptown" trend in 1878. Other retail stores quickly followed. On the right, William's mansion was flanked by the Eden Musée (1884–1916), a popular wax works collection and the last work of the German-born architect, Henry Fernbach (1828-1883)[19], one of Lienau's contemporaries. By the early '90s, Twenty-third Street had become exclusively a commercial thoroughfare. But Mr. and Mrs. Schermerhorn stubbornly refused to move; they lived in the house Lienau designed for them until they died. Finally, in 1911, the William Schermerhorn house was demolished—the last of the old landmarks on the block to go—and replaced by the present office building, 49-51 West 23rd Street, which runs through to Twenty-fourth Street.

Literary Sources

In effecting a reconstruction of these two notable houses, we can fortunately illustrate the literary references with the very complete sets of drawings preserved in the Lienau Collection and an excellent old photograph of William Schermerhorn's house (Fig. 50). With regard to the literary sources, the late Lloyd Morris's *Incredible New York*, a recent book, contains much valuable information concerning the Schermerhorns. Morris mentions that William's house was filled with notable, if disquieting, examples of European art. He relates how, at one of their affairs, a young debutante relative was greatly embarrassed to find herself standing beside an undressed statue and talking to a young man at the same time[20]. This anecdote is worth repeating for its authentic Victorian flavor and because it sheds light on the cosmopolitan taste of the Schermerhorns, which undoubtedly made them particularly receptive to Lienau's European background and personal taste.

Figure 50. William C. Schermerhorn House by Detlef Lienau (1907).

The dating of the Schermerhorn houses poses something of a problem, since none of the drawings was dated. The designs for 49 West 23rd Street, William's house, had been variously dated by J. Henry Lienau as 1850 and 1862. To those for Edmund's house at 45-47 West 23rd Street, he assigned a date of 1860[21]. However, city directories first list William at his new address in the volumes for 1859/1860. This date is corroborated by the Tax Assessment Records of 1859, indicating that the building was "in progress" at that time[22], and by an entry of May 18, 1859, in Strong's original manuscript, "Journal"[23]. On that day, Strong wrote, he dined with the Schermerhorns in their new *palazzo* on Twenty-third Street. Since the property had been purchased in 1857, the designs for the house may reasonably be assigned a date late in 1857 or early the next year, with the likelihood that construction began in the spring of 1858. As for the designs for Edmund's house, J. Henry Lienau's suggested date of 1860 seemed far too early for the advanced type of Second Empire style used. A probable date of c.1867-1869 is substantiated by contemporary sources such as Kennion's *Architects' and Builders' Guide*[24], the Tax Assessment Records, and listings for Edmund Schermerhorn in the *City Directory*[25].

William C. Schermerhorn Residence, c.1858-1859

Figure 51. William C. Schermerhorn House. Front elevation.

The design and rendering of this house (Fig. 51), solidly built of brick with brownstone trim, recalls in many ways the Shiff house of 1850 (Fig. 29)[26]. Here again, we find a simply handled elevation, with restrained classical detailing. Characteristic Lienau trademarks are the zoning of the façade into clearly defined areas, both horizontally and vertically, emphasized by careful corner quoining and prominent string courses[27]; the flat pilasters in the second and third stories with elongated panels interrupted by a conforming circular, or bull's eye, motif[28]; and the low-pitched mansard with prominent dormer windows.

Figure 52. Union Club House by Thomas & Son.

In comparison to the Shiff house, the general impression is one of greater monumentality and plasticity, though the decorative features (pilasters, panels, and pediments), which combine Italian and French Renaissance motifs, are still flattened against the surface plane. The overall effect of the Schermerhorn house is one of classic calm and restraint, and of order and logic, in contrast to, for example, Thomas & Sons' Union Club House of 1855 (Fig. 52). One cannot help but feel here some of the reticence and stolidity of the old Dutch tradition in New York—it obviously befitted the Schermerhorns—in spite of apparent Italian and French stylistic sources.

Figure 53. Rossiter House by Richard Morris Hunt.

This is particularly noticeable if one compares the Schermerhorn house with Richard Morris Hunt's Rossiter House (Fig. 53), which Hunt had designed in 1855 while he was still in Paris working under Lefeul. The Rossiter house was, as Montgomery Schuyler noted, "an unmistakable product of the Beaux-Arts"[29], directly inspired by Lefeul's Pavillon de la Bibliothèque du Louvre. Mention has already been made of Lienau's testimony on Hunt's behalf in the celebrated lawsuit, *Hunt v. Parmly* (1861)[30], which developed as a result of complications in the supervision of the construction of the Rossiter house, relegated to Joseph C. Wells during Hunt's absence in Washington.

Figure 54. Parish House by Frederick Diaper.

If Lienau's design was less obviously French and far less sophisticated than Hunt's, it nonetheless was an outstanding example of its period. This may perhaps be best understood by comparisons with other important, slightly earlier, and contemporary houses: Frederick Diaper's house for Daniel Parish (c.1854-1855) on the southeast corner of Sixteenth Street and Fifth Avenue (Fig. 54), a fine example of the influence of the English clubhouse tradition[31]; Dr. Townsend's $100,000 house (c.1854-1855) on the northwest corner of Twenty-fourth Street and Fifth Avenue[32], later replaced by the A.T. Stewart mansion, likewise a combination of Italian *palazzo* and villa traditions; and, finally, the much touted mansion of John Jacob Astor II. This brick and brownstone house (Fig. 55), built in 1859 on the northwest corner of Fifth Avenue and Twenty-third Street, was razed in 1893 to make way for Hardenbergh's Waldorf Hotel. Like the Schermerhorn house, it too was built "in the French style[33]," a mode most warmly advocated in *City and Suburban Architecture* (1859)[34] as worthy of imitation by Samuel Sloan after his trip to France. Comparison of the Astor and Schermerhorn mansions, built at about the same time, yields the conclusion that Astor's architect lacked the feeling for refined detailing and careful planning that was always apparent in Lienau's work. The architect of Astor's house is not known. Quite possibly, it was Thomas & Son, since the firm did a great deal of work for the Astors[35]. The Thomases were exceedingly astute businessmen, as well as competent architects; it is unlikely that they would have let such an opportunity slip away from them.

Figure 55. John Jacob Astor II Residence, New York (1887).

If the façade of the Schermerhorn house seems relatively austere, expressing little of the life within, we must remember that the old Knickerbocker families frowned upon the ostentatious display of wealth. But the interior was another story. A glance at the plan (Fig. 56) shows us a house in which the Schermerhorns could entertain graciously and display their works of art to advantage.

The broad hall, the impressive open-well staircase, the series of rooms *en suite*, which could easily be opened up to provide a free flow of space through which several hundred people could circulate easily—these features were important in a house for a leader of New York Society. Talbot Hamlin has commented on the freedom and magnificence of Lienau's carefully studied plan, as well as on his superb draftsmanship[36], which unfortunately does not show up well in the reproduction. Upstairs on the bedroom floors (Fig. 57), one sees evidence of the same careful planning: large bedrooms with generous dressing rooms and, rather unusual for the period, two bathrooms and water closets on the floor, each accessible not only from the adjoining bedrooms, but also from the hall. Notable also are the two water closets and a bath for the servants in the basement, as well as the provision of two dumbwaiters, one leading from the wine cellar in the sub-basement through to the upper bedroom floors, the other, as usual, connecting the kitchen in the basement with the butler's pantry on the parlor floor.

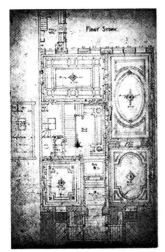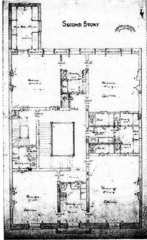

**Figures 56 and 57. Schermerhorn House. Left: Plan of first floor.
Right: Plan of second floor.**

Edmund Schermerhorn Residence, c.1867-1869

Far more important to a study of the influence of the French Second Empire style on American planning and design in the third quarter of the century are the drawings[37] for the Edmund Schermerhorn residence (Fig. 58). As indicated earlier, this house was an architectural curiosity. In the first place, it was planned as a double house: It had two entrances and an interior partition wall completely separating the two units (Fig. 59). The smaller house must have been occupied by a member of the family, or by Edmund's housekeeper[38] or secretary. (If Edmund Schermerhorn had a mistress, he certainly would not have had the audacity to set her up on Twenty-third Street.) Of far greater consequence for the architectural historian is the second point: In this house, the full impact of French influence, affecting plan as well as elevation, hit New York architecture. Edmund's house was almost literally a Parisian *hôtel particulier* transplanted. Particularly striking was the carriage drive that, as in many Parisian houses[39], ran through the center of the house leading to a grand staircase where passengers were discharged, and then continued past a stable in the courtyard[40] to an exit provided on Twenty-fourth Street. Lienau's introduction of French-planning practices into the New York private residence parallels Hunt's adaptation of the French flat tradition in the contemporary or slightly later Stuyvesant Apartments[41].

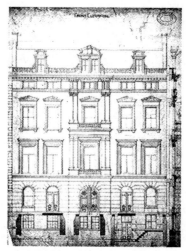

Figure 58. Schermerhorn House. Front elevation.

The elevation drawing for the house reveals that its materials, brick and brownstone, were the same as those used in William's building. The architectural vocabulary was almost identical. No doubt, this was intentional, for one of the important problems faced by the architect was to work out a scheme whereby Edmund's house would be brought into a harmonious design relationship with William's house next door, which had been built ten years earlier. It is evident that the most important visual factor to the architect of this period was the alignment, not of the various stories within the façade—which was out of the question, because of the difference in height of the two entrance floors—but of the roof line with its identical mansard design. This was cleverly achieved through the addition of a low attic story to make up for the loss of the half basement area under the stoop in William's house. String courses between stories, always prominent in Lienau's work, were eliminated, probably because the architect did not want to call attention to the disparity in the alignment of the two buildings.

Judging from the elevation drawing for Edmund's house, the net result was extremely successful. The design attains a degree of monumentality and quiet authority not encountered before in Lienau's work. The background was most certainly the Parisian *hôtel particulier*, with which Lienau was thoroughly familiar not only through English[42] and French books and magazines, but also from recent first-hand experience. He must have seen much of the new work in Paris when he went abroad in the spring of 1864[43], such as commercial and domestic architecture in progress or recently completed, and important public edifices built since his departure from Paris in 1847—the new Louvre, Duban's L'Ecole des Beaux-Arts, Bailly's Tribunal de Commerce and Lycée St.-Louis, Garnier's plans for the opera, etc. Even before this trip, he would have been cognizant of French architectural trends through the many publications of the late '50s and early '60s, such as Calliat's *Parallèle des maisons de Paris construites depuis 1830* (2 volumes, 1857 and 1864), Adams's *Receuil des maisons modernes les plus remarquables* (1858), Vacquer's *Maisons le plus remarquables construites pendant les trois dernieres années* (1863), and Daly's *L'Architecture privée du XIXe siècle* in the first edition (1864)[44].

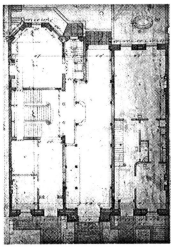

Figure 59. Schermerhorn House. Plan of first floor.

The closest parallels to the Edmund Schermerhorn house may be found in some of the plates in *L'Architecture privée*, though numerous examples, similar in spirit, may be referred to in Calliat's book, in *Le moniteur des architectes*, and in the *Revue générale*[45]. One of the illustrations in the *Revue*[46] is quite close to an unidentified Lienau study for a house (Fig. 60), which must date from about the same period as the Edmund Schermerhorn residence. Like the latter, it has a rusticated base with the entrance on the ground floor, but in this case the carriage drive is incorporated into the corner of the house.

Before jumping to any rash conclusions on the subject of French influence, one should bear in mind that there were isolated examples of French [*sic*] planning and prominent practitioners of the Second Empire style in Germany[47], as well as in France. Like most styles before and since, the Second Empire mode quickly became an international style, as Henry-Russell Hitchcock has so ably demonstrated in his investigations into Victorian architecture in England[48]. Renwick's Charity Hospital in New York (1858), his Corcoran Gallery (1859) in Washington, D.C., and Arthur Gilman's City Hall (1860-1862) in Boston illustrate the early extension of this style to official architecture in the United States. But the specific combination of Second Empire trademarks and Neo-Grec decorative motifs, so typical of Lienau's work, may be paralleled not only in France, but also in Germany, most particularly in the work of Hitzig in Berlin, whose buildings were published from the '50s onward[49].

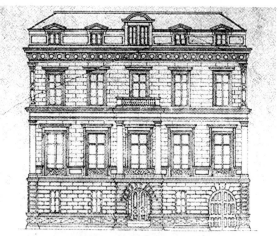

Figure 60. Unidentified study for a house by Detlef Lienau.

Whatever factors, conscious of unconscious, lay behind Lienau's designs for the Edmund Schermerhorn house, the important thing is the use to which he put them. Together, the two Schermerhorn houses provided New York with one of the most dignified, elegant, and refined bits of street architecture of the period. Judging from contemporary accounts and the two drawings in the Lienau Collection of decorative paneling for Edmund's house[50], the interiors must also have been handsome. Far less pretentious than John Kellum's million-dollar palace (1867-1869) on Fifth Avenue for A.T. Stewart (Fig. 61)[51], Edmund Schermerhorn's mansion was certainly one of the finest examples of the stylistic tendencies of the late '60s. It was a fitting compliment to the full blown, somewhat bombastic Second Empire style of public architecture on Twenty-third Street: Booth's Theatre, the YMCA building, and the Masonic Temple down the block.

Figure 61. A.T. Stewart Residence (Marble Palace) by John Kellum.

The Terrace: Colford Jones Block, Fifth Avenue, 1868-1870

Introduction

By far, the most ambitious of Lienau's work in urban residential architecture was the row of eight houses built from 1869 to 1870 for Rebecca (Mrs. Colford) Jones, forming the block front between Fifty-fifth and Fifty-sixth Streets on the east side of Fifth Avenue (Fig. 62). It has doubtless not gone unnoticed that, with the passing of the years, the buildings under discussion are located farther uptown. Indeed, this type of study provides interesting evidence of the wondrous growth of the city within a few decades.

The great impetus to building in this section of town came with the development of Central Park. Under the expert supervision of Frederick Law Olmstead and Calvert Vaux, the area above Fifty-ninth Street, formerly inhabited by miserably poor squatters living in squalid shanties[52], was gradually transformed into a section of town of which New Yorkers became justifiably proud. Although work had begun in 1857, Central Park was far from being finished even by the late '60s. Empty lots, bleak and barren, still lined Fifth Avenue between Renwick's St. Patrick's Cathedral at Fiftieth Street, and the lower section of the park, which at this time was far from "central". As late as 1864, Strong dismissed as completely preposterous the idea that he assume the presidency of Columbia College and emigrate to what he called the "frontier settlement" at Forty-ninth Street[53]. Nonetheless, prominent landowners in the vicinity, such as

Mrs. Jones, felt that the development of the area was inevitable—and held on to their property.

Figure 62. Colford Jones Block by Detlef Lienau.

Rebecca Jones (1802-1870) and her sister, Mary Jason Jones (1801-1891), who owned a corresponding block front on Fifth Avenue between Fifty-seventh and Fifty-eighth Streets, both were widowed early in life. They had married two cousins, [Isaac] Colford Jones and Isaac Jones, members of a wealthy and socially prominent New York family[54]. The sisters had acquired their property in 1855 from the estate of their father, John Mason, a millionaire New York merchant and banker, who for many years before had purchased from the city a large tract of land running from Fifty-fourth to Sixty-third Streets and from Fifth to Fourth Avenues[55]. This investment was to pay off handsomely for his two daughters. The tax valuations relating to the two properties provide one with a remarkably graphic picture of how the fabulous fortunes in New York real estate were built up. In 1855, Mary's parcel, originally purchased by her father for $1,500, was valued at $35,000, and Rebecca's at $30,600. By 1865, the latter's property was assessed at $292,000; Mary's had jumped to $319,000[56]. Obviously, the land had become too valuable to hold without improving it. Mary, the elder sister, pacesetter in architectural as well as economic matters, whose word was law in Society circles for over half a century[57], started the ball rolling late in 1867 by building on the northeast corner of Fifth Avenue and Fifty-seventh Street. Using Robert Mook as her architect, she erected a large mansion for herself on the corner and, next to it, a smaller house, followed in 1869 by five other houses, thus forming a solid block front from Fifty-seventh to Fifty-eighth Street[58]. This was the famed block, 737-745 Fifth Avenue, known until its final demolition in 1929 as "Marble Row" (Fig. 63)[59]. Rebecca, following the lead of her sister and using Lienau as her architect, began building in the summer of 1869. A year later, the "Colford Jones Row" at 705-719 Fifth Avenue, built of cream-colored Ohio stone, was finished[60].

Figure 63. Mary Mason Jones Block by Robert Mook.

These two blocks, so eminently successful as a real estate investment[61], marked a real turning point in the history of New York's residential architecture. They not only set a standard for luxury unequaled in New York until the 1880s, but also established important precedents in principles of planning and construction. Most noteworthy were: (1) a deliberate break with the brownstone tradition and (2) the transformation of the conventional additive "row" plan into an integrated monumental design comparable to the best of continental and English terrace planning.

Description

The history and architectural development of the Colford Jones Row is recorded not only in the usual sources, such as the records of the Department of Buildings, the Tax Assessment Records, and contemporary descriptions, but also by the magnificent portfolio of thirty-nine drawings, an excellent photograph, and a statement of costs, in Lienau's hand, all preserved in the Lienau Collection[62]. There is also a portfolio of large photographs at the Museum of the City of New York[63]. A lack of similar material on Marble Row is compensated for by many descriptions, the most valuable of which is by Edith Wharton, who knew the houses well. Mrs. Wharton, née Jones, was a niece of Mary Mason Jones; her unforgettable portrait of Mrs. Mingott, the headstrong old matriarch in *The Age of Innocence* (1920), was modeled after her aunt. Mary Mason Jones, having arrived at an age when conformity was no longer important, deliberately removed herself and her *ménage* to the "wilds" of Central Park[64]. She might as well have been moving to California[65], or so it seemed to her contemporaries who wishfully closed their eyes to the fact that the lower section of Fifth Avenue was already being taken over by business[66]. Even more shocking to Society was the house she built (Fig. 63): Flagrantly Parisian in design, with its tall mansard roofs, corner pavilions, and French windows opening onto balconies with graceful balustrades, it was decorated inside according to the latest Parisian taste[67]. According to one report, Marble Row was built from Mrs. Jones's own plans, modeled after fond recollections of Fontainebleau and the Tuileries[68]. Actually, as already indicated, the houses were designed by Robert Mook[69], an architect whose name is completely unknown today, but who did considerable building in the metropolitan area from the mid-1860s to the early '80s, when he retired from active practice.

Robert Mook (1830-1917) was born in New York City. His family, originally of Dutch origin, had emigrated to this country from England shortly before the Revolution. Thomas Mook, his father, a butcher by trade, amassed a considerable fortune and was the owner of the Bull's Head Cattle Yard on Fifth Avenue between Forty-fourth and Forty-sixth Streets, still shown on the *Dripps Map* of 1850. Leaving the butchering business to his father and brothers, Robert Mook went to work in the architectural office of Thomas & Son. It is said that "Grif" Thomas would not let him get ahead as fast as he wanted, so he opened his own office c.1856 at 111 Broadway.

Judging from the records of the Department of Buildings, Mook had an extensive practice. Among his clients, he counted James Cruikshank, the prominent real estate man, for whom he built two houses adjoining Mrs. Jones's row on East 58th Street; Amos R. Eno, later the owner of the Shiff house, was one of his best customers. He did a great deal of commercial building in downtown New York, but perhaps his best known building was Shearith Israel (1859-1860), formerly located at 3-5 West 19th Street, New York, the first domed synagogue in the U.S., which Madame Wischnitzer believes introduced the Neo-Baroque style to this country. Mook's plans for the William E. Ward house (1873-1876) in Port Chester,

New York, are still in the possession of the Ward family; this house was in all likelihood the first structure erected in reinforced concrete, and was planned by Mr. Ward, a mechanical engineer.

Figure 64. Colford Jones Block. Study.

Rebecca, to whom Strong often refers as "little Mrs. Jones," was not to be outclassed by her sister Mary in architectural matters. How she came to choose Lienau, rather than Mook, as her architect is not difficult to guess. William and Edmund Schermerhorn were her nephews; both she and her son, Lewis Colford Jones (like William, a member of the Patriarchs), had always been on the friendliest terms with the younger of the Schermerhorn brothers.

The kinship between clients in the small world that made up polite Society in New York in those days was often close; but the relationship of the two architects, Lienau and Mook, is not so simple to ascertain. It is entirely possible that the two architects may have consulted one another; both had offices in Upjohn's Trinity Building at 111 Broadway. Though Mook's design for the corner houses on Fifty-seventh Street predates even Lienau's earliest studies for the Colford Jones Row, Mook may very well have turned to Lienau for advice. Lienau was the older man, more experienced in the Second Empire mode than Mook, and familiar at first hand with the French buildings that Mook admired so much.

Lienau's design was considerably less showy than Mook's, but it probably suited the requirements of his client perfectly. We know from the number of studies for the houses and adjoining stable that he worked very hard to please Mrs. Jones; he certainly earned his commission of $20,976.50—a very large sum at the time[70]. But then, these were no ordinary row houses. Not only the owner, but also the prospective tenants, required a distinguished residential environment comparable in prestige to Davis's earlier Colonnade Row at Astor

Place. This no doubt explains the change in design from the conventional type of New York house with a high stoop, still seen in one late study (Fig. 64), to the monumental and definitely Parisian look of other drawings for the houses.

Figure 65. Colford Jones Block. Study.

Figure 66. Colford Jones Block. Presentation drawing.

Lienau gradually evolved an imposing terrace scheme resting on a rusticated base and crowned with four pavilions. First came a design calling for four stories, accented by two pavilions on houses Nos. 3 and 4 (Fig. 65). Then, the height of the row was raised from four to five stories. In searching for a formula to unify the long façade, Lienau adapted a system long in favor in France[71]. In the large beautifully rendered presentation drawing (Fig. 66), the elevation was divided into three main sections: (1) a two-story rusticated base, of which the basement was below the level of the sidewalk, customary in New York, but not in Paris; (2) second, third, and fourth floors featuring balconies at the second-story level and a giant order linking the third and fourth stories; and (3) a fifth story mansard plus a low sixth-story attic, lighted by bull's eyes in the tall center pavilions. The increase from two to four pavilions in the final drawings strengthened the design considerably, though the use of a low terminal pavilion and the indecisive treatment of the chamfered corner at roof level is less effective than Mook's stronger, more striking design. This restraint, however, is quite typical of contemporary or slightly earlier French apartment houses, which provided the general prototypes for the Colford Jones Row.

Figure 67. Colford Jones Block. Study for plan of first floor.

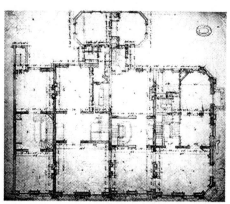

Figure 68. Colford Jones Block. Working drawing of first-floor plan.

Rusticated lower stories, giant orders, low mansards, occasional use of pavilions, and chamfered corners all may be found in Parisian and French provincial architecture of the period[72]. Also typical is the carefully studied vertical rhythm of the façade, given variety here by an "a-b-c-dd-c-b-a" arrangement. In a study of November 22, 1868 (Fig. 67), the plans also show a radical change from the conventional New York townhouse type with a cramped entrance hall and straight stairs to a more gracious open plan in the working drawing (Fig. 68). Relatively broad halls led to open-well or elliptical geometric stairways; in the corner houses, a good-size octagonal hall provided an impressive reception or waiting room at ground-floor level[73].

Historical Importance

While a more detailed examination and discussion of the many drawings for the houses would certainly reveal many interesting points[74], it is more important now to place Marble Row and the Colford Jones block within the general line of development of domestic architecture in New York. To understand their significance fully, we must try to visualize Fifth Avenue as it was in the late '60s. Everyone agreed that a brownstone house was dignified and imposing. But architectural critics were beginning to find the endless succession of high-stooped brownstones—once the symbol *par excellence* of affluence[75] and respectability—not only monotonous, but depressing[76]. Edith Wharton's description of New York in the '70s perfectly expresses the attitude of the younger generation, which characterized the architecture of the "brown decades" as "deplorable" and "monstrous"[77]. Commenting on the city following her return from Europe, Mrs. Wharton wrote:

One of the most depressing recollections of my childhood is my recollection of the intolerable ugliness of New York, of its untended streets and the narrow houses so lacking in external dignity, so crammed with smug and suffocating upholstery. How could I understand that people who had seen Rome and Seville, Paris and London, could come back to live contentedly between Washington Square and the Central Park? What I could not guess was that this little low-studded rectangular New York, cursed with its universal, chocolate-coloured coating of the most hideous stone ever quarried, this cramped gridiron of a town without towers, porticoes, fountains or perspectives, hide-bound in its deadly uniformity of mean ugliness, would fifty years later be as much a vanished city as Atlantis or the lowest layer of Schliemann's Troy...[78]

The reaction against the brownstone front is perhaps best expressed by Junius Henri Browne's typically moralistic description of the houses on Fifth Avenue in his fascinating book, *The Great Metropolis*, published in 1869, but based on sketches begun a few years earlier:

It is the habit of New-Yorkers to style Fifth Avenue the first street in America... The architecture is not only impressive, it is oppressive. Its great defect is in its monotony... A variation, a contrast—would be a relief...

Block after block, mile upon mile, of the same lofty brownstone, high stoop, broad-staired fronts wearies the eye... One longs in the Avenue for more marble, more brick, more iron, more wood even—some change in the style and aspect of these sombre-seeming houses...

The stately mansions give the impression that they have all dreamed the same dream of beauty the same night, and in the morning have found it realized; so they frown sternly upon one another, for each has what the other wished, and should have had alone.

It is a grievous pity that where there is so much money, there is so little taste[79].

The two Jones rows, one in marble, the other in light-colored Ohio Berea stone, provided the answer to the longing for a change in building materials, which Browne expressed so well. If we can trust descriptions published in the early '70s, reaction to the two rows was extremely favorable. Both rows were described in *Redfield's Traveler's Guide to the City of New York* (1871), one of the best guides of the period. After commenting on the exorbitant cost of the A.T. Stewart mansion, the writer continued:

The visitor, if he is a careful observer, will note changes in the style of building as he wends his way up the avenue. Houses which were considered to be "just one thing" ten years ago, are out of date today. Observe the style of the houses above Fourteenth street...; then, at Twenty-fifth to Thirtieth streets, and again, those which are being erected ten or twenty streets farther up. Between Fifty-fifth and Fifty-sixth streets, for example, a block of houses has just been built of Ohio stone—a material fast coming into use, and destined to supplant brownstone. These houses are finished with mansard roofs, and are vastly more attractive than the houses of ten years ago... Another block that will attract attention has just been finished, between Fifty-seventh and Fifty-eighth streets. These houses are of white marble, and when one is a little distance away, the effect has been so contrived that the block may very well be mistaken for a church [*sic*][80].

Thus, the erection of these two blocks definitely marked the end of the era of the brownstone front in fashionable architecture[81], though it continued for years, of course, in speculative middle-class housing and lingered on as late as the early 1880s in isolated examples along Fifth and Madison Avenues (*e.g.*, the twin William H. Vanderbilt mansions [1879-1881] and Villard residences [1883-1885]). Equally important is the second point, implied in Redfield's description and also in that of the Colford Jones Row furnished by *Appleton's New York Illustrated*, where it is called "a handsome block... The style is simple, yet the *general effect* [author's italics] is one that elicits only the most favorable criticism"[82]. Here, we sense the new realization of the importance of large-scale planning of sufficient breadth and sweep to be effective from a distance. Discussing the new opportunities for architecture in the vicinity of Central Park, Kennion voiced the hope that architects would take full advantage of the opportunities now (1867) open to them. He still thought, however, in terms of single buildings in which each mansion would be "an architectural poem of itself"[83]. The gridiron plan of New York and the relative lack of parks and open vistas had not been congenial to the development of large-scale architectural schemes[84]. In a city where each block was subdivided into equal twenty-five-foot lots, of which the average property owner had one (or at the most two) at his disposal, such planning was admittedly difficult to accomplish. Until now, the architect and his client generally had to satisfy their aesthetic longings and egos by the insertion, let us say, of a pint-size edition of an Italian *palazzo* or a Gothic castle, which might—and usually did—find itself in thoroughly uncongenial surroundings. Contemporary writers had much to say of these palaces "*à la sandwich*"[85]. A lead editorial in the *Architects' and Mechanics' Journal* of 1860 describes how sad it is to see all the fine features of a façade, cornices, string courses, and arcades, "meet with a sudden and untimely death in the midst of their career" as soon as they "come in rude and unexpected contact with the fatal party line"[86].

Solutions to the problems posed by the design of street architecture were manifold, and received much attention in the journals of the time, both here and in England. Some called for terminal features to isolate one building from the next[87]. Others suggested the use of projecting bays, pavilions, and the French mansard roof: These features, it was argued, would impart to the individual building in a block a sense of completeness, individuality, and dignity, as well as a striking skyline[88]—the latter all important to the Victorians. On the other hand, a few writers, admittedly in the minority, turned away from the aggressive individualism of the period, which expressed itself violently, even in the Victorian cemetery[89]; they suggested the possibility of cooperation among the various owners of lots in any given block[90]. The most radical plan of all, which will be discussed later, called for the submission of all designs to a planning board in order to eliminate all possibility of architectural conflict.

If the individual client were fortunate enough to own a large piece of property, as did Mesdames Jones, he (or she) still had to be convinced of the advantages, aesthetic and economic, to be gained from designing a block of houses as one integrated unit, rather than as a mere sum of identical parts. In New York, such clients had previously been rare. Le Roy Place (c.1827) was an early example of terrace planning. Later blocks were Depau Row[91], London Terrace (1832), and Chelsea Cottages on West Twenty-third and Twenty-fourth Streets respectively. Both London Terrace and Colonnade Row (1836) at Astor Place had been designed by A.J. Davis and built by Seth Gear. Characteristic of the 1840s was a long row of Gothicized houses on Twentieth Street off Sixth Avenue. More interesting are two rows of the early '50s, one a group of houses opposite St. George's Church on East Sixteenth Street[92], the other a five-house unit still standing at 139-147 East Fifteenth Street (Fig. 69). The latter row (1852-1854) was built for L.M. Rutherfurd[93], noted astrophysicist and the father of Rutherfurd Stuyvesant (whose Stuyvesant Apartments made history later)[94].

Figure 69. Rutherfurd Row by an unknown architect.

The latter row is one of New York's outstanding extant examples of the *Rundbogenstil*, which Mr. Rutherfurd had come to love in the course of several years of travel in France, Germany, and Italy in the late 1840s and early '50s. The unknown architect of the row cleverly played against each other plane surfaces and voids, and contrasting textures of brick and brownstone. It is distinguished by an unusually fine composition in which a center section is flanked by two projecting wings linked by an arcaded *loggia*. One wonders who the architect was. Saeltzer perhaps? The interesting brickwork suggests some German influence; stylistically, the building is more closely related to the Astor Library (Fig. 17) than to anything else. The last important row built before the Civil War was George Higgins's interesting but ill-fated enterprise, the block known as the "House of Mansions" (Fig. 71).

HOUSE OF MANSIONS

FIFTH AVENUE, OPPOSITE THE CROTON RESERVOIR.

Designed by Alex'r J. Davis, Architect, and erected by Geo. Higgins, Esq.

This block should recommend itself to all patriotic citizens, lovers of architecture, "the protector, preserver, and promulgator of all other arts," as well as to those who would purchase from its superior, practical, scientific construction, of brick hollow walls, and solid partitions;—most of what appear as good buildings, (fine and imposing we grant them), being constructed with wood-battened, faced brick, unbacked walls, and hollow wood partitions,—a most incendiary practice, constituting the worst manner of building, and against which there is no protection from the laws;—fire building for their own security, but rather for outward gaudy show and speculation.

This block contains eleven independent dwellings, differing in size, price and amount of accommodation. They have from twelve to eighteen rooms each. The pile is altogether unique in its character and plan, the eleven dwellings being combined as in one palace, or massive edifice, thereby exhibiting a unity in mass, not before attempted, though often desired by critics—the usual mode of building in cities, from the number of dissentient proprietors,—being *forced* in the extreme, one house five or six stories in the heavy Roman style, the next adjoining, one of two stories, in no style at all, and the two contrasting most oppositely in size and cost, making both, however costly the one, poor and mean, and the disagreed, unwilling owner loth to occupy his house, "neighbored by those of lesser quality."

For the aesthetic, or artistic expression of this block of buildings, and its value in this respect we leave to the mercy of the critics, we shall hold it worthy of imitation for city building architecture.

rally considered; and may we not esteem it as conducive to domestic comfort as well? From the "strength found in union;" in its continued terrace plantation, and varied yet elegant perspective from its windows, unobstructed light, air and ventilation; absence of street front areas; neatly kept walks, and terrace railing.

The prominent noticeable points in this row of buildings, are, the durable fire brick, of pleasing cheerful tint of color, without paint; the stair vestibule, or rotunda connecting the parlors with more elegance and variety than a third more private room would do. From its dome light, and stairs of unusual size and ease. The large and cheerful windows, balconies, bays, oriels, and terraced walks. Its crowning parapet, and convenient distribution of offices, closets, pantries, bath rooms and chambers. Almost all tastes are consulted in respect to entry vestibules, reception rooms, passages through mail-chambers, or by-passages, spacious or more confined, for summer air, or furnace heat; for light, cheerful kitchens, store rooms, and the rear alley of access for servants and market stores.

The view from the windows and summit is unrivalled, commanding the whole island with its surroundings; the Hudson and East rivers, Staten Island, the Palisades, and far into Westchester county, and over Long Island. The water in the Croton Reservoir, like an artificial pool or lake, of oriental magnificence, is seen from the upper windows, a bright mirror, reflecting the gay promenade surrounding. It will not suffer, in whole or part, by an inspection. Its liberal owner offers it to the Public, until it is made private by company. *Apply at the central house.*

(Fig. 70, see p. 171)
Figure 71. House of Mansions by Alexander Jackson Davis

Built in 1856, the row was designed by A.J. Davis in castellated Gothic style. It stood on Fifth Avenue between Forty-first and Forty-second Street, directly opposite the Reservoir. In 1859, the southern half of the block was put up for auction; the northern portion was purchased at auction for only $60,000 by the Rutgers Female Institute. One reason for its failure was probably the panic of 1857, which temporarily depressed the real estate market[95] and cut off the supply of ready capital for mortgage payments; another may have been the *retardataire* style of the building. While the composition as a whole was progressive—it was advertised as "altogether unique in its character and plan, the eleven buildings being combined as in one palace... exhibiting a unity... not before attempted"[96]—castellated Gothic was definitely *passé*. It might still be used in country residences, as was indeed the case with many of the Davis houses of the mid-'50s, but not for city architecture.

As for the run-of-the-mill speculative builder of the 1860s, he was content, like the builders of ranch houses today, with one standard model—a high-stooped brownstone, repeated *ad infinitum*. A thorough investigation of the beginnings of row architecture and terrace planning in New York is needed. The architectural historian, the sociologist, and the city planner would find much of interest in such a study. As is apparent from the foregoing rather cursory discussion, only a very few of the early rows were meant to be more than a sum of identical or similar individual units. The visual factor, the desire to plan a row or block that would have mass and coherence, yet still possess variety[97] and picturesque appeal, came in the '50s, as seen in the Rutherfurd and Higgins rows. Sociologically, these early rows are evidently of considerable importance. The acceptance among the well-to-do of the idea of the attached row house from the late 1820s on may well have been the first break with the Colonial tradition of the isolated house. Indeed, it may even have helped prepare the way for the belated acceptance here of the apartment house system, a subject to which we shall return.

Further development of the terrace plan in New York had to await the end of the Civil War, when fluid capital for investment again became plentiful. Architects then quite naturally turned to France for inspiration—large-scale projects such as Hittorf's and Rohault de Fleury's monumental buildings surrounding the Place L'Etoile were published early[98]—and also to England where the terrace tradition, long established, continued with renewed vigor from the late 1840s on. Henry-Russell Hitchcock devotes a number of interesting pages to the early Victorian terrace; examples of its later development, doubtless followed with interest on this side of the Atlantic, were published sporadically in the English architectural journals such as *Building News*[99] and the *Builder*.

Figure 70. The Terrace by H.H. Holly (1863).

One of the earliest American architects who was alerted to the design problems of large-scale urban street architecture was, oddly enough, a specialist in country houses, Henry Hudson Holly (1834-1892). Holly, a native New Yorker, had been to England in the late '50s and remained all his life under strong English influence. His first book, *Holly's Country Seats* (1863), whose publication was delayed for two years by the outbreak of the Civil War, was one of the most influential plan books of the period. Only one of the designs in the book, No. 30, was devoted to city architecture, but significantly it was called "The Terrace" (Fig. 70). Its kinship to the English-terrace tradition and resemblance to Knowles's mansard-roof terraces at Clapham, also erected at the edge of a park, is probably not fortuitous: The latter was published in the *Builder* of 1860[100]. In discussing the construction of buildings that are to rise around our parks and thus may be seen from a considerable distance, Holly wrote:

> Occupying sites so conspicuous, these blocks should be carefully studied in masses and outline, so that each house may not be entirely independent and individual as now, but a reasonable part of a general design. This can only be effected by an agreement of all the parties proposing to build in the block, or by care being taken that each successive house, as it is erected, may form an harmonious union with those which have preceded it. It is not meant that all should build alike—far from it, since irregularity, with due attention to the harmony, is an important source of beauty in architecture.

He goes on to describe how these differences may be reconciled with one another. Turning to the question of speculators of large property owners, he said:

> It is to be regretted that they make use of this privilege not to create a *unity* of design, but rather a *uniformity*—a weary and monotonous repetition of general features and details, the whole having the appearance of cheap contract work turned out with a

machine, and the unfortunate purchaser, in the middle of each block, can only recognize his own house by his name on the doorplate...

The design we offer is an attempt to prove that houses of different heights and of different degrees of finish and costliness, may be put together so as to produce an harmonious whole[101].

He concluded his essay with the suggestion that, with other governments having successfully legislated on the subject of street architecture, it might be possible to offer special inducements, such as temporary reduction in taxes

to those who will submit their plans to the censorship of a public officer, chosen by architects whose duty it shall be to observe certain approved aesthetic standards of design of generous, and not tyrannical, application, as well as to preside over the operations of the laws for the protection against unsafe buildings[102].

The creation of the Department for the Survey and Inspection of Buildings of New York in 1860 had been the first step in this direction.

It is noteworthy that the design offered by Holly, like that adopted by Lienau and Mook a few years later, was already definitely Second Empire in style. This was no accident for, from the late '50s on, the Second Empire mode was almost as much used in England as in France, particularly for large-scale commercial projects such as hotels[103]. After its precocious introduction by Lienau in the United States, followed by its rapid development by other architects, by the late '60s the Second Empire style was unchallenged in the New York area as the favorite architectural idiom. Mention has already been made of the important buildings on Twenty-third Street carried out in this style. Most of the city's large commercial buildings and institutions fit into the same general pattern, inaugurated by Griffith Thomas's Continental Life Insurance Company Building (1862-1863). Well known examples were John Kellum's New York Herald Building (1865-1867) and the offices of the Mutual Life Insurance Building (1863-1865), the National Park Bank (1866-1868) by Griffith Thomas, and Henry Fernbach's Staats-Zeitung Building (1870-1872), which stood on the site of the present Municipal Building. These are only a few, chosen because they were generally much admired in their day[104].

Summary and Conclusion

The rows designed by Robert Mook and Detlef Lienau have to be understood as reflections of general stylistic tendencies of the times to which they gave powerful expression. There is no doubt, however, that Mook's design owed much to the additions of Lefeul to the Louvre, and perhaps something also to the terraces along Grosvenor Place in London, begun in 1867[105]. Lienau's design, as we have seen, is also much closer to French sources than to the English prototypes that lay behind Holly's Terrace or the colossal project of 1867 by Gilman and Bryant for a hotel on Fifth Avenue and Fifty-ninth Street. This was published in *Builder*; the architects publicly acknowledged their indebtedness to Henry F. Garling's prize-winning design of 1857 for the Foreign Office[106]. In the case of the Colford Jones Row, unlike Marble Row, one cannot put his finger on any specific building that might directly have inspired the architect. All that can be said is that Lienau's design is generally close in spirit to slightly earlier Parisian work and to contemporary building in the French provinces; it is an excellent example of "synthetic" eclecticism.

The later history of Marble Row and the Colford Jones Block[107] reflects the slow but inexorable advance of trade northward up Fifth Avenue. The northern end (Fifty-eighth Street) of Marble Row was remodeled, probably in the late 1880s, by Richard Howland Hunt[108], son of Richard Morris Hunt, for use by the Plaza Bank, as our cut shows (Fig. 63). No. 741, the house next to Mary Mason Jones's Fifty-seventh Street corner, likewise was taken over by a commercial enterprise. Solomon R. Guggenheim occupied No. 743 for some years; the house was finally demolished in 1915 and replaced by the present narrow office building. The rest of the row remained residential. After Mrs. Jones's death in 1891, her house was leased to Mrs. Paran Stevens, wife of the hotel owner; in 1895, it passed to Mrs. Hermann Oelrichs, who had the interior redecorated by Stanford White. Mrs. and Mrs. William E. Iselin remained at 745 until the final demolition of the row in 1929, when it was replaced by the Squibb Building on the Fifty-eighth Street end and by the office building at Fifty-seventh Street, now occupied at street level by the Manufacturers Trust Company. The Colford Jones Row fared less well, for the northern half was razed in 1911; the southern section, in 1925. E.H. Harriman, the railroad magnate and father of the present governor of New York, lived in Mrs. Colford Jones's house on the corner of Fifty-fifth Street for some years until c.1907; later, the corner was occupied by several art dealers, the last tenant being Jacques Seligmann & Company. The entire block was occupied until recently by a large office building, 707-711 Fifth Avenue, which is still standing, and the Hotel Langdon at the Fifty-sixth Street corner. The latter was razed this summer (1957) to make way for the new home of the Corning Glass Works, to be erected on this site by Harrison, Abramovitz & Abbe.

A Country Estate: The Lockwood Mansion, Norwalk, Connecticut, c.1864-1868

[*The editor is grateful to Foreword author Mimi Findlay for updating key facts and descriptions in this section.*]

Figure 72. Lockwood Mansion by Detlef Lienau.

Introduction

To some wealthy New Yorkers, a house on Twenty-third Street or on Fifth Avenue, however grand, did not represent the *ne plus ultra*. For them, only the country estate would provide the definitive answer to their search for prestige. The Lockwood Mansion (Fig. 72), to which we turn now, is one of the most interesting examples of that period of our history, so aptly characterized by Mark Twain as 'The Gilded Age"[109]. It was the largest private house Lienau ever built and is still referred to as "The Mansion" in a tone of marked deference by the citizens of Norwalk. It stands today in Mathews Park, named after the second owner of the Mansion, and since 1966 has been leased by the Lockwood-Mathews corporation [and operated as a museum]. The former carriage house currently houses a non-profit printmakers workshop and art gallery. Since 1966, about $2-million has been spent on the Mansion to re-slate the roof (twice), rebuild the veranda, steam-clean and re-point the granite walls, repair and paint the windows, restore the rotunda's glass roof and rebuild the destroyed conservatory, restore the painted plaster decoration of most of the major rooms on the first floor, install bathrooms in the basement, and more[110].

LeGrand Lockwood (1820-1872)[111], for whom the house was built, was a native son of Norwalk, whose family had been associated with the development of the town since 1645. He was the head of one of Wall Street's best known and most reputable brokerage concerns. Lockwood had made a fortune in stocks and government bonds during the Civil War; he sunk part of these funds into the purchase of land and the construction of his million-dollar mansion in Norwalk. From there, he could easily keep in touch with his New York office, the Stock Exchange, and the several other enterprises in which he had an interest. Lockwood was active in the development of early horse-drawn railcar lines in Norwalk (1862) and New York; he was on the board of several railroad companies and the Pacific Mail Steamship Company[112]. The tracks of the Danbury-Norwalk Railroad, of which he was a Vice-President, ran directly to the east of his property. It was he who floated a $2,000,000 bond issue for the New York, New Haven & Hartford railroad line at a crucial time in its history. In short, LeGrand Lockwood was one of a new breed of men who emerged in this period—the Wall Street tycoon and railroad man. He was Norwalk's first millionaire and, while he was not in the same league as Cornelius Vanderbilt, he possessed certain qualities that the elder man lacked. Lockwood, according to all accounts, was a man of considerable personal charm, well liked by all who knew him; he was generous, public spirited, and had the reputation of being a man of his word—he was a gentleman. Unlike Jay Cooke, the famous financier of the Civil War (to whom he was distantly related), Lockwood had overcome his lack of a formal education (he went to work at age 18) by extensively traveling abroad, and he cultivated the role of a lover and patron of the arts and sciences[113].

Both as Norwalk's first millionaire and as a man of "taste," Lockwood must have felt a certain obligation, architecturally speaking, toward the town of his birth. Quite understandably, the house Lienau designed for him was no picturesque cottage retreat. It was a country mansion in the grand manner, destined to be the showplace of the community. Particular mention was made of the house in an article in *The New York Times* of August 5, 1867, describing the fine residences of Norwalk:

> One of these, now in the course of erection by Mr. Le Grand Lockwood... will cost, with the grounds, nearly two millions of dollars and, when completed, will stand with scarcely a rival in the United States. The designs were furnished by an eminent European architect, who has planned many of the palatial residences beyond the pond [*sic*][114]

The mistaken attribution to Lienau of the design of great mansions abroad is easily explained by the conscious aping of the French *chateau* tradition in the Lockwood mansion, a point to which we shall return. The passage is quoted here primarily for two reasons: one, it was useful in dating the house (the sources are contradictory, and the Lienau drawings at the Avery Library[115] are undated); two, for its statement regarding the cost and relative quality of the house.

First, the date of the mansion: We know that Lockwood purchased the most important parcels of land, which constituted Elm Park, as the estate was called, between November 1863 and March of the following year, rounding it out with purchases in 1865[116]. We may assume that the plans for the building were either furnished before Lienau's trip to Europe in the spring of 1864 (one writer maintains that construction began that spring)[117] or, following his return, in which case the start of construction would probably have been delayed until the spring of 1865. According to tradition[118], the Lockwoods (including their older children) occupied the gate lodge while awaiting completion of the mansion. This is substantiated by the listing of LeGrand Lockwood, Jr., in Connecticut in the New York directories of 1866/1867. According to the same source, LeGrand Lockwood, Sr., moved from New York to Connecticut only in 1868, thus corroborating the *Times* article above, which described the house as "in the course of erection" the summer before. A date of 1864/1865 to 1868 would therefore cover the actual dates of construction of the various buildings on the estate, gate lodge, gardener's cottage, main house, stables, carriage house, greenhouses, etc. If this seems a long time, we should remember that much of the material for the house was imported from Europe; furthermore, everything had to be hauled by ox-cart either from the railroad station in South Norwalk, two miles away, or up from barges on the Norwalk River.

LeGrand Lockwood must have felt that it was worthwhile when the house was completed. While the present generation may find Lockwood's taste a bit on the heavy side, there is no doubt that he, like A.T. Stewart, Jay Cooke, and others, fully understood the prestige value of architecture. No expense was spared to make this house one of the largest and most elaborately appointed country mansions of the time in America[119]. Unlike Cooke, who prided himself on the fact that everything in his famous mansion, Ogontz (1865-1866), had been made in the United States by American workmen[120], Lockwood is supposed to have traveled far and wide in search of materials for his house. Egyptian porphyry, Florentine marble carved to order in Italy, the rarest and best of domestic and imported woods beautifully inlaid, huge mantels rich with carving—these were mere details of interior decoration that indicate the *recherché* quality of planning and design that both the client and architect put into the house. Consider, moreover, that the house contained some 21 bedrooms (including seven servants bedrooms) on the second and third floors, that it had six bathrooms and about five water closets (unheard of in those days, even for a family with half a dozen children!), a picture gallery, not one but two connecting billiard rooms, a private theatre in the attic, and a bowling alley in the basement. This descendant of the Puritans was assuredly no ascetic, judging by the capacity of the wine cellar! The house was heated by two huge coal-fired boilers in the basement, one at each end of the house (still intact); water was supplied by a private spring located at some distance from the house and piped into a 2,000-gallon tank on the fourth story of the house. An annunciator at the kitchen door had twenty-three bells connecting with all the principal rooms. There was a burglar alarm connected to every window and door on the first two floors, and a fire and burglar-proof vault for silver next to the dining room[121].

Description and Analysis

This fabulous house, described by one writer as a "sumptuous and striking example of architectural invention"[122], was built like a fortress. The outer walls rest on concrete foundations three feet thick; the basement, entirely vaulted with brick arches, recalls North German traditions, which Lienau also used in the house he built for his brother Michael in 1872 in Ütersen[123] and later advocated as an excellent method of fireproofing[124]. The walls were double: the outer of granite slabs twenty inches thick, the inner of eight-inch thick brick with an air chamber of four inches between. In addition, the lath of the ceilings supports a four-inch layer of clay, which was put in for sound-deadening purposes. The exterior granite facing, finely cut, here and there shows signs of weathering. Leading into the house is a rather ponderous *porte-cochère* with LeGrand's initials worked into the keystone in heraldic fashion[125]—an interesting detail, which may be seen in Lienau's elevation drawing (Fig. 73).

Figure 73. Lockwood Mansion. West elevation.

The mansion then builds up gradually behind low flanking wings[126] and high central gable to a mansard roof finished off with an iron balustrade of delicate Neo-Grec design. The overall impression is decidedly reminiscent of the French Renaissance *chateau* tradition, which both Lienau and his client must have known at first hand and which was promoted by recent French publications[127] and restoration projects. While the Norwalk River winding its way at the foot of the property was hardly comparable to the Loire, it is quite possible that such an analogy existed in the minds of Lienau and Lockwood. As an example of this trend of thought, we have only to recall the wall built "to resemble the ruined castle of some ancient nobleman" at the end of Jay Cooke's Italian garden[128]. Lockwood was not going to be outdone by Cooke. Moreover, he evidently enjoyed playing the role of *grand seigneur*. Had he not handed out crisp new ten-dollar bills to every soldier who would enlist in the Union cause in Norwalk's "Fighting Seventh" regiment?

A preliminary study for the house, to modern eyes a far better design than the one finally adopted, makes clear the close relationship to the French tradition. The mansard roofs, dormer windows placed immediately above the cornice line, the emphasis on corner quoining, the tall chimneys decorated with Lienau's favorite bull's eye panels (replaced in the executed design by banded chimneys), the effort to make a balanced composition in spite of unavoidable asymmetries—these are all obviously French in origin. In the working drawings, certain significant changes were made, presumably at Lockwood's request: Note the raising of the mansard roof to make room for a fourth story, the elaboration of the pediments capping the second-story dormers, and the increased use of incised ornamentation on the dormers and *porte-cochère*. These changes bring to the building a certain top-heaviness—less readily apparent in photographs than in the actual building—and a fussy quality that relates it more closely to High Victorian taste. The conflict between Lockwood's tendencies toward monumentalization and display, and Lienau's simpler, more classical tendencies results in a building that cannot be cited as an altogether successful example of eclectic design. There is a certain over-elaboration, a coarseness in detailing (also apparent in the interior), a lack of subordination of parts to the whole, which again runs counter to modern critical standards, but as typical of the aesthetic of its own period. One unusual motif deserves mention, for which no exact parallels can be found: the introduction of a strongly projecting horizontal cornice in the gable immediately above the second-story window. This extremely mannerist device, whereby the pedimental scrollwork is disengaged completely from the window of which it is ostensibly a part (repeated in other parts of the house and in the gardener's cottage), had been introduced by Lienau years earlier in the Kane villa[129]. Similar motifs are found occasionally in French 17th century work where, however, they are still used functionally[130]. One wonders if the segmentation of the gable, reflected also in the transformation of the functional window lintel into a decorative horizontal band joining with the surround, may not ultimately reflect the influence of traditional North European gable treatments, particularly North German and Danish.

Figure 74. Lockwood Mansion. Detail from southwest.

Other features of the exterior deserve mention as interesting examples of the amalgam of European and American traditions. The porch (Fig. 74) encircling the southern side of the mansion is one of its most effective features, and stems, of course, from American, not French, traditions. The charming turret capping the octagonal oriel at the southeast corner may call to mind contemporary published French work where, however, even in Gothicized houses, turrets were generally used in pairs to bring symmetry and focus to the façade, rather than as a single picturesque accent, as in the Norwalk house[131]. In this respect, Lienau again is closer to American traditions of the 1840s and '50s, best illustrated by A.J. Davis's work, though one can also point to early French traditions of asymmetry, as in the turreted *chateaux* published by Victor Petit in *Chateaux de France du XVe et XVIe siècles* (c.1855).

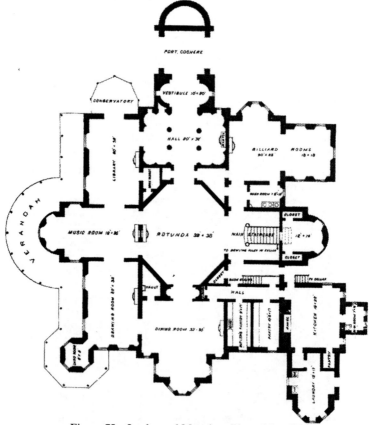

Figure 75a. Lockwood Mansion. Plan of first floor.

Figure 75b. Lockwood Mansion. Plan of second floor.

In plan (Figs. 75a, 75b, 75c), the house represents an interesting compromise between a strongly axial centralized scheme and centrifugal tendencies toward spatial expansion and picturesque irregularity. The core of the house is a large octagonal hall or rotunda, roofed over by a double lantern, from which the rooms radiate. This is a completely traditional scheme, known to all students of Serlio and Palladio[132]. Developed very successfully in France from the 17th century on in the *chateaux* and mansions of the kings and the nobility and in a number of English great houses[133], this type of plan had been popular in the United States from the early Republic on. The rotunda plan had been a favorite of Jefferson[134]; Latrobe built a number of such houses[135]; and Fiske Kimball noted that, particularly after 1830, many Greek Revival houses were built around a central rotunda or saloon of circular or polygonal shape[136]. In the 1850s and '60s, the central octagonal hall usually took one of two forms: It was either an elongated rectangle with squared-off corners, as in examples in Lafever's *Architectural Instructor* and Vaux's *Villas and Cottages*[137], or conceived as a true octagon, as in two examples by Sloan, one by Holly, and one by Hobbs, a Philadelphia architect[138].

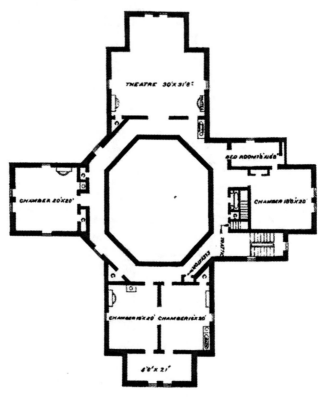

Figure 75c. Lockwood Mansion. Plan of third floor.

One should note that none of these plans, with the exception of Hobbs's project, an ambitious $150,000 scheme, even remotely approached the scale of the Lockwood rotunda, whose dimensions (32 feet by 38 feet) more or less corresponded to those of Palladio's Villa Capri (35 feet by 35 feet). In the Norwalk house, the rotunda, preceded by an impressive marble vestibule and flanked to the left by a grand staircase, has something of the flavor of a public hall in a municipal building, as is apparent from a photograph of the interior (Fig. 76). It is big, impressive, and grand—but hardly cozy in the sense of the living hall type plan developed in the '70s. Perhaps the only private house with central rotunda in this country up to this time that at all approached the scale of the Lockwood example is

Stevens's Castle, built considerably earlier, which has been mentioned in connection with the Cottenet villa[139]. While the Palladian tradition and local American variations on the rotunda theme are certainly most important for furnishing us with the immediate background of the Lockwood plan, it is interesting to note that the large open central space was also a recurrent feature of contemporary North German house plans. Usually square or rectangular, but occasionally octagonal, the central gallery or hall was often as large or larger than the reception and family rooms[140], as is the case here also. Lienau used a large rectangular gallery in Düneck, his brother's house in Ütersen (Fig. 82) but, again, none of the German examples compares in scale with Elm Park. For comparable dimensions, we have to look elsewhere, to the large Italian villas published by Petit in his *Villas cosmopolites*[141].

Figure 76. Lockwood Mansion. Rotunda.

If the plan is vaguely Palladian, one should note that Lienau intentionally broke with the tradition of perfect symmetry and balance associated with the concept. The basic rectangular outline, usually rigidly maintained in German examples, is repeatedly broken by polygonal excrescences, expressed in bay windows, the corner turret, the encircling veranda, the conservatory, etc. The sense of space as a self-contained unit, of symmetry and balance, is destroyed. In its place, there is substituted a conception of space as something palpably real, flowing from one room to the next. Openings between rooms were made wider than usual. On the right side of the plan, the *enfilade* of library, music room, and parlor provided an uninterrupted vista of eighty-two feet in length when the sliding doors, over eight feet wide, were open. The fireplace seen on the right side of the court in the plan also deserves special comment. It has a low grate; the mantel is surmounted by a large piece of lightly frosted glass on which is delicately etched a classical flying female figure (Pomona)— selected from two optional designs offered by Pierre-Victor Galland—and through which one can almost see into the music room from the central court[142].

Figure 77. Lockwood Mansion. Grand staircase.

It is fortunate that a number of old photographs of the interiors have survived to give us some idea of the opulence of the mansion's furnishings and its interior decoration. Although the Lockwood house was evidently not quite as large as Jay Cooke's fifty-two room Ogontz, the most famous mansion in America during the Grant administration, the former was far more sophisticated. One cannot help but wonder if there was a conscious effort on Lockwood's part to rival Ogontz. The magnification of scale and splendor of the interior of the Norwalk house indicate that the search for prestige, as expressed in architecture, had reached new heights in the post-Civil War period. The historian Robert Tomes, writing in *Harper's* in 1865, had this to say of the houses of the period: "What care they the ambitious patrons for taste and proportion? They want magnitude and show, the largest possible visible manifestation of expense."[143]

Figure 78. Lockwood Mansion. Music room.

Interiors such as those of the Lockwood mansion provide palpable proof that the extravagant living standards we generally associate with the '80s and '90s were merely refinements of tastes acquired much earlier. The entrance hall sets the tone: It is large, cold, and impressive; the floor is marble, it has corner niches for marble statues[144], and the frescoed ceiling, now restored, is supported by four columns of highly polished, heavily mottled Florentine marble on porphery bases. On the left, a heavy black-walnut mantel with a marble fireplace reaches almost to the ceiling. The interior architecture of the entrance hall and its four armchairs were designed by Herter Brothers. The pair of sculptures by J. Mozier were purchased in 1869 by the Lockwoods when they were in Rome. (They are now on loan to the museum, which has an option to purchase them.) The entrance hall leads into the monumental central court (Fig. 76), whose plan has already been discussed; its parquet floor, also now restored, was inlaid with five different kinds of wood in an intricate abstract design oddly preminiscent of linoleum patterns of the 1920s and '30s. The grand staircase to the left (Fig. 77), whose dramatic sweep was perhaps unparalleled in American domestic architecture of the period[145], was designed in black walnut and rosewood inlaid with satinwood, and executed by Herter

Brothers with four sofas, which match the inlays and carvings as an extension of the architecture. The staircase leads up to the second-story gallery, which encircles the court and affords easy access to all the bedroom suites. The balusters of the gallery are black walnut and bronze, and the railing is covered with scarlet plush velvet, supported by gilded standards.

Figure 79. Lockwood Mansion. Drawing room.

Returning to the ground floor, the rooms, counterclockwise, were as follows: first, a large and pleasant library trimmed in black walnut, opening onto a tiled conservatory; second, the music room (Fig. 78) with its woodwork of bird's-eye maple and rosewood, frescoed ceiling panels and side walls, gilded moldings, elaborately draped windows, French furniture, plush ottoman and suite of upholstered pieces all covered in lavender silk satin (which were designed and made by Herter Brothers to coordinate with the interior architecture), and fancy candelabra; and third, the *grand salon* (Fig. 79) with woodwork of rosewood inlaid with boxwood, ebony, and Lebanon cedar, gilded moldings, frescoed ceiling, Louis XV furniture, and a charming little oriel in the turret, which served as a card room. The center table with cabriole legs and inlaid top was designed and made by Herter Brothers; the sofa and the side cabinet (where the fireplace would later be installed) are American made, as is the small oval-back chair (near the windows by the card room), which was made by Léon Marcotte. A Herter Brothers-designed rosewood parlor suite, also matching the interior architecture, is also to be installed. The dining room, in the center of the house directly opposite the entrance, is (with the library) the best preserved room on the ground floor. Here, we can still see the dark oak, walnut, and Brazil-wood wainscoting, the huge mantels and sideboards so popular before the Eastlakian revolution, "inconceivably ponderous monuments to stability"[146]. In sum, the interiors of the Lockwood mansion are probably the finest and best preserved of their kind in the United States[147]. Each of the upstairs bedrooms was originally decorated and frescoed in a different style (*e.g.*, Louis XV, Moorish, etc.). All the bedroom suites were furnished with elaborate dressing rooms fitted out "with every convenience that ingenuity can suggest or the most generous expenditure procure"[148]. Even the bathroom fixtures are interesting: Each washstand—of marble, of course—had its own drinking fountain in addition to hot and cold running water. Returning downstairs once again, note to the left of the plan the two billiard rooms, forty-five feet in length, with adjoining washroom and "lunch room", located under the grand staircase. Incidentally, the kitchen facilities in the rear were evidently extended in the course of construction: The pantry and laundry wing, polygonal in shape and capped on the exterior by a picturesque turret, were not a feature of the original working drawings.

The place of this house in Lienau's total stylistic development will be discussed in a later chapter[149]. With regard to Elm Park, it may be seen from the description above that Lockwood and his architect had thought of just about everything to make his home the most princely establishment of the period, a perfect expression of the era of black walnut, marble, and silk in America. Most of the window treatments and upholstery on the first and second floors was silk—silk satin, silk lampas, silk damask, or silk velvet. The only plush velvet was on the two armchairs in the library. There was, in fact, only one thing Lockwood had not foreseen: that there might be an end to the years of speculation and boom, that this beautiful golden bubble might burst. And burst it did—suddenly—without warning.

On September 24, 1869, "Black Friday," the bottom dropped out of the stock market. Lockwood, along with many others, was ruined. But Monday morning, so the story goes, he was back on Wall Street. The first thing he did was turn over his house, which he owned free and clear, to his creditors. A few months later, he was able to regain title to Elm Park, which he then mortgaged heavily— for some $400,000—to the Lake Shore Railroad of which he was conveniently the treasurer. But legend says that he never really got over Black Friday. He died of pneumonia on February 24, 1872, and the New York Stock Exchange closed for the day of his funeral[150].

Later History of the Mansion

In 1873, following the panic of that year, the house with its thirty-four acres of land was put up for sale (as was Cooke's Ogontz) and advertised as "the perfect home for a gentleman of taste, culture, and fortune, who is able to avail himself of this singular opportunity to obtain a princely mansion at the cost of a moderate establishment"[151]. After a lengthy description, the advertisement concluded that it was "perhaps, the most perfect and elegant mansion in America". The estate, in addition to the house, contained a gate lodge, gardener's cottage, stables and stalls for twelve horses, carriage house for twenty vehicles, an ice house, barn, greenhouses, and extensive gardens. But this was 1873... The house remained on the market for three years before it found a buyer in the person of Charles D. Mathews, carbonated beverage king of New York, who purchased it for a fraction of its original cost (sums of $60,000 and $90,000 are variously reported). The estate remained in the hands of the Mathews family[152] until 1939, when it was leased to the City of Norwalk and finally purchased by the city in 1941 for $175,000 for a park, and conversion to civic use[153]. In September 1951, the mansion was the scene of Norwalk's Tricentennial celebration. Recently, the mansion was threatened by the new New England Thruway; however, the pike was rerouted and demolition averted through joint action by the Daughters of the American Revolution, the Society for the Preservation of the Antiquities of Norwalk, and the former mayor of Norwalk, Irving C. Freese. Although no action has yet been taken, plans are still under consideration for the conversion of the building to a city hall or community center for the city of Norwalk[154].

The Lockwood Mansion thus brings alive the fabulous era of the late 1860s, personified in the career of LeGrand Lockwood himself. It illustrates very well the faults, as well as the virtues, of the architecture and the psychological orientation of the period. More than that, the recent history of the building serves to remind us that vigilance is needed to preserve these precious and irreplaceable monuments of our architectural heritage[155].

Two Houses in Germany

If time permitted, a lengthier discussion of several other examples of Lienau's country houses would illustrate interesting variations on his style. However, Schloss Düneck (Figs. 80-82), Michael Lienau's villa (c.1872-1873) near Ütersen, mentioned previously, and a house for his brother Jacob in the same town, demonstrate Detlef's knowledge of standard North German design, planning, and construction techniques.

Close comparisons to Düneck are offered by some of the houses published in *Hamburg's Privatbauten*[156]. The small house for Jacob is not particularly outstanding, yet it is still interesting as an example of fusion of German and American ideas in planning (it has a typically American porch). The brickwork is completely in the North German tradition: The use of light yellowish brick with banding in a darker color, usually red or brown, may be paralleled not only in the publication cited above, but also in Hitzig's country houses[157]. Both these houses were still in existence in 1953[158]. Lienau's other work of the early '70s, notably his additions to the Wilks house in Canada and his plans for the Bech villa in Poughkeepsie will be mentioned briefly in Chapter VIII.

Figure 80. Michael Lienau Villa (Düneck) in Germany by brother Detlef.

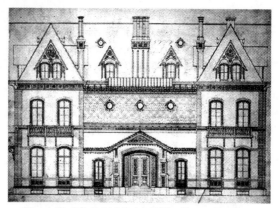

Figure 81. Michael Lienau Villa. Front elevation.

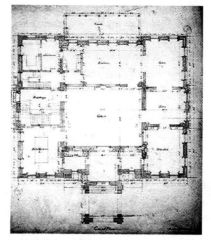

Figure 82. Michael Lienau Villa. Plan of first floor.

Chapter VII.
Urban Housing of the Early 1870s

Thus far, our discussion has centered on houses designed to satisfy well-to-do families like the Schermerhorns, the Joneses, and the Lockwoods. Turning now to four of Lienau's commissions of the early '70s—the Booræm Row, the Schermerhorn Apartments, Grosvenor House, and the American Jockey Club—we shall see how Lienau endeavored to provide housing for all levels of society from upper-class families down to the modest suburban commuter. Lienau thus takes his place among progressive architects of the day, Vaux, Hunt, Gilman, Jenney[1], and many others who strove to find workable solutions to the pressing housing problems of the post-war years[2].

Middle-Class Housing

Introduction

The plight of the growing urban middle classes—teachers, lawyers, shopkeepers—was acute. They had neither the capital nor the income required for the purchase or maintenance of even a modest private house in the city. Newspapers and periodicals called attention to the seriousness of the situation again and again, entreating architects and builders to give thought to the problem. It is perhaps hard to realize, from the vantage point of nearly a century later, that there actually was no place for these people to live. New York was characterized by one writer as "a city of paradoxes... full of palatial dwellings and homeless people"[3]. We must remember that the apartment house as we know it today was then hardly more than a visionary sketch on the drawing boards of a handful of architects. James H. Richardson, quoted above, was the author of an extremely informative article entitled "The New Homes of New York—A Study of Flats," which appeared in *Scribner's Monthly* in 1874. It is by far the best analysis of the post-war housing dilemma that I know. Pleading for the wholesale adoption of the French flat system, Richardson categorically stated that

> there is probably no great city in the world which needs a reform in domestic architecture more urgently than New York, as there is none

which contains such a preponderance of dwellings unsuited to the wants of those who inhabit them[4].

In this chapter, Lienau's answers to the problem will be discussed against the background of contemporary thought and writing on the subject, and solutions proposed by other architects of his generation. First, consider the chief causes that underlay the sad situation faced by the middle classes. New construction of one-family brownstones, brought to a virtual halt by the war, could take care of only a small proportion of the people: Prices, directly affected by skyrocketing land values and the increase in costs of construction[5] were prohibitive[6]. The middle classes steadfastly refused to live in the dilapidated tenements that were characteristic of old sections of the city downtown. Four possible courses of action were left open to them: One, they could rent a house, provided that they could find one to rent, and at a price they could afford[7]. Two, they could sublet a floor or one or two rooms in a private house, sharing meals with the owners or going out to eat. Three, they could "board" in a regular boarding house—New York had hundreds of such houses[8], converted private homes in neighborhoods, which had seen better days—or live in so-called "family hotels". The latter two solutions, needless to say, were far from satisfactory for families with children. Four, as a last resort, some of the people, those with a small amount of capital, could move to the suburbs and buy or rent small houses at a more reasonable price[9]. But this had its drawbacks: In addition to the need for a cash outlay in the event of purchase, daily commuting to the city would become a necessity for the breadwinner of the family.

The Suburban Row House: Booræm Block, Jersey City, 1871

To illustrate the fourth alternative, there was a good example in a suburban row house of the period, a block of ten three-story attached houses, built in 1871 on Second Street in Jersey City for Lienau's brother-in-law, Henry A. Booræm. Jersey City was one of the more popular suburban districts in the metropolitan area, because ferry service to downtown New York was excellent. Brooklyn, Richmond [Staten Island], and the towns of Westchester County were also gaining rapidly as a result of the housing shortage within the city limits. The newspapers of the period were full of articles and advertisements extolling the virtues of suburban living[10].

Figure 83. Booræm Row by Detlef Lienau.

The Booræm Row is no longer standing, but drawings for it are preserved in the Lienau Collection[11] (Fig. 83). Each narrow little house, eighteen feet wide, was identical with the next: Each had the same high brownstone stoop, decorative trim, and neatly fenced-in yard. Unpretentious to the extreme, these row houses were well suited to the requirements of the white-collar worker: a commuter to New York, office worker, or foreman in one of Jersey City's booming factories (*e.g.*, the New Jersey Sugar Refining Company, whose buildings had been designed by Lienau[12]). Each house was provided with a fully excavated sub-cellar, a basement with front dining room and rear kitchen, laundry, and water closet; on the first floor, a front and back parlor connected with sliding doors, plus the usual bedrooms and one bathroom upstairs. The houses were solidly and well built. But in vain do we search for a spark of imagination, some mark of distinction. Even the trim of the cornice, a variation on Lienau's characteristic bull's eye panel motif, is monotonous and dull. How uninteresting these houses seem—far inferior to Sloan's design of a decade earlier—when compared to a French solution of a somewhat similar problem[13]. They serve as a depressing reminder that even a good architect, perhaps under the pressure of adverse circumstances, could sink to the level of a speculative builder.

The French Flat: Background

In the last analysis, houses such as these side-stepped the real problem. The crying need was for the creation of middle-class housing *within* the city limits. Commuting was expensive, time-consuming, and often cost men their jobs[14]. Since the single-family brownstone offered no real answer to the housing problems of these people, some other solution had to be found. Given the high cost of land and the physical limitations of the typical 25-ft. by 100-ft. city lot, the only practical procedure lay in the adaptation of the continental apartment house system, long advocated by both laymen with foresight and progressive architects. Multiple tenancy was the only logical answer, a system whereby several families could, by virtual superposition, occupy the same space as that formerly devoted to the single-family unit in the now-obsolete brownstone. The development of the "French flat," as it was called in the early days, has been discussed by Alan Burnham in his interesting, but still unpublished manuscript, "The Dwelling in Greater Manhattan, 1850-1895". This subject merits an even more thorough investigation, including a painstaking search of the city's building records and of early extant examples before they are demolished.

It is generally acknowledged that Richard Morris Hunt's Stuyvesant Apartments at 142 East 18th Street—soon to be demolished[15]—were the first successful and certainly the most outstanding example of the new French-flat system in New York. It is also quite clear, even from our present fragmentary knowledge, that other architects, Lienau among them, were putting their weight behind the new idea. Nor should it be forgotten that Calvert Vaux, undoubtedly influenced by recent British propaganda and Henry Ashton's Victoria Street flats of 1852-1854[16], had already proposed the adoption of the French flat for American city dwellers in 1857[17]. The *Architects' and Mechanics' Journal* had been one of the earliest and most persistent champions of the apartment house system, and the lay press had taken up the cry. A combination of factors, psychological and economic, made the apartment house system a reality from c.1869 on. First, an *avant-garde* public was prepared to accept the new mode of living, until then socially unacceptable. Only then could architects give substantial form to drawing-board dreams. Encouragement also came from the municipal authorities, particularly James McGregor, New York's second Superintendent of Buildings, who was fully aware of the desperate need for this kind of dwelling[18]. The well known economic facts—the dramatic rise in New York's population after the Civil War, the high cost of land as a result of a wave of wild speculation, the availability of ready cash (plus certain psychological factors, all working together)—convinced wealthy landowners like Rutherfurd Stuyvesant and, as we shall see, William Schermerhorn, that they had more to gain than to lose by promoting the new French flats. These gentlemen were sound businessmen. The figures proved that returns on such investments could be expected to exceed by far those from a series of one-family houses on the one hand or third-class tenement houses on the other. Construction costs did not greatly exceed those for a single-family brownstone of the better class, while the rent roll would far surpass it. There were additional advantages to be realized from investing in French flats rather than in tenements. The arguments most frequently advanced were—due to occupancy by a better class of tenants—fewer vacancies, decreased turnover, relative stability of income, and lower operating costs[19]. When the French flat was combined with ground-floor shops, as was common practice in France[20], the monetary returns were even greater.

Before proceeding further, we should remember that the Stuyvesant Apartments and other famous examples of early French flats in New York (*e.g.*, Haight House and Stevens House[21]) were planned as havens for wealthy families that no longer desired the cares associated with the upkeep of a private house. Rents were high, definitely far out of reach of the average person. These early high-class apartment houses did, however, perform one extremely valuable service. They taught the rich that it was perfectly proper for gentlemen to live on shelves, one on top of the other, under a common roof[22]. This new-fangled notion, once adopted, canceled out the old Anglo-Saxon tradition (subscribed to by all except the Scots) that "every man's house is his castle"[23]. Gradually, the French flat became socially acceptable and perfectly respectable. Sauce for the goose was sauce for the gander, and so the apartment house system rapidly gained acceptance among the middle classes.

One question—an important one—may be raised here. Was there any possible relationship between the general acceptance of the French flat in the '70s and the national origins and social status of the first occupants of New York's less expensive apartments? If we take as an example the fastest growing part in the city, the 19th Ward[24], where the greatest number of so-called "second-class"[25] buildings were erected in the early '70s[26], is it merely a coincidence that so large a proportion of its population was of German origin[27]? Most of these people were first- and second-generation Americans, still close enough perhaps to continental traditions[28] to accept the fundamental premise of multiple tenancy on which the apartment house system is based. Furthermore, they were respectable members of the middle class. Although the first great wave of German immigrants who settled in New York following the Revolution of 1848 sprang largely from the ranks of the working and lower middle classes[29], it was highly characteristic of the Germans that, once in this country, they tended to rise rapidly on the social and economic scale[30]. At this time, although they constituted a relatively small proportion of the urban population, the Germans were already taking over leadership in many professions, in business and commercial enterprises, and in most of the skilled trades[31]. They were industrious, enterprising, and thrifty. They weren't satisfied, as were the Irish (who for the most part arrived in this country as paupers, without any special skills), to live in decrepit shanties and foul tenement houses. It should finally be noted that the extension of the apartment house system coincides with the second wave of German immigration, which came after the Civil War. For the first time, the arrivals from Germany at the port of New York outstripped the number from Ireland[32]. It is, therefore, extremely interesting that it was precisely in the 19th Ward that Lienau was commissioned by William C. Schermerhorn, his old client (acting on behalf of the estate of Peter Schermerhorn), to design four houses, among the earliest French flats erected for middle-class occupancy in New York.

The Schermerhorn Apartments, Third Avenue, New York, 1870-1871

**Figure 84. Schermerhorn Apartments by Detlef Lienau.
Front elevation.**

The row of four buildings at 2131-2137 Third Avenue and 201 East 71st Street (Fig. 84) was probably the earliest of the many Schermerhorn projects in the neighborhood[33]. Land values and consequently taxes in the 19th Ward had increased so phenomenally in the late '60s and early '70s that is was no longer economically sound to hold property vacant. The fabulous post-war boom in uptown East Side real estate[34] was, of course, directly attributable to the extension of the city's transit system. By the end of the 1860s, when Sixty-eighth Street was still considered a suburb[35], it was quite obvious that elevated railroads would soon replace the old Second and Third Avenue horse-drawn railcar lines, which had done so much to develop the East Side. By the end of 1878—it would have been much earlier had not the depression years intervened—the Third Avenue elevated line was completed as far north as One hundred twenty-ninth Street.

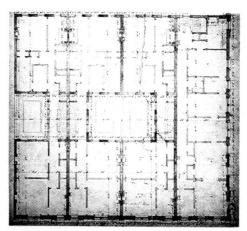

Figure 85. Schermerhorn Apartments. Plan of second floor.

The Lienau buildings are still standing today. The interior, however, was completely altered in 1935 when the Union Dime Savings Bank cut up the large apartments into smaller units[36]. Lienau's plans have been preserved in the Lienau Collection[37], plans corroborated by a sketch appended to the original building application on file at the Department of Buildings[38]. Each house consisted of a shop at ground-floor level with three single flats above. These drawings, as well as the official classification of the buildings as "second-class" dwellings, clearly indicate that the houses were not planned as tenements, but as comfortable apartments for families of moderate means. Originally, each flat consisted of six rooms (eight in the corner house), including kitchen, laundry, bathroom, and water closet (Fig. 85). All rooms were private, and the living and sleeping chambers were well lighted and ventilated, at least according to the standards of 1870[39]. Each apartment was furnished with the following conveniences, unusually complete equipment for the period: a wash trap, sink and hot water boiler in the kitchen, a pump and cistern near the bathroom, chute for the disposal of ashes, and a dumbwaiter for the raising and lowering of coal, supplies, and garbage[40]. A number of closets were built in. These conveniences, incidentally, would have been quite extraordinary even in a real Paris flat.

A comparison of these four buildings with the four situated immediately to the north of them, erected the following year by John C. Prague[41], makes clear two important points: one, the clarity and coherence of Lienau's elevation design; and two, the unusual plan he adopted to bring light and air into the center of the building. The neighboring buildings (Nos. 2139-2143 Third Avenue) were designed as four separate units, one of 36 feet and three of 22 feet. While some attempt was made to unify the design, the effort bogs down in meaningless detail. Moreover, with the structure having a frontage of 102 feet, Prague could have used something better than the regulation narrow shafts between each building, which brought only foul air and no light into the back bedrooms. Lienau's elevation (Fig. 84), at least from the second story up, has a quiet, uncluttered open feeling, largely due to unadorned brickwork and simply treated openings—again, decidedly close in spirit to some of Hitzig's early work[42]. In the cornice, a variation on Lienau's favorite rosette motif is introduced. The ground-story shop front, completely altered today, was originally designed with very fancy banded cast-iron piers in imitation of rusticated stonework and more simply treated arcades. This must have produced an oddly elaborate effect in contrast to the simple wall surfaces above. The rear elevation, relieved only by segmental headed windows and a stepped corbel frieze under the eaves, is decidedly plain and recalls Lienau's German background and training.

Lienau's plan provides the most significant contrast to the other buildings. With a frontage of 102 feet at his disposal, Lienau made a determined effort to bring illumination and light into the center of the buildings. This he accomplished by the introduction of interior courts between the houses, nearly 32 feet wide by 20 feet deep. The existence of these courts may in part be responsible for the difference in character today between the Lienau and Prague buildings. The latter, though they too have had the benefit of some remodeling, are definitely in a much lower category than the Schermerhorn buildings: The latter have the "high-class" tone of many of the better East Side remodeling jobs. The system of interior courts that Lienau used here was largely based on French precedent[43]. So too is the combination of ground floor shops with flats above, a scheme that began to be used both in England and elsewhere on the continent in the early '50s[44]. The use of interior courts had often been recommended, but to my knowledge had not been used by any architect before Lienau in the planning of early apartment houses or tenements in Manhattan; one example in Brooklyn is mentioned by James B. Runnion in an interesting article on "Our City Homes—What They Are and What They Should Be," published in the *American Builder and Journal of Art* of 1869[45]. A decade later, the large central courtyard with carriage entrance, directly based on French tradition, became standard in the ultra-fashionable French flats, such as Hardenbergh's Dakota Apartments, the first of New York's super-block apartments, which still stands today at Seventy-second Street and Central Park West. The fact that Hardenbergh was still working in Lienau's office as a draftsman when the Schermerhorn Apartments were designed should not pass unnoticed. In his description of Hardenbergh's first large apartment house, the Van Corlear (1878-1879), now demolished, but also planned around a central court[46], Montgomery Schuyler commented on the survival of Neo-Grec design elements[47], which he correctly assumed were a result of the architect's years of apprenticeship in Lienau's office.

Before taking leave of the Schermerhorn flats, one other item, somewhat technical in nature, should be noted. On the rear elevation drawing are two designs for fire escapes, lightly penciled, as though they had been added later. In Lienau's application form at the Department of Buildings, he states that fire escapes will be provided "if required by law". At the time the buildings were planned in 1870, the law of 1867 was still in effect. This provided that fire escapes had to be provided for all buildings over three stories in height that housed four or more families; therefore, it did not apply to these buildings. The law was amended in 1871, the year the buildings were completed. It then became mandatory for all buildings over two stories in height that housed two or more families above the ground floor, and for buildings over three stories accommodating three or more families above the first floor, to provide proper means of escape. The penciled additions thus faithfully reflect changes in the laws of the City of New York—a result of the growing concern by both the public and municipal authorities for the safety of the people. In years to come, the Department for the Survey and Inspection of Buildings, as it was originally called, extended its jurisdiction far beyond the powers grudgingly given to it in 1871 until, with other agencies, it was at last able to attack the housing problems of the poorest segment of the city's population. The question of tenement house reform, in which Lienau also played a part, would lead us far beyond the period of the early '70s and into a mountainous pile of literature. The reader is referred to a brief mention of Lienau's tenement house work in my article, "Detlef Lienau, an Architect of the Brown Decades[48]," and, as a starter, to the basic two-volume work, *The Tenement House Problem*, edited by Robert W. De Forest and Laurence Veiller[49].

Upper Class Housing

The Apartment Hotel: The Grosvenor, Fifth Avenue, 1871-1872

The expense and responsibilities involved in the year-round maintenance of a large townhouse, or even of one of the new French flats, was deemed undesirable by a small but nonetheless important segment of society. This was particularly true of Society people who traveled abroad a great deal, of young couples with small families, or elderly people whose children had left home. Many articles were written about simplifying housekeeping arrangements[50], since good servants were becoming increasingly hard to find. With the supply of "Bridgets" rapidly falling below the demand[51], the ladies must have welcomed the plea made by *The New York Times* in 1871 for the establishment of a "homey" sort of hotel[52]. And so, beginning in the early '70s in New York, the system now known as the apartment hotel evolved, whereby the management provided certain conveniences and services, such as a central kitchen and laundry, a restaurant, and most importantly a staff of trained "servants" at one's beck and call.

Lienau's Grosvenor House (Fig. 86), which stood until 1925 on the site of the present Grosvenor Hotel on Fifth Avenue and Tenth Street, has been called New York's first apartment hotel[53]. Strictly speaking, this is not quite true: The Haight House, altered into elevator apartments in 1870/1871[54], was in fact the first "family hotel" in the city. We know too that other architects, such as Gilman and Holly (Fig. 87)[55], were experimenting along the same lines elsewhere. Grosvenor House was, however, probably the first apartment hotel in New York City to have been planned as a family hotel from the beginning. Commissioned by Lienau's old client, Francis Cottenet, it was built on the site of his former residence at 35-37 Fifth Avenue, the northeast corner of Tenth Street. Although none of Lienau's original drawings for the building appear to have been preserved, we do have an old photograph of the hotel reproduced in the illustrations. The building is fully documented by municipal records, which indicate that it was begun in October 1871 and completed the following March[56]. It was opened to the public in October 1872.

Figure 86. Grosvenor House by Detlef Lienau.

If we can trust contemporary descriptions, Grosvenor House appears to have created quite a stir when it was built. James Richardson described it in these words:

> The Grosvenor... is a type unique. Starting with a singularly clear conception of the wants of a particular class of New York families—a class possessing wealth, culture, refinement, and love of ease, and desiring the security and comfort of home life with none of its cares—the designer of the Grosvenor brought to the task of supplying the demand a rare experience as a hotel manager [*sic*], a genius for organization, ample means, and untiring vigilance in the carrying out of his plans. The result is an establishment which may well be considered a model, since it secures the economy of multiple tenancy and co-operative living, with the atmosphere of home, and combines all the advantages of English exclusiveness and solid elegance, with the utmost independence in all that pertains to individual life. It is, in fact, a nest of elegant homes, each distinct and thoroughly secluded, yet all provided for with the elaborate machinery and systematic service of a first-class hotel.

> The Grosvenor was a success from the start. It opened with all its rooms leased for terms of years, while scores of desirable tenants eagerly enrolled themselves as candidates for the first vacancies that might occur[57].

Figure 87. Family Hotel by H.H. Holly.

From a newspaper account, probably written shortly after its opening, we learn that Grosvenor was considered the "model house" of its kind[58]. It is described as "a home and a hotel at the same time," and the writer gives a full account of many details concerning the management and, fortunately, the construction of the building. Tenants furnished their own apartments, but meals and all details of domestic service were the responsibility of the management. According to this account, the tenants had the option of dining downstairs in the restaurant or having their meals brought upstairs to be served in their own dining rooms. The description of the building follows:

> The house is built on two sides of a square lot, giving a court 40 feet square, opening on the inner sides, and dispensing with dark rooms entirely. The ventilation is as near perfection as anything ever yet seen, and might be the envy of many a fine private house on the avenue. The sunny exposure of all the suites to the south and west, and the use of elevators, render all the rooms desirable. Some of the suites are examples of the most luxurious furnishing in New York, and the happy possessors find themselves as free from the ordinary cares of domestic life as the most visionary could wish. Inspection of the kitchen and laundries showed everywhere the same system and shining neatness that bespoke competent direction. Suites rent from $650 to $2,200 a year, and some of the wealthiest families in the city have taken refuge in this manner from the uncertainty of American housekeeping in its present chaotic state.

The Grosvenor maintained its reputation as a first-class establishment until the very end. James L. Ford, in an article published in 1924 on "Famous New York Hotels of the Seventies," mentioned the Berkeley and the Grosvenor as "quiet family hotels entertaining no transient guests and depending entirely on a wealthy and refined clientele. The policy of both houses has not changed with the years"[59].

Stylistically, the building was an extremely restrained example of the Second Empire mode. Indeed, with its low mansard roof, stone balconies, and plain segmental headed windows, it seems closer in style to houses of the '50s and early '60s[60] than to contemporary examples in New York, Boston[61], and Paris. It may be that Mr. Cottenet asked Lienau to design along the general lines of the Shiff house across the avenue. The sober design provides a striking contrast to both the polychromatic Victorian Gothic of Holly's Family Hotel (Fig. 87) and the rather showy Second Empire mode used by Stephen D. Hatch (1839-1894) in the Gilsey House (1869-1871) or by Hunt in the Stevens House (c.1872)[62]. Perhaps, this was a deliberate attempt to appeal to the solid older generation, to people like the Cottenets, who frowned upon display, architectural or otherwise.

If the building is stylistically *retardataire*, it was abreast of the times, or even in advance, in other ways. For one thing, the open court around which the building was erected in an L shape was unusually spacious[63]. In those days, property owners could, and usually did, insist upon maximum coverage of the lot. Laws regulating the ratio of solids to voids were still in their infancy in New York. The Tenement House Law of 1867—oddly enough, Grosvenor House was assigned to the category of a third-class tenement by the authorities—provided that all new tenements must provide a space of ten feet at the rear between it and any other building. Where there was no building behind it, the architect could with perfect impunity build right up to the lot line. This loophole was closed by the New Tenement House Law of 1879, which specified that no tenement could occupy more than 65 percent of the lot[64]. As we have seen in the Schermerhorn Apartments, Lienau was keenly aware of the need for providing air and light to rear apartments.

The second progressive feature of the building was the provision by the architect of a means of vertical ascent. We have seen that Lienau constantly made use of the dumbwaiter in private homes; in his commercial buildings of the period, he used hoists of various kinds. But Grosvenor House was the first building in which, to my knowledge, Lienau introduced an elevator. The elevator, mentioned in connection with Haight House, had become a necessity by the early '70s, not only in commercial buildings vying with one another in height, but also in better-class apartment houses and hotels.

Following its rather unsuccessful debut in the Latting Observatory in 1853, the elevator was improved and developed rapidly in the course of the next two decades. At first, it was looked upon with good-natured skepticism by men like the editor of *Harper's* "Easy Chair," who envisaged the possibility of indefinite suspension, were such a contraption installed in an apartment house (Vol. VII [June 1853], p. 130). As is common knowledge, the first regular passenger elevator was installed by Elisha G. Otis in 1857 in the Haughwout store, at the corner of Broadway and Broome Street. Two years later, his competitor, Tufts of Boston (whose first name curiously was Otis), introduced the vertical screw elevator in the Fifth Avenue Hotel. Architects were quick to see that the solution of technical problems connected with the elevator would herald "the opening of a new era in the construction of buildings" [65].

Figure 88. American Jockey Club by Detlef Lienau (1871).

The upper floors thereby became at least as desirable as the lower ones, and rent rolls consequently increased. Contrast Grosvenor House with the Stuyvesant Apartments—Richardson found the lack of elevators a distinct disadvantage[66]; apartment rentals were graduated downward as the height from the ground increased[67]. The ladies and gentlemen who made the Grosvenor their home were freed, not only from the tedium of housekeeping, but also from the constant stair-climbing associated with the typical four-story New York townhouse. There was not even a stoop to climb:

The entrance to the Grosvenor was almost level with the curb, a point to which we shall return in discussing the Howland house later.

The Clubhouse: American Jockey Club, Madison Avenue, 1871

More closely related to Lienau's other work of the early '70s was a narrow four-story building, which served for many years as headquarters of two of New York's swankiest clubs, the American Jockey Club and the New York Yacht Club. It stood at the southwest corner of Madison Avenue and Twenty-seventh Street until 1909, when it was replaced by the present office building. The files of Brown Brothers turned up an old photograph (Fig. 88)[68] to supplement the six original drawings preserved in the Lienau Collection[69].

This building was commissioned early in 1871 by Judge Alonzo Castle Monson (c.1820-1901)[70], Vice-President and Treasurer of the American Jockey Club. Monson, who had been a classmate of William Schermerhorn at Columbia, was a well known club man and politician[71]. He was closely connected with August Belmont's racing interests; it was undoubtedly at the suggestion of Belmont as president of the club, that Lienau got the commission: He had only recently finished building a house on Long Island for the wealthy financier[72]. The location of the clubhouse is interesting. It was in the heart of the racing district. The Hotel Brunswick (1871-1885) on Fifth Avenue and Twenty-sixth Street, the favorite rendezvous of New York's "horsey set" and later the headquarters of the Coaching Club, has been mentioned in connection with Colonel DeLancey Kane[73]. At Twenty-sixth Street was Leonard Jerome's Jockey Club; next to it, fronting on Madison Avenue, is a building that today houses the Manhattan Club, which was Jerome's former mansion, converted since 1868 for use by the Union League Club. The latter building is mistakenly identified as the first city headquarters of the New York Yacht Club in its commemorative pamphlet, *The New York Yacht Club. A Centennial, 1844-1944*[74]. There can be no doubt that the New York Yacht Club was lodged on the second floor of the American Jockey Club building on Twenty-seventh Street, erected by Lienau, and not in either of the buildings built for Jerome by Thomas R. Jackson[75]. This is borne out not only by the listings for the Yacht Club in the city directories, but also in penciled notations by Lienau on the plans for the clubhouse[76]. The Yacht Club, of which Samuel Nicholson Kane (DeLancey's son) served as

Commodore from 1877 to 1879, moved to its own clubhouse at 67 Madison Avenue in 1884; the Jockey Club remained in the building for many years thereafter, facing McKim, Mead & White's Madison Square Garden (1891-1925), of which we catch a glimpse in the photograph.

Figure 89. American Jockey Club. Side elevation.

Although considerably less pretentious than the Jones houses, the American Jockey Club is stylistically quite close to them and to other contemporary Lienau buildings such as the Sage Library in New Brunswick[77]. The chamfered corner, the regulation combination of brick and brownstone, the arched windows with corner rosettes, the familiar decorative vocabulary (including the variation of the familiar bull's eye panel) are thoroughly typical of Lienau's work. These details may be seen on the side elevation drawing (Fig. 89). The placing of the stoop leading to the main entrance on Twenty-seventh Street is hardly a happy solution to the problem of monumentalizing the entrance to the narrow building. A second flight of stairs at the rear of the building gave access to the Yacht Club on the second floor. A private room for Mr. Monson, a Director's Room for the Jockey Club, as well as quarters for the Jockey and Yacht Club personnel, two separate kitchens, and a janitor's apartment were all located in the basement and sub-basement of the building. More interesting to our study of modes of living of the early '70s were the layouts of the third and fourth floors. These were planned as small bachelor apartments, two to a floor, and consisted of two or three rooms, furnished with a private bathroom, but no kitchen. The gay young blades who lived here doubtless needed small apartments for private entertaining. If refreshments were desired, these could be sent upstairs easily via the dumbwaiter from the club kitchens below.

This concludes an all too rapid survey of housing conditions after the Civil War. If Lienau emerges as an architect who dealt honestly and intelligently with the housing problems of the period, this chapter will have served its purpose.

Chapter VIII.
Lienau's Stylistic Development

The preceding chapters have dealt with Lienau's residential work from 1850 through the early '70s, a period of some twenty-odd years, which saw great changes in the political, social, and economic structure of the nation and which came to an end with the panic of 1873. This last chapter will begin with a summary of Lienau's stylistic development based on the material presented in the foregoing pages, followed by a résumé of his domestic architecture of the later '70s and early '80s. In the conclusion, several subjects of more general interest will be touched on, some of which have already been mentioned briefly, and perhaps then Lienau's place within the overall picture of American architecture of the period will emerge more clearly. These concluding remarks will be all the more important, since the arbitrary restriction of the book topic—to a report on Lienau's domestic work—by necessity eliminated many buildings and documents that would have given us a less one-sided view of Lienau's *oeuvre* and of his activities. For example, an account of his role in the American Institute of Architects would bring out many interesting details concerning the early history of the organization and would show us the kind of person Lienau was—but this more comprehensive treatment will have to await a more opportune moment.

Summary: Stylistic Development, 1850-1872

Even within the self-imposed limits of this study, the general outlines of Lienau's development and the character of his contributions to American architecture are clear. Within the confines of his own work, his designs evolved from a fundamentally classic conception to ones at least partially influenced by picturesque trends of the third quarter of the century. This is quite apparent if we compare an early work, the Shiff house, with designs of the middle period. Both in its elevation (Fig. 27) and plan (Fig. 30)—linear, flat, closed, and precisely defined—the New York house still reflects the heritage of the French tradition of the 1840s, which Lienau brought with him to this country. This is also true of other works of his early period, houses such as the Cottenet and Kane villas in Dobbs Ferry and Newport (Figs. 32 and 42) and even the study for Michael Lienau's cottage in Jersey City (Fig. 20). By the end of the '50s, this classical balance began to give way to a definitely picturesque tendency, particularly noticeable in the Toler house in Newark (Figs. 40 and 41). Though still organized around a traditional center hall, the house pushed out asymmetrically in all directions. The architect evidently wished to create an effect of gradual transition between interior volumes and the space outside; hence, the use of large polygonal bay windows[1] and the lightly shaded porch, which envelops the house on three sides. Lienau's romantic, almost painterly approach to the house, closely related to the ideas of Upjohn, Davis, and Holly, is in decided contrast to attitudes implied in his designs for the Cottenet villa a few years earlier. This may best be illustrated by a comparison of the sketches for the two houses. While both are presented as perspective views, according to English, rather than French, traditions of architectural rendering, the Cottenet villa (Fig. 32) is crisply drawn in pen and ink, a technique eminently well suited to expressing the sharp rectangular outlines of the Italian villa style and smooth ashlar construction. The study for the Toler house is a watercolor sketch, delicately tinted, in which the house is envisaged in a much closer relationship to surrounding landscape elements (Fig. 40). The substitution of random ashlar in varied tones of warm brownstone for the regularly cut light-colored Caen stone of the Cottenet villa still further enhances the painterly quality of the Toler house. In the latter, the abandonment of French Renaissance and Italianate stylistic features and the adoption of a style closer to English and American cottage traditions are likewise significant.

As one might expect, the French classical tradition lingered much longer in Lienau's city work. But, when we compare his houses of the late '60s, such as the Edmund Schermerhorn residence (Fig. 58) and the Jones Block (Fig. 63) to the Second Empire mode of other New York architects, they seem extremely restrained. In John Kellum's Stewart Mansion (Fig. 61), a strong mannerist tendency is clearly discernible. Buildings such as the New York Post Office (1867-1868) with its rich applied orders, striking contrasts of light and shade, and massive composition carried back in receding planes, brought Neo-Baroque trends to the fore[2]. It has been pointed out that Lienau's classical heritage and basic conservatism occasionally gave a mid-century, almost archaic character, to some of his buildings of the early '70s, such as Grosvenor House (Fig. 86) and the Schermerhorn Apartments (Fig. 84).

In the later '60s, Lienau allowed himself more latitude in the design of his country houses, as we have seen in the Lockwood Mansion. In contrast to his early domestic work, the Norwalk house brought Lienau's anti-classical tendencies, usually submerged, into the foreground. As noted in the descriptive text, the plan is basically academic and self-contained, yet a strong centripetal movement breaks through the basic rectangle at numerous points. The space seems deliberately to push the walls out, into large bay windows in every room, erupting first into one and later into two picturesque corner turrets (Fig. 75), and creating a deeply shaded porch on the south side of the house (Fig. 74). An almost Baroque conception of space has replaced Lienau's more casual classical leanings. In elevation, too, the house is in marked contrast to the restraint, planarity, and precision that is seen not only in Lienau's early work, but also in his roughly contemporary urban designs for Edmund Schermerhorn and Mrs. Jones. The Lockwood Mansion is far more plastic in conception than any of Lienau's other buildings. It is composed, both vertically and horizontally, as a series of gradually receding masses (Fig. 72). The visitor is quite conscious of the fact that the house must be seen from all sides; the building composes as well from an oblique angle as from a view straight on, a fact that clearly demonstrates a new and unexpected turn in Lienau's development. It is particularly important to call attention to this fact, since the elevation drawing for the façade (Fig. 73) is completely misleading: It is one of the flattest, most linear renderings in the entire Lienau Collection. The ornamental elaboration (still very restrained, however, when compared with the work of Lienau's contemporaries), the occasional overlapping and lack of clarity in the relationship on one element to the next, the exaggeration of single features (*e.g.*, the over-scaled dormer windows), all tend to produce an impression of greater-than-usual visual intricacy and a certain top-heaviness of effect, which Carroll Meeks has found so typical of the period after 1860. Yet, it is important to note that this is still very far from being a "typical" example of High Victorian style, the architecture of the Grant era, or the middle phase of Meek's "picturesque eclecticism"[3]. The classical balance between vertical and horizontal elements is still largely operative; surfaces are smooth; with the exception of the corner turrets, there are no sudden picturesque breaks in the total composition. Even the conception of interior space—typical, with the center hollowed out and built up in tiers of galleries—tends to create an impression of lateral extension rather than of vertical compression, which is atypical. The exterior is monochromatic and rather cold in color; the interior, with its dark woodwork and mottled marble, is rich, but rather somber. The brilliant, often garish effects of color, so often associated with High Victorian architecture, are conspicuous by their absence here. If this building reflects contemporary taste (as it most certainly does in many respects), it does so only to a limited degree. Lienau's classical point of view, strongly tinged here by Baroque (but not by Victorian Gothic) ideas, still retained the upper hand; as we have seen, it reasserted itself again very strongly in his urban work of the late '60s and early '70s.

Lienau's Late Work: The '70s and '80s

Lienau's houses of the later '70s and early '80s were, as might be expected, generally conservative in character, though we shall see that he made certain concessions to contemporary trends in planning and design. Echoes of German traditions appear from time to time. More important, perhaps, is the gradual recession of French influence, all pervasive in Lienau's work of the previous decades; by the '80s, it disappears almost entirely beneath the strong tide of English influence.

Country Houses

Bech House, Poughkeepsie, New York, c. 1875

A reflection of German traditions of planning and design, so appropriately adapted in Schloss Düneck, reappears a few years later in Lienau's studies of 1875 for the Bech villa outside of Poughkeepsie, New York[4]. The Bech estate, originally called Roselawn, has been owned since 1905 by the Marists, a Catholic teaching order, and is the home of Marist College[5]. Of the original buildings on the property, only two small houses, the former gate lodge, and the gardener's cottage retain any resemblance to their original form. Other buildings, such as the stable and carriage house, of which a drawing was published in the *New York Sketch-book of Architecture*[6], have either been demolished or altered beyond recognition. Moreover, it is not quite clear whether or not the main house, for which Lienau made a number of studies, was actually ever built. Among these studies, only one includes an elevation (Fig. 90).

The interest of this drawing lies chiefly in its picturesque asymmetrical massing, strong contrasts of plane surfaces and voids (particularly noticeable in the west elevation), and the echoes of North German brickwork traditions. This is especially evident in the segmental headed windows, the use of a red-brick string course and corner quoining as a contrast to the gray-blue ashlar, and the step design of the dormer pediments. These German touches, seen also in Lienau's dormitory building (1867-1868) at St. Mary's Hall, Burlington, New Jersey[7], are likewise evident in the plan studies for the Bech villa. All four variants include a small office, corresponding to the German *Bureau* or *Comptoir*, a feature often found in German middle-class houses.

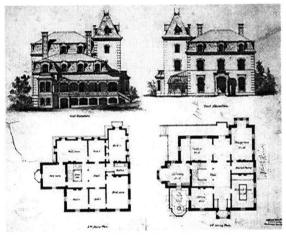

Figure 90. Bech Villa by Detlef Lienau. Study.

These Germanic reminiscences, incidentally, were fitting in a house for the widow of Edward Bech, Danish consul in New York during the 1840s and early '50s. Bech had begun his career, like Michael Lienau (whom he probably knew) as an importer of wines and liquors, then had gone into shipping, becoming a partner in the Cunard Steamship Company. In the early '50s, he moved to Poughkeepsie where, as co-owner with Tuckerman of the Poughkeepsie Iron Works, he played an important role in the development of the new pig-iron industry[8]. Bech, who died in Stuttgart in 1873, is buried in the Poughkeepsie Rural Cemetery in a vault designed by Lienau in 1874[9]. Two of his daughters were married to members of the German and Danish nobility; one, Countess Von Oxholm, whose husband was Count Chamberlain to the King of Denmark, is said to have called her castle "Rosenfeldt," in fond remembrance of Roselawn.

Though Lienau was certainly aware of contemporary trends of design and spatial organization, his later houses show that he never fully accepted them. For example, while the design for the Bech villa makes use of a characteristic feature of the picturesque style—the single asymmetrically placed tower—the emphasis on horizontals rather than verticals in the general massing, on relatively smooth surfaces, and on a pleasant but subdued color scheme[10], is far from typical of the architecture of the mid-'70s. The light blue and gray ashlar, sparing use of red brick in the trim, blue-slate roof, and touches of brown wood, are a far cry from the violent striation and strong color contrasts so often seen in contemporary work[11].

Moreover, there is not even the slightest reflection of the Queen Anne vogue, which was soon to become the hallmark of many houses designed by progressive young architects, as the plates of the New York and Boston *Sketch-books* show[12]. Given Lienau's German and Parisian training, and his personal stylistic preferences, it is quite understandable that, even in later years, he was "no admirer of the Queen Anne style"[13]. If we consider briefly two or three works by Lienau of the early '80s in order to bring this survey of his stylistic development to a logical conclusion, it should not come as a great surprise that he was relatively little influenced by the popular Queen Anne style. By means of these examples, we shall see to what extent Lienau kept up with the times and in what ways he was *retardataire*. He must have watched with a certain degree of detachment the gradual transformation of Queen Anne into a genuinely American idiom, which Scully has called the "Shingle Style"[14].

Anglesea, Newport, Rhode Island, c.1880

As an example of Lienau's late "cottage style," we take his villa in Newport built around 1880[15] for the New York City dry-goods merchant, Walter H. Lewis (1828-1901), and his wife Arabella (Fig. 92)[16], now owned by the Bogert family[17]. Still called by its original name—Anglesea[18]—the villa is beautifully located overlooking Ochre Point, one of Newport's most picturesque sites. Preliminary studies in the Lienau Collection[19] called for a brick house combined with half-timber construction. This distant echo of Norman Shaw and the Queen Anne mode, which by 1880 had become thoroughly acclimatized here, is rather oddly combined with bracketed elements reminiscent of the old Stick Style. In the contract drawings for the house, wood was substituted for brick (Fig. 93). While certain concessions were made to contemporary taste (note the slight asymmetry of the façade and the interest in surface textures, particularly the use of cut shingles in a variety of patterns), the design is not by any stretch of the imagination typical of either Shavian Manorial or Shingle Style. To be sure, one may point to a few isolated motifs derived from the ornamental stock-in-trade of the "Queen Anne" architect, such as the favorite sunflower (Fig. 96). Yet, the emphasis on Stick Style elements in the porches and framing, on verticality, on steep gables decorated with fancy verge boards, on the basic formality in the organization of design elements, all recall the work of the previous decades, rather than that of the '80s. Nor is there any evidence of the assimilation of concepts basic to the Shingle Style. True, there are shingles above and clapboards below, but instead of creating a continuous free-flowing surface, the materials are treated as decorative elements applied to the exterior and rigidly contained within the framing studs.

Just as there is no continuity of surface on the exterior, on the interior there is little flow of space from room to room, in contrast to the open plan adopted by progressive architects of the period. The plan of Anglesea (Fig. 94) actually differs very little from that of the Kane villa of almost thirty years earlier (Fig. 44). The rooms, however well related they may be, are envisaged as rather tall cubes or boxes separated from each other and from the center hall by relatively narrow doorways. Although the beamed ceilings are most certainly a reflection of contemporary taste (compare the French Renaissance types used in the Kane or Schermerhorn house [Fig. 56]), the beams are used structurally, as Stick Style elements, rather than as a means of bringing to the house a sense of horizontal continuity. The ceilings, moreover, are quite high[20]. This gives the house a light, cheerful, airy quality, which is quite the opposite of the low, cozy, intimate, but often dark, effect sought by architects of the Shingle Style. The only concession Lienau made to the spatial innovations of the '70s is seen in the introduction of a fireplace in the broad transverse hall, thus assimilating it, to a degree, with the "living hall" concept.

Figure 91. Study by J. August Lienau for an unidentified house.

In sum, Anglesea must certainly be considered somewhat *retardataire* for 1880, even when compared with the work of less *avant-garde* architects. Compare it to houses designed by men like Bloor & Oakey, Holly[21], and to one by Jenney in Illinois, where there is somewhat similar survival of Stick Style elements more or less successfully integrated with Queen Anne[22]. In a cottage in Cohasset by the Boston firm of Kirby & Lewis, we note the unresolved tension between vertical Stick Style elements and horizontal clapboarding, plus a fine roof. Almost no attempt was made to integrate the picturesque pavilion, jutting out from the porch on one side. A pavilion such as this, an extremely popular feature of country houses from the late '70s on, also appears in elevation studies for an unidentified project in the Lienau Collection (Fig. 91). On the basis of the rendering and the altogether wholehearted adoption of Queen Anne stylistic features (half timbering, shingling, banks of windows, fluted chimneys, etc.), I am inclined to attribute these sketches to Lienau's architect son, J. August Lienau, who worked in his father's office from c.1874 on. When Detlef Lienau designed Anglesea in 1880, he was a man of sixty-two. The retrospective character of the house becomes understandable as the product of a very able and conscientious architect who was no longer particularly interested in establishing new precedents or blazing new trails.

Figure 92. Lewis Cottage (Anglesea) by Detlef Lienau.

As a postscript, it is interesting to observe that the fundamentally conservative appearance of the Lewis house was greatly accented when it was renovated and altered by Peabody & Stearns in 1917. Beyond the stated fact that "certain alterations" were made[23], I have been unable to ascertain exactly what changes were made at this time. It seems reasonable to assume that it was then that the fine old shingling was completely stripped off, except on the west façade of the house (Fig. 96). The entire house is now painted a dead white, giving it a definitely Georgian look (Fig. 95). Other alterations, such as the substitution of heavy columns on the *porte-cochère* for the original thin-bracketed structure, are in line with the revolt of the later 19th and early 20th century Colonial Revivalists against the taste of the previous generation, a reaction that, interestingly enough, can be seen very clearly in the work of Lienau's own son[24]. Incidentally, the Lewis house provides an interesting illustration of the change in direction of the firm of Peabody & Stearns. Directly to the northeast of Anglesea was the original Breakers, built by them for Pierre Lorillard in 1877-1878, of which one can catch a glimpse in Fig. 92. This handsome house was a natural shingled structure, unpainted, and decidedly picturesque in general effect, though its plan and several details already betrayed the interest of the firm in the Colonial[25].

The Living Hall Plan

Brief mention has been made of the living hall type of plan in the discussion of Anglesea. In order to avoid any misunderstanding as to what is meant by the term "living hall" as used to describe the planning of the 1870s, '80s, and '90s, the following description by Bruce Price is enlightening. Summarizing the evolution of the suburban house, he tells us that, in the type current a quarter of a century ago, the porch opened into a narrow passageway rather than into a hall, of which a goodly portion was taken up by the stairs, placed only a few steps from the entry. The house of today [1893] was developed step by step:

> First, the passageway was attacked, and being broadened became a hall; the staircase fell away from near the threshold to a less obtrusive place, with landings and returns, and windows opening upon them. As the hall grew, the parlor, as its uses and purposes were absorbed by the hall, became of less importance. The fireplace became a prominent feature, and placed in the hall and more elaborately treated, became an ingle-nook, with the mantel over it, forming an imposing chimney piece. Improving thus its separate features upon the old, the newer plan advanced further in the disposition of these features. The new hall having become broad and ample, and the rendezvous and seat of home life, took its position in the most desirable place in the advanced plan. The house grew up about it, following it with the other features and details in their proper sequence...[26]

Figure 93. Lewis Cottage. North elevation.

The origins of this type of plan, in which the hall, formerly a mere passageway, becomes the center of both the agglutinated plan and of family life, have been studied by Vincent Scully in *The Shingle Style*[27]. Scully's emphasis on English prototypes almost exclusively[28] still leaves certain questions unanswered.

The following remarks are a summary of my own rather sporadic research into the subject. Was—as Scully would have us believe—Richardson's early use of the living hall influenced only by contemporary English publications, such as Richard Kerr's *Gentleman's House*, which reproduced the plan of Waterhouse's Hinderton in its second edition (1865), and the *Builder*[29]? Or did romantic memories of old Southern traditions[30] have something to do with his introduction of a living hall in the Codman house of c.1871? In addition to the varying types of living halls or saloons, so widely diffused throughout the South[31], one might also point to the plan type characteristic of the region where Richardson grew up, that of French Louisiana and the Bayou Country, where entrance into the house leads from a porch into a family room of one sort or another, and not into a stair hall (the stairs were generally outside the house)[32]. While it is perfectly true that Colonial influence was much stronger after the Centennial Exposition, not before it, must one necessarily assume that pre-Revolutionary houses with living halls were completely forgotten or ignored by architects and clients alike?

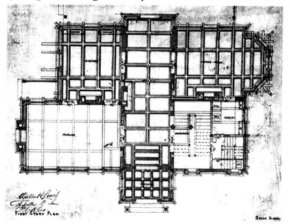

Figure 94. Lewis Cottage. Plan of first floor.

The nostalgic desire for a return to the "good old days" was a recurrent theme in America from the mid-century on; it does not appear out of the blue in the late '60s and early '70s[33]. The retrospective quality—part and parcel of the entire stylistic idiom of the period, which is so well illustrated by the popularity of the Queen Anne mode—is likewise seen in the re-adoption of a plan type long associated with the landed gentry, English and American, of olden days. It remained for Richardson and the architects of his generation to adapt the living hall plan to the need for large-scale but relatively informal entertaining, typical of American seaside resorts like Newport, and to the social aspirations of well-to-do Northerners after the Civil War. For a brilliant study of the later development of the living hall plan and its transformation of traditional spatial concepts—one of the great contributions of the later 19th century to modern planning—the reader is referred to the closing chapters in Scully's *Shingle Style.*

Figure 95. Lewis Cottage. View from northeast (1953).

Figure 96. Lewis Cottage. Detail of shingling.

Another source for the living hall of the 1870s—American plan books of the 1840s, '50s, and '60s, which in turn reflected English ideas—is perhaps dealt with in too summary a fashion by Scully in his book[34]. The expansion of the hall and the frequent suggestion that it be used for dining or as a living room in Downing's *Country Houses* (1850), Cleaveland and Backus's *Village and Farm Cottages*

(1856), and Vaux's *Villas and Cottages* (1857) cannot be dismissed as unimportant[35]. These publications had a tremendous influence on public taste and, indirectly, on the work of other architects. In addition to the definitely English type of stair hall used by Vaux & Withers in the Nathan Reeves project (Design XXIII), it is instructive to read the descriptive text accompanying Vaux's plates. Here, there is clearly a new spatial concept in the making, a feeling for space as an almost palpable entity, freely flowing from room to room and from the interior to the exterior. In the text referring to the Findley house in Newport, Vaux describes the large 18-ft. by 14-ft. hall that communicates, by means of sliding doors, with the three main rooms on the ground floor. From the hall in the center of the house, one

> could see clear through the house, north, south, east, and west... the porch, hall, vestibule, library, dining-room, drawing-room, and veranda, are converted, as it were, into a single apartment. All idea of the moderate size of the single rooms... is thus done away with, and the house necessarily seems roomy, open, and ample in its accommodations[36].

Professor Hitchcock has noted that it is somewhat difficult to establish a connection between these early plan books and the new cycle of development in the 1870s[37]. Consider, however, that Downing's *Country Houses* went through nine editions to 1866, that Vaux's *Villas and Cottages* was re-issued in 1864, and that other architects were publishing books in the '60s that carried the same message. The work of John Notman, who Bruce Price mentions in this connection[38], of Samuel Sloan in Philadelphia, and of George Woodward should also be investigated[39]. Another link in the chain was Henry Hudson Holly, whose ideas reached a large and apparently receptive audience after the publication of *Holly's Country Seats* in 1863. In some of his designs, he completely eliminated the drawing room, arguing that the dining room and/or the hall could easily take over its function[40]. He described one of his designs, No. 6, in these words:

> The hall serves as a large sitting room, and communicates with the drawing room by folding doors, while the stairs are so secluded as to obviate the necessity of a private staircase.
> It must be admitted that to enter at once into a large hall, treated somewhat like one of the living rooms of the house, and perhaps with a wood fire blazing cheerfully on one side in a wide open chimney, gives to the stranger the impression of generous hospitality and cordial

greeting, as if the house itself at once had received him into its arms. This is frequent in England[41].

Thus, while the idea of the living hall was certainly English in origin, as a plan feature it was far from dead in America in the second and third quarters of the century. Richardson, like so many great geniuses mistakenly credited with invention, took a plan type well known both here and in Britain, expanded it, and infused it with new life, meaning, and form to suit the requirements of his own day.

Wilks Residence, Blair, Ontario (Canada), 1872-1873

Returning once more to Lienau's work, we shall see that, in spite of the minimal concession to the living hall type of plan in the Lewis house, Lienau did make use of it on more than one occasion. A notable early example may be seen in the plans of 1872[42] for an extension wing to a house owned by Matthew Wilks, a wealthy New York financier, on his 1,000-acre estate, Cruickston Park, near Blair, Ontario (Fig. 97). In 1957, the estate was still owned by his descendants; and the house altered very little[43]. [Today, the Wilks mansion is part of Cruickston Park, which is owned by the Cruickston Charitable Research Reserve (CCRR). With 913 acres (370 hectares), the CCRR is one of the largest urban green spaces in Canada.]

Figure 97. Wilks Mansion (Cruickston Park) by Detlef Lienau.

The accommodation of Lienau's design to the pre-existing house is interesting. Of greater importance, however, is the introduction of a large hall with a fireplace in the center of the new wing (Fig. 98). Larger than any of the other rooms, this "hall," as it is labeled on the working drawings, was surely meant to be more than a mere passageway. For example, care was taken to bring light into the rear of the hall by means of a window opening onto a covered courtyard. As in the case of the Shiff house, with its French mansard roof, the client's background and preferences—British—may very well have been a decisive factor in the introduction (at so early a date) of a planning feature associated most closely with English tradition.

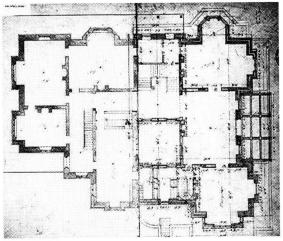

Figure 98. Wilks Mansion. Plan of first floor.

Matthew Wilks (1816-1899)[44] was born in England, but educated in Paris, where his father served as Chaplain of the British Embassy. He arrived in this country at the age of twenty-two, armed with a letter of introduction to John Jacob Astor. Soon afterward, he married one of Astor's granddaughter's, Eliza Langdon. Like his brother-in-law, DeLancey Kane, Wilks amassed a fortune in the ensuing years. Following the Astor tradition, he invested heavily in New York real estate; the Wilks Building (1889) at 15 Wall Street, designed by Clinton & Russell, was named after him[45]. In later years, however, he preferred the quiet seclusion of his Canadian estate, where during the last twenty-five years of his life he retired to the style of an English country squire, taking special delight in his stables and his garden, laid out in the English fashion. It was his son, Matthew Astor Wilks, who married the daughter of millionairess Hetty Green[46].

Another example showing Lienau's interest in the new plan type may be seen in the plans for the Bech villa, mentioned previously. Two out of four schemes, not including the one illustrated (Fig. 90) show a more developed type of hall with a fireplace. The new scheme must have been made at the request of Mrs. Bech. On one of the studies, dated June 24, 1875, Lienau made the following notations: "hall to be continued through end and to be more important".

Williams Cottage, New Brunswick, New Jersey, 1883

Several years later, we meet the true living hall plan in a modest clapboard house in New Brunswick, New Jersey. It was built in 1883 by Detlef and J. August Lienau as a summer house for Mary M. (Mrs. John) Williams[47], whose daughter Elizabeth married J. August the following year. The exterior shows not a trace of the popular Queen Anne mode[48]; indeed, it is so simply treated that it is almost devoid of identifiable style (Fig. 99). The clapboard sheathing is certainly related, however, to the current revival of interest in Colonial architecture. The house originally had a dining room, but no parlor. This function was taken over by the central transverse hall, which measured approximately 30 feet by 18 feet, serving both as a means of circulation and as the "seat of the home life," as is illustrated by the accompanying photograph (Fig. 100). This somewhat unusual plan type, mentioned years earlier by Holly[49], in which the hall completely takes over the function of the non-existent parlor (thus becoming a living hall in the true sense of the word), may be found occasionally in small seaside cottages of the period, which were planned, like this house, with the "simple life" in mind[50].

Figure 99. Williams Cottage by Detlef and J. August Lienau.

The antiquarian touches in the Williams house, particularly noticeable in the Dutch hutch doorway and the Georgian-type mantel, are typical of the period[51] and should probably be attributed to J. August, not Detlef. According to the Misses Mary M. and Catherine Lienau, his daughters, J. August Lienau (1854-1906)[52], true to his generation, was extremely fond of Colonial houses. Shortly after his marriage to Miss Williams, he purchased a pre-Revolutionary War house in New Brunswick, had it moved from its original site, and then lived in it for a number of years, altering it from time to time. His own work, mentioned in passing in connection with the Colonial Revival alterations to Anglesea, was often closely modeled on Georgian prototypes, as is only too obvious in a house he built in 1899 for Mrs. William M. Carson at East Hampton (Long Island), which followed its model, nearby Rock Hall, extremely closely[53].

Figure 100. Williams Cottage. Interior view of living hall.

City Houses

Lienau's later urban residential architecture also indicates a partial assimilation of "modern" features of planning and design. Mention has been made of the transformation of the traditional New York house plan in the Colford Jones Block (Fig. 68). In this row and in Edmund Schermerhorn's residence and Grosvenor House (Figs. 62, 58, and 86), a lowering of the entrance to the house—indeed, the actual disappearance of the traditional stoop in the latter two buildings—was also noted in passing as a significant feature; this point will be expanded and related to general trends of the '80s.

Mosle Residence, West Fifty-first Street, New York, 1878-1879

In a brick and brownstone house designed in 1878 for the German-born New York merchant, George Mosle[54], which stood at 5 West 51st Street (immediately adjoining the William H. Vanderbilt houses [1879-1881] on Fifth Avenue[55]), Lienau reverted to a more traditional type of plan with a long narrow hall[56]. There is perhaps more feeling for an uninterrupted flow of space than would have been the case earlier, particularly in the *enfilade* of three rooms separated by fairly wide sliding doors. But the Mosle house was definitely not *avant-garde*, nor even particularly up-to-date.

Figure 101. Mosle House by Detlef Lienau. Front elevation.

If we compare its elevation (Fig. 101) with that of Potter & Robertson's R.C. Pruyn house in Albany[57], one of the most stunning city house designs produced in the Queen Anne mode, Lienau's façade appears still, vertical, even reactionary, with its mid-century handling of the trim and vague reminiscences of Neo-Grec ornamentation[58]. In contrast to less advanced houses of the period to which it may also be compared, such as a residence in Washington by John Fraser[59], note the severely restrained treatment of the roof. In the unusually low-pitched pediments surmounting the attic windows, Lienau introduced a reminiscence of the old stepped gables of northern Europe, a motif that appears some years later in a row of houses on Eighty-second Street (Fig. 105). North European and Dutch design motifs were also a great favorite of Lienau's pupil, Henry J. Hardenbergh, a partiality that may be attributed chiefly to his own background, but perhaps also to his contact with North German brickwork traditions in Lienau's office.

Howland Residence, West Eighteenth Street, New York, 1881-1882

In 1881, Lienau designed a townhouse for Samuel S. Howland, which formerly stood at 10 West 18th Street. The drawings at the Avery Library, our only visual documents, were rendered by J. August Lienau[60]. While the elevation is not strikingly original (Fig. 102), the introduction of certain specifically contemporary features of design and planning here must in all likelihood be attributed to Lienau's youthful client and perhaps also to suggestions made by his own son. Howland, born in 1849[61], was the son of Gardiner Greene Howland, one of New York's great shipping merchants and railroad financiers. He was also—and this is more to the point—a son-in-law of Lienau's old client, August Belmont. At just about this time, Lienau was also busy making sketches for projected alterations to Belmont's own house a few steps down the block, on the corner of Fifth Avenue. The project came to naught when Belmont, a notoriously difficult client[62], lost his temper; Lienau, who always had a mind of his own, refused to go on with the job and requested the return of his drawings[63].

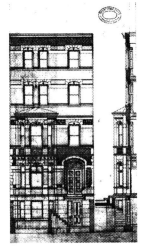

Figure 102. Howland House by Detlef Lienau. Front elevation.

The Howland residence, built from 1881 to 1882[64], is important in Lienau's architectural development for several reasons. First, note the appearance of far more developed Queen Anne vocabulary than had been the case at Anglesea. This is reflected in the emphasis given to the two-story bay window, the cut brickwork in varied patterns, the use of terra cotta panels under the second-story windows, and the substitution of a flat roof for the mansard. By the early 1880s, the mansard was somewhat *déclassé*. On the other hand, the persistence of Neo-Grec elements, seen particularly in the incised ornamentation of the window trim and interior decoration, and the emphasis on the flatness of the wall give to the building a somewhat old-fashioned flavor, if we compare it to contemporary work by architects of the younger generation. One of the best designs of the period was a house by Robert H. Robertson (1849-1919), a restrained yet effectively handled example of Queen Anne in its more severe Palladian phase; equally interesting is a project by William A. Bates (1853-1922), in which Shavian influence has been cleverly used to produce one of the most handsome designs of the time[65]. Occasionally, one may feel that Lienau's moderation, restraint, and retention of the surface plane is a pleasant relief from the cluttered effect so often produced by unbridled enthusiasm for Queen Anne, as seen in a Bruce Price (1843-1903) project of 1879 and a good many of the designs submitted in the competition sponsored by the Architectural League in 1881[66].

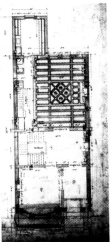

Figure 103. Howland House. Plan of first floor.

Second, an English basement plan has been substituted for the traditional high stoop, still seen in the Mosle residence. The victory of the English basement type, raised only three steps above the curb line—and also of the contemporary American basement type[67]—reflects in still another way the rebellion of the 1880s and the younger generation (typified by both Howland and J. August Lienau) against Victorian Gothic and Second Empire verticality. The emphasis on horizontal elements in the elevation and the omission of the mansard roof, noted above, is of course tied up with the same reaction. The original plans called for a very long house with a higher stoop and all family rooms on the first floor; a more shallow plan was substituted, in which the first two stories, as in the English townhouse, were devoted to living rooms (Fig. 103). The first floor was given over to the library and dining room; the second was occupied by a front parlor with an ell over the space devoted to the entry downstairs, and a rear drawing room. It is this ell that constitutes the new feature. A decade earlier, it would have been partitioned off; now, it is thought of as a part of the parlor, from which it could, however, be visually separated by drawing the *portières*, turning it into a "cozy corner". The new feeling for spatial flow implied here is also seen in the increase in the width of the sliding doors opening onto the hall, accompanied by a slight but nonetheless important decrease in their height. The decrease in the total height of the rooms, between 12 feet, 10 inches, and 13 feet, 5 inches here, versus as much as 15 feet in Lienau's earlier houses, likewise is typical of the 1880s.

Finally, there is the new importance given to the central stair hall with its fireplace. The hall, even in this relatively small city house, occupies the entire central portion of the first floor. In Russell Sturgis's informative article, "The City House in the East and South," published in *Homes in City and Country* in 1893[68], he pointed out the advantages and disadvantages of recent modifications in the plan of the New York house:

> The main peculiarity... is the resolute insistence on something in the way of the hall, which shall replace the long, narrow entranceway called by that name by former generations. Out of this square hall, the staircase to the upper stories must necessarily lead, and the completeness of the screening of this staircase from the hall... is the main point of differences among modern houses. In some, an architectural screen is arranged, amounting almost to a complete partition... in others... this separation is effected by means of an open arcade, or row of columns, with curtains that can be adjusted at pleasure. Whether this plan is agreeable or not... depends on the habits of the family... It seems to be largely founded on the idea that a hall and staircase should be handsome and spacious, and that a house that has not a handsome and spacious hall is an inferior one. This theory cannot be maintained in all cases. It may often be better to reduce the entrance way and the staircase to the narrowest and humblest dimensions reconcilable with convenience, in order that the rooms actually lived in may be larger... The square hall in the middle of the house, as it has been introduced into such New York houses as cost,

with the land, from $20,000 to $35,000, is certainly open to the objection that it is not a comfortable or agreeable sitting room, because too public and because not easily made warm, while, on the other hand, it is altogether unnecessary as a means of communication... It remains to be seen whether the whole scheme will be abandoned, as a temporary "fad," or whether modifications should be introduced into it, which will make it a permanent feature of our residences.

This same plan feature was used in at least one of the three rows Lienau built a few years later on the Upper West Side.

Row Houses on New York's Upper West Side, 1883-1886

Of the three rows erected by Lienau from 1883 to early in 1887 on West Eighty-second and Eight-third Streets just off Central Park West, only one remains today. The first two rows, built back to back, one on the south side of Eighty-third Street, the other on the north side of Eighty-second Street, were commissioned in 1883 by the same Mrs. Mary M. Williams mentioned in connection with the cottage in New Brunswick; both rows have long since been replaced by apartment houses[69]. Mrs. Williams was the widow of John H. Williams, co-partner in the Williams & Guion Steamship Company, incorporators of the famous Black Star Line of packets to Liverpool in the mid-century. She evidently built these rows for speculative purposes; each row consisted of six 16-ft. wide houses valued at $11,500 each. By the early 1880s, there was a tremendous demand for single-family, moderately priced houses within easy reach of New York's downtown district. The city had entirely recovered from the effects of the panic of 1873, the ensuing years of depression, and stagnation in the real estate market and building trades. People had money again, and prospects for the future looked promising. Not everyone wanted to live in one of the new-fangled French flats; others, tired of long years of commuting from outlying districts, were loath to give up the advantages of home ownership. For these people, the opening up of a completely new residential area on New York's Upper West Side was made to order.

The development of this section of the city[70], envisaged already in 1867 by the Board of Commissioners of Central Park, but held back by the lack of investment capital during the '70s, and the absence of adequate transportation services, proceeded with incredible rapidity after the extension of rapid transit to the West Side in 1879. At that time, the area consisted largely of empty lots and was almost totally uninhabited; in fact, the New York correspondent of the *American Architect and Building News*, writing in April 1879, saw no future for the West Side, which he described as "yet a desert"[71]. In an effort to remedy this situation, Edgbert L. Viele, engineer and city surveyor, published a pamphlet that same year entitled *The West Side Plateau of the City of New York*[72]. After comparing the region favorably to residential districts in European cities, he went on to present the West Side as an ideal place of residence for people who were moderately well-to-do and appreciated the finer things in life. He wound up with an appeal to citizens of taste to build there, in the hope that current styles of domestic architecture, of which he disapproved, would change for the better. This is what he wrote:

> The west side plateau will undoubtedly always [*sic*] be held intact for the development of a higher order of architecture than it has been the good fortune of New York hitherto to possess. We have become so accustomed to being victimized and led by speculative builders that the average citizen has come to believe that any attempt of his own to form a conception of the house he would desire to live in, or any expectation of finding such a house... would be perfectly absurd. It is time for us to ask ourselves if such a state of things is absolutely necessary. If we are to go on and be shelved away in a continuous interminable series of brown-stone boxes, the dimensions of which are growing less year by year until they finally become but little larger than the vaults into which our mortal remains are to be thrust away out of sight forever... The truth is that... we have lost the idea of what a real house is. The few attempts at architectural display have been principally made on "corner lots". This unfortunate fancy... we say unfortunate, because out of it has come that style of corner lot architecture that has dominated for so many years at the expense of symmetry and completeness, and has almost given a permanent stamp to domestic architecture in the city...
>
> The plans of improvement in the west end... afford the opportunity for that change in style of house construction that has so long been a desideratum with us[73].

He clinched his argument by pointing out that, for the price of one lot on Fifth Avenue, one could buy four to six on the West Side. Mrs. Williams followed his advice, no doubt also influenced in her decision by the forthcoming marriage of her daughter into a family of architects. Her husband's former partner, Mr. Guion, did not follow his advice: Charles W. Clinton (1838-1910) built a fancy house on Fifth Avenue for him.

In spite of the fact that J.C. Cady's Museum of Natural History at Seventy-seventh Street was opened late in 1877, the so-called

"West Side movement" did not begin in earnest until Edward Clark, president of the Singer Sewing Machine Company, aided by his favorite architect, none other than Henry J. Hardenbergh, began building twenty-six dwellings on Seventy-third Street in 1879[74]. One year later, in 1880, Hardenbergh filed plans with the city for the construction of Clark's "mammoth" Dakota Apartments on the northwest corner of Seventy-second Street and Central Park West. In the course of the next few years, small clusters of houses began springing up around the Elevated Railroad stations on Ninth (Columbus) Avenue, particularly in the vicinity of the Seventy-second, Eighty-first, and Ninety-third Street stations. Lienau's three rows were among the earliest buildings in the neighborhood[75] and were located in the heart of the area, which witnessed the greatest building activity in the 1880s[76].

Figure 104. Williams Row by Detlef Lienau.

Turning first to the Williams row on the north side of Eighty-second Street, of which two early photographs have fortunately been preserved, it will be seen that, in spite of the relative simplicity of means, an effort was made to give the row a certain interest and coherence (Fig. 104). In discussing the troublesome problem of row architecture, Montgomery Schuyler had this to say:

> A more complicated problem than the design of a single street-front is the design of a row, so as to preserve a unity of aspect while individualizing the various buildings that make it up. A generation ago, this was not a problem at all. The speculative builder, who at that time housed the well-to-do..., after his draftsman had produced one

elevation of a brown-stone front with the conventional "trimmings" merely repeated that front in the same material as many times as he had houses to do. Unity was doubtless preserved, but inasmuch as the single design that was repeated was of no interest whatsoever, it became exceedingly dismal by repetition. There are few things more depressing than a blockfront in a fashionable quarter erected between 1860 and 1880, and it may well have seemed that nothing could be worse. But worse remained behind. When the West Side was opened up for settlement and the speculative builder was credibly informed that the buyers and even the tenants of dwelling houses demanded "variety" in the fronts, he set himself to supply the new demand by instructing the same incompetent draftsman whom he had before instructed to make the fronts all alike, to make them all different. The results were awful...[77]

In reverting to the same subject some years later, Schuyler quoted the reaction of an eminent architect to the rows upon rows of variegated and individualized 16-ft. house fronts: "They made him seasick"[78].

Figure 105. Lienau-Williams Row by Detlef Lienau. Front elevation.

The row of four houses at 48-54 West 82nd Street, built in 1886 by Lienau for himself and various members of the Lienau and Williams family[79], has long since been converted into rooming houses. If the elevation drawing[80] for the row is neither particularly distinguished nor progressive (Fig. 105), one should remember that Lienau was faced with the problem so well described by Montgomery Schuyler—designing a row of houses that would have some measure of interest in its own right and yet not stick out like a sore thumb in relation to neighboring buildings. The Lienau-Williams row has at least the virtues of simplicity, clarity, and general fitness. Its directness contrasts strongly to a contemporary row like one erected by James E. Ware (1846-1918) on East Sixty-seventh Street which, judging by the published drawings, was a *pot-pourri* of the best of Norman Shaw[81].

A comparison of the Lienau row with the three buildings next to it, 56-60 West 82nd Street, built a few months earlier by H.L. Harris[82], is exceedingly instructive, first for the insight it affords into Lienau's construction techniques, and second, for its corroboration of our impression that certain basic premises underlay any and all styles Lienau used and remained fairly constant throughout his career. Lienau, who was a recognized authority on construction—he served for many years as a trusted member of the Committee on Examinations of the American Institute of Architects[83]—sank the foundation walls of this row considerably deeper than those of the neighboring houses. The foundations were laid in 12-in. depths of concrete and ranged in width from 24 to 40 inches versus 24 to 28 inches next door. Heavy timbers, 3 inches by 12 inches and 10 inches, supported the floors, which as a consequence have stood up well, in spite of considerable abuse. It is obvious from the figures cited above that these houses were built in a most substantial manner, unlike so many of the structures on the West Side put up for quick sale by speculators.

It is also interesting to compare the designs of the Lienau and Harris rows. Though the gabled silhouette of the two units is strikingly similar, a likeness that was undoubtedly intentional on Lienau's part, closer examination reveals interesting differences between the ways the two architects worked out a similar problem. A stroller on Eighty-second Street will note the contrast between Lienau's solution on the one hand and Harris's on the other: horizontal versus vertical emphasis; smooth surfaces (in spite of a lightly rusticated base) as against plasticity and surface texture, in all likelihood a reflection of Richardsonian influence on Harris; and classical balance (despite the disparity in the sizes of the houses) and picturesque irregularity. The reappearance of the high stoop is typical of middle-class housing on the West Side, as is the use of a mansard in combination with a flat roof. The angular stepped design in the gables of the Lienau row and the large coarse scrollwork used to ornament the Williams row across the street (Fig. 104) are vaguely Germanic in origin.

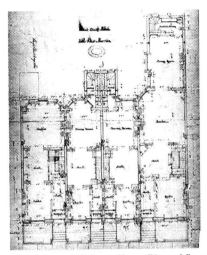

Figure 106. Lienau-Williams Row. Plan of first floor.

In three of the houses in the Lienau-Williams row, a relatively large stair hall occupies about one-third of the total floor space on the parlor floor (Fig. 106); it is just as important in the fourth and largest house, which belonged to Mrs. Williams. Of the elaborately carved screens separating the stairs from the halls, for which drawings are preserved, only the one at No. 48 is still in fair condition. The Harris houses, incidentally, retained the traditional long narrow hall. The objections raised by Sturgis to the use of an expanded hall in small city houses are certainly valid here. Too large to serve merely as passageways, the space was too dark and probably too drafty to serve as a sitting room. The incorporation of the great hall of the English tradition in the large country houses of the period is, as we have seen, readily understandable from both a sociological and an architectural point of view. The adoption of this type of plan in small middle-class houses, where it was actually a complete waste of space, must be explained in other terms. Almost its only *raison d'être* was the fact that it provided these houses with an impressive "front," an attitude that continued to plague a good deal of later 19th and, alas, 20th century architecture as well.

Lienau's Work: An Index to the Growth of the City

It was in one of these houses, No. 48, that Lienau died of typhoid fever on August 29, 1887. Only a few months before, he had moved to New York from Jersey City, where he had lived for over three decades and had obviously become a veteran commuter. His death was sudden; it is thought that he contracted the disease while superintending the construction of the Telfair Academy of Arts and Sciences in Savannah, Georgia. [A similar fate befell Richard Morris Hunt eight years later, when he caught a cold during an unusually hectic travel schedule, which aggravated several chronic and usually benign ailments. For more information on Lienau's family and survivors, see Editor's Epilogue.]

It must have been a source of immense gratification to Lienau that he had lived long enough to contribute to the development of still another section of the city to which he had come as an immigrant nearly forty years before. If we pinpoint Lienau's New York houses from 1850 to 1886 on an imaginary map of the city, we can readily see that they provide a remarkably accurate picture of the rate and direction of growth of the metropolis. For example,

1850—Tenth Street and Fifth Avenue (Shiff House)

1858—West Twenty-third Street (William C. Schermerhorn House)

1869—Fifth Avenue and Fifty-fifth Street (Colford Jones Row)

1871—Third Avenue and Seventy-first Street (Schermerhorn Flats)

1883-1887—West Eighty-second and Eighty-third Streets (Lienau-Williams Rows)

Lienau had seen New York grow from a relatively small provincial city of a half million people in 1848, with its northernmost boundaries at Union Square, to a great sprawling metropolis reaching far out into areas that had formerly been a half day's journey from the center of town. By 1887, the year of his death, New York had a population of one and a half million—three times what it was when Lienau arrived. It had become one of the most cosmopolitan cities in the world, a great cultural and artistic center[84]. It had a new opera house and grandiose plans for a museum of art. Hotels, apartment houses, and office buildings were growing taller each year, for the most part the creation of the new younger generation of architects, men like Hardenbergh, Post, McKim, Mead & White, and others. The old-timers, like Lienau, were disappearing. Of the pioneers of the profession, only Hunt, Le Brun, and Eidlitz were still building.

Chapter IX.
Conclusion

Lienau's Influence

There is no doubt that Lienau's most important contributions to American architecture were made in the decades of the 1850s, '60s, and early '70s, and that his buildings of the late '70s and early '80s, while still interesting to compare with contemporary work, no longer have the intrinsic interest of those earlier years. Nor was Lienau's later work particularly progressive from a structural point of view: None of his office buildings was over seven stories high, though tall structures, leading eventually to the skyscraper concept, were built in New York already in the early '70s. It may also be significant that Lienau's later work was more widely dispersed geographically, perhaps because important commissions in the metropolitan area were going to younger architects. Even William Schermerhorn, his good client of days gone by, turned to Lienau's pupil, Hardenbergh[1].

Nevertheless, we should not underestimate his influence on the younger generation of architects. Henry Janeway Hardenbergh (1847-1918) was quite conscious of the debt he owed to Lienau, whom he called "a remarkable man for his time"[2]. In response to the statement, "I suppose you served a real German apprenticeship at Lienau's," which was posed by Sadakichi Hartmann regarding his years in Lienau's office (1863-1870), Hardenbergh said, "Yes, it was a true apprenticeship. Conditions were different: He never had more than six men in his office. He could really devote some time to them. Now [1906], many offices have forty to fifty men on the payroll." Montgomery Schuyler, who several times commented very favorably on Lienau's work[3], had this to say about Lienau's influence on Hardenbergh:

> Mr. Lienau's work shows qualities that were quite independent of this special [Neo-Grec] style that were calculated to be of great advantage to an apt pupil. Chief among these was what I have called the straightforward and structural treatment of his designs, that habit of considering the artistic problem as inextricably connected with the mechanical problem, of regarding his paper design as the drawing of a building, rather than the execution of it as the building of a drawing[4].

This interest in structure and rational design Lienau also communicated to another well known later architect, Paul Johannes

Pelz (1841-1918). Pelz served as a draftsman in Lienau's office from 1859 to 1866, becoming Chief Draftsman in 1864. He is probably best remembered for the part he and his partner, John L. Smithmeyer (1832-1908), played in the design of the Congressional Library (1873 ff.) in Washington, D.C.[5] Lienau's eldest son, J. August Lienau, who has been mentioned in connection with the Williams cottage in New Brunswick, worked in his father's office from 1874 after training in Europe[6]. He took over his father's practice upon the latter's death in 1887, later forming a partnership with Thomas Nash. Thus, through the work of his pupils, Lienau's influence continued down through the early years of the 20th century.

Turning now to a consideration of Lienau's place in the development of American architecture as a whole, there can be no question of the real importance of Lienau's role in the origin and diffusion of the Second Empire style in the United States, as I have endeavored to show in the early chapters, particularly in the sections dealing with the Shiff house, the Edmund Schermerhorn residence, and the Jones block. In addition, this survey of Lienau's suburban and country houses over a period of four decades has enabled us to follow changing currents of architectural taste on many different levels. From simple cottage to great mansion, we have seen how the architect used first one, then another, mode to express his own ideas and the wishes of his clients in what he considered to be their most appropriate form. The Chalet and "Stick Style" of the early cottages, the Italian Villa, and the monumental French Renaissance tradition, reflections of the picturesque High Victorian Gothic of the late '60s and early '70s, and finally echoes of the "Queen Anne" and of the Colonial Revival—all found expression in Lienau's work. Eclectic? Yes, but an eclecticism that was never used capriciously[7], always held in check by Lienau's basic conservatism and rational point of view. Of course, the Second Empire mode, on which Lienau staked his early reputation, was itself eclectic. It is a mode difficult to define, precisely because it was made up of elements borrowed from many sources, from Italian and French Renaissance architecture, from 17th century France, and—as developed by architects such as Lienau—from motifs carried over from the Neo-Grec of the 1830s and '40s.

The word "eclecticism" itself, formerly used chiefly as a term of opprobrium, is even more difficult to define properly, even though we all know in general what it means. In recent years, several writers, notably Carroll Meeks[8] and Henry-Russell Hitchcock, have redefined and reinterpreted it. Eclecticism has now become "respectable" again. In explaining the self-conscious selection of styles from the past, so characteristic of the period, Hitchcock has stated the case extremely well:

> The obvious readiness of the mid-19th century to utilize alternative [sic] stylistic forms in different fields, already deprecated by severe critics at the time, seems peculiarly reprehensible to us in a way it did not to the Late Victorians or even to most men of the early 20th century... Even those mid-19th century architects who were positive fanatics about "style" generally employed without shame a more or less extensive variety of modes when their practice included various different types of edifices. Other leaders of taste were quite frank in defense of a studied eclecticism, intentionally varied according to purpose and location[9].

It may be difficult for us, indoctrinated by the 20th century's cult of originality at all costs[10], to understand that architects of Lienau's generation saw nothing wrong with borrowing from time-honored traditions in their search for solutions to new problems of design and construction. They were not yet ready for a complete break with the past. This had been true of Labrouste, of Barry, and of Viollet-le-Duc. Even Leopold Eidlitz, one of the most stringent critics of eclecticism, never advocated a negation of the past:

> Shall we refer to the architecture of the past, or must we ignore it to become good architects? By all means, let us keep in view the work of the past, not for the purpose of utilizing its forms, but for the purpose of utilizing the accumulated knowledge and technical skills manifested in its work[11].

This was the same man who sarcastically described American architecture as "the art of covering one thing with another thing to imitate a third thing which, if genuine, would not be desirable"[12]. Eidlitz, incidentally, is an excellent example of the typical 19th century dichotomy between architectural theory and practice, understandable only if we place him properly against dominant trends of thought of his own period.

From the point of view of a Louis Sullivan, Lienau's work may appear academic and revivalistic. Yet, it would be a mistake to suppose that his approach to the past was that of a naive schoolboy, lifting one detail from here and another from there. His mind was a rich storehouse from which he could pick at will, discard or recombine elements according to the exigencies of the particular situation. He was, if we adopt Meeks's terminology, a "synthetic" eclectic, combining, re-shuffling elements from the past, and adapting them to new conditions. This is very evident when one attempts, almost always unsuccessfully, to find prototypes for his designs. Even in early works such as the Shiff house and Grace Church, one cannot put his finger on exact sources. In the best of his buildings, such as the Schermerhorn houses and the Jones Block, he achieved a real unity of design. The outcome was, of course, not always so happy, as we have seen in a few examples, notably the Kane cottage in Newport, where there is undeniable friction between elements drawn from disparate sources.

It is extremely important to emphasize the fact that, while Lienau had great respect for the past, he fully understood the need for adapting it to contemporary requirements. In this respect, he was a true disciple of Schinkel and Labrouste[13]. In the only statement of his aesthetic theory that has come down to us—a paper "On Classic and Romantic Architecture," read at one of the monthly meetings of the American Institute of Architects in New York on May 4, 1858[14]—one notes that his criteria were essentially determined by a rational and functional point of view. Thus, while he stated that the forms of Greek architecture "have never been surpassed or equaled," he defined "classic" [*sic*] periods of art as times when "the devotee to Art seems so far lost in the admiration of a former period, that he actually becomes unable to create independently," an evident confusion of classic with classicistic art. On the other hand, he maintained that

> romantic art is... just the opposite; it invents, it creates new ideas, new systems, and expresses these ideas through new forms and new modes of construction. With the continually changing requirements of human society, with the progress of civilization, it advances step by step; romantic architecture creates new structures, entirely adapted to the purposes for which they are intended, adapted to the climate of the country in which they are erected, and out of materials supplied by the locality; it gives to the materials the forms most expressive of their nature and most expressive of the degree of perfection and *taste* and mechanical skill of the time; in short, structures reflecting like a mirror, the people, the country, the climate, and the wants of the times for which they are erected.

In the analysis of Greek and Egyptian architecture that follows, the criterion is always whether or not the forms expressed the *nature of the service* [the italics are Lienau's] for which they were intended. In the architect's own work, a deliberate effort was almost always made to adapt whatever mode he chose to the functional requirements of the building and the psychological needs of the client. As Talbot Hamlin observed:

these systems were strained through his mind, and that mind was deeply and soundly trained... Whatever style he used, however outlandish it may appear to us, the work is always strongly and skillfully composed, ornamented with discretion, and logically planned[15].

For example, when Lienau advocated the use of the old North German brick architecture and vaulting system (in a paper read at the eleventh annual convention of the American Institute of Architects in Boston in 1877[16]), his plea was based on the assumption that its excellent qualities of fire resistance would provide an answer to the desperate need for such a material, on which attention had recently been focused because of the disastrous fires of the early '70s in Boston and Chicago. The symbolic, associative values of the Second Empire style to some of Lienau's well-to-do clients have been stressed; Germanic traditions mentioned briefly in connection with Schloss Düneck, St. Mary's Hall, the Bech villa, and the row houses on the Upper West Side; and English planning traditions in the discussion of the Matthew Wilks house in Canada. When Lienau was commissioned in the 1860s by F.O. Matthiessen to design a sugar refinery in Jersey City, he turned to the stark simplicity of the Romanesque as the most expressive symbol of the new industrial age. The Romanesque mode had come to be accepted in this country, as it had in Germany and Austria[17], as suitable not only for churches, but also for other architectural types, particularly for railroad stations and manufactories. Notable early examples were Tefft's Union Depot (1848) in Providence, Rhode Island, and J.C. Hoxie's Horstmann factory in Philadelphia (c.1852-1853)[18]. Lienau's factory buildings in Jersey City, which once dominated the city's skyline, were among his most powerful works. In terms of their own period, they were an exceptionally fine demonstration of the integration of plan, form, and function[19]. How can one consider these buildings as merely derivative, the product of a mind content merely to copy and adapt the past?

It should be noted, finally, that Lienau's eclecticism was of a very particular variety. He was not interested in the styles of the past for their picturesque qualities. If we accept Carroll Meeks's thesis that picturesque eclecticism was "the dominant aesthetic of the whole 19th century[20]—an all-inclusive view, which (as we learn more and more about the period) may have to be qualified—then Lienau's work is almost always atypical. Quite characteristically, for example, Lienau used the Gothic mode only rarely in domestic architecture, and then only in minor buildings, such as gate lodges. When he was called upon to design a "Gothic" church, he preferred the earliest, simplest phase of the style in contrast to most of his contemporaries[21]. His general anti-Gothic feeling is made quite clear in the discussion that followed Charles Babcock's advocacy at a meeting of the American Institute of Architects in 1858[22] of Gothic, finally narrowed down to Italian Gothic, as the best style for New York's proposed new City Hall. Richard Upjohn and Leopold Eidlitz supported Babcock against Lienau, who stood alone against the medievalists. As we have seen, the emphasis in Lienau's work was generally on the precisely defined, closed, regular contour, on a relatively smooth wall surface, on symmetry, order, and restraint. Nor was he concerned with obtaining special effects of color or texture. The bold surface treatment and striking color contrasts achieved by architects like Mould, Eidlitz, Wight, the Potters, and later Richardson, were alien to his nature. His was a rational, classical approach. Indeed, by his own admission, he preferred classical forms to all others. In a period of American architecture, when picturesque effects were valued above all else[23], Lienau stood his ground. He stuck to the precepts taught by Labrouste. His work may have seemed out-of-date to practitioners of the Victorian Gothic and later of the Queen Anne styles. But his colleagues recognized that he stood for what they called the "classical" tradition in design, and honesty in construction. At the twenty-first annual convention of the American Institute of Architects, held in Chicago in October 1887, a few weeks after his death, the following tribute, prepared by Messrs. Congdon and Upjohn, was read by A.J. Bloor:

> One of the founders of the Institute, and sometime a member of your Board of Trustees..., [Lienau] for many years furthered its interests, and was always a faithful and honored member. Thorough, conscientious, and painstaking in every work in which he was engaged, he always endeavored to avoid shams, and to practice truth in his art. In disposition, he was kind and sympathetic, and ever ready to promote the best interests of the profession. Having a high aim, he lived up to it. In his practice quiet and studious, his influence for good was felt by those near to him in official relations; and his loss will be keenly felt by all with whom he came in contact...[24]

Lienau's Place in American Architecture

Lienau's chief importance to American architecture of the period from 1850 to the mid-'80s lies, then, not in his use of the Second Empire mode *per se*, nor in his general eclecticism, but in the classical orientation of his entire *oeuvre*. His work represents a continuing current of conservatism in American architecture, which for a time was submerged beneath the more dominant picturesque modes of the period, the High Victorian Gothic *and* the Second Empire—the latter quite as anti-classical in its later style phase as the former. He served as a bridge between the classical traditions of design of the second quarter of the 19th century and their re-emergence in the 1880s of the movement led in New York by the firm of McKim, Mead & White.

Figure 107. Loft building by Detlef Lienau for Kane estate. Front elevation.

This point may be illustrated by four buildings erected for the Kane family, beginning with Detlef's villa for DeLancey Kane in Newport (Fig. 42). If we jump from this building, in which the architect made a tentative effort to synthesize the monumental French classical tradition with the American vernacular style, to an office building he erected in 1873 for the Kane estate at 676 Broadway (Fig. 107)[24], we may conclude that the influence of the Renaissance tradition still remained strong in a period when other architects were turning more and more to the Victorian Gothic.

Let us compare Lienau's office building to two well known and popular examples of the period: R.G. Hatfield's office building of 1874 on Broad Street in New York[25] and, a few years later, C.W. Clinton's and J.W. Pirsson's Queens Insurance Company Building (1877) on Wall Street (Fig. 108)[26]. While the Kane building is far

from a brilliant piece of design, it provides a foretaste of trends that
became dominant only much later in the 1880s. The third example,
Arthur Gilman's house of 1877 for the Colonel, DeLancey Kane's
second son, in New Rochelle, New York, may be chosen to
demonstrate the change in taste of the younger generation[27]. Though
Gilman's design is not a typical example of Queen Anne, its
picturesque and distinctly antiquarian flavor (seen in the English
half-timber construction and the hooded Dutch stoop, the latter
built at the expressed wish of the owner) are a far cry from both the
French character of the Kane villa of 1852 and the dry classicism of
Lienau's office building of 1873.

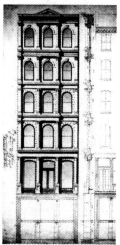

Figure 108. Queens Insurance Company by Clinton & Pirrson.

The full swing of the pendulum—the return to classical and
Renaissance precedents—may be illustrated by McKim, Mead &
White's Fifth Avenue residence for John Innes Kane, the youngest
member of the family (Fig. 109). This house, built in 1907, is a fine
example of the firm's superbly restrained work in the Italian *palazzo*
tradition, inaugurated many years earlier in the Villard houses on
Madison Avenue[28]. Thus, while the classicism and academic flavor of
Lienau's work of 1873 may seem *retardataire* when compared to
contemporary picturesque trends, it actually may be said to have
presaged architectural developments of the later 1880s and '90s.

Before turning to other matters, one question concerning the
eclecticism of the third quarter of the 19th century remains
unanswered. The term has been defined, and Lienau's role within the
movement has been discussed. But, after the relatively clear-cut
opposition to the Classical and Gothic revivals of the second quarter

of the century, why didn't the struggle resolve itself into a single dominant style, such as the Italian villa mode, rather than develop into what has so often been described as "the battle of the styles"[29]? Why the co-existence of various modes? Why eclecticism at all? This is a complicated, but fascinating question. Finding a definitive answer, or answers, to this problem cannot be attempted here. However, what we can do is suggest a few avenues of approach, which would call for far more serious and thorough investigations.

Figure 109. Kane House by McKim, Mead & White (1907).

An editorial on "Eclecticism in Architecture," resignedly critical in tone and published in one of the very first issues of *American Architect*[30], called attention to several factors that were of unquestioned importance to its development in this country. First, our lack of a unified, long-established tradition and the varied origins and sympathies of the architects of Lienau's generation, men like Upjohn, Wells, Mould, Petersen, Eidlitz, and Saeltzer, to mention only a few. In a short speech at the second annual dinner of the American Institute of Architects in 1859, Lienau himself noted that the diversity of nationalities, background, and education of its members had given rise to a variety of styles and opinions. He went on to say that, though this sometimes led to heated discussions, it "augurs well for the future of our Institute and for the future of Art in this country"[31]. In later years, the tendencies toward eclecticism were further encouraged by the years of study of the younger architects at L'Ecole des Beaux-Arts. This brings us to the second point, namely, the broadening base of American culture in the third quarter of the century. This was true not only of the education of architects, but also of the general public and of patrons of art and architecture, especially after the Centennial Exposition. What was characteristic of them had been true a generation earlier in the case of the wealthy upper middle classes. When architects had clients like the Schermerhorns, Joneses, Belmonts, and Lockwoods, who had traveled extensively abroad, they were dealing with people who prided themselves on their cultivated taste. Moreover, as a class, they were highly conscious of the prestige value of architecture, as we have seen, and of art in general[32]. The educated upper middle classes, not only the *nouveau riche*, as has been maintained[33], liked to cloak themselves in aristocratic garb. And what style could express this better than a combination of the "best" elements from the approved styles of the past[34]? Architects vied with one another in their endeavor to give substance to the fabulous dreams that easy money made possible. Money, and the open flaunting of the architectural creations it could buy, had not yet become generally suspect. The climax came, of course, in the period of the '80s and '90s with the creations of Hunt for the Vanderbilts and the Astors.

The Victorian Period Reconsidered

American Architect touches on many other factors that were of prime importance for the development of the eclectic point of view, such as the free interchange of ideas among nations—bringing design elements from many quarters—and the varied processes of reproduction, following closely upon the heels of the great archæological discoveries of the 19th century. The reluctance of architects to work outside the framework of tradition has been mentioned. But even more important, perhaps, is the historical fact that the period of the 1860s and early '70s was a very different one from that of the 1840s. These years were among the most remarkable in our history. The days of a stable balance between architecture and industry were over, blown sky-high by the roar of the cannon. The sense of equilibrium had vanished. Everything was changing; everyone was on the move. The West was opening up, transportation and the means of communication became cheap, fast, and easy. Railroads were beginning to cover the country, steamboats and barges were plying up and down the rivers and canals with the products of our fast-expanding industries. Steamships replacing the old clipper ships and packets, and the Atlantic Cable, assured the quick exchange of news and ideas from abroad. Immigrants by the millions—and one should remember that Detlef Lienau had been one of them—poured into this promised land, bringing with them their own traditions, which in due course were being absorbed into the mainstream of our culture[35]. Our urban population, reinforced by recruits from the farms, doubled within a generation. The social and economic foundations of the old South were knocked out from under her. Feudalism was dead. In the intellectual sphere, science, the spirit of skepticism, and of free inquiry were here, sweeping away long-accepted standards of absolute truth and beauty. In short, the entire cultural atmosphere—the political, social, and economic fabric of the country—was being completely transformed within the memory of a single generation[36].

It is against this background of change, of the Civil War, of the emergence of power of the industrial North, that one must try to understand the architecture of these crucial decades. A single dominant style, such as the Classical Revival, was no longer capable of expressing the complicated tensions of the period. The delicate balance between the Greek and Gothic Revivals, so long maintained, was impossible now. There was no time to cope adequately with all the problems raised by the new needs, much less to work consciously toward the creation of an "American style". Architects had to work quickly just to keep up with the tremendous demand for buildings of all types. In these circumstances, it is only natural that they relied on the past[37].

When art historians first began writing about the architecture of the third quarter of the century, they were revolted by what they saw. Borrowing from the invectives heaped upon the era by social historians, architectural writers used the term "Victorian" as an epithet and saw "naught but an abyss of taste, a riot of ugliness, that is almost unique in history"[38]. Some, like Fiske Kimball, ventured to suggest that perhaps these "Dark Ages" had been painted blacker than they actually were, but he joined in the chorus and saw the architecture of the period largely as "A Confusion of Tongues" and "A Battle of the Styles"[39]. Lewis Mumford, in 1924, wrote gloomily:

> By 1860, the halcyon day of American civilization was over... The sun had already sunk below the horizon and what seemed a promise was in reality an afterglow. By the time the Civil War came, architecture had recorded faithfully the social transformation; it was sullen, grim, gauche, unstable. Romanticism had not restored the past, nor had industrialization made the future more welcome. Architecture wandered between two worlds, 'one dead, the other powerless to be born'[40].

Parrington, whose third volume of *Main Currents in American Thought* reflected the thinking of the architectural historians of the first quarter of the 20th century, was no less emphatic:

> It was in the seventies that good taste reached its lowest ebb... A veritable *débâcle* of the arts was in process... In no other field is the sprawling formlessness of the seventies more grotesquely suggested than in its architecture and interior decoration. Upon the buildings of the times the hallmark of the Gilded Age is stamped in gaudy colors... It was the golden age of the jig saw, of the brownstone front, of the veranda that ran around the house like a spider web, of the mansard roof, of the cupola... Architecture sank to the level of the jerry-builder. Bad taste could go no further[41].

The first hint of a change of attitude came with the publication in 1931 of Lewis Mumford's *Brown Decades*, wherein he stated unequivocally that "it is time that we cease to be dominated by the negative aspects of the Brown Decades". He went on to say that

> there was, without doubt, something pitifully inadequate, indeed grotesque, in the post bellum scene; and the epithets that have been applied to it, the Gilded Age, the Tragic Era, the Dreadful Decade, the Pragmatic Acquiescence, are too full of truth ever to disappear. But neither epithet nor description, however adequately documented, tells the whole story. Beneath the crass surface, a new life was stirring... For the Brown Decades are not merely a mirror of our vices and infirmities; they are also a source of some of the most important elements in our contemporary culture[42].

Then came several monographs, of which the most important was unquestionably Henry-Russell Hitchcock's book on Richardson (1936), followed by Everard M. Upjohn's biography of his great-grandfather, Richard Upjohn (1939).

It may perhaps be questioned whether modern writers, in an effort to correct the earlier jaundiced view of the late Victorian era, have not sometimes swung too far in the opposite direction. The deserved emphasis by James Marston Fitch on the great technological contributions of the post-war period[43], of Vincent Scully on the creativity and genuine American quality of the Stick and Shingle styles, of Carroll Meeks on the development of the new aesthetic based upon picturesque eclectic principles—all are highly provocative and extremely valuable in correcting our earlier distorted view of 19th century architecture. Nonetheless, there is quite a natural temptation for each writer to eliminate material that doesn't quite fit into his general thesis. Some of the richness of the period, its extraordinary juxtaposition of contradictory elements—yes, its "confusion of tongues"—is lost through the necessary processes of condensation and elimination, a danger that Henry-Russell Hitchcock has most carefully avoided in his exhaustive and thoroughly stimulating *Early Victorian Architecture in Britain* (1954).

Lienau's work, which consistently exhibits a clarity in plan, honesty in execution[44], and restraint in design—all too rare in this period of American architecture—illustrates eminently well the dangers of over-simplification in the analysis of stylistic trends, as well as the utter falsity of the old glib generalizations, even when amusingly phrased[45], concerning Victorian architecture, the dearth of educated architects in America, and so on. In any case, the research of the last twenty years has proven beyond all measure of doubt that this was a period when the architects of America were not content merely to wander aimlessly between two worlds, "one dead, the other powerless to be born". This was a time of preparation, of "gathering of the forces[46]," and of experimentation, all necessary before a synthesis could be achieved.

In truth, "new life was stirring".

Endnotes.

(**Note:** Some footnotes were deleted when they referred to pages in the original dissertation that weren't relevant to the book manuscript. These deletions are noted by the phrase, "Refers to page in original dissertation". Also, a few question marks indicate alphabetic or numeric characters that I found undecipherable in the original typed dissertation.—Editor)

Introduction

[1]In addition to J. Henry Lienau's "Detlef Lienau, Architect, 1818-1887; Biography, Memorabilia: [New York? 1842?], which includes Talbot Hamlin's typescript, "The Place of Detlef Lienau in American Architecture" (pp.5-7), see the following: Elie Brault, *Les architectes par leurs oeuvres*, Paris [1893], III, pp. 429-30, two articles by Hamlin on Lienau, *Dictionary of American Biography*, XXI, pp. 493-94; and *National Cyclopedia of American Biography*, XXIX, pp. 16-17, and Ellen W. Kramer, "Detlef Lienau, An Architect of the Brown Decades," *SAH Journal*, Vol. XIV (March 1955), pp. 17-25. The recently published *Biographical Dictionary of American Architects (Deceased)* by Henry F. and Elsie Rathburn Withey, Los Angeles, 1956, is a generally useful compendium, but should be used with caution since, regrettably, it does contain a number of careless errors.

[2]Tabulation drawn from printed summaries of this census cited in Robert Ernst's fine study, *Immigrant Life in New York City*, 1825-1863, New York, 1949, Table 27, p. 216. City census records are preserved in the County Clerk's Office, Hall of Records, of their respective boroughs. The State Census of 1855, taken in June and July of that year, is a little known but invaluable research tool to which my attention was called by Rosalie Fellows Bailey, author of the extremely helpful *Guide to Genealogical and Bibliographical Sources for New York City (Manhattan), 1783-1898*, New York, 1954. The Census supplies the following information for each household: value of dwelling, material of which it is built, and number of families occupying it. Each individual member of the household is listed by name, age, sex, and relation to the head of the family; marital status, place of birth, profession, trade or occupation, number of years resident in New York City, voting status (naturalized or alien). A word of warning: Since the listings are in no special order, it may take considerable time to track down one individual in a heavily populated district, unless his profession is an unusual one. Architects are quite easily spotted by scanning the column devoted to "Profession".

[3]Many of these names will recur repeatedly here.

[4]Henry Dudley, FAIA, and a founder of the AIA, practiced in Exeter, England, before coming to this country in 1851. Shortly thereafter, he entered into partnership with Frank Wills. Perhaps the best known examples of their work are two churches in Nashville, Tenn., Holy Trinity

(1852) and the Church of the Advent (1857-1866). As a specialist in church architecture, he was proposed as an alternate to Eidlitz for a lecture on this subject to AIA members at a meeting of August 2, 1859, reported in the *Architects' and Mechanics' Journal*, Vol. VI (September 1859), p. 278. An expert on construction, he served with Lienau, Hatfield, Upjohn, and Draper on the AIA's Committee on Examinations, and was first listed in *Doggett's New York City Directory of 1851/1852*; New York State Census, 1855, King's County, Brooklyn, Tenth Ward, 3rd Election District, Dwelling #345, Family #683; his own testimony in the famous case of *Hunt vs. Parmly*, Superior Court of New York, February 21, 22, 25, and 26, 1861, which established the legal status of the architect in the U.S. (*Architect's and Mechanics' Journal*, Vol. III [March 16, 1861], p. 233). A complete transcript in this case is contained in Vols. III and IV of this publication, issues of March 9, 16, 30, and April 6, 1861; as will be seen, it is a very useful source of information concerning the architects who testified on Hunt's behalf.

⁵Petersen (1808-1885), FAIA, a founder, indeed one of the incorporators of the AIA, was trained as an architect and civil engineer. He was born in Prussia and served with the Corps of Engineers of the Prussian Army; later, he was attached to the Royal Staff. In 1848, however, his pro-revolutionary sympathies landed him in jail; he eventually escaped and landed in New York in 1851. In addition to Cooper Union, where he made a speech on the occasion of the laying of the cornerstone (*New York Daily Times*, September 19, 1853, p. 3, col. 3), he built the Washington Market (1851, demolished 1957, specifications in *Evening Post*, October 7, 1851, p. 2, col. 3), the Essex Market, Polytechnic Institute, Brooklyn, as well as a number of other structures. Apparently, he never lost interest in military affairs; see his pamphlet, *A Military Review of the Campaign in Virginia and Maryland*, New York [1862-1863]—first listed in *Doggett's Directory of 1851/1852*; New York State Census, 1855, King's County, Brooklyn, 10th Ward, 2nd Election District, Dwelling #38, Family #93; testimony in *Hunt vs. Parmly*, *Architect's and Mechanics' Journal*, Vol. III [March 16, 1861], p. 233; *New York Graphic*, cited in his obituary, *American Architect*, Vol. XVII (May 30, 1885), p. 253. A quick check of the Peter Cooper Papers in the collection known as the Cooper-Hewitt Manuscripts at Cooper Union, which I examined through the courtesy of Aaron L. Fessler, Librarian, revealed nothing of interest. A search of the records of New York's Department of Buildings would doubtless prove valuable.

Chapter I

¹Though officially, Detlef's surname was Lienau, he used the spelling Linau until 1841. See early drawings, Lienau Collection, Avery Library, Columbia University.

²For information on this point, I am indebted to my cousin, Eva Marie (Frau Werner) Lienau of Gosler, Germany (letter of August 20, 1952, citing an article by Johann Lienau) and to Carl C. Lienau of Orange, NJ, for

forwarding to me a pamphlet by Robert Lienau, *Nachrichten des Sippenverbendes Lienau*, Lübeck, 1973.

[3]These notebooks, given to the Avery Library by J. Henry Lienau in May 1954, are entitled as follows: (1) *Die Metalle*; (2) *Physik... nach dem Vortrage des Herrn Direktors Klöden ausgearbeitet von Detlef Lienau von Ostern 1835 bis Ost: 36*; (3) *Technologie nach dem Vortrage des Herrn Dir. Klöden ausgearbeitet von Detlef Lienau. v. Ostern 36 bis Ost. 37*, XII pls.

[4]For a picture of the German education system in the first half of the 19th century, see Gustav Thaulov, *Plan einer National-Erziehung und zur Begutechtung allen Lehrern Deutschlands besonders aber dem Lehrstands im Schleswig-Holstein*, Kiel, 1848; Georges Dumesnil, *La pédagogie dans l'Allemagne du nord*, Paris, 1885, especially chapter xi; and Friedrich Paulsen, *German Education: Past and Present*, translated by T. Lorentz, New York, 1908, pp. 133, 212.

[5]S. Grumbach, *Die Entwicklung des Berlinischen Fortbil?ungschulwesens*, Berlin, 1898, p.17.

[6]Henry Wenston Barron's *A Few Notes on the Public Schools and Universities of Holland and Germany*, London, 1840, is particularly valuable for its detailed descriptions of schools and courses of study in the various regions of Germany.

[7]See certificate from the Carpenter's Guild in Berlin, dated March 30, 1840 (Lienau, "Memorabilia," p. 22), which states that Dettlef [*sic*] Linau has completed a three-year course of apprenticeship under Master Schultz from April 1837 to the present, that he has done excellent work and conducted himself well. A certificate from the Carpenter's Guild in Hamburg, dated October 4, 1841 (*ibid*, p. 23) asserts that, in the seventeen weeks that Detlef has worked as an apprentice, he has been faithful, hard-working, amiable, and honorable.

[8]It is interesting to note that the Avery Library's copy of this standard work, a gift of J. Henry Lienau, originally belonged to Detlef. He may have brought it to the United States with him, since the publication dates of both volumes predate his departure from Europe (Vol. I, *Mauerkunst*, 3rd edition, Berlin, 1841; Vol. II, *Zimmerwerk*, 2nd edition, Berlin, 1835).

[9]Cf. definitions of "Tischler" and "Zimmerman" in Muret-Sanders' *Encyclopëdisches Wörterbuch*, Berlin [1906?], with the meanings given to "Carpenter" in *Webster's New International Dictionary*, 1931 edition. See also *Obersicht über das Fortbildungeschulwesen und die gewerblich??n Unterrichssanstalten der Stadt Berlin*, Berlin, 1900, for courses respectively at the Fachschule für Mauerer und Zimmerer (pp. 145 ff.) and at the Berliner Tischlerschule (pp. 150 ff.).

[10]His testimony in the case of *Hunt vs. Parmly*, February 22, 1861, begins with the words, "I have been an architect for twenty-four years..." (*Architects' and Mechanics' Journal*, Vol. III [March 16, 1861], p. 233).

[11]For exact plate references, see my "Catalog of Student Drawings," p. 1.

[12]Barron's list of the topics covered in lectures on architecture at the Heidelberg School of Arts is particularly informative. In addition to

construction and planning, details such as locks, bolts, and hinges, as well as ornaments of all sorts, were discussed (pp. 80-81). He notes that the drawing classes copied these ornaments from pattern books.

[13]Published in Leipzig [1846?-1851?], the first section of the 1st edition appeared c.1818. The third part, published after Moller's death, was by Ernst Gladbach. Cf. Series II, Nos. 10, 25, 36, 37, and plate references in my "Catalog," pp. 2, 3, and 4.

[14]In general, see publications such as Nicolas Marie Joseph Chapuy's five-volume *Moyen-âge pittoresque*, Paris, 1837-1840, and his *Moyen-âge monumental et archeologique*, 3 vols., Paris, 1843; Sulpice Boisseree, *Monuments d'architecture du septième au treizième siècle... du Rhin inferieure*, Munich, 1842. Important monographs are Frenz Werner, *Der Dom zu Mainz*, 3 vols., Mainz, 1836, and Johann Geissel, *Der Kaiser-Dom zu Spayer*, 3 vols. Mainz, 1828, both cited in Jules Gailhabaud's *Monuments anciens et modernes*, Paris, 1865, Vol. III, unpaginated; Christian Wilhelm Schmidt, *Romische, byzantinische und germanische Baudenkmale in Trier...*, Trier, 1836-1845; Bernard Bundeshagen, *Kaiser Friedrichs I Barbarossa Palast in der Burg zu Gelnhausen...*, 2nd edition, [Mainz], 1819; Chapuy, *Vuss pittoresques de la cathedrale de Strasbourg*, Strasbourg, 1827.

[15]Stuttgart, 1872. For plate references, see my "Catalog," p. 2.

[16]Cf. Series II, Nos. 11-13, and Augustus [Charles] Pugin, *A Series of Ornamental Timber Gables...*, 2nd edition, London, 1839, plates 28, 30; Series II, No. 22, with *Gothic Ornaments...*, London, 1831, plates 62, No. 1.

[17]Four volumes, Nurnberg, 1838-1855. See numerous book reviews of works of this type in Franz Kugler's *Kleine Schriften und Studien zur Kunstgeschichte*, 3 vols., Stuttgart, 1853-1854, *e.g.*. Heinrich A??us, *Hsue Ornamente Musterblatter für Architekten, Fabrikanten, Bauhandwerker und Kunstler...*, Berlin, [1845?] (*ibid.*, III, pp. 427-428).

[18]See certificate of Lienau, "Memorabilia," p. 24.

[19]See F. Sander, "Baugewerksschulen," *Lexikon der Pedagogik*, Breslau, 1889, p.45. Described as continuation schools for workers in the building trades who had had some years of trade experience, the first of these schools was founded in 1831 in Holzmindern, Brunswick, and was soon followed by others elsewhere in Germany. For further information on the type of program in these schools, I am indebted to Professor Paul Zucker, interview on March 30, 1953.

[20]*E.g.*, H. Haberlin's project of 1828 in Architekten- und Ingenieur-verein, *Architektonische Entwurfe...*, Potsdam, 1837-1842, plate 4.

[21]*E.g.*, Stuler and Strack's railway station in *Architektonisches Album* [bound together with *ibid.*], Potsdam, 1838-1846, Heft I (1838), plate 9; *Architektonisches Skizzen-buch*, Vol. I (1855), *passim; Zeitschrift für Bauwesen*, Vol. II (1852), plate 82; *Allgemeine Bauzeitung*, Vol. VIII (1843), *passim*, and other volumes of the '40s.

[22]*Die Holzarchitektur der Schweiz*, Zurich, 1876. See also rural buildings in C.F. de Wiebeking's important seven-volume work, *Architecture civile theorique et pratique...*, Munich, 1827-1831, *e.g.* Vol. V, plates between pp. 122-125.

Perhaps the most charming publication of this type is Graffenried & Sturler's *Schweizerische Architektur*, Bern, 1844.

[23]Series II, Nos. 23, 45. Cf. Wiebeking, VIII, pp. 94 ff., and J. Ch. Krafft, *Traite sur l'art de la charpente...*, 2nd edition, Paris, 1820.

[24]Series V, *Krankenhaus für eine Stadt von 10 bis 12000 Einwohner.*

[25]Refers to page in original dissertation.

[26]This certificate states that Lienau had received third prize in design out of a class of 157 students and makes special mention of his talent in design and woodcarving.

[27]Henry-Russell Hitchcock, letter of June 25, 1954. Lienau's project is close in style to a hospital and retirement home in Kempten, published the same year in *Allgemeine Bauzeitung*, Vol. VII (1842), plate CDLVXXV.

[28]See, however, Talbot Hamlin's sympathetic discussion in *Architecture Through the Ages*, revised edition, New York, 1953, pp. 551 ff. A comprehensive well illustrated account is David Joseph's *Geschichte der Baukunst des XIX Jahrhunderts*, Vol. III[1]: *Geschichte der Baukunst von Altertum bis zur Neuzeit*, Berlin [1902-1909]. Fritz Schumaker's *Stromungen in der deutscher Baukunst seit 1800*, Leipzig [1935], is probably the best modern survey.

[29]Hans Vogel, *Deutsche Bankunst des Klassizismus*, Berlin, 1937, deals at length with this question.

[30]Schumaker (p. 20 and *passim*) puts great emphasis upon the tendency towards *Sechlichkeit* in German architecture of the period. See also Karl Heinz Clasen, "Schinkel und die Tradition," Berlin, Deutsche Bauakademie, *Über Karl Friedrich Schinkel*, Berlin, 1951, pp. 42 ff.; Nicolaus Pevsner, "Schinkel," *RIBA Journal*, Vol. LIX (January 1952), p. 94; Brune Taut, *Modern Architecture*, London, 1929, pp. 35-36.

[31]Pevsner, *ibid.*, p. 95.

[32]Kugler's essay, "Karl Friedrich Schinkel," written a year after the architect's death, already makes this point (*Kleine Schriftan*, III, p. 340).

[33]Schinkel's early interest in Italian brick architecture was strengthened by his later visits to North Germany, Holland, and England, where in 1826 he saw the new architecture of the English industrial towns. For the latter, see Ettlinger's article in *Architectural Review*, Vol. XCVII (1945), cited by Pevsner, *RIBA Journal*, Vol. LIX (January 1952), p. 94. In turn, Schinkel's work in brick greatly impressed a visiting Englishman—and must have been admired by Lienau also—see W. Howitt, *The Rural and Domestic Life of Germany*, London, 1842, p. 433, cited by Carl von Lorck, *Karl Friedrich Schinkel*, Berlin, 1939, pp. 72-73. Schinkel's Bauakademie was published immediately in *Allgemeine Bauzeitung*, Vol. I (1836), plates I ff. Other architects in Berlin began to use brick, particularly for commercial work, *e.g.*, G. Stier's fine warehouse of 1837, *Architectural Album*, Heft V (1840), p. 6 and plates XXVIII-XXIX. For Schinkel's brick architecture, see August Grisebach, *Carl Friedrich Schinkel*, Leipzig, 1924, Figs. 80-87.

[34]*E.g.*, sugar refineries erected for the Matthiessen-Weichers and New Jersey Sugar Refining Companies, Jersey City, 1862 ff., St. Mary's Hall, Burlington, NJ, etc. The most comprehensive and best illustrated book on

North German brickwork tradition is Otto Stiehl's *Backsteinbauten in Norddeutschland und Danemark*, Stuttgart [1923].

[35]Refers to page in original dissertation.

[36]Schinkel, *Aus Schinkel's Nachlass; Reisetagebuchner, Briefe und Aphorismen*, edited by Alfred von Wolzogen, 4 vols., Berlin, 1862-1864.

[37]The most concise statement of Schinkel's ideas is contained in a letter of 1834 to Crown Prince Maximilian of Bavaria, cited in *ibid.*, III, p. 333: "... dass das Ideal in der Baukunst nur dann vollig erreicht ist, wenn ein Gebaude seinem Zwecke in allen Theilen und im Genzen in geistigenund physicher Rucksicht vollkommen entspricht." A favorite Schinkel aphorism was "die Kunst ist nichts, wenn sie nicht neu ist" (quoted in Moeller van der Bruck, *Der Preussische Stil*, new edition, Munchen, 1922, p. 179). For discussions of Schinkel's theory, see Clasen, *Über... Schinkel, passim;* Pevsner, *RIBA Journal*, Vol. LIX, p. 94; Leopold Ettlinger, *Gottfried Semper und die Antike...* (Bleicherode am Harz, 1937), *passim*.

[38]For Persius' work in Potsdam, see *Arch. Entwurfe* (1843-1845), bound with earlier issues of this important publication. Valuable modern works dealing with Potsdam and Berlin are Burkhard Meier's *Potsdam, Palaces and Gardens...*, 4th edition, Berlin: Deutscher Kunstverlag, 1930, Otto Zieler's *Potsdam, ein Stadtbild des 18. Jahrhunderts*. Bd. I: *Stadtarchitektur*, Berlin: Weiss, 1913, and most particularly the series issued by the Preussische Akademie des Beuwesens, Berlin, *Schinkel Ausshus. Karl Friedrich Schinkel* [Schriftleitung von Paul Ortwin Rave, Berlin, Akademie des Beuwesens, [1939], of which 8 volumes have appeared so far. The last were issued under a different title: *Karl Friedrich Schinkel: Lebenswerk*. For individual volumes, see under Hans Kania, Gunther Grundmann, Johannes Sievers, P.O. Rave, J. Sievers, Hans Vogel, and J. Sievers, the authors respectively of [Bd. 1, 2, 4, T. 2-3, 5, 6, 7, and 8].

[39]*Allgemeine Bauzeitung.*, Vol. IV (1839), plates CCXCII ff.; Carl Schellenberg's small, but well illustrated book, *Das alte Hamburg*, Leipzig, 1936, Fig. 116; Joseph, III[1], Fig. 107.

[40]See the wonderful series of lithographs in *Hamburg. Heubau: Sa??lung Facaden der Gebaude an den neugebauten Strassen...*, Hamburg [1844-1848].

[41]Vol. XII (1847), plates 80, 81, 91, 92, etc. De Chateauneuf's work is discussed most enthusiastically by Schumaker, pp. 51-53.

[42]Barron, p. 66.

[43]See *e.g.*, Karl Mollinger, *Elemente des Rundbogenstiles...*, Munshen, 1845-1847, and the great interest in French and German Romanesque church architecture, evidenced by publication in journals, such as *Allgemaine Bauzeitung.*, Vol. X (1845), *passim*, etc. For further details on the development of the *Rundbogenstil*, see Carroll L.V. Meeks, "Romanesque before Richardson in the United States," *Art Bulletin*, Vol. XXXV (March 1953), p. 21 and n. 18.

[44]Refers to page in original dissertation.

[45]Series II, Nos. 7, 8. No. 8 evidently represents the old synagogue in Munich, rebuilt in the mid-'80s according to Bayerischer Architekten- und Ingenieurversin, Munich, *Munchen und seine Beuten*, Munchen, 1912, p. 228.

[46]Kugler, "Kunstreise im Jahre 1845," *Kleine Schriften*, III, pp. 517 ff.

[47]See his descriptions of Beaux-Arts training, *ibid.*, III, pp. 432-33, and *passim*.

[48]Felix Pigeory (1813-73) lamented the timidity of the architects of the period and repeatedly attacked the constant use of the classical style without regard to function in buildings of the preceding generation, as Brongniart's Stock Exchange and the Madeleine (*Les monuments de Paris; histoire de l'architecture... sous le regne du roi Louis Philippe*, Paris, 1847, pp. 271-272 and 128 ff.). For illustrations, see Pierre Gourlier *et al.*, *Choix d'edifices publics projêtes et construits en France depuis le commencement du XIXe siècle*, 3 vols., Paris, 1825-1850. The most recent survey is Louis Hautecoeur's *La restauration et le gouvernement de juillet*, 1815-1848, Vol. VI: *Histoire de l'architecture classique en France*, Paris, 1943-1957.

[49]See Hautecoeur's discussion of "Le rationalisme classique" (Vol. VI, pp. 238-253) and especially the excellent résumé of the revolt of both romantics and rationalists by Cesar Daly, "Discours prononce sur la tombe de Felix Duben...," le 7 octobre 1871, reprinted in *Souvenirs d'Henri Labrouste. Notes recueillies et classées par ses enfants*, Fontainebleau, 1928, pp. 40-41. I am greatly indebted to James C. Palmes, Librarian, RIBA, for his kindness in forwarding to me from London this small booklet, which provided information on Labrouste not available here; a photostatic copy is now on deposit at the Avery Library. See also Adolphe Lance on the transitional role of Elouet in preparing the way ("Les professeurs s'en vont," 1856 in *ibid.*, pp. 35-36) and Lucien Magne, *l'Architecture française du siècle*, Paris, 1890, pp. 20 ff.

[50]Neo-Grec is one of those amorphous terms that is difficult to define. According to Alexandre Sandier, the term was first used in France after 1860 ("Neo-Grec," in Russel Sturgis' *Dictionary of Architecture and Building*, New York, 1901-1902, Vol. II, col. 1025). Perhaps the best general definition of the mode is that offered by the *Encyclopedia Britannica*, 14th edition, 1929, Vol. XVI, p. 213:

> "Neo-Grec, in architecture and applied arts, is a style developed in the second quarter of the 19th century in France, in which an attempt was made to instill into generally classic design a spirit at once modern, original and yet full of restraint, delicacy and perfection of Greek details. It was largely the result of the efforts of three men—J. Duban, H. Labrouste and L. Duc. It found its most complete expression in Paris, especially in the Colonne de Juillet (1831-1840) by Duc; the library of S. Geneviève (1843-1850) by Labrouste; the Ecole des Beaux-Arts (1820-1839) by Duban; the west wing of the Palais de Justice (1857-1868) by Duc. The style is important less for these complete works, than for its tremendously widespread influence throughout the middle of the 19th century, not only in Europe, but also in America. Its chief characteristics are modified orders; imaginatively modernized classic detail; much use of simple,

flat surfaces, often with chamfered edges; pediment forms without horizontal cornices; and delicate, refined, incised ornament."

[51]Objections to the term were raised early. Charles Garnier, after paying tribute to Duban, Labrouste, and Duc, specifically made the point that the only thing Greek about the style was its name (*A travers les arts* [1869], cited in *Souvenirs*, pp. 47-48). Later, J. Gaudet also made strenuous objections to the term in an article in *L'Architecture* (1890), quoted in *ibid.*, p. 38.

[52]*E.g.*, Magne, p. 22; the section entitled "Ecole rationaliste ou logicienne," *Souvenirs*, pp. 40-51; Hautecouer's terminology.

[53]See the sarcastic editorial commentary on the program given out by Louis Pierre Baltard (1764-1846) at the Ecole for a parochial school—in classical style, *bien entendu*—and its outrageous specifications ("Enseignement de l'architecture à L'Ecole des Beaux-Arts," *Revue générale de l'architecture*, Vol. II [1841], cols. 634-639). Subsequently, Daly reported with incredulity that a course on the architecture of the Middle Ages would be introduced at the Beaux-Arts (*ibid.*, Vol. IV [1843], col. 96). For further details on the battle between classicists and gothicists, see Hautecoeur, Vol. VI, pp. 332 ff., and pp. 336-341, on the role of Viollet-le-Duc and Lassus following the pitched battle conducted by Daly in the *Revue générale* in 1846.

[54]Daly, *ibid.*, Vol. II (1841), cols. 466 ff.

[55]For a full account of this battle, see Henry Lapauze, *Histoire de l'Academie de France à Rome*, Paris, 1924, Vol. II, pp. 190-200, in which the correspondence of Vernet and Quatremere is given in full.

[56]See Hautecoeur, Vol. VI, pp. 239-240, on the beginnings of the Labrouste *atelier* and his role as the leader of the reform party, which after the Revolution of 1830, tried to introduce desirable changes in architectural training.

[57]Lienau was in Munich at least until the end of March 1842. He was in Paris in May, as is documented by two signed drawings. (Series IV, Nos. 19, 52), dated respectively "mai 42" and "9 mai 42". No. 52, as well as others executed subsequently, was definitely connected with assignments given out by Labrouste to his pupils. See Appendix I.

[58]Series V, three drawings connected with work for Waldmann & Conrad at St.-Denis. Note the appearance of the acute accent in the signature, an indication that Lienau had become quite assimilated to French ways.

[59]Vol. I (1840), cols. 58-60. Viollet-le-Duc came back to this point years later in his article on "Construction," *Dictionaire raisonne de l'architecture du XI au XVIe siècle*, Paris, 1854-1868, Vol. IV, p. 1.

[60]Translated from *Souvenirs*, p. 29.

[61]*Ibid*, p. 24. The following, a translation of the second and third paragraphs, differs in minor respects from that of Sigfried Giedion in *Space, Time and Architecture*, 3rd edition (revised and enlarged), Cambridge, Mass., 1954, pp. 217-218:

> I have devised a few programs of study to drill beginners in something useful. I want to teach them to compose by very simple means. First of all, they

must see clearly the destination of their work so that they may arrange the parts according to the importance which can be reasonably given them. Then I explain to them that solidity depends more on the way materials are put together than upon their mass and, as soon as they are acquainted with the first principles of construction. I tell them that they must derive from the construction itself an ornament which is reasonable and expressive.

I often repeat to them that the arts have the power of making everything beautiful. But I insist that they understand that in architecture, *form must always be appropriate to the function for which it is intended*."

See also Vandoyer's aims expressed in a letter to his cousin Le Bas, quoted in *L'Art en Europe et en Amerique au XIXe siècle et au debut du XXe*, Vol. VIII, Part 1; André Michel (editor), *Histoire de l'art*, Paris [1905-1929], p. 31; Hautecoeur, VI, pp. 263-264. Edward Robert De Zurko points out that Labrouste's functionalism was the logical development of (1) the rationalist functionalism of Cordemoy and Laugier, (2) the *architecture parlante* functionalism of Boullee and Ledoux, and (3) the efficient functionalism of Durand, to whose point of view he probably was closest (letter of July 16, 1954). See also De Zurko's "Functionalist Trends in Writings Pertaining to Architecture...," unpublished, Ph.D. dissertation, Institute of Fine Arts, New York University, 1954, and *Origins of Functionalist Theory*, New York, 1957.

[62]See Henri Delaborde's excellent article, "La vie et les ouvrages de Henri Labrouste," Notice lue à l'Academie des Beaux-Arts, le 19 october 1878, *Encyclopedie d'architecture*, Vol. VII (1878), pp. 83, 87; Daly, "Henri Labrouste," *Revue générale de l'architecture*, Vol. XXXIV [1877], col. 63; Julien Gaudet, "Notice sur la vie et les oeuvres de M. André" (1890), quoted in *Souvenirs*, p. 34.

[63]Jean Baptiste Antoine Lessus, *Album de Villard de Honnecourt*, Paris, 1858, foreword.

[64]*E.g.*, Giedion, pp. 218-219; *Souvenirs*, pp. 61-67. Giedion characterized Labrouste as "without a doubt the architect of the middle of the 19th century whose work possessed the most significance for the future" (p. 225). A new structural concept, in which stability is recognized as no longer dependent on mass, is clearly stated in Labrouste's letter cited above, p.22.

[65]Delacorte, *Encyclopedie d'architecture*, Vol. VII, p. 86. For a survey of the uses to which iron had been put previously in France, see Jean Rondelet, *Traite theorique et pratique de l'art de batir*, 8th edition, Paris, 1838, III, Livre VII, pp. 279-344. A fine reproduction of Labrouste's perspective rendering of the façade was published in *Revue générale de l'architecture*, Vol. XI (1853), plate 31. See also *Allgemaine Bauzeitung*, Vol. XVII (1852), plates 469-475, and *Ballou's*, Vol. II (1852), p. 412.

[66]Series IV, Nos. 50 and 55, discussed in my "Catalog," pp. 13-14.

[67]Series II, Nos. 27, 28, 33, 34, and 71-73. See last three, mostly studies of iron roof trusses (Theatre des Nouveautes, Hittorf and Lecointe's Theatre de l'Ambigu Comique, etc.), which are especially interesting for their early structural use of iron. Cf. Hautecoeur, Vol. VI, Figs. 72-74.

[68]*Revue générale de l'architecture*, Vol. XI (1853), plate 32; general view in Hautecoeur, Vol. VI, Fig. 212.

[69]Lienau, "Biography, Memorabilia," p. 3; Montgomery Schuyler, "Henri Janeway Hardenbergh," *Architectural Record*, Vol. VI (January-March 1897), p. 335; Sedakichi Hartman, "A Conversation with Henry Janeway Hardenbergh," *ibid*, Vol. XIX (May 1906), p. 378.

[70]Antoine Desgodetz, *Les edifices antiques de Rome...*, Carlo Fea, editor of work first published in 1682, Roma, 1822; M.P. Gauthier, *Les plus beaux edifices de la ville de Genes...*, Paris, 1830-1832; A. Grandjean de Montiguy et A. Famin, *Architecture toscane...*, Paris, 1815; Paul Marie Latarouilly, *Edifices de Rome moderne...*, Paris, 1840; Charles Percier et P.F.L. Fontaine, *Palais maisons et autres edifices modernes dessines a Rome*, Paris, 1798; F.L. Sehault, *Recueil d'architecture...*, Paris, 1821; P.T. Suys et L.P. Haudebourt, *Palais Massimi a Rome*, Paris, 1818.

[71]Livre III: *Restaurations des monuments antiques par less architectes pensionnaires de l'Academie de France a Rome*, Paris, 1877-1890. Cf. Series III, No. 7, with Labrouste's plate II.

[72]Series IV, Nos. 5, 8, 9, 10, 15, 16, 17, 19, 21, and 52.

[73]Series IV, Nos. 19 and 52.

[74]Delaborde, *Encyclopedie d'architecture*, Vol. VII, pp. 83 and 85; Eugene Millet, "Notice sur la vie et les ouvrages de Labrouste," lue à l'Assemblée générale de la Societé [centrale des architectes], le 26 octobre 1876, quoted in *Souvenirs*, p. 25.

[75]Delaborde, *Encyclopedie d'architecture*, Vol. VII, p. 85; Millet, quoted in *Souvenirs*, p. 16. For assistance in identifying the Etruscan subjects of the Lienau drawings (Series IV, Nos. 35-38), in which their appearance at the time of discovery may be studied, I am indebted to Professor Luisa Banti of the University of Florence, Visiting Professor of Fine Arts and Archeology, Bernard College, 1953-1954.

[76]Cf. Series IV, Nos. 8, 9, and 9a, and Gailhabaud, Vol. II, plates II, IV, I, and III respectively.

[77]I learned of this exhibition through J. Renoult, Curator, Bibliotheque Mazarine (letters of February 25 and March 12, 1954) and Madame Bouleau-Rabaud, Curator, Bibliotheque de L'Ecole des Beaux-Arts, Paris (letter of March 1, 1954), to whom I had written for information regarding the possible survival of Labrouste drawings.

[78]Paris, 1953. My thanks go to Jean Vallery-Redot, Curator of Prints, Bibliotheque Nationale, for forwarding this catalog to me and for his letters of April and June 4, 1954. His introduction, which includes a useful bibliography, "Henri Labrouste, 1801-1875," is followed by a three-part catalog by M. Weigert: (1) "La carriere et les oeuvres..."; (2) "Souvenirs divers..."; (3) "Inventaire des dessins d'architecture de l'antiquite à l'epoque moderne executes par Henri Labrouste en Italie (1825-1830)."

[79]Cf. Series IV, Nos. 36 and 53 and plates III and V in *ibid*.

[80]For details, see Appendix I and my "Catalog," *passim*.

[81]Series IV, No. 21. See also Nos. 10, 12, and 13 as evidence of the growing interest in Islamic, as well as Byzantine, art, reflected in the superb publications of the 1830s and '40s, *e.g.*, J.J. [*sic*] Hittorf et L. Zenth, *Architecture moderne de la Sicile...*, Paris, 1835; Philibert Joseph Girault de Prangey, *Monuments arabes et moresques de Cordone, Seville et Grenada*, Paris [1836-1839]; Domenico lo Faso Pietrasanta, duca di Serradifalco, *Del duomo di Monreale et di altre chiese siculo normanne...*, Palermo, 1838; Henry Gally Knight, *Saracenic & Norman Remains...*, London [1840]; Jules Goury and Owen Jones, *Plans... of the Alhambra...*, 2 vols., London, 1842-1845.

[82]Dates based on earliest dated drawing, surely copied from Labrouste, Series IV, No. 52, and watermarked date (1846) on Whatman paper of No. 15, Series III.

[83]*E.g.*, Series IV, Nos. 7, 11, 50, etc.

[84]Reference is made by several writers to the wise mixture of reform and traditional elements in Labrouste's teaching, *e.g.* Rapine, "Notice necrologique sur M. Juste Lisch," 1910, in *Souvenirs*, p. 32; Daly, *Revue générale de l'architecture*, Vol. XXXIV, col. 61. A deserved emphasis on traditional elements in the work of Labrouste and his circle has appeared in recent modern criticism, *e.g.*, Hautecour, VII, pp. 133-134. This final volume of the series, *Le fin de l'architecture classique, 1848-1900*, Paris, 1957, was very kindly lent to me by Professor Hitchcock, since it is not yet available here.

[85]Daly, "La bibliotheque Sainte-Genéviève," *Revue générale de l'architecture*, Vol. X (1852), cols. 380-381.

[86]From an undated letter regarding annual awards to students, addressed in all probability to Juste Lisch, cited in *Souvenirs*, p. 39. Below is an English translation:

> We want to encourage studies of past works, like the resurrection of ancient monuments and restoration of the buildings of our own country; but in my opinion we should concentrate more on projects of a general interest, with contemporary inspirations and proposals for the future. It is regrettable to me to see architects, despite strong educations, resign themselves to borrowing forms which were invented, with reason, of course, for other periods; and restrained to seek for themselves creative solutions that actually respond to our needs, our manners, and our artistic sensibilities.

[87]*Entretiens sur l'architecture*, Paris, 1863-1872, II, pp. 167-168.

[88]2nd edition, Paris, 1907, pp. 157, 366, 403, and 311 respectively.

[89]Series II, Nos. 41 and 62. Gaspard George later became an important architect and writer: See Delaire, p. 273, and E.L.G. Charvet, *Lyon artistique...*, Lyon, 1899, p. 169.

[90]Series II, Nos. 62 and 63. For Jean Baptiste Vanginot, see Delaire, p. 419.

[91]Letters dated March 8 and April 4, 1865, to Lienau, "Biography, Memorabilia," pp. 14-15.

[92]Series IV, Nos. 46 and 47.

[93]Kugler, III, p. 432.

[94]Letter of December 14, 1951. This undoubtedly was the Dien engraving of the pencil portrait of Labrouste made by Ingres at the special

request of Labrouste's students in 1852. A copy was sent to almost all of his former students.

[95]Pages 25-26. A number of pamphlets dealing with the French railways by [Pierre A.] Adolphe Jullien are listed in *Catalogue générale des livres imprimes de la Bibliotheque Nationale*, Vol. 79, cols. 968-969.

[96]Lienau, "Biography, Memorabilia," p. 27.

[97]Queyron is listed by Daly (*Revue générale de l'architecture*, Vol. XXXIV, col. 61) as a student of Labrouste's. For illustrations of Langlais' work, see Pierre Chabat, *Batiments des chemins de fer...*, 2 vols., Paris, 1862-1866, *passim*.

[98]Leonce Reynaud stresses this point particularly in his *Traite d'architecture*, Paris, Vol. II (2nd edition, 1863), p. 459.

[99]Talbot Hamlin's exhibition, "The Architecture of Railroads" (Avery Library, January 1939), was a pioneer enquiry into this field, which has been so brilliantly covered by Carroll Meeks in *The Railroad Station: An Architectural History*, New Haven, 1956.

[100]For the Gare du Nord I and Gare de l'Est, see *ibid.*, Figs. 47, 48, and 50.

[101]Since the sources of information regarding Cendrier are widely scattered, the following references, used in conjunction with the illustrative material cited below, may be helpful: Bauchal, *Nouveau dictionnaire... des architectes français*, Paris, 1887, p. 620; Brault, III, 60; Delaire, p. 207; Thieme-Becker, III, 61.

[102]G. Abel Blouet, *Supplement* to Rondelet's *L'Art de Batir*, Paris, 1868, I, p. 50. For the Paris station, see *ibid.*, plates XV, XVI, and especially "Vues panoramique du chemin de fer de Paris à Orleans," The William Barclay Parson Railroad Prints, Special Collections, Columbia University, No. 1 (Paris station), No. 2 (Orleans), No. 3 (14th print, Paris shed). See also James Kip Finch and Talbot Faulkner Hamlin, *The William Barclay Parsons Railroad Prints*, [New York], 1935.

[103]Daly, "L'Architecture des chemins de fer. Gare de Paris...," *Revue générale de l'architecture*, Vol. XVII (1859), cols. 27-33, plates 12-22, and Reynaud, Vol. I (3rd edition, 1867), plate 84, Figs. 1-5.

[104]Chabat, I, p. 8 and plate 20.

[105]Daly, "L'Architecture des chemins de fer. Gare de Lyon...," *Revue générale de l'architecture*, Vol. XVIII (1860), cols. 130-132, plates 16-26; *Allgemaine Bauzeitung*, Vol. XXIV (1859), plate 243.

[106]See Appendix II.

[107]Series V, sheet of studies for Altona Hospital.

[108]This program, deeply affected by Socialist doctrines of 1848, called for a good deal of public construction. New bathing establishments were first on the agendum according to Daly (see his review of architectural accomplishments in France since 1830, *Revue générale de l'architecture*, Vol. XVIII [1860], 3). Cf. also bathing establishments in Germany: *e.g.* Architekten und Ingenieur-Verein zu Hamburg, *Hamburg und Seine Bauten...* (Hamburg: Selbstverlag, 1890), chapter xiii, pp. 214-230.

[109]Series V, sheet of undated studies.

[110]*Altonaer Mercur*, No. 160, p. 738, col. 1. For information pertaining to the competition, the subsequent history of the building, and photographs, thanks are due to J. Gierlinger, Municipal Archives, Hamburg (letters of December 6, 1952, and February 23, 1957).

[111]Refers to page in original dissertation.

[112]See lists in Henry C. Burdett, *Hospitals and Asylums of the World*, London, 1891-1893, III, p. 187, including Bethanien Hospital (1847), Berlin, Hamburg General (1823 plus wings of 1848), and Bremen General (1850).

[113]For a succinct, well illustrated discussion of hospitals both in England and on the continent, see F. Oppert, *Hospitals, Infirmaries, and Dispensaries...*, London, 1867. The corridor type continued in use throughout the fifth decade of the century in Germany until the publication of Oppert's *Die Einrichtung von Krankenhausern...*, Berlin, 1859, cited in Armand Husson's monumental study, *Etude sur les hopitaux...*, Paris, 1862, p. 403, n. 1. The change to pavilion planning in Germany came with Ludwig Degen's recommendations in *Der Bau der Krankenhauser...*, Munchen, 1862, p. 190.

[114]Begun in 1846 according to plans by Martin Pierre Gauthier (1789-1855), Lariboisiere was the first large hospital to put into practice the revolutionary recommendations of the Commission of the French Academy of Sciences made in 1786 and 1788 (see Husson, Appendix III, pp. 347 ff.; *Allgemaine Bauzeitung*, Vol. XXIII (1858), plates 182-184). Other early hospitals with progressive planning features were those in Bordeaux (Gourlier, Vol. I, plates 105-108 [5-54], and St.-Jean in Brussels.

[115]Th[eodor] Stein, *Das Krankenhaus der Diakonissen Ansttalt Bethanien zu Berlin*, Berlin, 1850, plate II. Begun by Stein under Persius' supervision, the design was completed after the latter's death (1845) with the help of Stuler and Romer. See also Ludwig Rellstab, *Berlin und seinenachsyen Umgebungen...*, Darmstadt, 1852, pp. 163-167.

[116]*Hamburg und seine Bauten*, pp. 249-250. For other examples of his work, see, *e.g., ibid.*, p. 631; Architekten- und Ingenieur-Verein, Hamburg, *Hamburg's Privatbauten*, Hamburg, 1877, plate XLIX.

[117]Refers to page in original dissertation.

[118]III, pp. 429-430.

[119]Lienau, p. 3, and letter of December 14, 1951.

[120]For immigration statistics for the port of New York at this period, see Ernst, Appendix II, Table 9. Compared to the 50,000 to 100,000 arriving from Ireland and Germany, very few emigrated from Denmark: 95 in 1847, 52 in 1848, 159 in 1849. Cf. also figures in Edward Young, *Special Report on Immigration*, Washington, 1872, Table No. 1, pp xii ff.; U.S. Treasury Department, *Tables Showing Arrivals of Alien Passengers and Immigrants... 1820 to 1880*, Washington, 1889, p. 16. The standard work on German immigration, which will be referred to again, is still Albert Bernhardt Faust's *The German Element in the United States...*, new edition, 2 vols., New York, 1927.

[121]*E.g.*, Traugott Bromme, *Neuestes vollstandiges Hand- und Reisebuch für Auswanderer...*, 3rd edition, Bayreuth, 1846, pp. 319-320; Charles Norton, *Dar treue Fuhrer des Auswanderers...*, 2nd edition, Regensburg, 1848, p. 11.

[122]See seal on Lienau's passport in Lienau, p. 31a.

[123]Advice on ports of embarkation, optimum time of the year for emigrating to the States, etc., were always included in the German guide books. One of the best is Georg Treu's *Das Buch der Auswandererung...*, Bamberg, 1848, which contains reprints of the informative booklets issued by the Deutscher Gesellschaft und Volksverein, with which Leinau was doubtless familiar: *Bekanntmachnung der deutschen Gesellschaft zum Schutze deutscher Auswanderer nach Amerika* (pp. 83-118). On the excellent work of this organization, of which Lienau became a member in 1854, see Christof Vetter, *Zwee Jahre in New York...*, Hof: Selbstverlag, 1849, pp. 41-45, and Alexander Ziegler, *Skizzen einer Reise nach Nordamerika und Westindian...*, Dresden, 1848, I, pp. 24-25. Many of these guide books make fascinating reading.

[124]Robert Greenlalgh Albion's *The Rise of New York Port (1815-1860)*, New York, 1939, the authoritative work on this topic, contains much information on commercial activities in general and an extensive bibliography, both of which were extremely useful.

The tremendous excitement and great hopes for the future engendered by the new age of speed is reflected in a wonderful passage in J[ohn] C. Myer's *Sketches on a Tour through the Northern and Eastern States, the Canadas & Nova Scotia*, Harrisonburg, 1849, pp. 426-427 and "Steam-Bridge Across the Atlantic," *Harper's New Monthly Magazine*, Vol. I (August 1850), p. 412. On the intense rivalry between the American Collins Line and the British Cunarders, see "The Editor's Easy Chair," *ibid*, Vol. VII (September 1853), p. 577, and *The Diary of Philip Hone, 1828-1851*, edited by Allan Nevins, new and enlarged edition, New York, 1936, pp. 915, 928, entries of June 10 and November 14, 1850. The *Hone Diary* is one of the best sources for New York in the second quarter of the 19th century.

[125]Since passenger lists for the two vessels (Brig Celeritas and Bark Edinburg) on which Lienau could conceivably have sailed are lost (see marine lists, *Shipping and Commercial List*, Vol. XXIV [October-December] 1848, and letters of August 25 and December 2, 1954, from N. Neil Franklin, Chief, General Reference Section, National Archives and Records Service, Washington, D.C.), the *Evening Post* notice ("Marine Intelligence," p. 3, col. 3) was a lucky find.

[126]According to Talbot Hamlin, recalling a conversation with J. Henry Lienau.

[127]For information concerning this Marcotte (1822-1885), see Delaire, p. 339, and Daly, *Revue générale de l'architecture*, Vol. XXXIV, col. 61, n. 2.

Chapter II

[1]For a picture of the city at about the time Lienau arrived here, see Henry Hoff's remarkable series of lithographs, *Views of New York* (1850),

Eno Collection of New York City Views, Nos. 252-270, Print Room, New York Public Library. Nos. 252 and 274 are particularly fine views of the harbor. Other views of New York, in some cases duplicates of those in the *Eno Collection*, may be found in the *Stokes Collection, American Historical Prints, Early Views of American Cities*, also at the New York Public Library. Convenient sources for illustrations of New York material are at the New York Public Library, *American Historical Prints...* by Daniel C. Haskell, New York, 1933; I[saac] N[ewton] Phelps Stoke's monumental six-volume work, *The Iconography of Manhattan Island, 1649-1909*, New York, 1915-1929, especially Vol. III; John Atlee Kouwenhoven, *The Columbia Historical Portrait of New York...* [1st edition], Garden City, NY, 1953.

[2]See N. Currier's color lithograph, "City of New York from Jersey City," 1849, *Eno Collection*, No. 235.

[3]My information is derived chiefly from a copy of his obituary, dated February 27, 1893, clipped from an unidentified newspaper, kindly given to me by Talbot Hamlin.

[4]Refers to page in original dissertation.

[5]These directories, published by Longworth, J. Doggett, H. Wilson, C.R. Rode, J.F. Trow, and later by Goulding, have been an invaluable source of information for this study. Microfilm copies are available in the General Reading Room, New York Public Library.

[6]He was sole agent in the States for a number of French wine export firms: see Michael Lienau's advertisements in the *Shipping and Commercial List*, Vol. XXXIV (November 11, 1848), p. 364, col. 4, and subsequent issues. It appears from other ads (*ibid., passim*), that he also dealt in commodities of such varied character as spelter and sardines!

[7]He was listed in Reuben Vose, *The Rich Men of New York*, New York, 1861, Series 4, No. 2, as having an income of $100,000 yearly. One of his early business associates was H.G. Eilshemius, father of the artist Louis Michael Eilshemius (1864-1941).

[8]See Appendix II.

[9]On the great success of German merchants in New York, see Karl Quentin's excellent study, *Reisebilder und Studien aus dem Norden der Vereinigten Staaten...*, Arnsberg, 1851, I, pp. 8-11; Faust, *passim*.

[10][Joseph A. Scoville], *The Old Merchants of New York City*, by Walter Barrett, clerk [pseudonym], New York, 1863, I, p. 158.

[11]Refers to page in original dissertation.

[12]W. Jay Mills, *Historic Houses of New Jersey*, Philadelphia, 1902, opposite p. 28.

[13]He was so listed in *Doggett's... Directory*, 1849/1850.

[14]See N. Reiss, *Excursion a New-York, en 1850*, Bruxelles, 1851, *passim*, an interesting account by a Belgian doctor; Ernst, *passim*.

[15]Fig. 11 reproduces only one plate of *The Ultimate Pictorial Directory of New York*, New York, 1848, No. 1, plate 6, *Eno Collection*, No. 222. Nos. 2, 3, and 4 of this valuable series are known as *Jones and Newman's Pictorial Directory...* and are available in the Reserve Room, New York Public Library.

The aim of the editors, who hoped to continue the series—which actually only illustrates Broadway from the Battery to Pearl Street—was to provide "a literal Picture of the Western Emporium of Commerce in the noon of the 19th century."

[16]While similarities in the general appearance of New York in the late 1840s and very early '50s to British towns was noted by many (*e.g.*, Robert Playfair, *Recollections of a Visit to the United States... 1847, 1848, and 1849*, Edinburgh, 1856, p. 19; Moritz Wagner and Karl Scherzer, *Reisen in Nordamerika... in 1852 and 1853*, Leipzig, 1854, I, p. 239), not a few found that these comparisons were greatly exaggerated. Robert Baird dismissed these claims as "pure nonsense" in *Impressions and Experiences of the West Indies and North America in 1849*, [Philadelphia, 1850], p. 264.

[17]See comments by Cooper to his wife, letter of November 22, 1850, in James Fenimore Cooper (editor), *Correspondence of James Fenimore Cooper*, New Haven, 1922, II, p. 693.

[18]Refers to page in original dissertation.

[19]Myers, *Tour through the... States*, pp. 50-51. The last sentence of this quotation echoes Walt Whitman's opening paragraph in an article entitled "Tear Down and Build Over Again," *American Review*, Vol. II (November 1845), pp. 536-538, reprinted in Emory Holloway, *The Uncollected Poetry and Prose of Walt Whitman...*, Garden City, NY, 1921, p. 92:

> "He who at some future time shall take upon himself the office of writing the early history of what was done in America and of how the American character was started, formed and finished... will surely have much cause to mention what may be called 'the pull-down-and-build-over-again-spirit'."

[20]*E.g.*, Dr. A.R. Thummel, *Die Natur und das Leben in den Vereinigten Staaten...*, Erlangen, 1848, pp. 159-160, and, much later, Henry James's fine sketch of the city in *The American Scene* (1907), reprinted in *The American Scene, together with Three Essays from Portraits of Places*, edited by W.H. Auden, New York, 1946, pp. 110-111.

[21]*E.g.*, Reiss, pp. 25-26.

[22]The situation had been bad for years. See Asa Greene's well known essay, "The Sidewalks of New York" in *A Glance at New York* (1837), reprinted in Warren S. Tryon (editor), *A Mirror for Americans; Life and Manners in the United States, 1790-1870, as Recorded by American Travellers* [Chicago, 1952], I, p. 168. Cf. T. Horner's etching, "Broadway, New-York," 1835, *Stokes Collection*, PL835-E103, New York Public Library.

[23]John Randel, *The Elevated Rail-way... for Broadway*, New York, 1848, and R.J. Rayner's print, "View of Broadway... with the Proposed Elevated Railway," 1848, *Stokes Collection*, 1848-E128, in Stokes, Vol. III, plate 133-A.

[24]J.W. Orr's wood engraving, "Genin's New and Novel Bridge Extending across Broadway," 1852 (*Eno Collection*, No. 287) is actually a far better illustration than Fig. 12 here of the many wonderful verbal descriptions of Broadway contained in books such as Dr. Joel H. Ross's *What I Saw in New York...*, Auburn, NY, 1851, pp. 164-165, and accounts such as "Stray Notes from a Southerner Adrift," the *New York Daily Times*,

September 7, 1853, p. 2, col. 5. The latter contains a remarkable sketch of the ear-splitting din of Broadway, the clatter of the horses' hooves over the rough pavement, the cries of the vendors, the raucous swearing—all coming to a climax with the blaring of the band from early morn till evening at Barnum's Museum.

[25]The subject of one of Whitman's best known essays, Broadway to him represented the living symbol of American democracy, the "open road" along which streamed the vast procession of humanity, a quite different interpretation from that of Baron Joseph A. Hubner some years later. Hubner described Broadway as an "enormous railway station, a 'depot'… both of travellers and goods"—the quintessence of the "principle of mobility". For Whitman, see an excerpt from his series, "New York Dissected," *Life Illustrated*, August 9, 1856, reprinted in Walt Whitman, *New York Dissected… A Sheaf of Recently Discovered Newspaper Articles by the Author of 'Leaves of Grass'*, annotated by Emory Holloway and Ralph Adamari, New York, 1936, pp. 119-122; for Hubner, see his *Ramble around the World* (1871), translated by Lady Herbert, London, 1874, I, pp. 23-24.

[26]See the fine lithograph, "Bird's-eye View of New York from Union Square Looking South," Stokes, III, plate 135.

[27]Hone, II, p. 784, entry of January 28, 1847.

[28]Edited by Allan Nevins and Milton Halsey Thomas, New York, 1952, I, p. 40, entry of October 16, 1836, and *passim*. Microfilm proofs of the original "Journal," which has now been returned to its owner, Mr. Hasket Derby of Portland, Maine, is available upon special request to Mr. Thomas, Curator of Columbiana, Columbia University; a microfilm copy is also at the New York Public Library. Reference has already been made to my manuscript, "George Templeton Strong: Architectural Historian".

[29]An excellent description of this type of house is contained in Karl W?chardt, *Die Vereinigten Staaten…*, Leipzig, 1848, p. 23. See also Schramke, "Einrichtung und Konstruckzion der Waarebnagazube, Stadt- und Landhauser in den Vereinigten Staaten von Nord-Amerika, mit besonderer Rucksicht auf die Stadt und Landschaft New-York," *Allgemaine Bauzeitung*, Vol. XI (1846), pp. 73-110 and plates 22-24; Montgomery Schuyler, "The Small New York City House," *Architectural Record*, Vol. VIII (April-June 1899), pp. 357-388; Talbot Hamlin, *Greek Revival Architecture in America*, London, 1943, pp. 125-134.

[30]There are many delightful prints of the Battery in the '40s and early '50s: See Stokes, Vol. III, plate 137 (top); *Eno Collection*, Nos. 219, 253, 272, etc. See descriptions in Myers, p. 428; N. Parker Willis, "Open-air Musings in the City," *Rural Letters and Other Records of Thoughts at Leisure*, New York, 1849, p. 238.

[31]Two panoramas of Broadway at this time survive: the *Pictorial Directory* and a watercolor scroll about 25-feet long, painted by a schoolboy, James William Pirrson, "Panorama of the East Side of Broadway," c.1848-1850 (Print Room, New York Public Library), which runs from Bleecker Street south to Cedar. For the conversion of Broadway, see Hone, II, p. 896, entry

of May 31, 1850; Charles H. Haswell, *Reminiscences of an Octogenarian of the City of New York (1816-1860)*, New York, 1896, p. 461, a chatty book packed with information; Charles Astor Bristed's biting satire, *The Upper Ten Thousand: Sketches of American Society*, New York, 1852, p. 17, etc. An especially interesting description of Broadway and its architecture a few years later is in (editor) Charles A. Dana's *The United States Illustrated...*, New York, 1854, I, pp. 156-159.

[32]Ross, *What I Saw in New York*, p. 178.

[33]Lady Emmeline [Charlotte Armstrong] Stuart Wortley, *Travels in the United States... during 1849 and 1850*, London, 1851, I, pp. 2 and 5.

[34]A phrase used by the famous Swedish novelist Frederika Bremer, letter of March 15, 1850, in *Homes of the New World...* (1853), reprinted in *America of the Fifties: Letters of Frederika Bremer*, edited by Adolph B. Benson, New York, 1924, pp. 92 ff.

[35]*Things as They Are in America*, Philadelphia, 1854, p. 178.

[36]See excerpts from the *Evening Post* and New York *Herald*, cited in Stokes, V, 1785, under date of June 22, 1844, and V, 1789, February 26, 1845.

[37]See Edwin Williams (editor), *New York as It Is, in 1833*, New York, 1833, pp. 12-13; Schramke, *Allgemeine Bauzeitung*, Vol. XI (1846), pp. 80-94, and plates 19-21; A.J. Bloor, "Annual Address," October 12, 1876, *AIA Proceedings* (1876), p. 19—an interesting account of the development of American architecture, with special emphasis on New York, to which reference will be made repeatedly; Roger Hale Newton, *Town and Davis, Architects...*, New York, 1942, pp. 181-184; Hamlin, *Greek Revival Architecture*, p. 149. The original drawing for the Tappan store is in the Davis Collection, Avery Library, No. Fl-5.

[38]An early edifice built for commercial use was the U.S. Bonded Warehouse at 52-56 Broadway (Fig. 11), a fine example of Greek Revival style.

[39]Hone, II, p. 772, under date of September 10, 1846. The building was extended to encompass the entire block on Broadway between Chambers and Reade Streets during the summer of 1850, according to *idem*, II, pp. 896-897; Cooper, II, p. 687.

[40]Since this chapter was first written, an excellent study has appeared by Winston Weisman: "Commercial Palaces of New York: 1845-1875," *Art Bulletin*, Vol. XXXVI (December 1954), pp. 285-302.

[41]*Harper's New Monthly Magazine*, Vol. VIII (July 1854), p. 261. This interesting description, which was forwarded to Winston Weisman for use in his article (p. 288), was probably written by George William Curtis (1824-1892), distinguished author and journalist, who for many years was associated with *Harper's* and *Putnam's*. According to H. Henry Harper (*The House of Harper...*, New York, 1912, p. 127), he was not the sole contributor to the "Easy Chair" for several years. Cf., however, accounts of his activities in *National Dictionary of American Biography*, Vol. III, pp. 96-97; *Appleton's*

Cyclopedia of American Biography, Vol. II, pp. 35-36; *Lamb's Biographic Dictionary of the U.S.*, Vol. II, pp. 287-288.

[42]In his discussion of the Stewart building, Bloor credited Ottoviano Gori, a marble cutter, with its design (*ALA Proceedings* [1876], p. 19), an attribution that was later echoed in *History of Architecture and the Building Trades of Greater New York...*, New York, 1899, Vol. I, p. 146. This two-volume work, available in Room 328, New York Public Library, is one of the best reference books for the period.

[43]Manhattan, 18th Ward, Electoral District 1.

[44]*Art Bulletin*, Vol. XXXVI, p. 288, n. 18.

[45]P.B. W[ight], "A Millionaire's Architectural Investment," *American Architect*, Vol. I (May 6, 1876), p. 148. The Stewart building is also attributed to him in [John Franklin Sprague], *New York, The Metropolis. Its noted business and professional men...*, New York, 1893, Part II, p. 34.

[46]*North America* [1862], editors Donald Smalley and Bradford Allen Booth, New York, 1951, p. 212. Wight [*ibid*] still thought very well of it in 1876. Progressive critics of the early 1850s were unanimous in their praise of the building: See particularly the critique in *Putnam's Monthly Magazine*, Vol. I (February 1853), p. 358, and *New-York Quarterly*, Vol. IV (April 1855), p. 118—two excellent sources for New York architecture.

[47]Initiated by Pugin's Travellers' Club (1829-1831), the Manchester Atheneum and the Reform Club (1838-1840), the mode was quickly transposed to commercial architecture in A. & G. Williams' Brunswick Building (1841-1842), Liverpool. See Hitchcock's "Victorian Monuments in Commerce," *Architectural Review*, Vol. CV (February 1949), p. 62. For a more detailed account of Barry's role in the creation of the palace style, see *idem., Early Victorian Architecture in Britain*, New Haven, 1954, I, pp. 162 ff. Barry, according to Hitchcock, was "the really representative Early Victorian architect... and Pugin's equal in influence" (p. 162).

[48]This unsigned article, attributed in the index to Gilman ("Architecture in the United States," *ibid*, LVIII [April 1844], pp. 436-480), was ostensibly a review of Edward Shaw's *Rural Architecture...* (1843). The espousal of the Barryesque mode here (pp. 454-455) was not the only new note: Hamlin's interpretation of the young Gilman's point of view as eclectic and as a complete rejection of the Gothic Revival is open to question. See his *Greek Revival Architecture*, pp. 335-336, and 375-376: cf. Gilman, *ibid*, pp. 463 ff.

[49]Robert C. Smith, *John Notman and the Atheneum Building*, Philadelphia, 1951, pp. 15-17; Philadelphia Art Alliance, *Philadelphia Architecture in the Nineteenth Century*, Thomas B. White, edited by William P. Harbeson *et al*, Philadelphia, 1953, plate 37.

[50]Hitchcock, *Early Victorian Architecture*, I, p. 176.

[51]See the biographical sketch of Stewart in Junius Henri Browne's *The Great Metropolis: A Mirror of New York...*, Hartford, 1869, chapter xxxii, and *Appleton's Cyclopedia of American Biography*, Vol. V, pp. 681-683. The most famous buildings associated with Stewart were the Tenth Street store (1859-1862), later Wanamaker's, destroyed by fire in August 1956, described by

Alan Burnham, "Last Look at a Structural Landmark...," *Architectural Record*, Vol. CXX (September 1957), pp. 273-279; his "marble palace" (c.1867-c.1869) on Fifth Avenue (Fig. 61); the $3,000,000 Hotel for Working Women, planned in 1869, but not built until 1877-1879, later converted into the Park Avenue Hotel; and his grandiose schemes in Garden City, Long Island, which included the Cathedral and his own mausoleum. His ideas were given fitting expression by the architect John Kellum, of whom more will be said later.

[52]Cf. Weisman's date of 1848-1849. It is clear from contemporary sources that the building, described as in the process of erection on September 22, 1849 ("The New Buildings on Broadway," *Evening Post*, p. 2, cols. 3-4), was not completed until 1850. Cf. city directories of 1849/1850 and 1850/1851 for change of address and date of 1850 consistently cited in contemporary sources: *Andrews & Co.'s Stranger's Guide in the City of New-York*, New York, 1852, p. 12; date on building in advertisement for Bowen-McNamee in *The Citizen and Strangers' Pictorial and Business Directory for the City of New York... 1853*, edited by Solyman Brown, New York, 1853, p. 32; W. Frothingham, "Stewart and the Dry Goods Trade of New York," *Continental Monthly*, Vol. II (October 1862), p. 530.

[53]*Andrews Stranger's Guide*, p. 54. The Hoskins-Hieskel dry goods store (1853), 213 Market Street, Philadelphia, by Sloan and Stewart, appears to be quite literally a copy of Bowen-McNamee, according to a Winston Weisman photograph.

[54]The Venetian Sansovinesque mode was introduced into England by Sydney Smirke in the new front for the Carlton Club, Pall Mall (1847): See Hitchcock, *Early Victorian Architecture*, I, p. 173, and II, Fig. VI, No. 7.

[55]Wells was one of a committee of five (the others were Charles Babcock, Henry Dudley, Edward Gardiner, and Frederick A. Petersen) that drew up the Constitution of the AIA. He apparently first established independent practice here in 1839 and built a number of charming villas in the metropolitan area, mostly in the Italian, English Gothic and Elizabethan styles (see his advertisement in the *Evening Post*, July 3, 1844, cited in *History of Architecture and Building Trades*, I, p. 127). Wells also erected a number of churches in New York, of which the best known is the First Presbyterian (1844-1846), Fifth Avenue and 11st Street. For illustrations of his work, see *Villas on the Hudson...*, New York, 1860 [plates 47, 48]; Wayne Andrews, Architectural Photographs, New York [pp. 194 ff.], Series V[2], No. 634, VIII, p. 1028; [Frank John Urquhart *et al*], *A History of the City of Newark... 1866-1913*, New York, 1913, II, pp. 771-772, description and photograph of Newark Public Library (1848). Commercial buildings are discussed in *The Crayon*, Vol. IV (June 1857), pp. 183-184, and *Architects' and Mechanics' Journal*, Vol. I (March 17, 1860), pp. 191-192; Vol. II (September 8, 1860), p. 223. First listed in *Longworth's American Almanac, New York... Directory, 1839-1840*; New York State Census, 1855, Manhattan, 15th Ward, Election District 3, Dwelling #254, Family #284; obituary, *The Crayon*, Vol. VII

(September 1860), p. 270; Hobart B. Upjohn, manuscript material on the early years of the AIA, very kindly lent to me by Everard M. Upjohn.

[56]I (February 1853), p. 130. This series, whose authorship has long puzzled historians, was attributed to Clarence Cook by the anonymous but apparently well informed author of two articles, "New York Fifty Years Ago," which appeared in *The Critic and Literary World...*, Vol. XLV (December 1904), pp. 500-501, and Vol. XLVI (January 1905), pp. 58-69. The articles, largely a rehash of the *Putnam's* series, are illustrated with a selection of the same prints. For biographical information on Cook and other attributions to him, see comments on several anonymous articles on New York architecture listed in Bibliography, Part III.

[57]Weisman, "New York and the Problem of the First Skyscraper,: *SAH Journal*, Vol. XII (March 1953), Fig. 3.

[58]Cf. Hitchcock, *Early Victorian Architecture*, Vol. II, Fig. XII, Nos. 1, 5, and 18, and *passim*.

[59]As late as 1857, Walt Whitman, who generally disliked the derivative connotations of Greek Revival style, expressed his admiration of its "simple and massive elegance" and claimed that it was "unsurpassed" among the buildings of New York "as a specimen of exquisite design and proportion" ("Grand Buildings in New York City," an article dated June 5, 1857, reprinted in Whitman, *I Sit and Look Out, Editorials from the Brooklyn Daily Times*, edited by Emory Holloway and Vernolian Schwarz, New York, 1932, p. 128).

[60]Thummel, p. 167.

[61]The Metropolitan, originally called Niblo's Hotel (described and illustrated in *Ballou's*, Vol. I [September 13, 1851], p. 305), was owned by William Niblo, not by A.T. Stewart (cf. Weisman, *Art Bulletin*, Vol. XXXVI, p. 291, n. 30). The hotel was steam-heated throughout and luxuriously furnished; it cost the hitherto unheard of sum of $1,000,000. In an article describing the Metropolitan, the *Evening Post* of August 21, 1852, remarked that our public houses were beginning to rival the palaces of Europe.

The attribution to Trench & Snook rests chiefly on The Architectural Iron Works of the City of New York, *Illustrations of Iron Architecture...*, New York, 1865, p. 28—a rare and extremely useful reference work available at the Avery Library. This is corroborated by a reference to Mr. French [*sic*] in the *Evening Post* (June 15, 1850). The substitution of French for Trench, possibly attributable to the penmanship of the period, is repeated in Snook's obituary (*American Architect*, Vol. LXXIV [1901], p. 41), wherein it is stated that he first practiced with Joseph French. According to Weisman (conversation of August 28, 1954), Snook probably should be given full credit for the design, since Trench may already have left for California at this time. (Note, however, that Trench maintained listings in the New York directories when he supposedly was in California.) John B. Snook (1815-1901), who reportedly came to this country from England at the tender age of two, will be mentioned from time to time. He erected many buildings in

New York, of which the best known is the old Grand Central Station (1869-1871).

[62]Weisman, *ibid.*, p. 291, n. 34. Note, however, that the attribution to Griffith Thomas (which should be Thomas & Son, since Thomas Thomas, the father, was the head of the firm until 1860), is based on a relatively late, though usually reliable source: John W. Kennion, *The Architects' and Builders' Guide...*, New York, 1868, p. 67. Earlier sources favor Snook: the *Morning Courier* and *New York Enquirer* (December 4, 1852) says that the hotel was built on a novel plan projected by Mr. Haight, the owner, but carried out by Trench & Snooks [*sic*]; *The St. Nicholas Hotel, Its Plan and Arrangements* (1856), a pamphlet issued by the hotel, states that plans and designs were prepared by D.H. Haight; *Illustrations of Iron Architecture*, p. 28, gives credit for the design of the 470-foot front to Snook. My thanks for the references of 1852 and 1856 go to Alan Hodge, "Early Boston and New York Hotels," unpublished paper, 1955, n. 133.

Contemporary descriptions of the hotel's fabulous interiors are many. One of the best is that of an English M.P., who visited America in 1853-1854, W.E. Baxter's *America and the Americans*, London, 1855, p. 33. He was completely "bamboozled" by the profusion of mirrors, gilding, tapestry, and crystal, and claimed that even the embroidery on the mosquito nettings might be exhibited to royalty. (An amusing anecdote is retold by Russell Lynes in *The Tastemakers*, [1st edition, New York, 1954], p. 86: An English comedian claimed that he was afraid to put his boots outside his door for fear that the management might gild them.)

[63]*E.g.*, *Harper's*, Vol. V (November 1852), p. 843; *Harper's Weekly*, Vol. I (September 5 and December 26, 1857), pp. 563 and 824-826. The evils of hotel life were always pointed out in shocking detail by British visitors to America, *e.g.* the former British consul in Massachusetts, Thomas Colley Grattan, *Civilized America*, London, 1859, I, p. 109 ff.

[64]"American Architecture," *U.S. Magazine and Democratic Review* (1843), reprinted in *Form and Function: Remarks on Art by Horatio Greenough*, edited by Harold A. Small, Berkeley, 1947, p. 53. Cf. also De Zurko, *Origins of Functionalist Theory*, pp. 218-230. British writers, in contrast to those from the continent, were usually favorably impressed by Trinity [*e.g.* Alexander Mackay, *The Western World; or Travels in the United States in 1846-1847...*, 3rd edition, London, 1850, I, p. 85). Cf. the opinion of Madame Pulszky, who visited this country in 1851-1852 as a member of the *entourage* of Kossuth, the Hungarian patriot, recorded in her interesting diary (Francis and Theresa Pulszky, *White, Red, Black, Sketches of American Society...*, New York, 1853, I, p. 71, entry of December 16, [1851]); E[ugene] Jouve's sarcastic comments on naive New Yorkers who consider Trinity a masterpiece (*Voyage en Amerique. Extrait du Courier de Lyon*, Lyon, 1853, pp. 23-24); and Schramke, who calls Trinity "eine leidliche Kompilazion" (*Allgemaine Bauzeitung*, Vol. XI [1846], p. 73).

[65]See Whitman's two articles of March 9 and 30, 1846, "Splendid Churches," *The Brooklyn Daily Eagle*, reprinted in *idem.*, *The Gathering of the*

Forces. Editorials. Essays... Written by Walt Whitman as Editor of The Brooklyn Eagle, edited by Cleveland Rogers and John Black, New York, 1920, II, pp. 91-93, and 93-96; Strong, I, pp. 256-267, entries of March 3 and August 1, 1845. Strong much preferred Trinity, with whose architectural progress he, as vestryman, was closely identified.

[66]He reports, not without humor, that its "lofty arches resound with astute criticism upon *Gothic architecture* from fair ladies who have had the advantage of foreign travel" (Hone, II, p. 754, entry of February 5, 1846).

[67]See Basil F.L. Clarke, *Church Builders of the Nineteenth Century...*, London, 1938, Chapter V, pp. 75 ff; Kenneth Clark, *The Gothic Revival...*, revised edition, London, 1950, Chapter VIII, pp. 204-239; Hitchcock, *Early Victorian Architecture*, I, *passim*.

[68]See the articles on church architecture that appeared in the *New York Ecclesiologist* in 1848-1849, based on lectures given to the society by Frank Wills, an English architect who had recently established himself in the States, especially "Reality in Church Architecture," *ibid.*, (I [April 1848], pp. 8-12), a thinly veiled attack on Grace Church, and two articles on church planning (I [January 1849], pp. 53 ff. and 175 ff.). See also the emphasis on "truth" in *A Book of Plans for Churches and Parishes...*, New York, 1853, p. 21.

[69]Expressive use of building materials was one of Andrew Jackson Downing's favorite subjects of discussion (*Cottage Residences...* [New York, 1842], pp. 18-19; *The Architecture of Country Houses*, New York, 1850, pp. 35 ff.). Vincent J. Skully, Jr., has thoroughly investigated this question in "Romantic Rationalism and the Expression of Structure in Wood: Downing, Wheeler, Gardner and the 'Stick Style,' 1840-1876," *Art Bulletin*, Vol. XXXV (June 1953), p. 133. The educated laity, such as George Templeton Strong, became even more familiar with the principle of truth to material following the publication of Ruskin's books, beginning with *The Seven Lamps of Architecture* in 1849. The Avery Library's copy of this book, interestingly enough, came from the library of Detlef Lienau.

[70]The *Evening Post* of October 8, 1845 (quoted in *History of Architecture and Building Trades*, I, p. 129) said that it looked like "an embellished paper horn for sugar plums" and that "whoever countenanced its erection should be decorated with [what] it [most] nearly resembles—a paper fool's cap. It is better to have a 'Church without a Bishop' than a marble edifice with a wooden spire." In all fairness to Renwick, one should note that it was originally designed in marble, but that wood was substituted as an economy measure. The present spire is marble.

[71]Strong, I, p. 256, under date of March 3, 1845. The passage reads "... the pipe cleaners of columns that support the clearstory will tend to impress the congregation with the uncertainty of human life and suggest profitable meditation of the instability of things temporal."

[72]For a penetrating discussion of ecclesiological functionalism, see Hitchcock, *Early Victorian Architecture*, I, p. 57.

[73]*Putnam's*, Vol. II (September 1853), p. 247.

[74]*Ibid.*, pp. 247-248, view of the side elevation, p. 245. St. George's was one of the early commissions of the firm of Blesch & Eidlitz, a partnership which, according to the city directories, existed from 1845 to 1852/1853. In any case, it launched Leopold Eidlitz (1823-1908) on a long and successful architectural career. Born in Prague, Eidlitz had come to America at the age of twenty after studying architecture and engineering at the Imperial Polytechnic Institute in Vienna. Upon his arrival here (c.1843), he worked as a draftsman for Richard Upjohn before going unto partnership with Blesch. Although slightly younger than Lienau, he had a somewhat similar background, so it will be interesting to compare the work of the two architects in the course of this study. To Montgomery Schuyler, we are indebted for the only account of his work that has so far been published: "A Great American Architect: Leopold Eidlitz," *Architectural Record*, Vol. XXIV (1908), pp. 164-170, 277-292, 364-378. Cf. also Rachel Wischnitzer, *Synagogue Architecture in the United States...*, Philadelphia, 1955, *passim*.

[75]I, p. 355, entry of November 30, 1848, written shortly after the church was opened.

[76]After walking home from a party with Renwick, Strong wrote that he was an "infatuated monkey" without "the slightest trace or germ of feeling for his art... who degrades, vulgarizes, and pollutes every glorious idea and form of the successive eras of Christian art that he travesties and tampers with, as a sacrifice to the stolidity of the building committees and his own love of fat jobs and profitable contracts" (*ibid.*, I, p. 292, under date of April 16, 1847).

[77]Cf., however, Robert Dale Owen's enthusiastic concluding remarks in *Hints on Public Architecture...*, New York, 1849, which deals chiefly with Renwick's Smithsonian Institute (1846-1852), Washington, D.C. Renwick's best known works of the '40s in New York, in addition to Grace Church, were Calvary Church (1846-1847) and the Church of the Puritans (1846). On Renwick, see Effingham P. Humphrey, "The Churches of James Renwick, Jr.," M.A. thesis, Institute of Fine Arts, New York University, 1942, and Rosalie Thorne McKenna, "A Study of the Architecture of the Main Building and the Landscaping of Vassar College, 1860-1870," M.A. thesis, Vassar College, 1949, kindly lent to me by Mrs. McKenna. An abridged version of the latter is "James Renwick, Jr., and the Second Empire Style in the United States," *Magazine of Art*, Vol. XLIV (March 1951), pp. 97-101. Ms. McKenna's discussion demonstrates that Renwick was certainly one of the most interesting architects of the mid-century.

[78]Fine views of the building, including rare ones of the interior, are in the *Eno Collection*, No. 303. For contemporary opinion, see *Putnam's*, Vol. II (July 1853), p. 5. A criticism of the building that appeared years later, written by an anonymous author [Clarence Cook?] of "Our Streets," a remarkable series of essays in the *New York Weekly Review* (March 4, 1865), plate 1), is interesting both as a reaction against the older phase of the Gothic Revival and as one of the most abusive pieces of architectural criticism ever penned. After calling the Free Academy "the most hideous

building to be found in this whole city of mongrel manifestations," the author continued:

> "The design or plan of this nondescript caricature was, we understand, one of the masterpieces of that credit to his country, *Sir Christopher WRenwick*, the distinguished architect (?) of *Dis*grace Church and of... other sundry perpetuations too numerous and too horrible to mention. Renwick has applied... Yankee genius, to what has usually been called Go*thick* architecture; and has succeeded in patenting a style which could not be better known or described than as Go*thin*. The Free Academy is decidedly in the Gothin style..."

[79]*Putnam's*, Vol. I (April 1853), p. 358.

[80]Weisman, *Art Bulletin*, XXXVI, p. 286.

[81]Cf. Hitchcock, *Early Victorian Architecture*, Vol. II, Fig. XII, *passim*.

[82]Weisman, *Art Bulletin*, Vol. XXXVI, p. 289. This is essentially the same principle as the modern cubical loft building with its repetitive bay system, as Vincent Scully pointed out to me.

[83]A prize essay by Ralph Nicholas Wornum, "The Exhibition as a Lesson in Taste," published in the *Art Journal*, may perhaps help to clarify this confusing terminology: Lombard and Norman are classified as varieties of the Byzantine style, and the three together are called "Romanesque" (cited by Pevsner, *High Victorian Design, a Study of the Exhibits of 1851* [London, 1951], p. 67). Strong, who examined the plans for the Astor Library at Saeltzer's office, objected to its description as "Byzantine," saying that he would prefer to call it "Romanesque" or "Lombard," but that "all these terms seem to be very loosely employed" (I, pp. 256-257, entry of June 29, 1849). The building is also quite close to the German *Rundbogenstil*. *Ballou's* described it as an example of the "style of the royal palaces of Florence" (III [September 25, 1852], p. 200). Perhaps the closest comparison is the Spinelli Palace, published by A. Rosengarten, "Die Architektur und die Architekten Venedigs," *Allgemeine Bauzeitung*, Vol. XIV (1849), plate 238, Fig. 1.

The question of pre-Ruskin interest in Venetian *palazzi*, touched on by Alan Hodge in a seminar report dealing chiefly with the work of Mould and Wight (Institute of Fine Arts, New York University, March 1957), deserves further study. Cf. letter of August 6, 1835, by William Cullen Bryant, *Letters of a Traveller...*, New York, 1850, pp. 42-43.

[84]Harry Miller Lydenburg, *History of the New York Public Library*, New York, 1923, pp. 15-16 and 24-35 for history and description; the *Evening Post*, September 14, 1849, p. 2, cols. 3-4.

[85]In spite of the fact that Saeltzer had an important practice in the 1850s in New York, information regarding the man and his work remains distressingly scant. According to *Ballou's* (Vol. III [September 25, 1852], p. 200), he came from Berlin; in the Census of 1855 (18th Ward, Electoral District 4, Dwelling #529, Family #2443), he gave his birthplace simply as Germany, his age as forty-one, and stated that he had been in the city for thirteen years. His first listing was in *Doggett's Directory of 1844/1845*; he maintained an architectural office throughout the years (in partnership with Lawrence B. Valk, 1860-1861) until 1882-1883, when his name disappears

from the directories, indicating probable death or removal from the city. I have not found any obituaries in New York papers, nor in architectural magazines. Very little is known of his work in later years: He was awarded a premium of $500 for a design submitted to the Post Office competition of 1867; a slim volume by Saeltzer, *A Treatise on Acoustics in Connection with Ventilation*, New York, 1872, which is preserved at the New York Public Library, shows that he maintained contact with Germany.

In addition to the Astor Library, Saeltzer designed the following buildings in New York: (1) Anshe Chesed (1849-1850), 60 Norfolk Street, in Gothic style, the largest synagogue in the U.S. in the 1850s, still in use today by Congregation Beth Hamedrash Hagodol; attributed to Saeltzer by Reiss, *Excursion a New-York*, p. 65, corroborated by extensive records and memorabilia of Anshe Chesed preserved in the Archives of Temple Emanu-El, access to which was kindly granted to me by the late Samual Berliner, formerly Comptroller, Temple Emanu-El, to whom I was referred by Rabbi I.S. Meyer, Librarian-Editor, American Jewish Historical Society, New York. The folio volume, "Minutes 1848-1850," written in fine German script, shed interesting light on the awarding of contracts at this time and on the parts played by Diaper, Sloan, Keely, and Eidlitz & Blesch in connection with the building. (2) Academy of Music (1853-1854), Lexington Avenue at 14th Street, destroyed by fire in 1866: illustrated in *Ballou's*, Vol. X (March 29, 1856), p. 200; *Harper's Weekly*, Vol. III (January 1, 1859), p. 4; described by Walt Whitman in Holloway, *Whitman*, II, pp. 97-101; and scathingly criticized in *New York Weekly Review*, May 6, 1865, p. 5. (3) Duncan and Sherman, banking house (1856), Nassau and Pine Streets, described in *The Crayon*, Vol. III (July 1856), pp. 214-215. Other buildings that might tentatively be attributed to him are Rutherfurd Row. In any case, Saeltzer's extensive use of iron and partiality to the *palazzo* or *Rundbogenstil* certainly place him among the ranks of progressive architects of New York in the '50s.

[86]A check of the Astor Library Records (manuscripts Division, New York Public Library) revealed nothing of interest, except two slips of paper entitling the winners of the first and second prizes to collect their premiums of $300 and $500 each.

[87]See discussion in *History of Architecture and the Building Trades*, I, p. 170. *Ballou's* published an excellent view of the interior (Vol. VI [1854], p. 124).

[88]For a discussion of Bogardus's work, see [Charles Edward Lester], *Glances at the Metropolis*, New York [1854], p. 79. Two years later, Bogardus, aided by John W. Thompson, published *Cast Iron Buildings: Their Construction and Advantages...*, New York, 1856. Cf. *History of Architecture and Building Trades*, II, pp. 168-170; Giedon, pp. 193-198; Walter Knight Sturges, "Cast Iron in New York," *Architectural Review*, Vol. CXIV (October 1953), pp. 232-237; and most particularly, Turpin C. Bannister, "Bogardus Revisited," *SAH Journal*, Vol. XV (December 1956), pp. 12-22, and Vol. XVI (March 1957), pp. 11-19.

[89]City Hall (1802-1812) by Joseph Mangin and John McComb (plans preserved at the Municipal Archives and Records Center, New York Public Library, 238 William Street); Haviland's "Tombs" (1836-1838), which was called a "dismal fronted pile of bastard Egyptian" by Charles Dickens, an opinion with which other visitors from the Continent generally concurred (*American Notes...*, 3rd edition, London, 1842, I, p. 199); the Custom House, now the Sub-Treasury Building, by Town & Davis, Frazee and Ross (1834-1842); the Merchants' Exchange (1836-1841 ff.) by Isaiah Rogers. For a discussion of these buildings, see Hamlin, *Greek Revival Architecture*, pp. 119 ff.

[90]The French were particularly disappointed with our public architecture. With the exception of City Hall, of which the best view at this period is the Bechmann lithograph (*Eno Collection*, No. 242), Jouve (*Voyage en Amerique*) characterized the public buildings of New York as pretentious and maladroit on style, "cathedrales gothiques ou temples grecs d'un gout et d'une execution à faire dresser les cheveux sur la tête d'un architecte" (pp. 23-24). F. Dizac flatly stated, "Il n'y a pas un seul monument public digne d'attention" (*Excursion aux Indes occidentales et aux Estats-Unis...* [1853-1854], Brive, 1855, p. 47). Schramke (*Allgemaine Bauzeitung*, Vol. XI [1846], p. 73) also was critical of the Custom House. "B.," the author of an interesting article, "Erste Eindrucke von New-York," discussing the merits of German and New York architecture, wrote that though he had always thought contemporary German architecture was bad, in retrospect it seemed a solid masterpiece in comparison to American building! (*Atlantische Studien. Von Deutschen in Amerika*, Gottingen, 1853-1857, I, p. 124).

[91]A term used already by Madame Pulszky in her fine description of Wall Street (*White, Red, Black*, I, pp. 71-72, entry of December 16 [1851]). Many visitors commented upon the strange juxtaposition of Trinity Church and Wall Street.

[92]See *The Stranger's Guide around New York and Its Vicinity...* New York, W.H. Graham, 1853, pp. 34-35, and especially *Putnam's*, Vol. I (1853), p. 136 (quoted in Weisman, *Art Bulletin*, Vol. XXXVI, p. 289) and pp. 353-354. Whitman criticized the classic style of the Custom House as completely inappropriate to its setting, period, and function ("Grand Buildings of New York," *I Sit and Look Out*, p. 130). The more usual laudatory attitude is represented by the descriptions of the Custom House and Merchants' Exchange in the most noteworthy guide book to New York in the mid-century, E[zekiel] Porter Belden's *New York, Past, Present, and Future...* New York, 1849, pp. 62-64, which has a fine view of the Exchange opposite p. 59.

[93]This was noted by English and continental visitors alike, *e.g.*, Mackay, *The Western World*, I, p. 84; Grattan, *Civilized America*, I, p. 22, in a passage recalling his early impressions of years ago of Wall Street; *Schliemann's First Visit to America, 1850-1851*, edited by Shirley H. Weber, Cambridge, Mass., 1942, p. 23; "B.," *Atlantische Studien*, I, p. 123.

[94]*Putnam's*, Vol. I (1853), p. 132.

[95]The law offices of George Templeton Strong and William Colford Schermerhorn, who later became one of Lienau's best clients, were housed in one such converted residence at 68 Wall Street (see view in Strong, IV, opposite p. 18).

[96]Dated by newspaper sources cited by Stokes, V, 1822, under dates of May 26 and October 8, 1849. For later building on this site, see Fig. 108.

[97]The old building was torn down in 1847 and replaced by a new building of granite, described in the *Evening Post* of February 11, 1848 (quoted in *ibid.*, V, 1809, under that date). For a view of the building, see *New-York Pictorial Business Directory of Wall Street, 1850*, New York, c.1849, plate IV, *Eno Collection*, No. 230, as good a reference for Wall Street as the *Pictorial Directory* is for Broadway.

[98]*Putnam's*, Vol. I (1853), p. 132. Demolition was reported in the *Evening Post* of May 6, 1851 (p. 2, col. 4), which pointed out the novelty of the Italian style as adapted to a bank building. Work began on May 24, 1851 (*The New York Herald*, cited in Stokes, V, 1833). For other descriptions and illustrations, see *Putnam's*, Vol. I (1853), pp. 132-133, and Weisman, *Art Bulletin*, Vol. XXXVI, p. 291, and Fig. 7. The architect wasn't Thomas & Son, as Weisman assumed (n. 33), but Hurry & Rogers, according to the *Evening Post* article cited above. This firm, located at 13 Wall Street, consisted of William Hurry and John Rogers; I have little information concerning them.

[99]Cf. particularly the corner fenestration with contemporary English examples such as Sancton Woods's Queen's Assurance and Commercial Chambers (1851-1852), London (Hitchcock, *Early Victorian Architecture*, Vol. II, Fig. XI, No. 15). The relation of our palace mode to that of the British was pointed out by the German writer, "B." (*Atlantische Studien*, II, p. 183); he devotes considerable space to an analysis of the special fondness of New York architects for the "sogenannte italienische Styl der aber nach hiesiger Behandlung nichtsweiter als ein geschmackloser Zopfstyl ist" (*ibid.*, II, p. 184). *Zopfstyl* is untranslatable, but its derogatory connotation is made clear in the paragraph following, wherein the author complains that the Italian style was handled by these architects as mere surface decoration, without regard for its original structural basis and general principles of composition.

[100]"Emigration Advice from an American," 1792, reprinted in *Profile of America: An Autobiography of the U.S.A.*, edited by Emily Davis *et al*, New York, 1954, p. 52.

Chapter III

[1]Portfolio, I,. No. 1. According to J. Henry Lienau (letters of December 13, 1951, and January 29, 1954), the house was located at Jersey Avenue and Third Street. This checks with listings for Michael Lienau at 44 Jersey Avenue, or Jersey Avenue and South Sixth Street, in *Gopsill's Jersey City Directories* from 1855/1856 to 1867/1868. Sixth Street was originally Third Street: Cf. *Map of Jersey City, Hoboken and Hudson Counties* by William H. Wood, 1855, Jersey City, 1855, and *Map of Jersey City and Environs* by Edlon

W. Harrison, Hudson County, NJ, 1879, Map Division, New York Public Library. Michael's cottage was probably demolished when the tracks of the Pennsylvania Railroad (see map of 1879) were laid down.

[2]A term coined by Downing in *Cottage Residences* (1842), p. 99, and more fully described in *Country Houses* (1850), pp. 393-394. Discussed by Vincent J. Scully, Jr., and then in a series of publications: "Nineteenth Century Resort Architecture," Part IV of Antoinette F. Downing and Vincent J. Scully, Jr., *The Architectural Heritage of Newport, Rhode Island, 1640-1915*, Cambridge, Mass., 1952, especially pp. 120 ff.; *Art Bulletin*, Vol. XXXV, pp. 130 ff.; "American Villas; Intventiveness in the American Suburb from Downing to Wright," *Architectural Review*, Vol. CXV (March 1954), pp. 178-170.

[3]Refers to page in original dissertation.

[4]One of the earliest speculative suburban developments in metropolitan New York was Ravenswood (c.1840), Astoria, Long Island: See Newton, pp. 250, 268, and label for Davis' Roach House in Ravenswood, used in Talbot Hamlin's exhibition, "A Century of American Architectural Drawing," Avery Library, March 1937. A plea for better suburban planning and the expression of a hope that the advantages of English cottage life might soon be made available to more people appeared in the "Easy Chair," *Harper's*, Vol. VII (June 1953), pp. 123-130—a reflection, perhaps, of current interest in Llewellyn Park, Orange, NJ, first projected by Llewellyn Haskell in 1851, and developed by Downing's friend and associate A.J. Davis from 1852-1870. See Newton, pp. 268-269, Samuel Swift, "Llewellyn Park, Orange, NJ," *House and Garden*, Vol. III (June 1903), pp. 327-335, and Christopher Tunnard, "The Romantic Suburb in America," *Magazine of Art*, Vol. XL (May 1947), pp. 184-187, cited in Dora Wiebenson's interesting seminar report, "City Planning: 1850-1875," April 29, 1957, Institute of Fine Arts, New York University.

[5]See Edythe Norton July, "Andrew Jackson Downing; a Guide to American Architectural Taste," unpublished master's thesis, Institute of Fine Arts, New York University, 1945; Lynes, *The Tastemakers*, chapter iii. George Tatum's forthcoming book on Downing should prove extremely interesting. Contemporaries had a high regard for Downing's contribution to the American scene: See Curtis, *Lotus-eating: a Summer Book*, New York, 1852, p. 11 (his first page of text); Frederika Bremer, letters of October 4 and October 7, 1849, pp. 2 and 4.

[6]Paris [1848]. Cf. also the numerous Swiss chalets in Louis Marie Normand, *Paris moderne...* Liege, no date, Vol. III, especially plates 124 and 129, and references in Hautecoeur, VI, pp. 321-322, and Fig. 264.

[7]The type goes far back into the 18th century: See Hugh Morrison, *Early American Architecture...*, New York, 1952, p. 474, Fig. 395, No. 2. Cf. Downing's description (*Country Houses*, p. 272) of current [1850] practice of locating the kitchen on the first floor of houses, rather than in the basement, in a wing of less height than the main building, with sleeping quarters for the servant in the garret above. Examples of this type are very

common in the period, *e.g.*, an Upjohn house in Taunton, Mass., dated August 15, 184?, Upjohn Collection, Avery Library, B-4, 1; William R. Ranlett, *The Architect, a Series of Designs for Domestic and Ornamental Cottages and Villas...*, New York, 1847-1849, Vol. II, plate 50; Samuel Sloan, *The Model Architect...*, Philadelphia, 1852, Vol. I, Design XI, plate L; etc.

[8]Page 34.

[9]*E.g.*, Vol. I, Designs XII and XIII, and pp. 51-52.

[10]Page 2, col. 4.

[11]Refers to page in original dissertation.

[12]New York, 1857, p. 24. The full title of this reveals the eclectic taste of the time and the desire of architects to accommodate themselves to the whims of their clients: *Rural Architecture; or Designs for Villas, Cottages, etc., in the Italian, Gothic, Elizabethan, Old English and Swiss Styles...*

[13]By Henry W. Cleaveland, William Backus and Samuel D. Backus, New York, 1856, pp. 68 and 91-92. Adaptation of house to site was accepted as a basic principle by the writers of the plan books, all of whom followed Downing's example: See his *Treatise on the Theory and Practice of Landscape Gardening... with Remarks on Rural Architecture...*, New York, 1841, p. 298, and *Cottage Residences...*, pp. 22-23 and 33.

[14]For a detailed discussion of this point, developed by Downing in *Country Houses* (pp. 50-52), see Scully, *Art Bulletin*, Vol. XXXV, p. 133. Note that a few years later, Vaux completely reversed the rationalist stand of his former partner in *Villas and Cottages...*, New York, 1857, p. 59.

[15]See Downing, *ibid*, p. 45; Minard Lafever, *The Architectural Instructor...*, New York, 1856, p. 412, etc.

[16]See Downing in "Hints to Persons about Building in the Country," preface to George Wightwick's *Hints to Young Architects*, American edition, New York, 1847, p. xxii, note.

[17]Hoboken's famed "Elysian Fields" were the subject of many a delightful print of the period, *e.g.*, Clara Therese (Hill) Evans, "Scrapbook of Views of Old New York," [19??], I, [29], preserved at the Avery Library.

[18]Strong, I, p. 53, entry of March 25, 1837.

[19]*A Description of Cities, Townships, and Principal Villages within Thirty Miles of New York...*, New York: Colton & Disturnell, 1839, pp. 34-35.

[20]The construction of the Cunard docks in 1847 was decisive for the development of Jersey City; thereby, it automatically became a part of the port of New York. In a few years, the direct route from New York to Liverpool overshadowed the older Boston-Halifax-Liverpool route completely.

[21]For census figures, see "A Brief History... of Jersey City...," *Gopsill's Directory of Jersey City, 1855/1856*, p. 137.

[22]In 1849, the ferries ran regularly every fifteen minutes; by 1853, the interval had been cut to seven and a half minutes. Commutation tickets were procurable at a cost of $10 a year.

[23]*The New York Times*, August 26, 1853, p. 6, col. 3.

[24]For the history of the parish and church, see a pamphlet by the Reverend George Stephen Bennitt, Rector, *Historical Sermon Preached on the First Sunday in May, 1887, Being the Fortieth Anniversary of the Founding of Grace Church (Van Vorst), Jersey City, New Jersey*, New York, 1888; a souvenir edition prepared by Dr. Bennitt and printed in his memory, *Grace Church (Van Vorst) Messenger,* Jersey City, NJ, Whitsunday, 1914; "The Diamond Jubilee of Grace Church...," *The Newark Churchman*, Vol. XVI (June 1922), p. 65—all are in the Lienau Collection at the Avery Library.

[25]Alexander McLean, *History of Jersey City, New Jersey*, Jersey City, 1895, II, pp. 350-352.

[26]The land was donated by four women: Sarah Van Vorst, her daughters Cornelia (Mrs. Henry A. Booræm) and Sarah (Mrs. C. Bacot, later Mrs. Michael Lienau), and her daughter-in-law, Emily Bacot (Mrs. John Van Vorst).

[27]Portfolio III, No. 4. Forty-two drawings relating to Grace Church are preserved, among them four contract drawings signed by the contractors and Lienau, including plan, side elevation, transverse section through the chancel, elevations of east and west ends, all beautifully rendered in watercolor; also a signed detail of the first and second stage of the tower. Related to the building are a number of drawings of church furniture (pulpit, sedilla, etc.), all in early Gothic style, an elevation of the organ gallery, and a dozen designs of stained-glass windows. The three stained-glass windows were made in Paris and were the gift of Michael Lienau; the west windows were donated by Henry A. Booræm and his wife.

[28]Bennitt, p. 9.

[29]"Van Vorst Marks 100th Anniversary Today," a news clipping from *The Jersey Journal*, May 18, 1953, kindly forwarded to me by Richard J. Scheibner, First National Bank, Jersey City.

[30]*Ancient English Ecclesiastical Architecture and Its Principles, Applied to the Wants of the Church at the Present Day*, plate X, p. 62. See also Joseph Coleman Hart, *Designs for Parish Churches...*, New York, 1857, Design II, plates II and III.

[31]Refers to page in original dissertation.

[32]*New York Ecclesiologist*, Vol. II (June 1850), pp. 107-109.

[33]Edward F. Bataille, *Grace Church in Newark...*, Newark, 1937, frontispiece and illustrations opposite pp. 25 and 48.

[34]*Art Bulletin*, Vol. XXXV, pp. 17-33, and especially Figs. 1, 2, and 3, for Upjohn's Church of the Pilgrims, Brooklyn (1844-1846), Renwick's Church of the Puritans on Union Square, New York (1843-1846), then considered "Norman" or "Lombard" in style, and Eidlitz's St. George's Church (1846-1848)—all examples that Lienau surely knew well. See Fig. 16 for St. George's.

[35]Cf. *Wasmuth's Lexikon der Baukunst*, Berlin (c.1929-c.1937], II, p. 93, Fig. 10.

[36]Meeks first wrote of this question in "Creative Eclecticism," *SAH Journal*, Vol. XII (December 1953), pp. 15-18. One of the earliest champions

of eclecticism in the U.S. appears to have been Ranlett. See his discussion of a "Villa in the American Style" which, he points out, combines the best elements from many sources: Swiss brackets, English gables, French windows, Italian verandas (Vol. II, Design XLVIII, plate 50, and p. 70).

[37]See Portfolio III, No. 4, for the following: four drawings for two additional bays to the west (1863-1864); one sheet with elevations and plans for the Rectory (1867), now somewhat altered on the interior; eight sheets of drawings for the Sunday School (1879), which were not utilized. The present building was erected by Le Bau & Sons.

[38]*E.g.*, Church of the Ascension, New York, and Christ Church, Brooklyn, in Everard M. Upjohn, *Richard Upjohn, Architect and Churchman*, New York, 1939, Figs. 18 and 20.

[39]My thanks go to the Reverend Robert P. Pegram for his kindness in conducting me through Grace Church and the adjoining buildings.

[40]Portfolio III, under separate cover labeled "Church Projects, Unexecuted".

[41]Listed as "Mariotle & D. Sienna, architects, 654 Bway" and "Marcotte L. and D. Lieman, 654 Bwy" in *Doggett's New York City Directory, 1852/1853* and *Wilson's Business Directory of New York, 1852/1853*. For 1853/1854, see under "Architects," *Rode's New Business Directory*, in the back of *Trow's New York City Directory*.

[42]*E.g.*, Collegiate Dutch Church at 29th Street, opened October 1854; Fifth Avenue Baptist Church at 35th Street, dedicated 1856 (for exterior and interior views, see *Frank Leslie's Illustrated Newspaper*, Vol. I [May 24, 1856], p. 373); Meeks reproduces the interior in "Romanesque before Richardson," Fig. 14. Lienau's plans seem to correspond quite closely in general proportions and dimensions to the Collegiate Dutch Church: See E. Robinson and R.H. Pidgeon, *Robinson's Atlas of the City of New York*, New York, 1885, plates 12 and 13. Further research probably would provide a positive identification for the Lienau-Marcotte projects.

[43]Cf. the new synagogue, Kassel, *Allgemaine Bauzeitung*, Vol. X [1840], plate CCCL, which is similar in general silhouette and design, though the detailing is different.

[44]Cf. St. Paul's Church, Baltimore (Upjohn, Fig. 62); Christ Church, Bridgeport, CT, 1852-1853, is still another example of these early "Romanesque" churches (Meeks, Fig. 6).

Chapter IV

[1]Information in the State Census of 1855, however, checks neither with my information nor with the city directories. According to the census, L. Marcotte, aged thirty, born in France, a cabinetmaker by trade, had been a resident in the city for four years, *i.e.*, since 1851. His mother and a brother lived with him, all residents here for four years; also A. Hedin, a boarder, born in France, likewise a cabinet maker.

²Listings for Pierre-Emile Leprince-Ringuet (1874-?) and Jean-Jacques Eugene Ringuet (1858-?) in Delaire (pp. 325 and 388) may be for sons of Marcotte's former partners.

³*AIA Proceedings* (1870), p. 27 [227].

⁴Note from J. Henry Lienau to Talbot Hamlin, April 5, 1942, Lienau Folder, North Office, Avery Library.

⁵See records of the Department of Buildings, City of New York, Room 2000, Municipal Building, New York. Beginning in June 1866, a record of each new building erected in the city was entered in the volumes entitled, "New Buildings," and given a number. Reference will be made to New Building Docket (NBD), following by the appropriate number and year. These records contain the following information: owner and location of property, name of architect, type of building, description of construction, value of building, date of original building application, and from 1869 on beginning and end dates of construction. In some cases, original plans are still preserved at the Plan Desk, Room 2021. A similar set of volumes exists for alterations, entitled "Alteration Dockets". For Lienau's shops for Marcotte, see New Building Docket #1055 of 1867 and #879 of 1870 (see Appendix II). Both buildings were demolished in the early 1920s, according to the files of the Index, Room 2012, Municipal Building.

⁶For the influence of France on the U.S. in the middle 1840s, an excellent source is the memoirs of the British geologist, Sir Charles Lyell, *A Second Trip to the United States...*, New York, 1849, II, pp. 332-333, and *passim*. Howard Mumford Jones has a great deal of interesting material in *American and French Culture*, 1750-1848, Chapel Hill, NC, 1927, *passim*, but unfortunately, it stops just short of our period.

⁷Although Americans were outspoken in their disapproval of Louis-Napoleon and his methods (*e.g.*, "Easy Chair," *Harper's*, Vol. IV [February 1852], p. 418), even George Templeton Strong was much taken with *Eugénie* (II, p. 118, entry of February 18, 1853). Americans of the 1850s and '60s were kept well informed of events in France not only by the daily press, but also by the numerous articles on all phases of French life, including architecture, which appeared in periodicals such as *Harper's* and *Putnam's*, and in illustrated newspapers like *Ballou's*.

⁸*American Architect...*, Vol. I (1876), pp. 411-412.

⁹Clarence Cook, *The House Beautiful...*, New York, 1878, p. 223, and *passim*.

¹⁰Charles Eastlake's *Hints on Household Taste* (1868) appeared in an American edition in 1872. For an excellent analysis of his work, see Frances Lichten's *Decorative Art of Victoria's Era...*, New York, 1950, pp. 231 ff. This book, one of the milestones in Victorian criticism, cannot be too highly recommended. It is witty and thoroughly enjoyable, in spite of its erudition.

¹¹See, *e.g.*, Edith Wharton's description of Newland Archer's library in *The Age of Innocence*, New York, 1920, p. 206, and *passim*.

[12]The city directories list Marcotte's home as France from 1883/1884 through 1886/1887. Thereafter (1887/1888 ff.), only the firm name is given, and he is listed as deceased in *ALA Proceedings* (1887), p. 50.

[13]Downing strongly recommended French furniture for the drawing room to readers of *Country Houses* (pp. 432-440). See Miss Lichten's penetrating analysis of the Victorian predilection for the curvilinear and the ornate, which found expression in the revival of Louis XIV and XV styles (pp. 91-92 and 98); Pevsner, *High Victorian Design*, p. 49; Ralph Dutton, *The Victorian Home, Some Aspects of Nineteenth-Century Taste and Manners*, London, 1954, *passim*.

[14]*North America*, p. 204.

[15]Lichten, p. 218.

[16]Ward McAllister, *Society as I Have Found It*, New York, c.1890, pp. 126-127. James Fenimore Cooper's letter of April 9, 1850, to his wife describing a dinner at Thorn's (*Correspondence*, II, p. 676).

[17]Strong, *passim*.

[18]Refers to page in original dissertation.

[19]See the interesting book written by her leading man, Léon Beauvallet, *Rachel and the New World...*, translated from the French, New York, 1856.

[20]Cf. Franconi's Hippodrome in Paris, built by Hittorf in 1843 (Hautecoeur, VI, pp. 91-92, and Fig. 76).

[21]Wharton, p. 260.

[22]Wolfgang Born, "Introductory Remarks on the Crinoline and the Bustle," *Ciba Review*, Vol. XLVI (May 1943), p. 1677. The late Dr. Born's article is an astute analysis of the sociological implications of women's fashions of the Second Empire.

[23]See especially Harriet Beecher Stowe's essay, "Ravages of a Carpet," *House and Home Papers*, by Christopher Crowfield [pseudonym], Boston, 1865, pp. 12-13. The closed front parlor, of course, also goes back to New England tradition.

[24]*Godey's Lady's Book*, Vol. XXXVIII (March 1849), p. 228.

[25]The article, "America's Mightiest Inheritance," is reprinted in *New York Dissected*, pp. 61-65.

[26]*Godey's*, Vols. XXXVIII-XLVI (1849-1853), *passim*.

[27]First printed in *Harper's Weekly*, Vol. I (February 7, 1857), p. 84. Its author, as might be expected, was a man, William Allen Butler.

[28]Bristed, a millionaire in his own right, was the author of the satirical series of articles published in book form as *The Upper Ten Thousand: Sketches of American Society*, New York, 1852. In it, he describes the "ambitious upholstery attempts of young New York, which... goes ahead of Paris itself" and rages against "the constant appeal to France as the standard of dress, furniture and manners" (pp. 250 and 257).

[29]New York, 1853, chap. iii, pp. 97-98, for the passage quoted. These papers were originally published as articles in *Putnam's Magazine*. My attention to Curtis's fascinating book, now largely forgotten, was drawn by Theodore Roosevelt, who used it as source material for his acid description

of New York Society of the 1850s in *New York* (1895), new edition, New York, 1903, pp. 198-200.

[30]Strong, I, pp. 331 and 355, entries of September 30, 1848, and June 15, 1849.

[31]Entries in the original manuscript "Journal," III, pp. 252, 263, and 277, under dates of December 18, 1858, and May 10, 1859.

[32]*E.g.*, photograph of front drawing room, John Sloan House, 883 Fifth Avenue, decorated by Marcotte, Print Department, Museum of the City of New York; photographs of interiors of Mrs. Colford Jones houses on Fifth Avenue, designed by Lienau in "Colford Jones Block," Scrapbook, Museum of the City of New York. Marcotte's clientele was not restricted to New Yorkers. According to Mrs. E. Maitland Armstrong, he did considerable redecorating at Kingscote in Newport, RI, c.1867, none of which survives today (interview of August 16, 1953).

[33]Portfolio II, No. 3. The seventeen drawings include the following: one large-scale study; six small presentation drawings (elevations of *façade*, side view, plans of basement, parlor, second, third, and attic floors; five signed contract drawings dated May 4, 1850 (front elevation and four floor plans; one side elevation; one basement plan); one contract drawing for the stable; one study of paneled front door; one contractor's study with names of the various masons responsible for the setting of the stones.

[34]The first and only listing of H.M. Shiff is in *Doggett's... Directory 1850/1851*.

[35]For information concerning the Shiff family, thanks are due to Mrs. W. Kennedy Cromwell, Jr., of Baltimore, Maryland, a great-granddaughter (letters of June 29, 1951, and July 2, 1955); Mrs. Frances Bryson Moore, Acting Executive Director, Louisiana State Museum, New Orleans (letter of November 12, 1954). Mr. Shiff's obituary in the *Evening Post*, (February 28, 1851 (p. 3, col. 5) was located through an extremely useful typescript, Gertrude A. Barber's "Index to Deaths Taken from the New York Evening Post," XXVII, p. 67, available in Room 328, New York Public Library.

[36][Henri Dulac], *Almanac des 25000 adresses des principaux habitans de Paris. Anée 1840* (Paris: Pankouche, 1840). This is the only volume of the '40s available at the New York Public Library.

[37]Strong, I, pp. 339, 353, 358, and 362, under various dates from the end of 1848 to September 1849.

[38]Maitland Armstrong remembered that, as a young boy, he often saw large white sows asleep in the gutter at the corner of Fifth Avenue and Fourteenth Street (*Day Before Yesterday; Reminiscences of a Varied Life*), edited by Margaret Armstrong, New York, 1920, p. 36).

[39]*The New York Herald*, February 26, 1845, cited in Stokes, V, 1789.

[40]An adjective applied somewhat indiscriminately to all the "palaces" of his wealthy dinner hosts, such as William H. Aspinwall, Moses H. Grinnell, John Stevens, etc.

[41]Page 2, col. 4.

[42]This colloquialism became particularly popular after publication of Bristed's *The Upper Ten Thousand* in 1852.

[43]A comparison made by many European visitors to New York, among them Madame Pulszky (*White, Red, Black...*, I, p. 71, December 16 [1851]) and Chambers (*Things as They Are in America*, p. 172). The term became standard in all descriptions of Fifth Avenue in guide books to the city from the early 1850s on.

[44]A term used by Willis in the *Home Journal*, the smart set's favorite magazine, and quoted in the late Lloyd Morris's entertaining book, *Incredible New York; High Life and Low Life of the Last Hundred Years*, New York [1951]), p. 21.

[45]Hamlin, *Greek Revival Architecture*, plate XXX, lower right.

[46]See, *e.g.*, views of the Croton Reservoir at 42nd Street (site of the present New York Public Library) in Henry Collins Brown, *Old New York. Yesterday and Today*, New York, 1922, unnumbered, and Belden, opposite p. 40. A large cattle yard occupied the block between Forty-fourth and Forty-sixth Streets on the east side of the Avenue.

[47]The comments of Mrs. Bishop and Edgar Allan Poe are interesting in this connection. See [Isabella Lucy (Bird) Bishop], *The Englishwoman in America*, London, 1856, p. 360, and Poe's "The Philosophy of Furniture," p. 462.

[48]William S. Bobo, "High Life in New York," *Glimpses of New York City, written by a South Carolinian*, 1852, reprinted in Tryon, *A Mirror for Americans*, I, p. 209.

[49]This article first appeared in *Burton's Gentleman's Magazine* (May 1840), was reprinted in the *Broadway Journal*, Vol. I (1845), p. 18, and, in a German translation, in *Atlantische Studien*, Vol. II (1853), pp. 231 ff., which is where I stumbled across it. The following quotations are from Poe, *The Complete Tales and Poems*, with an introduction by Hervey Allen, New York, 1938, p. 462: Comparing us with other nationalities, he claimed that "the Yankees alone are preposterous".

> "How this happens, it is not difficult to see. We have no aristocracy of blood, and having therefore as a natural, and indeed as an inevitable thing, fashioned for ourselves an aristocracy of dollars, the *display of wealth* has here to take the place and perform the office of the heraldic display in monarchical countries. By a transition readily understood, and which might have been as readily foreseen, we have been brought to merge in simple *show* our notions of taste itself."

He went on to compare the situation in England with that in America, where the display of money

> "may be said, in general, to be the sole means of aristocratic distinction... The populace... are insensibly led to confound the two entirely separate ideas of magnificence and beauty. In short, the cost of an article of furniture has at length come to be, with us, nearly the sole test of its merit..."

[50]*E.g.*, Curtis, *Potiphar Papers*, especially chap. I, "Our Best Society," and *passim*; see also Frederick Saunders's comments on the tendency to

ostentatious display in his excellent book, *New-York in a Nutshell...*, New York, 1853, p. 102.

[51]*Putnam's* correspondent, like Reuben Vose later, rejoiced in this display, gently chiding those who attacked it on moral grounds (Vol. III [March 1854], p. 241; Reuben Vose, *Wealth of the World Displayed*, New York, 1859, pp. 37 ff.). For a sympathetic account of the social atmosphere of the 1850s, see Morris (*Incredible New York*, chap. 2, "A Farewell to Simplicity"). More recently, Wayne Andrews has suggested that "the most vital American architecture of any given time will usually be located in those communities where the most money was being made and enjoyed" (*Architecture, Ambition and Americans...*, New York [1955], p. xvii).

[52]Weisman, *Art Bulletin*, Vol. XXXVI, p. 290.

[53]Mrs. Bishop described the houses of the very wealthy as surpassing anything she had seen in the royal or ducal palaces at home (p. 258). J.S.C. Abbott, in the second of a series of articles on "The Palaces of France" (*Harper's*, Vol. V [October 1852], p. 609), found it necessary to remind his readers that "the glory of America consists not in the pride of palaces and the pomp of armies, but in the tasteful homes of a virtuous, intelligent, and happy people."

[54]In an article on "The Progress of American Architecture" in the *Evening Post*, January 12, 1901, Russell Sturgis commented on the fact that "the arrival of the year 1850 found no important architectural movement existing in the country" ("Scrapbook of Clippings on Architecture," III, p. 119, preserved at the Avery Library.

[55]See charming colored lithograph in Davis Collection, Avery Library, D3-1.

[56]John B. Snook's house for Richard J. Haight (c.1849) at Fifth Avenue and 15th Street was one of the earliest and easily the most outstanding example of the Italian *palazzo* style of the period. The building was later taken over by the New York Club. Its simple, elegant design (characterized as "Palladian") and interesting fenestration were described at some length (pp. 336-337) in "Private Residences," one of the articles in the series "New York Daguerreotyped," *Putnam's*, Vol. III (March 1854), pp. 333 ff. Described as having been built some five years ago, a date of c.1849 is confirmed by the first listing of Haight at this Fifth Avenue address in the directories of 1850/1851 and by the vivid description of its Italian winter garden, playing fountains, large saloons in the Parisian fashion, a drawing room in the style of the Taj Mahal, etc., in Madame Pulszky's diary (I, p. 71, December 16 [1851]). See the critique in the *New York Quarterly* of 1855 and in the New York *Weekly Review* (March 18, 1865, pp. 4-5), which calls it "one of the best specimens of the Anglo-Italian style we possess," but criticizes it for its poor construction.

[57]"Mason's Specifications" and contract drawings were signed May 4, 1850; "Carpenter's Specifications" are dated May 10, 1850.

[58]Cf. decorative features (*e.g.*, garlands and medallions over second-story columns, flame-like motifs and acroteria used as terminal finials) with

Labrouste's drawing of a doorway of the Bibliotheque Ste.-Geneviève, *Revue générale de l'architecture*, Vol. X (1852), plate 25.

[59]Refers to page in original dissertation.

[60]*Francis' New Guide to the Cities of New-York and Brooklyn, and the Vicinity...*, New York, 1853, p. 89. The house continued to rate special mention in most of the guide books of the following decades, *e.g., Miller's New York As It Is...*, New York, 1859-1875, wherein it is mentioned at least until 1869, the last volume checked.

[61]Page 234; illustrated p. 238.

[62]Pages 119-120. The attribution of this long and very informative article to Clarence Chatham Cook is based upon the catalog of the New York Public Library and a penciled notation in the article by the cataloguer. I have been assured by Mr. Gerald Doan McDonald, Chief, American History and Genealogy Divisions, that such an entry would not have been made unless the source were perfectly reliable. Clarence Cook, who in later years achieved fame as an architectural critic and arbiter of taste, studied architecture under A.J. Downing, his brother-in-law (they married the DeWint sisters), and Calvert Vaux; then, he taught and wrote for a number of years (*National Cyclopedia of American Biography*, Vol. X, p. 167; *Dictionary of American Biography*, Vol. IV, p. 371).

[63]*Richardson*, p. 15; letter of June 25, 1954.

[64]The revival of the style Louis XII and of the mansard roofs is discussed in very general terms by Hautecoeur, VII, pp. 293-294.

[65]The Liege edition at the Avery Library is undated. *Ante quam non* dates of c.1835, 1841, and 1846 for Vols. I, II, and III respectively are based on internal evidence, *e.g.*, Vol. I, plate 10 (1826), Vol. II, plates 100 and 130 (both 1835), and Vol. III, plate 138.

[66]Hautecoeur, VI, p. 59. Note, however, that the textual reference does not agree with the illustrations (Figs. 43-46), nor with Normand's illustration of No. 3 rue de la Tour des Dames (Vol. I, plate 53), which is identified as No. 1 rue de la Tour des Dames in Hautecoeur's Fig. 46.

[67]*Habitations champêtres*, plates 38, 74, and *passim*.

[68]For Visconti, see Normand, III, pp. 65 and 115; for Vaudoyer, see Hautecoeur, VI, Fig. 226; for Gisors, *ibid.*, Fig. 149; Gourlier, III, plate [40], and Pigeory, pp. 414-415.

[69]Attributions based on Gourlier, III, plate 389 [43].

[70]Paris, 1844-1856.

[71]*E.g.*, Imperial Polytechnic Institute, Vienna, a mansarded structure with pavilions, *Allgemeine Bauzeitung*, Vol. IV (1839), plate CCCV.

[72]Fiske Kimball, *Domestic Architecture of the American Colonies and of the Early Republic*, New York, 1922, p. 168, Fig. 128.

[73]*American Architecture*, New York, 1928, p. 120; Winsor, IV, p. 480, in reference to the Deacon House on Washington Street. The same data is contained in Charles S. Damrell's *A Half Century of Boston's Building*, Boston, 1895, p. 344. The name "J. Lemoulnier, archt" disappears from George Adams' *Boston Directory* after 1850/1851, only to reappear in New York

directories of the mid-1850s, which list a "Jean," alternating with "John Lemoulnier, archt," undoubtedly one and the same person.

[74]"Report on Mansard Roofs," a paper read October 16, 1873, *AIA Proceedings* (1873), p. 45, wherein he noted "its first appearance in this country, some twenty years ago, on a house executed by Messrs. Lienau and Marcotte... for Mrs. Shiff, on the Fifth avenue, in New York."

[75]Note, however, the very early appearance (1847) of two designs in the French style in Ranlett, Vol. I, Designs XX and XXI, plates 55 and 59. In his discussion of the French style (I, p. 76), Ranlett commented on its good taste, pleasing proportions, graceful ornament, and the picturesque qualities of the building silhouette. He took particular interest in the hipped roofs and concluded with this interesting prediction:

> "This style is so well adapted to the many portions of the country, and to the tastes and habits of our citizens, that it will not be a matter of surprise, if it should become a favorite style with us in a few years."

[76]McKenna, "... Vassar College," p. 72. Chap. xii, "The Second Empire Style in France and England," is an excellent survey of the subject.

[77]*Gazette des Beaux-Arts*, Series VI, Vol. XLII (1953), p. 130, and Fig. 13; *Early Victorian Architecture*, I, p. 215.

[78]Vaux extolled the virtues of the low French curved roof in "Hints for Country House Builders," *Harper's*, Vol. XI (November 1855), p. 733, Figs. A and B, later reproduced in *Villas and Cottages*, p. 54. He particularly liked the picturesque effect of the mansard when viewed from the opposite side of the street (*ibid.*, Design 29, p. 31).

[79]*E.g.*, Mrs. Burton Harrison in Mrs. Martha Lamb's *History of the City of New York...*, enlarged edition, New York [c.1877-1896], III, p. 41; James Philip Noffsinger, *The Influence of the Ecole des Beaux-Arts on the Architecture of the United States*, Washington, D.C., 1955, p. 14. Noffsinger, incidentally, mistakenly lists Lienau as an alumnus of the Ecole (p. 115). The best survey of Hunt's work is still Montgomery Schuyler's "Works of the Late William Morris Hunt," *Architectural Record*, Vol. V (1895), pp. 97-180; see also Alan Burnham, "The New York Architecture of Richard Morris Hunt," *SAH Journal*, Vol. XI (May 1952), pp. 9-14.

[80]It is quite evident that there were other architects in the U.S. who worked in the French tradition before Hunt's return. Vaux's predilection for the mansard, referred to by Kennion, has been noted above. Little is known of the work of other architects such as Alfred H. Piequenard (c.1826-1876), who settled in Springfield, Illinois, associate architect of the State Capitol of Iowa and other public buildings (see obituary, *American Architect*, Vol. I [1876], p. 399) or Peter [Pierre] Portois, a Belgian architect who settled in San Francisco c. 1849. There appears to be no direct corroborating evidence for Agnes Foster Buchanan's statement that he was the first Beaux-Arts architect in America ("Some Early Business Buildings in San Francisco," *Architectural Record*, Vol. XX [July 1906], p. 28), though strong French influence in the Nagler Building and "Wright's Folly" (illustrated in *ibid.*, pp. 18 and 21) is undeniable.

[81]Part I, p. 36. My thanks go to Mrs. Lois Dinnerstein for calling this amusing description to my attention in her seminar report, "The Influence of the Second Empire in the U.S.," April 27, 1957, Institute of Fine Arts, New York University. The passage reads as follows:

"We see this wonderful power of fashion in the sudden and universal application of the Mansard roof among us. A very short time ago, nobody seemed to know that buildings had roofs, and that roofs were not necessarily things to hide, but to be seen and ornamented; although Mr. Calvert Vaux had taught us better in a neat design for a residence on Fifth avenue... Suddenly, however, a sort of roof epidemic seemed to seize us; and now no building," etc.

[82]See the editorial, "An Architectural Affliction," *American Builder and Journal of Industrial Art*, Vol. X (January 1874), p. 32; *e.g.*, George E. Woodward, *Woodward's Country Homes*, New York: George E. Woodward [c.1865], Design 21 or *Woodward's Suburban and Country Houses*, New York, 1873, Design 18.

[83]See especially the spirited defense of the mansard by Albert G. Nash in his paper, "Mansard Roofs," November 13, 1872, *AIA Proceedings* (1872), pp. 48-49.

"Before abandoning a feature which has contributed so much to the scope of design in beautifying street architecture—a never-ending source of distinctive ideas—which breaks up monotony, marks a building..., a feature which has contributed more to picturesque effect in isolated structures and in domestic architecture generally, than any one idea that has been advanced since their invention—I say, before we abandon a roof which has done so much for architectural aesthetics; which has... been in use these three hundred years... and which has only been recently attacked... because it burnt where even granite crumbled—... would it not be well to inquire whether there is any other cause for combustion than the mere fact of the existence of a Mansard roof?"

[84]See Hamlin, *Greek Revival Architecture*, p. 129, Fig. 14, and [Robert Griffith Hatfield], *Plans of the Parish House* [New York, c.1848], of which a copy is preserved at the New York Public Library. Henry, the older brother of Daniel Parish, died in 1856; in 1863, the building was taken over by the Union League Club. In 1883, it was torn down to make way for a store for the Daniel Parish estate, designed by Lienau, which still stands, though much altered, at 860 Broadway.

Robert Griffith Hatfield (1815-1879), FAIA, born in Elizabeth, NJ, was one of the most influential architects of the period. He was one of the founders of the AIA and served for many years on its Committee of Examinations; he also was Treasurer of the New York Chapter. A member of the American Society for Civil Engineers, he was widely known as an authority on construction. His *American House Carpenter...*, New York, 1844, went through eleven editions to 1889; his *Theory of Transverse Strains*, New York, 1877, was widely acclaimed as a unique and much needed work. Hatfield is probably most famous for his design of the train shed for Grand Central Depot (1869-1871); earlier buildings were the depot for the New York-New Haven Railroad (1851), the Tiffany Store (1853-1854), and the Randall's Island School-house (1860). Oliver Perry Hatfield (1819-1891) was his younger brother.—Review of *Transverse Strains, American Architect,* Vol. II (October 13, 1877), pp. 326-327; obituary, *ibid.,* Vol. V (March 1, 1879), pp. 65, 69, and 77-78; Ada Louise Huxtable, "Grand Central Depot, 1869-1871," *Progressive Architecture,* Vol. XXXVII (October 1956), pp. 135-138.

[85]Strong, II, p. 208, January 21, 1855, referring to January 19. He could only have been referring to this house, since no other Shiffs (or Schiffs) are listed on Fifth Avenue in the directories of 1854/1855 and 1855/1856.

[86]Note that the second- and third-floor plans have penciled notations in Lienau's hand in French. One of the most interesting features of the house is the smoking room beyond the conservatory. Horace de Viel Castel, in his *Memoires sur le regne de Napoleon III,* Paris, 1883-1884, notes that the Emperor set the example of smoking after dinner in a room arranged as a winter garden in Princess Mathilde's new *hotel,* 24 rue de Courcelles (II, p. 121, entry of November 25, 1852, a reference I owe to Hautecoeur, VII, p. 249). French house plans, in contrast to English and American ones, often provided a *fumoir.* See Petit's *Maisons des environs de Paris,* plates 21, 29, 30, 41, etc.

[87]An old tradition (*e.g.,* Chateau de Villiers [Somme] in Petit's *Chateaux de France des XVe et XVIe siècles,* Paris [1855], plate 1), this type was occasionally used by Petit in his own designs (*e.g., Maisons de campagne,* plate 67).

[88]Morris, p. 26.

[89]Hamlin, *Greek Revival Architecture,* pp. 134-135, n. 16, item 5.

[90]According to Elizabeth Perkins's letter of January 10, 1926, to the editor of *The New York Times* (in J. Rosenfeld, "New York City Scrapbook," p. 5, New York Public Library, Room 328), the first brownstone house in New York was built c.1840 by her grandfather, Newton Perkins, at 11 West 9th Street. She also states that this was the first private residence with gas and water on the second floor.

[91]Downing's preference for drab or fawn colors in country houses (*Cottage Residences,* pp. 22-24, etc.) is echoed in the shift to brownstone for city residences. Early reactions against brownstone, or quite possibly a survival of the taste of the previous decades, may be noted in *The Citizen and Stranger's Pictorial and Business Directory for the City of New York... 1853,* p. 71. In describing the new houses on Fifth Avenue, "that Parisian Arrondissement," the editor comments on the unfitness of somber brownstone as a material suitable for city residences, though he concedes its possible suitability for Gothic churches "designed to perpetuate the memory of the Dark Ages..." See also the description of a new granite store in Philadelphia as a pleasant contrast to those buildings "of cheerless and unwelcome brownstone, which frown upon you at every step you take" (*Ballou's,* Vol. VI [February 18, 1854], p. 112). The funereal look of some country houses, whose builders apparently carried Downing's dictates to extremes, is noted by Lewis F. Allen, author of the popular plan book, *Rural Architecture...,* New York, 1852, p. 43.

⁹²See Bristed's sarcastic remarks concerning the social importance of the brownstone front and the total lack of interest in side and rear elevations (*The Upper Ten Thousand*, p. 41). A few years later, Charles D. Gambrill, in a paper read to a meeting of the AIA on March 16, 1861, "Reveries in a Back Yard," also spoke of the current neglect of the backs of houses: "We behold the anomaly of a Venetian palace joined to the expressionless [*sic*] façade of a New England factory" as soon as we turn the corner (*Architects' and Mechanics' Journal*, Vol. IV [April 6, 1861], p. 2).

⁹³Refers to page in original dissertation.

⁹⁴"Carpenter's Specifications," p. 14.

⁹⁵Regarding the Haight house, the author of the article in the New York *Weekly Review* (p. 4) says that the house is "replete with the worst New York vices of unthoroughness and unsubstantiality". He describes the stone work as a mere veneer with scarcely any bond, the cornice as a mere sham made of painted zinc or wood, and the interior "miserable," both in design and execution. Contemporary publications are filled with accounts of buildings collapsing while under construction, such as the accident recorded in the *Evening Post* of January 16, 1851 (p. 2, col. 4), in which over thirty workmen were injured and six killed (see also Ross, pp. 36-37). Philip Hone (p. 919, entry of August 6, 1850), after commenting on the collapse of two houses in the process of erection, says, "I have noticed... blocks of new buildings so slightly built that they could not stand alone, and, like drunken men, require the support of each other to keep from falling". The small study for the Shiff house mentioned above bears witness to the care with which the house was built. Minutely annotated, it shows how the master mason checked off the work of his helpers, Frank, Dominick, King, etc.

⁹⁶Its position on the lot is indicated in Robinson and Pidgeon's *Atlas*, plate 9.

⁹⁷Cf. *Architektur Skizzenbuch*, I, Heft XXII, plate 3. But one should also bear in mind that popularity of the chalet style in France around 1850 (see discussion in Hautecoeur, VI, p. 321, and VII, p. 246, Fig. 220, an illustration of the Summer chalet residences of Napoleon III in Vichy).

⁹⁸Refers to page in original dissertation.

⁹⁹Vol. III, plate 96.

¹⁰⁰Cf., however, Madame Pulszky's characterization of the architecture of the U.S., following English example, as "a chaotic conglomeration of all styles and all tastes, thrown together as if by chance" (I, p. 49); "B," *Atlantische Studien*, I, p. 185; J.J. Ampere, *Promenade en Amerique*, Paris, 1855, II, p. 81, with particular reference to Renwick's Smithsonian Institute.

¹⁰¹Refers to page in original dissertation.

¹⁰²A study of the sixty odd drawings on interior decoration in the Lienau Collection, including designs for mantels, staircases, etc., would provide an interesting footnote to changes in taste from the 1850s through the '80s. Quite unexpected are the Eastlakean touches in designs of 1880 for proposed alterations of August Belmont's house on Fifth Avenue, a

project that was abandoned because of a row between the architect and the client.

[103]Chambers, p. 178 for passage quoted; see also Bishop, *The English-woman in America*, pp. 335 ff.; Jouve, *Voyage en Amerique*, p. 22. Jouve was delighted with the houses on Fifth Avenue, although he disliked our public buildings and churches, maintaining that they were decorated with a taste Paris would not disavow.

[104]*E.g.*, "A Parlor in a New York Dwelling House," *Ballou's*, Vol. VII (1854), p. 300.

[105]According to a list of the work of L. Marcotte & Company in the "Advertiser's Trade Supplement," *American Architect*, Vol. XXI (June 4, 1887), they had installed the marble mosaics in Dr. Gautier's residence [formerly the Shiff house].

[106]Letter of June 29, 1951.

[107]Portfolio XXII, No. 46. The Shiff vault is a severely simple structure with thick walls faced with granite. A reflection of the spirit, though not of the detailing, of the Neo-Grec is felt here: See L. Normand aine, *Monuments funeraires...*, Paris [1847], *passim*. It is completely different from Upjohn's funerary monuments (see Upjohn Collection, Avery Library, Box IV, E-1, 18, etc.), all in Gothic style.

[108]The Tax Assessment Records of the City of New York are preserved at the Municipal Archives and Records Center, New York Public Library, 238 William Street, New York. They have proven singularly useful throughout this study, particularly for buildings erected before May 1866, after which the New Building Dockets at the Department of Buildings may be consulted. A change in assessed valuation is often accompanied by penciled notations regarding the progress of construction.

With reference to the Shiff house, the Map Book of the 15th Ward indicates that in 1850 Shiff owned one lot valued at $7,000; in 1851, the house and three lots, $30,000, with the notation "house unfinished" appended. In 1852 and 1853, the assessment was raised to $32,000, indicating probably completion of the house by the spring of 1852 (tax records ran from May to May in the 1850s).

[109]Completion also is corroborated by the *Map of the City of New-York Extending Northward to Fiftieth Street*, New York, 1852, Map Room, New York Public Library. Familiarly known as the Dripps Map, this map is a particularly useful one. Unlike those of other years, it differentiates between vacant (unshaded) and improved (shaded) lots.

[110]The directories also were useful in dating the construction of the house, particularly *Doggett's New York City Street Directory of 1851* (one of two New York directories of its kind), which informs us that 32 Fifth Avenue is "now building". Matthew Keiley, the carpentry contractor, listed his business address as "Av. 5 c. Tenth" in *Doggett's Directory of 1850/1851*; the following year, he had moved to 60 West 11th Street. It is most unlikely that he would have left the house had it been unfinished.

[111]See Census of 1855, Manhattan, 15th Ward, Election District 5, Dwelling #10, Family #18; listings in the city directories, and Vose, *Wealth of the World*, 1859, p. 115.

[112]Basilice Shiff's will (dated 1861, with addenda of 1869, proved June 15, 1877) indicates that she was a woman of considerable means. Records of wills for New York County, Surrogates Court, may be consulted in Room 402, Hall of Records, New York. For Mrs. Shiff's will, see Lib. 255, pp. 239 ff.

[113]For Gauter, see McLean, *History of Jersey City*, II, p. 231; Mills, *Historic Houses of New Jersey*, pp. 74 ff.; William H. Shaw, *History of Essex and Hudson Counties, New Jersey*, Philadelphia, 1884, II, p. 1151. In his will (dated May 2, 1893, proved April 16, 1895, Lib. 509, pp. 429 ff.), he bequeathed the house to his son Dudley rent free for one year (!).

[114]See editorial, "An Old New Yorker," *The New York Times*, October 23, 1915 (p. 10, cols. 3-4), written in tribute to him two days after his death.

[115]I owe this information to J. Henry Lienau (letter of December 14, 1951), who was so informed by Mr. Eno's niece. Interestingly enough, Train served as counsel for the contestants of Eno's will. He must have known the house well.

Chapter V

[1]Strong, II, p. 77, entry of December 16, 1851.

[2]Biographical data based on Cottenet's obituary, *The New York Times*, August 9, 1884 (p. 4, col. 7) and [Moses Yale Beach, editor], *Wealth and Biography of the Wealthy Citizens of New York City...*, 6th edition, New York, 1845, p. 10.

[3]*Ibid.*

[4]*The Hudson from the Wilderness to the Sea*, New York [1866], p. 355.

[5]According to the "Chain of Title," preserved by the present owners of the house, the deed transferring the property to Francis Cottenet was dated November 27, 1852, and recorded December 6, 1852 (Lib. 214, cp 289).

[6]Portfolio IV, No. 6. Over thirty drawings for the house are preserved, including the eight preliminary studies and eight working drawings for the original building, twelve studies and two working drawings for the extension, a study for a gardener's cottage, and a working drawing of a section through the greenhouse. See also an early photolithograph and the enlarged plan (Fig. 35 here), published in *Villas on the Hudson* [plates 8 and 9], and a view in Wayne Andrews's invaluable collection of "Architectural Photographs," New York [194?], Series VII, No. 879.

[7]I am much indebted to the Browns for permission to visit the house on several occasions and for sundry information.

[8]*The Hudson*, p. 355.

[9]I, p. 32. Sloan's very first design was an Italian villa. The reference to the popularity of the style in the old world undoubtedly referred chiefly to English sources, summarized by Meeks in "Henry Austin and the Italian

Villa," *Art Bulletin*, Vol. XXX (June 1948), pp. 145-149. See also Newton's discussion of the origins of Town & Davis's "Tuscan" style (pp. 244 ff.).

With reference to Lienau, one might point to the extensive use of the style in Germany, particularly by the Schinkelschuler. For Persius, see *Architektonische Entwurfe*, plates I, VII, and XIII; and *Architektonische Album*, Heft XII (1846), plate LXXII and p. 8, where reference is made to the many Italian villas he built in the vicinity of Potsdam. The apparent absence of Italian villas from French pattern books of the period is striking: See Petit's publications and Normand's *Paris moderne*. In the latter, there are a number of villas that feature a central *belvedere* or look-out, usually more classical than Tuscan in style (*e.g.*, Vol. I, plates 37, 70, 94, 145, etc.).

[10]I, p. 12. See also Downing, *Country Houses*, pp. 285-286. Of the thirty-one villas in *Villas on the Hudson*, all within the metropolitan area, nine were Italian villas. One of the finest was a stone house for James Cunningham in Irvington, near Dobbs Ferry, for which the architect is not given [plates 30 and 31).

[11]Downing, *Country Houses*, pp. 262-263.

[12]*Ibid.*, p. 263.

[13]It is abundantly clear that, even in the 1840s, a laborer's house might be a "Gothic cottage" or a *cottage orne*, but that "Tudor" was reserved for the wealthy gentry and rich merchants. The prestige value of the Italian villa is stressed in the quotation from Sloan above. It is interesting to note that Renlett (II, p. 13) disapproved of the elaborate Italian villa because he thought it out of keeping with our republican habits. As time went on, however, the high class limited edition Italian villa became available in simplified, crude, wood versions to people who took their plans "ready made" from the plan books or the period, paralleling the process by which the Paris "Original" finds it way to the bargain basement today. See especially John W. Ritch, *The American Architect, Comprising Original Designs of Cheap Country Houses and Village Residences...*, New York [1850-1851?], Design 1, 20; John Bullock, *The American Cottage Builder; a Series of Designs, Plans and Specifications from $200 to $20,000...*, New York, 1854, Design VII, pp. 50 and 97.

[14]The dominant vertical of the tower was usually emphasized not only by its height (four stories were more common than three), but also by its double- or triple-arcaded windows in the uppermost story. In an unidentified study for an Italian villa (in the Lienau Collection), we find the usual four-story tower with triplet window at the top. Since the style and rendering are clearly related to the Shiff house (1850) and the Kane villa (1852), it is possible that this was an alternate design for the Cottenet house.

[15]Cf. especially Upjohn's King house (discussed below) and Austin's Norton house of c.1849 in New Haven (Meeks, "Henry Austin," Fig. 9, and Andrews, *Photographs*, Series I, Nos. 9 and 10). Hitchcock has discussed the important role played by the irregular Italian villa type in breaking down the tradition of symmetry in American house design of this period in *Rhode Island Architecture*, Providence, 1939, p. 48.

[16]Meeks, *Art Bulletin*, Vol. XXX, p. 147. See Davis's villa for Llewellyn Haskell (1851) in Belleville, New Jersey, which Lienau may have known (Newton, Fig. 24, and Meeks, Fig. 4), his houses for John Munn in Utica, New York (1854) and E.C. Litchfield in Brooklyn, New York (Figs. 5 and 6 in Meeks) and his villa for Daniel Devlin, Manhattanville, New York (*Villas on the Hudson* [plate 35]).

[17]Design XXVII, pp. 317 ff. Plan on p. 318. An excellent photograph is in Hitchcock, *Rhode Island Architecture*, plate 54.

[18]Everard Upjohn, commenting on Downing's glowing comparison of the variety of the window openings to the complexities of a Beethoven symphony, adds that this was "probably as left-handed a compliment as that genius ever received" (*Richard Upjohn*, p. 94). This particular failing of Upjohn is seen again and again in the drawings in the Upjohn Collection, Avery Library (*e.g.*, drawings of 1851-1852 for Mrs. Heard's house in Watertown, Massachusetts [plates?], A-1, 16).

[19]Though Colonel Stevens himself has been credited with the design (*The New York Times*, April 17, 1951, p. 31, col. 5), Jackson is cited as the architect in *Villas on the Hudson* [plate 7]. This edifice replaced an earlier one that burned c.1852 (*The Herald-Tribune*, November 8, 1854, p. 17, col. 1). According to his obituary (*American Architect*, Vol. LXXI [1901], pp. 49-50), Thomas R. Jackson (1826-1901) came here from England in 1831 and trained in Upjohn's office. Late in life, he served as Superintendent of Federal Buildings in New York. The following important structures are attributed to him: the "old" Academy of Music on 14th Street (replacing Saeltzer's earlier building, which burned in 1866), Wallack's Theatre, Tammany Hall, and *The New York Times* Building, many of which are illustrated in *King's Handbook of New York*, 2nd edition, Boston, 1893. For additional examples of his early domestic architecture, see *Villas on the Hudson* [plates 11, 12, 45 and 46]. Reference will be made later to his work for Larry Jerome.

[20]Vol. I, Design VI, plates XXI and XXII. The emphasis on, and position of, the canopied window in the second story of the tower, with its little balustraded balcony, is similar. As Meeks has pointed out, such architectural features as balconies, canopies, etc., so typical of the work of the 1840s, tend to disappear in the '50s (*Art Bulletin*, Vol. XXX, p. 147).

[21]See Andrews's photograph, Series II, No. 236.

[22]See Meeks, Fig. 16, or Upjohn, Fig. 84. Many studies for the house, dated 1853 and 1855, are preserved in the Upjohn Collection, Avery Library, A-11.

[23]Statement of James G. Van Derpool, Avery Librarian.

[24]Refers to page in original dissertation.

[25]*E.g.*, Upjohn's C. Ely house of 1852-1854 in West Springfield, Mass. (Upjohn, Fig. 80; Andrews, *Photographs*, Series I, No. 5); Thomas S. Wall's villa in Inwood Park for Francis A. Thompson (c.1854) and house for S.D. Babcock in Riverdale (both in *Villas on the Hudson* [plates 41 and 25-26] respectively).

[26]*Villas and Cottages*, p. 69; also mentioned in *The Crayon* of November 21, 1855, as becoming popular (Vol. II, p. 329).

[27]Represented by the unshaded section of Fig. 35. The back drawing room was originally the dining room, and the sitting room, a billiard room.

[28]Cf. the King house, typical of many of the plans of the early period (Meeks, "Henry Austin," Fig. 13) with the use of polygonal or curved projections in Davis's and Upjohn's work of the later 1850s, as in the latter's E.B. Litchfield house (Meeks, Fig. 15, or Upjohn, Fig. 82). The square bay of very slight projection used in two of the rooms in "Nuits" are of the type used as early as the mid-'30s by Davis (Meeks, p. 148).

[29]While ascending cupboards of one sort or another had been in use for years (a famous early example in this country was installed by Jefferson at Monticello), they were not successfully mass produced and marketed until after 1855, when James Murtaugh of New York took out a patent. This dumbwaiter was a marked improvement over the older types, according to *Architects' and Mechanics' Journal*, Vol. II (April 14, 1860), p. 14, and *History of Real Estate, Building and Architecture in New York City*, New York, 1898, pp. 450-451. This extremely useful and well illustrated reference work may be consulted at the Avery Library and the New York Public Library.

[30]The date 1858 *ante quam non* is assured by the fact that, on the drawing for the greenhouse, Lienau's address is given as 111 Broadway, where he was first listed in 1858/1859 in the directories. The date *post quam non* of 1860 is given by the appearance of the illustrations, including the revised plan, in *Villas on the Hudson* [plate 9], published in that year.

[31]*Architects' and Mechanics' Journal*, Vol. I (1860), p. 117; also, editorial of February 25, 1860, in Vol. I, p. 159. For French plans, cf. Normand, *Paris moderne*, Vol. III, plates 57 and *passim*.

[32]For an interesting discussion of the rustic style, an outgrowth of the Victorian fondness for the picturesque, see Lichten, pp. 206 ff. Lienau's treatment of the ironwork is still structural and rather classical in feeling, in contrast to the extraordinarily fanciful effects often sought after in this material.

[33]The present firm, A.M. Hunter & Sons, no longer has any of the plans connected with the alteration.

[34]For biographic information, see Charles H. Winfield, *History of the County of Hudson, New Jersey...*, New York, 1874, p. 347, and McLean, *History of Jersey City*, p. 187. Tax lists of 1856 are very informative (*Gopsill's Directory of Jersey City and Hoboken, 1857-1858*, pp. 233 ff.). Miller's real estate was valued at $98,000, Michael Lienau's at $21,000, and Detlef's at $16,000; their personal estates were respectively $3,000, $2,000, and $500. While these figures may seem low to us today, even Detlef was in the higher income bracket in the town.

[35]Portfolio VI, No. 10. Four studies in pen and ink, including two elevations and plans of the parlor and second floor.

³⁶Cf. Petit, *Habitations champêtres*, plate 63. For the Tully-Bowen house, see Hitchcock, *Rhode Island Architecture*, plate 56, and Barbara Wriston, "The Architecture of Thomas Tefft," *Bulletin of the Museum of Art, Rhode Island School of Design*, Vol. XXVIII (November 1940), p. 42, and Fig. 29.

³⁷See "Elizabeth City, New Jersey," a well illustrated article in *Ballou's*, Vol. XI (1856), pp. 215-216.

³⁸*Boyd's Directory of Elizabeth, Rahway and Plainfield*, Elizabeth, New Jersey, 1869, the earliest directory available at both the New York Public Library and the Free Library of Elizabeth. According to Miss Helen J. Ferguson of the latter's Reference and Technical Department (letter of March 1, 1955), there is no house now at 138 West Jersey Street. Mrs. Mayo later moved to a different address.

³⁹Portfolio VI, No. 9. Four studies, including two elevations and plans of basement and first floor.

⁴⁰Refers to page in original dissertation.

⁴¹*E.g.*, T.C. Sherman house (1853), Springfield, Ohio, J.J. Johnson house (1851-1854), Flatbush, Brooklyn (Upjohn Collection, A-21, 6; A-10, 4, and Upjohn, Fig. 79).

⁴²See Hugh McD. Closkie, "William Pennington," *Dictionary of American Biography*, XIV, pp. 442-443, Governor of New Jersey (1837-1843) and Speaker of the U.S. House of Representatives in Washington (1860); *Biographical and Genealogical History of the City of Newark and Essex County, New Jersey*, New York, 1898, I, pp. 493-494; [Lyman Horace Weeks, editor], "Henry Pennington Toler," *Prominent Families of New York...*, revised edition, New York, 1898, p. 565. The latter, a very useful work, will be cited again.

⁴³C.G. Hine, *Woodside, the North End of Newark, N.J. Its History, Legends and Ghost Stories...*, Hines Annual, 1909, p. 37, a quotation sent to me by both Mrs. Maud H. Greene, corresponding secretary, New Jersey Historical Society, Newark, and Miss Julia Sabine, Chief Librarian, Art and Music Department, Newark Public Library (letters of November 16, and December 15, 1954, respectively). Thanks are due to Miss Sabine for data on the Tolers and the house (letters of February 18, 1955, and January 20, 1956).

⁴⁴Toler, who lived until 1902, was listed for the last time on Belleville Road in the *Newark Directory of 1862/1863*.

⁴⁵"Woodside Landmark Succumbs to Progress of Time," the Newark *Evening News*, June 28, 1924 (Julia Sabine, letter of January 20, 1956).

⁴⁶Portfolio VI, No. 11, including the watercolor rendering illustrated, two elevations, and four plans.

⁴⁷For a discussion of the English origins of the bay window and its subsequent development in the U.S., see Meeks, *Art Bulletin*, Vol. XXX, p. 148.

⁴⁸Cf. Belcher residence (1853-1854), Garrison, New York (Upjohn Collection, A-4, esp. No. 5), which is extremely close in plan to the Toler house; also the Atwater house (1854-1855) and Litchfield house (A-3, 1; A-11, both illustrated in Upjohn, Figs. 75 and 82).

[49]Henry Hudson Holly, *Holly's Country Seats...*, New York, 1863, Designs 12, 14, and 22. Since the publication of this book was delayed two years by the outbreak of the Civil War, it may be considered representative of the late 1850s, rather than of the '60s.

[50]This exhibition was entitled "A Century of Summer Architecture in the United States". Newton followed with "Our Summer Resort Architecture—An American Phenomenon and Social Document," *Art Quarterly*, Vol. IV (Fall 1941), pp. 297-322.

[51]*The Shingle Style; Architectural Theory and Design from Richardson to the Origins of Wright*, New Haven, 1955.

[52]Interest in the work of Stevens was stimulated by Talbot Hamlin's exhibition, "Drawings by John Calvin Stevens, 1856-1940," Avery Library, 1945. The Avery Library has considerable material on Stevens and Eyre. The Stevens Collection consists of 125 original drawings, the gift of his son, John Howard Stevens, in 1944. For a complete listing, see the catalog, "The Stevens Collection," typescript, Avery Library [1945]. The Wilson Eyre Collection consists of four packages of original drawings, indexed in "The Wilson Eyre Collection," typescript, Avery Library [1946], plus ten scrapbooks of drawings and two packages containing drawings, clippings, correspondence, and biographical material, the gift of Miss Roberta Yerkes, 1956, not indexed to date.

[53]A phrase coined by Mrs. May (King) Van Rensselaer, *Newport: Our Social Capital*, Philadelphia, 1905.

[54]Carl Bridenbaugh, "Colonial Newport as a Summer Resort," *Rhode Island Historical Society Collections*, Vol. XXVI (January 1933), pp. 1-23.

[55]In 1836, Strong called Newport "a mean, wooden, contemptible-looking place" (I, p. 18, May 6, 1836).

[56]To this "intellectual" period belong the familiar names of Longfellow, Julia Ward Howe, Bret Harte, the elder Holmes, the Jameses, George Bancroft, Mr. Agassiz, Professor Gibbs, William Morris Hunt, and John La Farge. Maud Howe Elliott's interesting memoirs, *This Was My Newport*, Cambridge, Massachuetts, 1944, has furnished recent writers with excellent source material. See Gibson Danes, "William Morris Hunt and his Newport Circle," *Magazine of Art*, Vol. XLIII (April 1950), pp. 144-150, and Cleveland Amory's best seller, *The Last Resorts*, New York, 1952. Amory maintains (pp. 23-24) that a sort of "Gresham's Law" holds true for 19th century resorts and summarizes Newport's development in these words:

> "*First*, [came] artists and writers in search of good scenery and solitude; *second*, professors and clergymen and other so-called 'solid' people with long vacations in search of the simple life; *third*, 'nice' millionaires in search of a good place for their children to lead the simple life as lived by the 'solid' people [he includes DeLancey Kane in this category]; *fourth*, 'naughty' millionaires who wished to associate with the 'nice' millionaires, but who built million-dollar cottages... and utterly destroyed the simple life; *fifth*, trouble..."

[57]William James, "Newport" (1870), reprinted in *Portraits of Places*, Boston, 1884, p. 348. The Indians called Rhode Island *Aquidneck*, or "Isle of Peace".

[58]*Idem.*, *Notes of a Son and Brother*, New York, 1914, p. 415.

[59]*Idem.*, *Portraits of Places*, pp. 341-342.

[60]For a clarification of the real estate background, I am indebted to Mrs. Gladys E. Bolhouse, Executive Secretary, Newport Historical Society, letters of September 26 and November 6, 1953. For Smith, see Junius Henri Browne, "The Queen of Aquidneck," *Harper's*, Vol. XLIX (August 1874), p. 310; Richard R. Bayles (editor), *History of Newport County, Rhode Island, from the Year 1683 to the Year 1887...*, New York, 1888, p. 489; Richmond Barrett, *Good Old Summer Days; Newport, Narragansett Pier, Saratoga, Long Branch, Bar Harbor*, New York, 1941, pp. 4 ff.

[61]Johnson, a Jamaica planter, is discussed in George Champlin Mason's *Reminiscences of Newport*, Newport, RI, 1884, chapter xxiv, pp. 186-190, and in a pamphlet written by his granddaughter, M.W. Powel, "The Old Easton Farm," *Bulletin of the Newport Historical Society*, No. 64 (January 1928), pp. 1-14, kindly forwarded to me by Mrs. Bolhouse.

[62]Letter of August 22, 1853, signed "Young America," *The New York Times*, August 26, 1853 (p. 2, cols. 5-6). The growing importance of Newport as a social center is indicated by the first appearance at this time of regular letters to the *Times*, paralleling those from Saratoga and other resorts.

[63]V, p. 413. For a really vivid description of a typical day at the United States, see Curtis, *Lotus-eating*, pp. 113-121; also Bristed, *The Upper Ten Thousand*, chapters iv and v. Bristed, incidentally, was a cousin of Mrs. DeLancey Kane.

[64]Vol. VII (June 1856), p. 659.

[65]In 1865, Saratoga was already described as a faded beauty, which had seen better days (Curtis, p. 109).

[66]*Newport Illustrated*, Newport, 1854, pp. 8-9. Mason (1820-1894) was a successful Rhode Island architect. In addition to this little book and *Reminiscences of Newport*, he wrote the handsomely illustrated *Newport and Its Cottages*, Boston, 1875, the best source for the early cottages, now a rare book; the Redwood Library, Newport, and the New York Public Library have copies.

[67]Pages 163-164.

[68]"The Age of McAllister" is discussed at some length in Barrett's *Good Old Summer Days*, p. 27 and *passim*.

[69]Though their owners might refer to their houses as "cottages," Ranlett pointed out in an essay on nomenclature of dwellings that "some of our wealthy merchants who reside in elegant country houses would be very likely to take offence at being called 'cotters'" (II, p. 21). Elsewhere (I, p. 21), he writes:

> "A cottage indicates a disposition in the proprietor to live within his income, and to appropriate his means rather for the convenience and comfort of his family, than for show, which he is ill prepared to sustain."

[70]Strong, IV, p. 94, summer of 1866. Mrs. Paran Stevens was the wife of the famous hotel owner.

[71]See Mrs. Elliott's memoirs, *This Was My Newport*, pp. 131 ff.

[72]"Flirtation at Newport," *Harper's Weekly*, Vol. I (September 12, 1857), p. 584. The sentence concludes, "it is only at Newport that you find people who do really nothing well."

[73]Walter W. Spooner (editor), *Historic Families of America*, New York, 1907-1908, I, p. 200. Other helpful sources of biographical and genealogical information have been: Elizabeth Dennistoun Kane, *The Story of John Kane of Dutchess County*, Philadelphia, 1921; Harvey O'Connor, *The Astors*, New York, 1941; Elliott, *passim*; Morris, *Incredible New York*, *passim*; Amory, *passim*; "Astor Genealogical Chart, 1764-1895," manuscript in Genealogy and Local History, Room 328, New York Public Library; obituary of DeLancey Kane, *The New York Times* and *Tribune*, March 24, 1874, pp. 5, cols. 7; copy of his "Last Will and Testament," dated August 28, 1871, Record of Wills, Lib. 221, pp. 125-127, Surrogates Court, New York County.

[74]Oliver and John Kane, who operated for a time under the firm name of Kane & Brothers, built up a large commission business, importing soft goods from Europe in exchange for American furs, potash, and wheat from upstate New York and points farther west.

[75]In Edith Wharton's *The Age of Innocence* (p. 125), there appears this revealing sentence: "... the crude fact of money-making was still regarded as derogatory, and the law, being a profession, was accounted a more gentlemanly pursuit".

[76]Lawrence S. Mayo, "Woodbury Langdon," *Dictionary of American Biography*, X, p. 590; William A. Robinson, "John Langdon," *ibid.*, pp. 587-588. Walter Langdon himself relied heavily on his family name, good looks, and his wife's fortune. Strong, who was his attorney, had very little regard for him (Strong, II, pp. 29 and 37, entries of November 22, 1850, and February 4, 1851). O'Connor (pp. 76-77) describes him as a man with no particular calling, who devoted himself to the life of a *grand seigneur* on his estate at Hyde Park when he was not in residence at Astor Place.

[77]It was a two-story and basement structure with a simple classical portico (see *Broadway, Bond Street to Eighth Street, 1865*, an old print, Scrapbook, No. 381, Print Department, Museum of the City of New York). The Kanes lived there from 1845/1846 through 1853/1854, according to the city directories of those years. For the building of 1873 that replaced it, see Fig. 107.

[78]For an interesting story of the Astor will, see O'Connor, pp. 80 ff. Louisa Kane contested the terms of the will and took her uncle, William Astor, to court—to no avail. Her inheritance, estimated at $200,000 in securities and real estate, increased phenomenally in the ensuing decades. DeLancey Kane is listed as worth $2,000,000 in *Reuben Vose's Wealth of the World Displayed*, p. 72.

[79]His brother, Samuel Nicholson Kane (1846-1906), the brains of the family, was a graduate of the Naval Academy in Annapolis and had been an aide to Admiral Farragut on his visits to the courts of Europe in 1867. After his resignation from the Navy, he studied at Cambridge University; then, he

studied law. Valedictorian of his class, he was admitted to the bar, but never practiced. He devoted his time to the family estate (it was he who signed the contract drawings for the Lienau building at 676 Broadway in 1873), various charities, and clubs. As a member of the New York Yacht Club and its Commodore from 1877 through 1879, he was probably the one who induced the club to make its headquarters in the American Jockey Club, which was designed by Lienau.

[80]Index of Deeds, City Clerk's Office, City Hall, Newport.

[81]For the history of the property, see Powell, *Bulletin of the Newport Historical Society* (January 1928).

[82]Kane and his family are mentioned by Philip Hone as passengers on the steamer Atlantic, which arrived in New York from Liverpool on June 9, 1850 (p. 915, entry of June 10, 1850).

[83]Downing and Scully, plate 162.

[84]Downing, A.J. Davis's good friend, cautioned against the folly of building castles: "Unless there is something of the castle in the man, it is very likely... to dwarf him to the stature of a mouse" (*Country Houses*, p. 261). The tradition of a castellated architecture did persist, however, notably in *retardataire* plan books such as Field's *Rural Architecture...* (1857) and in Davis's work of the '50s (see *Villas on the Hudson, passim*, and the Davis-Higgins terrace of 1856, "The House of Mansions," Fig. 71). A very early example of the revolt against castellated architecture is offered by the anonymous critic who reviewed Ranlett's *American Architect* for the New York *Mirror*, October 17, 1846 (cited by Hamlin, *Greek Revival Architecture*, p. 325). A tentative attribution to Henry W. Cleaveland is suggested by the similar phraseology in Cleaveland and Backus, *Village and Farm Cottages*, p. 66.

> "There can be nothing more grotesque, more absurd, or more affected, than for a quiet gentleman, who has made his fortune in the peaceful occupation of selling calicos, and who knows no more of the middle ages than they do of him, to erect for his family residence a gimcrack of a Gothic castle... as though he anticipated an attack upon his roost from some Front de Boeuf in the neighborhood."

[85]Downing and Scully, plate 160.

[86]Downing may well have had a house such as Kingscote in mind when he wrote in *Country Houses* (p. 263):

> "The man of sentiment... will seek for that house in whose aspect there is something to love. It will nestle in, or grow out of, the soil. It must not look all new and sunny, but must show secluded shadowy corners. There must be nooks... where one would love to linger; windows, where one can enjoy the quiet landscape leisurely; cozy rooms, where all domestic fireside joys are invited to dwell. It must, in short, have something in its aspect which the heart can fasten upon and become attached to, as naturally as the ivy attaches itself to the antique wall."

[87]Refers to page in original dissertation.

[88]This is particularly emphasized by Scully (Downing and Scully, p. 123).

[89]In discussing the Newport houses of the 1840s and '50s, Scully divides them into two groups, one emphasizing mass, and the other stressing articulated structure (*ibid.*, pp. 124 ff.).

[90]It was through this print (in folder labeled "Out of Town Residences of New York Families") that I learned the original name of the Kane house.

[91]James T. O'Connell, letter of August 27, 1953.

[92]Portfolio IV, No. 5. The seven small presentation drawings, dated 1852, include four elevations and three plans (basement, first, and attic stories). The date of completion of the house is not known. Information regarding tax valuations, which would probably have provided a clue, was contained in a letter from Mr. Kenneth Stein, Tax Collector's Office, Newport, unfortunately lost in the mail.

[93]According to the Index of Deeds, Beach Cliffe was sold by DeLancey Kane on October 22, 1867, to Charles J. Peterson, who named it Red Cross. It remained in the Peterson family until October 17, 1894; then, it was held by various owners for short periods of time until its purchase by Richard V. Mattison on July 22, 1899. Known as Bushy Park, the property was held by the Mattisons until 1934, when it was sold to Henry Whittington. In 1939, it was purchased by Eugene O'Reilly, who with his father-in-law, James T. O'Connell, subdivided the property into small parcels.

[94]Mason, *Newport and its Cottages*, pp. 47-48.

[95]Pages 139-140.

[96]Chateau-sur-mer's advanced stylistic character should, in all likelihood, be attributed to its owner, rather than to the mysterious Seth Bradford, who is mentioned in local newspapers as the builder. Mrs. Bolhouse of the Newport Historical Society knows nothing about him (letter of September 26, 1953). William Shepard Wetmore, a Vermonter who had made his fortune in the China trade, was one of New York's leading merchants and bankers. He was thoroughly cosmopolitan and spent much of his time traveling in England and on the Continent. See James C. Wetmore, *The Wetmore Family of America...*, Albany, 1861, p. 359.

[97]*E.g.*, *Maisons de campagne*, plate 89.

[98]The so-called *colonne française* or *colonne de l'Orme* was first used by Philibert de l'Orme at the Tuileries (pp. 1574 ff.).

[99]One is reminded of Downing's amusing description of a six-story brick house on Staten Island, which looked as if it had "strayed out of town, in a fit of insanity, and had lost the power of getting back again" (*Cottage Residences*, p. 33). One wonders why Lienau designed so citified a building for the beach at Newport. The wishes of the client may have had a great deal to do with it; relative lack of precedent was certainly another factor. Possibly, Lienau's French training may also have had a bearing on the question. As late as 1878, an American reports that French seaside houses are simply townhouses transplanted "such as might have been built in the heart of Paris" (letter signed "R" on "English and French Seaside Architecture," *American Architect*, Vol. IV [November 16, 1878], p. 165).

[100]*Treatise of Landscape Gardening*, p. 304; *Cottage Residences*, p. 21; etc.

[101]Curtis, *Lotus-eating*, p. 174. Ranlett (I, pp. 19-20) discusses the national tendency toward "amplification, "*i.e.*, exaggeration which James Fenimore Cooper had also ridiculed. Ranlett points out that we now [1847] have no residences in this country which deserve to be called villas, if by that we mean to compare them to the old Roman or even the modern Italian villas. "Then," he continues, "it would be quite proper to call the houses in Union Square, palaces, or our meeting places, Cathedrals..."—which is exactly what happened. The architectural descriptions of the period have to be taken with not one, but several, grains of salt.

[102]"Newport—Historical and Social," *Harper's*, Vol. IX (August 1854), p. 296; Van Rensselaer, p. 63.

[103]H. & D. Parish, occasionally misspelled as Parrish, was one of the largest dry goods firms in New York in the second quarter of the century, with branch offices in several southern cities. Henry, the older brother, retired from business in 1838 and restricted his activities to heavy investments in stocks and New York City real estate. Daniel Parish remained active in the business for several decades. In the '70s, he was President of the New York Life and Trust Company, for which Lienau designed a new building c.1866 (see Appendix II). Henry Parish's "palace" at Union Square has already been mentioned. Daniel's Fifth Avenue residence, built at about the same time as his Newport villa, was designed by Frederick Diaper.

[104]Clay Lancaster, "Ammi B. Young—His Work as First Supervising Architect of the United States Treasury Department," unpublished manuscript, 194?, pp. 15-16. See Ammi Burnham Young, *Specifications for the Custom House and Post Office at Bath, Maine*, Washington, 1853, etc.

[105]For the impact of Ruskin on the intelligent layman, see Strong's comments on *The Seven Lamps of Architecture* (Diary, I, p. 354, entry of June 6, 1849) and *Stones of Venice*, published 1851-1853 (II, p. 128, August 24, 1853).

[106]Paris [18??], especially plates 17, 26, 31, and 29, which is closest.

[107]*Model Architect*, Design XVIII, plate LXXII. A few years later, Vaux recommended the use of arcades for their value in producing pleasant contrasts of light and shade, adding that they deserve more attention than they commonly receive (*Villas and Cottages*, p. 98, Fig. 8, p. 99).

[108]Downing and Scully, p. 125.

[109]Suburban Cottage No. 4, discussed on p. 223; plates opposite pp. 221, 253, 272, and 289.

[110]There appears to be a close relationship between Eidlitz's chalets and slightly earlier German work: cf., *e.g.*, his cottage in New Jersey of 1860 (Schuyler, *Architectural Record*, Vol. XXIV [1908], p. 169, Fig. 6) and a house near Berlin (*Architektonisches Skizzenbuch*, Vol. I [1855], Heft XIX, plate 1). An anecdote told by Schuyler (p. 170) makes clear the fact that Eidlitz was interested in the Swiss style for its structural expressiveness, a point that is also stressed by Scully in his discussion of the chalet (p. 128).

¹¹¹One of the few non-stylistic designs suggested for use as a seaside cottage was the quite extraordinary "Marine Villa" built by Ranlett in Long Branch (II, p. 19). It had a flat roof and a deep two-story porch on the seaward side. There must have been many such cottages, but in all likelihood they were not deemed worthy of inclusion in the builders' guides of the period.

Chapter VI

¹See Henry Irving Dodge, "Forty Years on Twenty-third Street, *Valentine's Manual of Old New York*, edited by Henry Collins Brown, New York, VIII (1929?), pp. 81-106.

²Incredible as it may seem, the purchase price of Edmund's property at 45-47 West Twenty-third Street in 1857 was only $5,000 (Tax Assessment Records, Manhattan, 18th Ward).

³See Brown, *Fifth Avenue Old and New, 1824-1924*, New York, 1924, pp. 53 ff.

⁴The following sources credit Washburn: *The New York Herald* of August 25, 1859 (cited in Stokes, III, p. 978, and V, 1881, under date of August 23); *Architects' and Mechanics' Journal*, Vol. I (1859), p. 21, wherein he is identified as the architect of the American House in Boston (see *New York Illustrated News*, Vol. II [1860], p. 412). Kennion (p. xxi) names Olmsted & Fosgate. Other sources credit Thomas & Son (*Illustrations of Iron Architecture*, p. 8) or Griffith Thomas alone: *The New York Weekly Review*, January 28, 1865, p. 3; Thomas's obituary, *American Architect*, Vol. V (1879), p. 29; Schuyler, "Architectural Aberrations: The New Hoffman House," in "Architectural Essays, 1879-1913," Vol. III, unnumbered (a collection of Schuyler's articles bound for him and preserved at the Avery Library). An article on the "Fifth Avenue Hotel" in *Granite Monthly*, Vol. X (1887), p. 317, suggests that Thomas designed the exterior and Washburn the interior (cited by Alan Hodge, "Early Boston and New York Hotels," n. 136). Mention will be made subsequently of the revolutionary use of the elevator in this hotel.

⁵See Wight's "Reminiscences of Russell Sturgis" (*Architectural Record*, Vol. XXVI [August 1909], p. 123) for an interesting account of the influence of Ruskin and Mould on both architects at the beginning of their careers. Jacob Wrey Mould (1825-1886), an English architect who came to this country in 1853 to design All Souls Church in New York at the invitation of the merchant Moses Grinnell, had a colorful personality and varied career. All Souls (1853-1855) introduced New Yorkers, somewhat to their dismay, to High Victorian principles of design and coloration. Mould, a founder of the AIA, is remembered also for his work in Central Park. Readily available sources for his life and work include the *Strong Diary*, *passim*; obituary, *The New York Times*, June 16, 1886, p. 5, col. 2; Schuyler, "Italian Gothic in New York," *Architectural Record*, Vol. XXVI (July 1909), p. 46; *National Cyclopædia of American Biography*, III, pp. 415-416; seminar report

by Hodge dealing with his and Wight's early work, Institute of Fine Arts, New York University, March 1957.

⁶For a scathing critique, see "Our New York Letter," *American Builder and Journal of Art*, Vol. I (June 1869), pp. 119-120, attributed in a later issue (p. 232) to Mr. [Clarence] Cook.

⁷Le Brun, a Philadelphia architect trained in Thomas U. Walter's office, came to New York after the Civil War with a fine reputation established by the Cathedral of Saints Peter and Paul (1846-1864) and the Philadelphia Opera House (1853-1857), the latter work designed in collaboration with the German architect, Georg Runge. The most complete account of his work is in Schuyler's "The Work of N. Le Brun and Sons," *Architectural Record*, Vol. XXVII (1910), pp. 365-381. Regarding Masonic Hall, the *American Architect and Builders' Monthly*, a short-lived but valuable publication, contains illustrations not only of Le Brun's winning design (Vol. I [1870], opposite p. 92), but also of the competition drawings by Griffith Thomas (opposite p. 81) and Renwick & Sands (p. 24). Their design, an example of Victorian Gothic restlessness at its worst, reflects strong English influence, specifically from the published competition drawings for the new Law Courts in London (*Building News*, Vol. XIV [1867], particularly Deane's design, pp. 442-443). Thomas's design, with its tall corner accents and magnified orders, is quite close to E. Salomon's Prince's Street *façade* for the Manchester Town Hall competition (*ibid.*, Vol. XV [1868], p. 417). Le Brun's design is closer to classical principles of competition; it apparently underwent minor alterations in the course of construction (cf. photograph in *King's Handbook*, p. 570).

⁸For the Schermerhorns, the following have been most useful: William C. Schermerhorn, Esq., "History of the Schermerhorn Family," *New York Genealogical and Biographic Record*, XXXVI (1905), pp. 141-147, 200, and 205; Richard Schermerhorn, Jr., *Schermerhorn Genealogy and Family Chronicles*, New York, 1914; Margherita A. Hamm, *Famous Families of New York*, New York, 1902, II, pp. 121-124. Also the following articles and pamphlets: clipping from the New York *Evening Post*, July 13, 1901 (APT+, n.c. 4, pp. 159-161, New York Public Library, Room 328); a copy of an article from an unidentified newspaper in Lienau, "Biography, Memorabilia," p. 11; obituaries of January 2, 1903, for William Schermerhorn in *The New York Times*, p. 1, col. 3, and the New York *Daily Tribune*, p. 7, col. 4, and for Edmund in the New York *Herald* of September 3, 1891, p. 8, col. 2. A less flattering picture of the Schermerhorn financial transactions is contained in that great classic, Gustavus Myers's *History of the Great American Fortunes*, 1st edition [c.1907], New York [c.1937], pp. 163, 171, and 184.

⁹Strong, II, p. 87, entry of March 18, 1852.

¹⁰Nevins, "George Templeton Strong, the Man and the Diarist," *ibid.*, I, p. iii.

¹¹*Ibid., passim.* The performance of Sandeau's Mademoiselle de la Seigliere was based on William Schermerhorn's own translation (*ibid.*, III, p. 27, entry of May 18, 1860). Evenings such as these impressed the English

lady, Mrs. Bishop, as evidence of the highly cultivated taste and cosmopolitan atmosphere of New York Society (*The Englishwoman in America*, pp. 370-373).

[12]For accounts of the ball, see Strong, II, p. 160, entry of March 2, 1854; "A Ball for the Bald," *Harper's Weekly*, Vol. I (1857), p. 66; Haswell's *Reminiscences*, p. 424; McAllister, *Society As I Have Found It*, pp. 15-16; Morris, *Incredible New York*, pp. 17-19.

[13]*A Backward Glance*, New York, 1934, p. 79.

[14]Refers to page in original dissertation.

[15]An impressive list, consisting of only half of his inherited property, is contained in Edmund's will of June 26, 1883 (New York County, Surrogates Court, Lib. 469, pp. 489-492).

[16]IV, p. 474, entry of April 1, 1873.

[17]The New York *Herald*, September 3, 1891, p. 8, col. 2.

[18]New Building Docket #619 of 1892, filed October 22, erected 1893-1894.

[19]Illustrated in *American Architect*, Vol. XV (May 24, 1884), No. 439. Henry Fernbach, FAIA, a native of Breslau and graduate of the Berliner Bauakademie, emigrated to the U.S. c.1855 or 1856, when he was first listed in the New York directories. He was an active member of the AIA, of which he served as treasurer in 1878-1879. Fernbach erected many important buildings in New York, particularly for the German and Jewish communities, of which quite a number are still standing today. The following is a partial list: Hebrew Orphan Asylum (1860-1863), 77th Street near Third Avenue; Harmonie Club (1866), formerly at 45 West 42nd Street; Allemania Club, 18 West 16th Street; German Bank for Savings (1870), Union Square at 14th Street, in collaboration with Edward Kendall, now the Bowery Savings Bank; Staats-Zeitung Building (1870-1872), on the site of the Municipal Building; New York Institute for Deaf Mutes (1880), still on Lexington Avenue, in collaboration with Leopold Eidlitz (both received equal compensation); Temple Shaaray Tefila (1869), West 44th Street, and Ahavath Chesed (1870), now Central Synagogue, Lexington Avenue at 55th Street; much commercial work, *e.g.*, stores for Frederic Loeser, 114-120 Greene Street and 102-104 Prince Street—Brault, III, p. 435, obituaries in *American Architect*, Vol. XIV (November 24, 1883), p. 241, *The New York Times*, November 13, 1883, p. 2, col. 3, *Architecture and Building*, Vol. II (1883), p. 36. For descriptions and illustrations of his work: *ibid.*, III, p. 83; *American Architect and Builders' Monthly*, Vol. I (1870), pp. 53, 69, and 119; Kennion, *passim*; *History of Real Estate, Architecture and Building, passim*; *King's Handbook, passim*; New Building Dockets, Department of Buildings, *passim*; *Valentine's Manual of Old New York*, VIII (1924), p. 239; Wischnitzer, pp. 80-81 and 84-85.

[20]Page 25.

[21]Lienau, p. 3, and penciled notations on drawings.

²²Tax Assessment Records, Manhattan, 18th Ward. The assessed valuation of $40,000 in 1859 was raised to $42,000 the following year, indicating probable completion.

²³Volume 1854-1862, folio 278.

²⁴Page xxi. Kennion's book, entered in 1867 but not published till 1868, includes buildings in the planning stage or already begun by November 1867, when the preface was written.

²⁵A search of the New Building Dockets failed to disclose any information, but tax records indicate that the building was "in progress" in 1868 and 1869. Edmund is listed at his new address in *Trow's City Directory of 1869/1870.*

²⁶Portfolio 5, No. 7. The ten working drawings include front and rear elevations, two details of roof construction, and six plans. An unidentified study, close in style to both the Shiff and Cottenet houses, may be considered a link between the two houses of the early '50s and the Schermerhorn residence. It is also interesting for the resemblance it bears to some of Hitzig's work.

²⁷If this point is emphasized again and again, it is done with a purpose. One of the most frequent criticisms of the architecture of the period made by contemporary writers was the general lack of feeling among architects for clear definition of areas.

²⁸Popular in France since the early 16th century, this motif becomes a Lienau trademark.

²⁹"Works of the late Richard Morris Hunt," *Architectural Record*, Vol. V (1895), p. 99. According to *History of Architecture and Building Trades* (I, p. 40), this house had an interesting plan with a central atrium.

³⁰Refers to page in original dissertation.

³¹Cf. garden front of Barry's Bridgewater House, Hitchcock, *Early Victorian Architecture*, Vol. II, Fig. VII, No. 10. Date of the house was based on listings for Parish in city directories. Very fine Pach photographs of the interior are preserved in the Print and Map Rooms, New-York Historical Society. Attribution to Diaper is based on Bloor, *Proceedings of the AIA* (1876), p. 19, and his letter to the New York *Tribune*, reprinted in *American Architect*, Vol. XC (1906), p. 94, the only reliable source of information concerning the architect. Bloor was his pupil.

Frederick Diaper (c.1810-1906), FAIA, one of the most respected members of the AIA, of which he was a founder, was born in Devonshire, England. He served his apprenticeship under Sir Robert Smirke and began his practice in England, where he was a member of the Royal Institute of British Architects. Diaper came to the U.S. some years after Upjohn, but was already active in the late 1830s and early '40s, when he erected several Greek Revival banks on Wall Street (*e.g.*, Bank of America, Seaman's Bank for Savings, etc.), the New York Society Library Building (1840), etc. He built a number of the early Fifth Avenue mansions, *e.g.*, August Belmont's house on Eighteenth Street, originally erected c.1853 for Mrs. Elizabeth Gihon, and others in the neighborhood of Union Square. Of his country houses, the best known is Bwerwyck, the Van Rensselaer Mansion (1839-1843) in Albany. Later on, he built almost exclusively in the Italian *palazzo* style, of which the Parish house is such a good example. His influence on New York architecture was decidedly on the conservative side.

[32]Best view is in Brown, *Fifth Avenue Old and New*, p. 79. Commenting on the razing of "Sarsaparilla," Townsend's house, Strong predicted that the Stewart mansion would be "ten times as ugly and barbaric as its predecessor, if that is conceivable" (III, p. 416, entry of March 21, 1864). It is difficult to understand why he found the house so displeasing. Doubtless, his opinion was influenced by personal prejudice, as in Renwick's case, for Townsend was a prime example of a breed that he despised—the newly rich, self-made man.

[33]See description in the New York *Tribune*, November 28, 1859, cited in Stokes, V, 1882, under that date.

[34]Philadelphia, pp. 96-97, and Design XXIX, plate 129.

[35]Mention is made of this fact in Griffith Thomas's obituary (*American Architect*, Vol. V, p. 29). Thomas Thomas and his son Griffith, both English by birth, were among the most prolific and successful architects in New York from the 1840s through the '70s. For further information, see Weisman, *Art Bulletin*, Vol. XXXV, p. 228, n. 19, and *passim*.

[36]*SAH Journal*, Vol. XI, p. 8.

[37]Portfolio 5, No. 8, including the eight working drawings (front and real elevations, six plans, and two studies of interior paneling).

[38]In his will (Lib. 469, p. 489), Edmund Schermerhorn left a substantial annuity to a certain Eliza Burkhill, identified as his "relative" and "for many years, a member of my father's household and subsequently of my own". Her own will, drawn on August 28, 1883, probated on December 9, 1890 (Lib. 441, p. 326), indicates that she was a person of limited means, without immediate family connections. Mr. Richard Schermerhorn, Jr., of New York, author of the *Family Chronicles*, has no idea who she was (conversation of September 26, 1956).

[39]*E.g.*, plans illustrated in *Zeitschrift für Bauwesen*, Vol. VI (1857), Atlas, plate 5; Victor Calliat, *Parallèle des maisons de Paris construites depuis 1830 jusqu'à nos jours...*, Paris, 1857-1864, II, p. 22, and *passim*; *Moniteur des architectes*, III (1868), plate 196; etc. Cf. the incorporation of this feature in Sanford E. Loring and W.L.B. Jenney, *Principles and Practice of Architecture... Also, an Explanation and Illustrations of the French System of Apartment Houses...*, Chicago, 1869, Ex. U., plate 1.

[40]The location of the stable is indicated in a sketch accompanying the *Herald* article of September 3, 1891.

[41]Refers to page in original dissertation.

[42]Although the popularity of the Second Empire plan here is generally credited to the influence of English magazines, particularly the *Building News* (*e.g.*, Hitchcock, *Richardson*, p. 27), there can be no doubt that in Lienau's case (as in Renwick's), the influence was more direct. For Renwick, see Mrs.

McKenna, "Vassar College," pp. 74-75, and *Magazine of Art*, Vol. XLIV, p. 98.

[43]The photograph of Lienau (frontispiece) was taken in Paris in 1864. Evidence of this trip abroad is corroborated by a visa dated May 24, 1864, from the Dutch consul in New York, granting him permission to pass through Holland on his return to the United States (photostat of passport in Lienau, p. 31a).

[44]See Bibliography, *passim*, for publication details. Other notable publications of the period, besides Calliat's *Hotel de Ville de Paris*, were *Paris dans sa splendeur...*, Paris, 1861, and Albert Lenoir's *Statistique monumentale de Paris...*, Paris, 1867.

[45]Daly, I, Ex. B[1], plates 1 and 2, B[2], plates 1 and 2; Calliat, *Parallèle*, Vol. II, plate 82, and *passim*; *Moniteur*, Vol. III (1868), plate 181.

[46]*Revue générale de l'architecture*, Vol. XXIII (1865), plate 16. Cf. also Calliat, *Parallèle*, I, plate 36, and Hautecoeur, VI, p. 197, Fig. 166, for use of bull's eye panel as a terminal motif.

[47]*E.g.*, Kyllman & Heyden's houses of a somewhat later date in Architekten-Verein zu Berlin, *Berlin und seine Bauten*, Berlin, 1896, Vol. III, Fig. 250.

[48]I, p. 213.

[49]*E.g.*, flat Neo-Grec incised ornament, acroteria, bull's eye panels, corner rosettes in window frames—these were favorites of Hitzig. See his houses on the Victoria Strasse, Berlin (*Zeitschrift für Bauwesen*, Vol. IX [1859], Album, plate 24, and *passim*), those in the Bellevue Strasse (*Berlin und seine Bauten*, III, Fig. 542), and especially Friedrich Hitzig, *Ausgeführte Bauwerke*, Berlin [1855-1862], *passim*, which includes plates that were published as early as 1850-1855 (Bd 1, Heft 1-4 and Supplement).

[50]Strong, IV, p. 350, entry of April 13, 1871; the *Herald* article, wherein the fittings are described as "elaborate even to gorgeousness".

[51]An enthusiastic, though not completely uncritical, description appeared in *Harper's Weekly*, Vol. XIII (August 14, 1869), pp. 525-526: It was predicted that this was one edifice "that, if not swallowed up by an earthquake, will stand as long as the city remains, and will ever be pointed to as a monument of individual enterprise, of far-seeing judgment and of disinterested philanthropy". Cf. Browne's contemporary characterization of the building as "a huge white marble pile... very elaborate and pretentious, but exceedingly dismal, reminding one of a vast tomb" (*Great Metropolis*, p. 292). He concluded with the remark that "Stewart's financial ability is extraordinary, but his architectural taste cannot be recommended". P.B. Wight apparently shared his sentiments. After quoting Ruskin to the effect that "many know the art of making money, and but few the art of spending it," he wrote that Kellum's buildings should be "a warning to the rising generation of architects and the great capitalists of the future" (*American Architect*, Vol. I, pp. 147 and 149).

For information on John Kellum (1809-1871), born in Hempstead, Long Island, where he began work as a carpenter before becoming Gamaliel

King's assistant, see *Appleton's Cyclopedia of American Biography*, III, p. 359. Kellum was one of New York's most successful architects on the '60s. In addition to his work for A.T. Stewart, he erected the Mutual Life Building (1863-1865), the Stock Exchange, the New York Herald Building (1865-1867), the New York City Court House, etc. (see Weisman, *Art Bulletin*, Vol. XXXVI, p. 296, and *passim* for a discussion and illustrations of some of these structures).

Kellum's colleagues, perhaps partly because of professional jealousy and a natural distrust of the self-made man, never had anything good to say of him. One comment was that he "acquired a goodly fortune, if not much renown" (*American Architect*, Vol. I [1876], p. 206). He was blacklisted by the AIA for taking kick-backs from contractors. Even A.J. Bloor, not unusually given to vindictive statements, maintained that he was entirely dependent on his assistants for design, as well as draftsmanship, and that he knew nothing in architectural matters (see his letter, "Two Popular Architects" [on Thomas and Kellum], *American Architect*, Vol. V [March 1, 1879], p. 71). Cook said that he stuck to the classic style because it was the neatest, as well as the cheapest, in the long run, thus giving large profits to the contractor (*American Builder*, Vol. I, pp. 119-120). See also the nasty comments on Stewart's uptown store in *New York Weekly Review*, February 18, 1865, p. 2. The combined impact of Stewart and Kellum on New York architecture might be an interesting topic for study.

[52]See the very graphic illustrations in *Harper's Weekly*, Vol. I (1857), pp. 756-757.

[53]*Strong Diary*, III, p. 409, entry of February 27, 1864. Anthony Trollope, the English novelist, had more foresight. In 1861, he prophesized that fashionable residences would soon line Fifth Avenue as far north as 90th Street (*North America*, p. 215).

[54]Marie Caroline de Trobriand Post's *Descendants of John Jones and John Mason*, New York, 1913, has been a great help in disentangling the confusing relationships among the Jones, Mason and Schermerhorn families. For additional information, I am also indebted to Mrs. A.E. Distelhurst, Parish Secretary, Grace Church, New York (letter of May 4, 1951).

[55]Exclusive of the block from 56th to 57th Streets.

[56]Figures from Tax Assessment Records, Manhattan, 19th Ward.

[57]See Strong, I, pp. 317-318, entry of April 24, 1848, and *passim*; "Death of Mary M. Jones, *The New York Times*, May 30, 1891, p. 2, col. 2. This article makes mention of the fact that her house at 122 Chambers Street, built in 1818, was the first in the city to be furnished with a bathtub and lighted by gas.

[58]See New Building Docket #1050 of 1867, filed October 30, wherein Robert Mook is named as architect. This refers to the two corner buildings only; a notation states that, although drawings for nine buildings were submitted, specifications called for only two. Plans for the five later buildings were filed on New Building Docket #468 of 1869 on April 26,

finished November 30. Mrs. Jones presumably moved in shortly thereafter, since *Trow's City Directory* lists her at 1 East 57th Street from 1871/1872 on.

⁵⁹The corner house was published already in *Valentine's Manual* of 1869, opposite p. 240 (the full title of this important and well illustrated series in New York City, Common Council, is *Manual of the Corporation of the City of New York*, New York, 1841-1870). The Jones Row was chosen as one of two views of Fifth Avenue contrasting "upper and lower crust" in Robert Macoy's *Centennial Illustrated: How to See New York and Its Environs*, New York [1875], p. 69. Excellent views are preserved in "Fifth Avenue. Scrapbook of Views, 51st to 149th Street," New York Public Library, Room 328, of which the most charming is "Coaching Day Scene in Fifth Avenue" with Marble Row in the background.

⁶⁰See Appendix II for records of the Department of Buildings. Though plans weren't filed until July 21, 1869, it is clear both from dated studies in the Lienau Collection and from an entry in the *Strong Diary* (IV, p. 239, January 2, 1869)—wherein he remarks that Mrs. Colford Jones, just home from Europe, "is about building on or near Central Park"—that the row was projected at least as early as 1868.

⁶¹Houses near the park brought in handsome rents. See "Prices of Dwellings," *The New York Times*, April 16, 1871, p. 3, col. 5; Ellis Paxton Oberholtzer mentions a figure of $6,000 a year as not unusual in *A History of the United States since the Civil War*, New York, 1922, I, p. 270.

⁶²The drawings (Portfolio VIII, Nos. 15 and 15a) consist of two plot surveys, eight studies, eleven working drawings (eight plans and three elevations), and thirteen details of stone work, as well as three studies and two working drawings for the stable. An itemized account in Lienau's hand, "Statement of Cost of Eight Houses Built for Mrs. Colford Jones on Fifth Avenue..." totals $556,456.54. Among the items listed was $4,488.32 for papier mache supplied by L. Marcotte.

⁶³"Colford Jones Block," Scrapbook, Print Room, New York Public Library.

⁶⁴For pictures of New York at this time, see "Panorama of New York," 1865, a colored lithograph by J. Bien published by John Bachman (Stokes P., 1865, G-83, Print Room, New York Public Library) and Matthew Dripps, *Plan of New York City, from the Battery to Spuyten Duyvil*, New York, 1868, plate 12. The country atmosphere of the block to the north of Rebecca's property (now the site of Bonwit Teller and Tiffany) may be seen in the E.P. Chrystie view in Kenneth Holscomb Dunshee, *As You Pass By*, New York [1952], p. 247, an extremely useful, well documented, and excellently illustrated book.

⁶⁵Wharton, *The Age of Innocence*, p. 152.

⁶⁶Kennion (Part III, pp. 29 and 58) describes how the advance of trade was forcing owners of downtown palaces to seek refuge farther uptown.

⁶⁷Wharton, pp. 10-11 and 24-25; Morris, *Incredible New York*, pp. 141-142. Morris's description is based on Mrs. Wharton's and also upon his own recollections of the house, which he knew well (letter to me of February 26,

1952). Excellent views of the interior are preserved in the Print Room, Museum of the City of New York.

⁶⁸Cf. Pavillon de Flore, Louvre, and Pavillon de Gabriel, Fontainebleau, Hautecoeur, Vol. I², Figs. 374 and 376; III, Fig. 475. Henry Collins Brown, commenting on the wave of Second Empire style that was sweeping the fashionable world of New York, wrote: "All good Americans went to Paris while they lived and brought home plans and specifications for replicas of the Tuileries on lots 50x100. The Stewart Mansion at 34th Street, a monumental futility having all the hospitable aspects of an iceberg, capped the climax of the style. The Mason houses at 57th Street were more rational exemplars of the expression..." (*Valentine's Manual of Old New York*, IX [1925], p. 337).

⁶⁹Documented by records of the Department of Buildings, by a letter of July 1, 1935, by Waldron Kintzing Post, quoting William E. Iselin, in turn citing Mary Hasell (Print Room, Museum of the City of New York), and by a letter of December 6, 1955, to me from Mrs. Jessie M. Hebert of Hartford, Connecticut, Robert Mook's daughter. Mrs. Hebert believes that her father introduced the first system of indirect lighting in the city in Mrs. Jones's ballroom.

The following sources have been helpful in effecting a reconstruction of Mook's work: (1) New Building Dockets, Department of Buildings. (2) Published accounts and illustrations: *American Architect and Mechanics' Journal* (1859 ff.), *passim*; *Illustrations of Iron Architecture*, plate XV, No. 7; for Shearith Israel, William Smith Pelletreau, *Early New York Houses...*, New York, 1900, p. 178, Fig. 39; Wischnitzer, *Synagogue Architecture*, pp. 58-59, Fig. 36; for the Ward house, see Aly Ahmed Raafat and Ellen W. Kramer, article in preparation. (3) Original drawings (unfortunately, mostly destroyed): two sketches of the original Crosby Street synagogue (1833) by Calvin Pollard, preserved at Shearith Israel, 2 West 70th Street, information I owe to Madame Wischnitzer; plans of the Ward house, of which I have photostats. (4) Raafat, "Reinforced Concrete and the Architecture It Creates," unpublished dissertation, Columbia University, 1956, pp. 23-26, to be published in 1958 by Reinhold. (5) Documents in the possession of Milton C. Mook of New York, whom I interviewed in December 1955 and on April 2 and 18, and May 9, 1956. (6) The late Warren L. Ward, letters of September 20 and October 22, 1951; Evans Ward, personal interview and visit to the Ward house in June 1957.

⁷⁰This figure, derived from the document on the cost of the houses, was computed at 4% of $524,414. The customary fee at this time was 5% for plans and supervision.

⁷¹Cf. Hautecoeur's discussion of French apartment house design, VI, especially pp. 206-208, Figs. 175, 177, and 178; VII, pp. 250 ff.

⁷²Cf. Adams, *Receuil*, plate 1; Calliat, *Parallèle*, I, plates 28 and 93, II, plates 11, 29, 70, and 87; [Vecquer] *Maisons... de Paris*, plates 32-33. A number of these examples were by Francois Rolland, an architect who erected many apartment houses in Paris. Examples of pavilion architecture

and chamfered corners likewise abound in a short-lived publication, *Paris architecte, e.g.,* Vol. 1868-1869, plate XXII. Cf. also the abundance of low mansards and stylistic features generally similar to those of Lienau in F. Barqui, *L'architecture moderne in France. Maisons les plus remarquables des departements,* Paris (1871), especially plates 88-89.

[73]Refers to page in original dissertation.

[74]*E.g.,* the third house from the 55th Street corner had a billiard room in the basement. Cf. also the basement bowling alley in the Lockwood Mansion, both early examples of conversion to recreational use of this area.

Attention has been called to the fact that the Lienau drawings not only are valuable for tracing architectural developments and the history of taste in this country, but also are important as examples of architectural drawings *per se* and of methods of practice of the period, *e.g.,* among the thirteen details of stone mason's work mentioned above, there is one duplicate on tracing paper. We are reminded of the fact that these were the days before blueprinting, when assistants in an architect's office were required to spend hours in laborious duplication. The copies were then handed over to the contractor, who in this case was Alexander M. Ross, one of the best known masons in the business.

[75]*E.g.,* John Jacob Astor's house of 1859 and Shook's mansion for William H. Vanderbilt at 40th Street and Fifth Avenue (Kennion, Part III, p. 29, and New Building Docket #116 of 1866).

[76]Foreigners were particularly struck by the somber aspect and monotony of New York's domestic architecture. See Camille Ferri-Pisani, *aide de camp* of Prince Napoleon who visited here in 1861, in *Lettres sur les Etats-Unis...,* Paris, 1862, pp. 44-45, and the impressions of the English correspondent Edward Dicey, *Six Months in the Federal States,* London, 1863, I, p. 12, as well as many others.

[77]Henry James, *A Small Boy and Others,* New York, 1913, p. 98.

[78]*A Backward Glance,* pp. 54-55.

[79]Pages 221-222, and quoted verbatim in *American Builder,* Vol. I (February 1869), p. 50. Almost equally picturesque is the description furnished by the author of the article from the *World,* cited in Kennion (Part I, p. 33):

> "What artist... needs any sketch-book in traversing our much vaunted Fifth Avenue...? When he has seen one house, he has seen them all. The same everlasting high stoops and gloomy brown-stone fronts; the same number of holes pinched in precisely the same places...; the same huge cornices bristling with overpowering consoles and projections, like whole regiments of petrified buffaloes leaping headling from the roof. To be sure, what we lack in invention, we can cover over by ornamentation... the largest merit being... which cost the most."

[80]New York, pp. 71-72.

[81]This was pointed out in *Fifth Avenue; Glances at the Vicissitudes and Romance of a World-renowned Thoroughfare,* Boston: Walton, 1915, p. 60; Brown, *Fifth Avenue,* p. 96.

[82]New York, 1876, p. 30.

[83]Part III, p. 59.

[84]Two important exceptions were Union Square and Gramercy Park, developed in the 1840s.

[85]"The Central Park and City Streets Criticized... by an Intelligent Zulu," *New York Weekly Review*, April 15, 1865, p. 2. The writer went on to recommend Holly's censorship plan. The anonymous writer of a fine article, "Our Houses," in *Harper's* (Vol. XIX [1859], pp. 513-518), describes amusingly how most buildings look as though they were "thrown together as if by chance—as if they met most reluctantly, and wished to fight each other" (p. 516).

[86]"The Architectural Errors of Progress," *Architects' and Mechanics' Journal*, Vol. III (1860), p. 21.

[87]Robert Tomes was of the opinion that many striking effects were lost for want of adaptation of a house to its site. He particularly recommended the corners of the house for architectural display and would have approved of the chamfered corner used by Lienau in the Jones and other houses (*Harper's*, Vol. XXX, p. 737). See also editorial, "Corners of Street Buildings," *American Architect and Builders' Monthly*, Vol. I (December 1870), p. 151.

[88]Cf. contemporary opinion in England: *e.g.*, "London Streets," an editorial composed largely of quotations from a paper read by James Edmeston before the Society for the Encouragement of the Fine Arts, in *Examples of the Architecture of the Victorian Age and Monthly Review of the World's Architectural Progress*, London, 1862, p. 21. The writer expresses wholehearted approval of the mansard roof, a fashion "lately" set in, citing as examples the Tuileries and the Duke of Buccleuch's house at Whitehall, Montagu House by William Burn, discussed in Hitchcock, *Early Victorian Architecture*, I, p. 208; he concludes with a discussion of the desireability of municipal controls.

[89]See Miss Lichten's description, p. 219.

[90]"Our Street Architecture," *Architectural Review and American Builders' Journal*, Vol. I (January 1869), pp. 469-472.

[91]Depau Row has been mentioned previously. A fine view of Le Roy Place is in Theodore S. Fay's *Views in New-York and its Environs from... Drawings... by Dekin, Architect...*, New York, 1831, plate 7.

[92]Many of these rows are illustrated in *Putnam's*, Vol. III (March 1854), p. iii. See pp. 246, 245, and 243 for London Terrace, 20th Street, and 16th Street rows.

[93]Ownership and dates are based on Map Book for 1845-1852 and Tax Assessment Records, Manhattan, 18th Ward. For Lewis M. Rutherford, see *Dictionary of American Biography*, XVI, pp. 256-259; for Rutherford Stuyvesant (originally Stuyvesant Rutherford), see Weeks, *Prominent Families of New York*, p. 540.

[94]Refers to page in original dissertation.

[95]See *Strong Diary* (II, p. 367, entry of October 22, 1857) for a graphic description of the effect of the panic on building operations in New York,

and the *Architects' and Mechanics' Journal* (Vol. II [1860], p. 84) for the decline of real estate values evidenced by recent auctions.

⁹⁶Quoted from an advertisement reproduced in Fig. 71 here. Reuben Vose waxed eloquent over Mr. Higgins's "Square," saying that we should thank Mr. Davis for "giving us a design that has originality, taste, and beauty to recommend it" (*Wealth of the World*, p. 114). He informs us that the Higgins brothers, originally from Maine, were the owners of a carpet factory on 43rd Street near the East River.

⁹⁷Sloan countered a possible charge of monotony by referring to the grandeur of effect produced by Parisian architecture (*City and Suburban Architecture...*, Philadelphia, 1859, p. 67). His own proposed design for a block of ten houses (No. XVII) is hardly calculated to forestall such criticism, however.

⁹⁸Vacquer, plates 8-9.

⁹⁹See *Early Victorian Architecture*, I, pp. 480 ff., on the beginnings of Victorian housing; Wiedenson, "City Planning: 1850-1875". For pertinent published material, see Beeston's houses at St. George's Place, Knightsbridge, and Tarring's Terrace, corner of Queen's Gate and Kensington Gore, London, *Building News*, Vol. V (1959), p. 653, and Vol. VI (1860), p. 293.

¹⁰⁰Vol. XVIII (June 16, 1860), pp. 380-381, described as "now in the course of erection".

¹⁰¹Holly, pp. 156-157.

¹⁰²*Ibid.*, p. 158. This espousal of French city planning practices, notwithstanding sporadic examples of English approval, was rare. More typical is the stringent criticism of French "despotic" rule by G.R. Burnell in "Studies of Modern Architecture at Home and Abroad," *Examples of the Architecture of the Victorian Age*, p. 69. The article continues with a long and vehement attack on all the stylistic practices of the Neo-Grec school as "violations of the laws of logic and optics".

¹⁰³Concluding his discussion of the Great Western and other large British hotels of the 1850s and '60s, Hitchcock writes" "This 'Second Empire' mode is almost as characteristically Victorian and Anglo-Saxon as is Victorian Gothic" (*Gazette des Beaux-Arts*, XLII, p. 126).

¹⁰⁴Cf., however, the sarcastic criticism of the "Thomasic" and "Kellumnar" style in *New York Weekly Review*, January 28, 1865, p. 3.

¹⁰⁵Discussed in "The Grosvenor-Place and Pimlico Improvements...," *Builder*, Vol. XXV (February 23, 1867), pp. 121-123, where they are attributed to Cundy (p. 122). See also Pevsner, *London. 1: The Cities of London and Westminster*, [Harmonsworth, Middlesex, 1957], pp. 509-510. (HE 12: *The Buildings of England.*)

¹⁰⁶Vol. XXV (1867), p. 561, elevation, p. 571. The hotel was planned for the block between Fifth and Madison Avenues from 59th to 60th Streets, a site now occupied in part by the Savoy Plaza Hotel.

¹⁰⁷This summary is based on records of the Plan Department, Department of Housing, the city directories, newspaper articles, and other

material preserved in the Print Room, Museum of the City of New York, Lloyd Morris's letter of February 26, 1952, and "Fifth Avenue from Start to Finish," New York, 1911, a volume of photographs preserved at the Fifth Avenue Association Offices, Empire State Building, New York.

[108]According to Schuyler, he was associated with his father from 1887 on (*Architectural Record*, Vol. VI, p. 176).

[109]Mark Twain and Charles Dudley Warner, *The Gilded Age, A Tale of Today*, Hartford, 1874, a study of the corruption of the period.

[110][According to Mimi Findlay, there is still an enormous amount left to do: for example, the restoration of the entire second and third floors, and the development of the basement for income-producing meeting space, all estimated to cost about another $2-million.]

[111]See Frederic A. Holden and E. Dunbar Lockwood, *Descendants of Robert Lockwood; Colonial and Revolutionary History of the Lockwood Family in America from A.D. 1630*, Philadelphia, 1889, I, p. 360, II, pp. 489-493. For information of a personal nature, I am indebted to a granddaughter, Hilda Lockwood (Mrs. John F.) O'Brien of New York and Franconia, New Hampshire (letter of October 3, 1952).

[112]For his testimony in the notorious Credit Mobilier scandal, see Myers, *History of the Great American Fortunes*, pp. 476-477.

[113]He financed Dr. Isaac I. Hayes's third expedition to the Arctic (1869), when he was accompanied by the marine painter, William Bradford. The LeGrand Lockwood Prize at Dartmouth College, awarded for excellence in debating, was established by him.

[114]Page 5, col. 3.

[115]Portfolio IX, No. 16, consisting of one study, seven working drawings and a study for the gate lodge.

[116]The Reverend Charles M. Selleck, *Norwalk*, Norwalk, Connecticut, 1895, n. 1, pp. 213-214; Elsie Nicholas Danenberg, *The Romance of Norwalk*, New York, 1929, p. 314. I am also indebted to Mr. Peter Collins, architect, of Norwalk, for information regarding the house culled from a clipping from *The Norwalk Hour*.

[117]Danenberg, p. 314.

[118]Many legends have grown up about the house and its owner, some of which have been told to me by Mrs. Dorothy B. Chase of Norwalk (Chairman of the Committee for Norwalk's Tricentennial Celebration, 1951), who conducted me through the house in 1952, and by Thomas B. Goggins, employed from 1897 on by the Mathews family, second owners of the house.

[119]A.J. Bloor mentioned this and Holly's residence for a Mr. Brooks, also of Connecticut, as the most important country houses of the period regarding cost and finish (*AIA Proceedings* [1876], p. 28).

[120]Oberholtzer, *Jay Cooke, Financier of the Civil War*, Philadelphia [1907], II, p. 448, and *passim*, with photograph in Vol. II, opposite p. 152; Henrietta Larson, *Jay Cooke, Private Banker*, Cambridge, Massachusetts, 1936, p. 195, with view of parlor opposite p. 196.

[121]Much of my information is derived from advertisements for the mansion when it was put up for sale in 1873. A copy of one such ad from a New York newspaper of March 1873 is in Lienau, "Biography, Memorabilia," p. 18; another, a description of the plans of "Elm Park," made by Weston in 1874, is in the possession of the City Planning Commission, of which photostats were kindly forwarded to me by Mr. Shapiro, formerly Chairman of the Commission.

[122]Selleck, p. 214.

[123]Refers to page in original dissertation.

[124]Refers to page in original dissertation.

[125]The yearning for aristocratic distinction, reflected architecturally in the adoption of the mansard roof and the Newport cottages, found one of its most direct expressions in the ever increasing number of establishments on Broadway devoted exclusively to furnishing impressive genealogies and family crests to the wealthy middle class. For the 1850s, see Chambers (*Things as They Are in America*, p. 179) and Grattan (*Civilized America*, I, p. 208). Browne's chapter, "Heraldry on the Hudson," in *The Great Metropolis* (pp. 596 ff.) indicates how important this fad had become by the later '60s. This same period saw the adoption of other social patterns based on those of the aristocracy, already mentioned in connection with Colonel DeLancey Kane and the Coaching Club. Note too the beginning of the trend for daughters of American millionaires to marry into the ranks of the nobility abroad, of which the most conspicuous example was that of Jennie, Larry Jerome's daughter, to Lord Randolph Churchill. Mary Mason Jones's daughter, also known as Mary Mason Jones (1820-1907) had anticipated this trend when she married Regis Denis de Keredern, Baron de Trobriand, afterwards Comte de Trobriand, and later Major General in the U.S. Army.

[126]The effect of an *avant-corps* recalls occasional French practice, as in an hotel rue d'Amsterdam (Calliat, *Parallèle*, II, plate 97), where it is used for stables and service quarters.

[127]E.g., Petit, *Chateaux de France...* [1855], and slightly later, Claude Sauvageot, *Palais, chateaux, hotels, et maisons de France du XVe au XVIIIe siècle*, Paris, 1867, in 4 volumes.

[128]Oberholtzer, *Jay Cooke*, II, p. 449.

[129]Particularly noticeable in the side elevations.

[130]E.g., Camille Martin, *La Renaissance en France...*, Paris [c.1913-c.1921], Vol. I, plates XC and *passim*.

[131]Cf. Lassus's hotel at avenue Montaigne #24 (Adams, *Recueil*, plates 30, 31, and 41 [plan]); Calliat, *Parallèle*, I, plates 104-105; Daly, *L'Architecture privée au XIXe siècle sous Napoleon III...*, Paris, 1864 [1st edition of this important work], II, Villa suburbaine Iere classe, Ex. A¹, plates 2, 3, 4, etc.; A. Normand, Chateau of Liancourt, *Moniteur des Architects*, Vol. III (1868), façade plates 176-177, plan plate 171.

[132]Cf. Sebastiano Serlio, *Tutte l'opere d'architettura...*, Venice, 1584, VII, p. 5, and *passim*; Bannister Fletcher's drawings of Palladio's Villa Capra,

Vicenza, gives its dimensions in English feet (*A History of Architecture...*), 13th edition, New York, 1946, p. 661).

[133]Mansart's Chateau de Marly (Hautecoeur, II², p. 573, Fig. 449) was the prototype for most later variants which, according to Hautecoeur, enjoyed widespread popularity at the end of the Ancien Regime (IV, pp. 373-374, and Figs. 216, 217, 219, and 220). For England, see, *e.g.*, Giorgina Masson, "Four Palladian Villas," *Country Life*, CVII² (June 2, 1950), pp. 1634-1638.

[134]See his rotunda projects for the Government House, Richmond, and his anonymous competition drawing for the White House, Fiske Kimball, *Domestic Architecture of the American Colonies and Early Republic*, p. 174, and Fig. 131, p. 171.

[135]*E.g.*, Pope house, Lexington, Kentucky, the Tayloe project, Washington, D.C., etc., in Hamlin, *Benjamin Henry Latrobe*, New York, 1955, pp. 102-110, Figs. 7, 8, and 10.

[136]Page 175.

[137]Lafever, Mansion No. 3, plate XCII; Vaux, Rogers house, Design No. 11 (1857 edition) and No. 13 (1864 edition).

[138]Sloan, *Model Architect*, Vol. I, Design IX, plate XXXVI, and *Homestead Architecture*, Philadelphia, 1867, Design XXXIV, opposite p. 253; Holly, Design 13, opposite p. 81; Isaac H. Hobbs and Son, *Hobbs' Architecture...*, Philadelphia, 1873, Design LXXI, p. 163 (Design LXX, p. 161 in 1876 edition).

[139]For the plan, see *Villas on the Hudson*, plate [7].

[140]Cf. Hamburg, Architekten- und Ingenieur-Verein, *Hamburg's Privatbauten*, Hamburg, 1877, plates II (1872), XIV (1858), XX (1876), XXIII-XXIV, especially Halle's villa for S. Lowenstein (1873), XXIX (1866), XXXIX (1874), and LV (1876); also plates L (1856) and XX (1876), examples with octagonal courts. Carl Weichert, *Das Stadthaus und die Villa...*, 2nd edition, Weimer, 1884, *passim*, and plates XXXVI and XXXVII.

[141]*E.g.*, plate 29, and *passim*.

[142]Robert Koch, whose study of Louis Comfort Tiffany (unpublished dissertation, Yale University, 1957) has made him thoroughly familiar with interiors of this period, knows of no earlier example of this type of unusual arrangement, though frosted glass doors and windows may be found between rooms in some Greek Revival houses; after 1870, painted-glass screens became very popular (see *Harper's*, Vol. LXIX [1869], pp. 655 ff.). Koch, letter of April 11, 1957.

[143]Vol. XXX, p. 738.

[144]This type of formal vestibule is often seen in early 18th century French architecture, *e.g.*, Cuvillies's Falkenlust, Chateau de Bruhl and Blondel's Maison Cramer in Coligny (Hautecoeur, Vol. III, p. 87, Fig. 66, and p. 101, Fig. 73).

[145]Cf., however, Henry Austin's Victoria mansion, Portland, Maine, called to my attention by Carroll Meeks.

[146]An apt phrase of Miss Lichten, p. 92.

[147]An opinion that is shared by Robert Koch of Norwalk, but not merely out of local patriotism; see also Weeks's statement in *Prominent Families of New York*, p. 400. I am indebted to Koch for several photographs of the interior decoration of the second-floor bedrooms. A sad postscript: A visit to the museum on September 28, 1957, revealed that the building has been permitted to deteriorate considerably in the last year or two. There has been a great deal of vandalism, and apparently almost all of the old furniture has disappeared. Many of the rooms are now locked.

[148]Quoted from 1873 newspaper advertisement in Lienau, p. 18.

[149]Refers to page in original dissertation.

[150]The resolutions passed by the Stock Exchange at a meeting of February 26, 1872, are cited in Holden and Laughlin (*Lockwood Family*, II, p. 491), together with others by the Danbury & Norwalk Railroad, the Pacific Mail Steam Ship Company, New York & Eastern Railroad, and Second Avenue Railroad (*ibid.*, pp. 491-494).

[151]Quoted from an 1873 newspaper advertisement.

[152]Charles Thompson Mathews (1864-1934), architect and author of the *Renaissance under the Valois*, New York, 1893, best known for the Lady Chapel of St. Patrick's Cathedral, was the son of the second owner.

[153]Interestingly enough, it was suggested already in 1874 (*The Sentinel*, November 17, cited by Danenberg, p. 315) that the grounds be used as a public park and the building converted to municipal use. In 1887, there was talk of using the building for a county courthouse, but Bridgeport outbid Norwalk.

[154]George R. Brunjes, Mayor of the City of Norwalk, letter of April 16, 1957. In 1950, Holden McLaughlin Associates of New York completed a preliminary survey on the cost ($197,000) of converting the mansion for use as a city hall. Mr. Arthur C. Holden recently informed me that nothing further has been done (conversation of April 13, 1957), though the plan has the partial backing of the Norwalk Planning Commission (see site plan, "Proposed Civic Center for Veterans Memorial Park," *Mark*, August 18, 1956, p. 1, kindly forwarded to me by Robert Koch). The editorial (*ibid.*, p. 12) pleads for the preservation of the mansion and conversion to use as a community center for lectures, exhibits, etc.

[155]This was the general tenor and, indeed, the purpose of a short talk made by this writer to the Kiwanis Club of Norwalk on March 14, 1954 (reported in *The Norwalk Hour*, March 5, pp. 1-2).

[156]Eighteen drawings for Düneck are preserved (Portfolio XIV, No. 25): five studies by J. August Lienau, Detlef's son, eight working drawings, of which several are dated February 3 and 5, 1872, and a number of others relating to the main house and to other buildings on the estate. For comparative material, see *Hamburg's Privatbauten*, plates X, XXXI, XXXII, LVIII (elevations), XXIII-XXXIV, XXXL, LV, etc. (plans).

[157]Portfolio XX, No. 38, 7 sheets. Located Kuhlenstrasse 14, Ütersen. Cf. Hitzig, *Ausgeführte Bauwerke*, Bd. I, Heft I and III, plates VI and V respectively; Bd. II, Heft III, and *passim*.

[158]Düneck, which apparently is quite a large estate, was used as a youth center during the Hitler regime. For information on these houses, my thanks go to Eva Marie Lienau, letter of February 1953, in turn citing data contained in a letter to her from Jacob's granddaughter, Anna Marie Lienau, of Wedel, Germany.

Chapter VII

[1]See Loring and Jenney's strong plea for the adoption of the French flat (*Principles and Practice of Architecture*, pp. 43-45 and 58-59). William Le Baron Jenney (1832-1907) was quite familiar with French planning practices. He studied at the Ecole Centrale, Paris.

[2]See *The New York Times* of June 23, 1865 (p. 1, col. 3) on the impossibility of keeping up with the tremendous demand for shelter for the tens of thousands "pouring" into the metropolitan area from the interior and from Europe.

[3]James H. Richardson, "The New Homes of New York—A Study of Flats," *Scribner's Monthly*, Vol. VIII (1874), p. 64. Thanks to Alan Burnham for calling my attention to this important article.

[4]*Ibid.*, p. 63.

[5]For wages in the building trades in 1869, see tables in Edward Young, *Special Report on Immigration*, pp. 219-221; also Michael A. Mikkelson, "A Review of the History of Real Estate on Manhattan Island," *A History of Real Estate, Building and Architecture*, table showing the cost of building materials in 1873 (p. 65) versus the table illustrating the decline in wages and prices in 1876 (p. 70).

[6]Pointing to the futility of building row upon row of houses for single occupancy, Richardson said that there were ten times as many such buildings as there were families "large enough to fill them or rich enough to support them" (*Scribner's*, Vol. VIII, p. 65).

[7]According to contemporary sources, rentals of $3,000 a year were not unusual. See James B. Runnion, "Our City Homes—What They Are and What They Should Be," *American Builder*, Vol. I (October 1869), p. 185, and statistics cited by C.W. Elliott, "Life in Great Cities. I: New York," *Putnam's*, Vol. XI (January 1868), p. 93. Using 1863 as an average year, Elliott tells us that the great majority earned less than $1,000 a year, only 15,000 families occupied a whole house, and only 18,034 earned over $5,000 per annum.

[8]In 1857, Pairpont (*Uncle Sam and His Country*, p. 26) had already commented on the habit New Yorkers had of living in boarding houses because of the enormous rentals. See the review in *Harper's Weekly* (Vol. I [1857], p. 652) of the satirical book with very amusing illustrations, T. Butler Gunn's *Physiology of New York Boarding Houses*, New York, 1857.

[9]This tendency is referred to regretfully by James M. MacGregor, Superintendent of Buildings, in his *Annual Report for the Year 1866*, bound together with those of other years, in New York Superintendent of Buildings, *Reports 1862-1872*, p. 213. These reports, of which a copy is preserved at the Avery Library, give the highlights of construction data; they

are a very convenient source of information, often saving endless hours of searching through New Building Dockets at the Municipal Building. Richardson predicted dire results for the political and social life of the city as a result of the banishment to the suburbs of the educated middle classes (*Scribner's*, Vol. VIII, p. 66).

[10]Cf. "New Jersey Improvements," the *World*, January 31, 1869 (p. 1, col. 1) for a good picture of suburban improvements in other areas, as well as "Suburban Homes: Homes for New York Business Men," *ibid.*, October 8, 1871 (p. 1, col. 6).

[11]Portfolio 16, No. 29. The set of six working drawings, dated August 21, 1871, consists of a plat plan; front, side, and real elevations; and three sheets of plans.

[12]See Appendix II.

[13]Cf. Sloan, *City and Suburban Architecture*, Design XVII, plates 79-81. The Sloan row was definitely more high class than Lienau's block, so the comparison is not quite fair. Though the plans are almost identical in arrangement, the rooms are much larger and a secondary servant's staircase is introduced, a luxury which Booræm's clients could probably not afford. The French row (Daly, *L'Architecture privée*, III, Villas suburbaines Troisième classé, Ex. A³, plates 1 ff.) must likewise have been planned for a somewhat higher-income group than the Booræm houses.

[14]The *World* of January 31, 1867 (p. 8, col. 2) noted that employers were becoming more and more reluctant to hire commuters whose ferries and trains were so often delayed by inclement winter weather.

[15]See the nostalgic article by Thomas W. Ennis, "City to Lose First Apartments as 'Stuyvesant's Folly' Fades," *The New York Times*, September 22, 1957, Section VIII, p. 1, cols. 5-6, and p. 8, col. 1.

[16]Beginning in the late 1840s, letters, articles, and editorials began appearing in the English architectural journals calling for the adoption of the Scottish or continental flat as a solution to London's housing problems. J.E.D.'s letter to the *Builder* (Vol. VI [October 28, 1848], pp. 524-525), titled "Improvement of Dwelling for Middle and Lower Classes," stated the case very well: "The growth of the mighty Babylon in length and breadth must henceforth be... superceded by... a re-arrangement in height." In the years following, the *Builder* published a number of papers on the subject, some of which are discussed and illustrated by Hitchcock (*Early Victorian Architecture*, I, pp. 475 ff.). The Victoria Street flats were the first practical application of the new idea in London; they were published immediately on the continent, as well as in England (*e.g.*, *Allgemeine Bauzeitung*, Vol. XIX [1854], p. 344 and plate 643). One of the best analyses of the situation was made by that prolific Scottish writer, William Chambers (1800-1883), to whom reference has already been made; see his well illustrated pamphlet urging the adoption of a compromise between the Scottish and French systems, *Improved Dwelling-Houses for the Humbler and Other Classes in Cities Based on the Scottish Dwelling-House System*, London, 1855.

[17]This paper, read before a meeting of the AIA in June 2, was published immediately in *The Crayon* (Vol. IV [July 1857], p. 218) and in *Harper's Weekly* (Vol. I [December 18, 1857], pp. 809-810). The latter is illustrated, as is the version that appeared under the title "Parisian Buildings for City Residents" in *Architects' and Mechanics' Journal* (Vol. II [July 21, 1860], pp. 154-157).

[18]See his *Annual Reports, passim.*

[19]*E.g., Architects' and Mechanics' Journal,* Vol. III (October 6, 1860), p. 1.

[20]For a discussion of the new type of apartment house that combined shops and flats, which was introduced in Paris after the Restoration, see Hautecoeur, VI, pp. 125 ff., and VII, pp. 250 ff., for later examples.

[21]Excellent descriptions of these two buildings may be found in the *World,* October 8, 1871, p. 3, cols. 1-2.

[22]See anecdote cited by Morris (*Incredible New York,* p. 110) and his discussion of the revolution in social attitudes brought about by the introduction of the French flat (pp. 109-110); also Burnham, "Dwelling in Greater Manhattan," *passim.*

[23]Richardson's comment is singularly apropos: "the genuine Briton puts his social trust only in vertical walls. He feels his privacy invaded the moment there is anyone above or below him in space...; a prejudice harmless enough where there is no lateral compression... but mischievous in a crowded community like ours," *Scribner's,* Vol. VIII, p. 66. Cf. the typical Parisian's reaction to current (1957) efforts to move him out of city slums into the suburbs: "What do you think I am, an Englishman?" ("Parisians Resist Plea to Move into Suburbs," *The New York Times,* March 17, 1957, Section VIII, p. 7, cols. 2-3).

[24]Cf. tables, "New Buildings Commenced" and "New Buildings Completed," in New York Superintendent of Buildings, *Annual Reports* (pp. 408-409 for 1868, pp. 627-628 for 1869, and pp. 14-15 for 1870).

[25]This term was used loosely to designate either second-class single-family dwellings or buildings for several families, which did not fall into the category of "third-class" dwellings, *i.e.* tenements.

[26]Cf. figure of 115 in 1870 cited in *Annual Report of 1871,* p. 8, with number erected in previous years.

[27]Further research among the census reports, etc., might provide a definite answer to this question. Cf., *e.g.,* "Map of the City of New York Showing the Density of Population Born of Irish (German) Mothers...1890" in Kate H. Klaghorn's classic study, "The Foreign Immigrant in New York City," *United States Industrial Commission Reports,* Washington, D.C., 1901, XV, following p. 470.

[28]The following quotation from Marcus Lee Hansen's *The Immigrant in American History,* Cambridge, Mass., 1949, pp. 129-130, is particularly apropos:

"But if the physical luggage counted for little, every man, woman and child brought with him something else that no student of American society can ignore... Each newcomer carried with him habits of life and belief and intellectual and aesthetic tastes. Planted in American soil, these inbred attitudes were to grow and bear fruit long after the humble individuals who had introduced them had vanished from the scene."

[29]It has often been pointed out that many Germans who immigrated to this country were of middle-class origin and formed with their descendants an "intellectual aristocracy" in American cities, in contrast to their Irish counterparts of 1846-1850 (*e.g.*, John R. Common, *Races and Immigrants in America*, new edition, New York, 1927, p. 48).

[30]See a report of 1864 characterizing the Germans and Swiss as "the most enterprising and thrifty" and figures pertaining to German versus Irish applications for relief (Klaghorn, *U.S. Industrial Commission Reports*, XV, p. 460 and 464). All seem to be in agreement with this view: See Common, *ibid.*, Edward Alsworth Ross, *The Old World in the New*, New York, 1914, p. 59, etc.

[31]See statistics concerning representation in various occupations and trades of the different nationalities culled from the Tenth Census (1880), cited in Richmond Mayo-Smith's classic book, *The Influence of the Immigrant on the United States...*, Rome, 1888, Tables 23, 25, and 27, pp. 68 and 71.

[32]The *World*, January 15, 1867, p. 4, col. 2. See also percentages cited by Mayo-Smith, *Emigration and Immigration*, New York, 1890, p. 67; New York State, Commissioners of Emigration, *Annual Reports*, 1861-1869; Young, *Special Report on Immigration, passim*, especially the table dealing with the years 1859-1870, p. xviii.

[33]Hardenbergh later built a number of houses for the Schermerhorns in the area. A handsome block front consisting of six five-story French flats on the east side of Third Avenue between 68th and 69th Streets (New Building Docket #922-925 of 1882) was demolished in August and September 1956 to make way for the new building for the Foundling Hospital. The original specifications and plans of one of the buildings are preserved at the Plan Desk, Department of Buildings (envelope for Block 1423, Lot 48).

[34]For details, see Mikkelson, *History of Real Estate, Architecture, and Building*, pp. 58 ff.

[35]See *Appleton's New York Illustrated*, New York, 1870, p. 45.

[36]See Alteration Docket #3110 of 1935 (in envelope for Block 1426, Lot 4, Plan Desk) and plans in the possession of the Misses Mary M. and Catherine Lienau, Detlef's granddaughters, who have lived in the corner building ever since it was renovated.

[37]Portfolio XVI, No. 30, consisting of five working drawings dated May 18 and 21, 1870 (side and end elevations, plans of basement, and first and second stories), three studies (including one of rear elevation), plus two details of the iron work on tracing paper.

[38]New Building Docket #837 of 1870 in envelope pertaining to Block 1426, Lot 4, Plan Desk; for complete information, see Appendix II.

[39]No provision was made for external venting of the bathroom and water closet.

[40]In the original building application, however, there is no indication that such a hoist was actually provided. Since the building has been greatly altered, there is no way of checking on the discrepancy.

[41]New Building Docket #1087 of 1871. Prague was the architect of a huge seaside hotel, The Brighton, at Coney Island (see *American Architect*, Vol. IV [September 7, 1878], No. 141) and was later very active in the development of the upper West Side of New York (Mikkelson, pp. 96 and 104).

[42]Cf. one of his early apartment houses in Berlin in Hitzig, *Hamburg's Privatbauten*, Vol. I, Heft II, plate V.

[43]While German examples are not lacking (*e.g.*, *ibid.*, and *Hamburg's Privatbauten*, plate XLVIII), the French examples are probably more pertinent, such as Paul Mesnard's apartment house at rue de la Chausée d'Antin, No. 21 (Vacquer, *Maisons... de Paris*, plates 34-38), etc. Interior courts were usually considerably larger in the French examples: *e.g.*, Sedille's apartment house at Boulevard Sebastopol, No. 124 (Calliat, *Parallèle*, plate 29). Rolland is mentioned by Hautecoeur (VI, p. 128) as one of the architects most interested in the development of apartment house planning; he is represented in Daly's *L'Architecture privée* by three apartment houses in the Boulevard Beaumarchais, another interesting comparison to the Lienau plans (I, Maisons a louer, troisieme classe, Ex. A³, plate 1).

[44]See, *e.g.*, Hitzig, *ibid.*; for England, see Hitchcock, *Early Victorian Architecture*, I, p. 375 and *passim*.

[45]I, p. 186. A check of the area, now largely rebuilt, corroborated by the local post office, revealed that the street on which the example was located is no longer in existence.

[46]Illustrated in *American Architect*, Vol. III (May 4, 1878), No. 123.

[47]Schuyler, *Architectural Record*, Vol. VI, p. 336.

[48]*SAH Journal*, Vol. XIV, p. 22 and Fig. 8.

[49]New York, 1903.

[50]A relatively late example is an article in *The New York Times* of February 12, 1873 (p. 4, cols. 5-6), wherein it is pointed out that, while there is an eight-hour day in industry and division of labor, conditions within the home "are still as primitive as in Biblical days". The writer looks forward to the day when outside specialists will be called in to take care of the necessary work, giving wives more time "to elevate their minds"[!].

[51]Immigration had slackened considerably during the Civil War; moreover, the post-war years saw a decline in the ratio of Irish to German immigrants, as noted above and in the *World*, January 15, 1867 (p. 4, col. 2).

[52]January 16, 1871, p. 4, col. 5.

[53]Lienau, "Biography, Memorabilia," p. 3.

[54]See Fig. 28. It was divided into twenty family and fifteen bachelor suites and was described by Richardson as "the chosen refuge of artistic and literary people" (*Scribner's*, Vol. VIII, p. 69). Later, it became the home of the New York Club.

[55]Holly's Family Hotel was planned for Trinity College, Hartford, Connecticut. It differed from Grosvenor House and later versions of the apartment hotel in providing six separate entrances to the apartments, thus maintaining, on the exterior at least, the general feeling of the individual row house. Each family was expected to furnish its own house maid.

[56]New Building Docket #658 of 1871. Tax records also indicate replacement of a three-story building by a six-story building in 1871 (Tax Assesssment Records, Manhattan, 15th Ward).

[57]*Scribner's*, Vol. VIII, p. 69.

[58]Copy of an undated clipping from an unidentified newspaper in Lienau, pp. 9-10. Believed to date in the autumn of 1872 by Mr. [J. Henry] Lienau (letter of December 14, 1951.

[59]*Valentine's Manual of Old New York*, Vol. VIII (1924), pp. 167-168.

[60]It is extremely close in style to an apartment house by one of the older architects, Lesueur (Calliat, *Parallèle*, Vol. II, plate 70).

[61]One of the earliest apartment hotels in Boston was Ware & Van Brunt's Hotel Hamilton, illustrated in *American Architect*, Vol. I (1876), p. 373 (elevations), plans between pp. 272-273. It was a much larger building than the Grosvenor; it too was a rather restrained example of Second Empire style, though its picturesque roofline and truncated corner pavilions are definitely of the '70s.

[62]Gilsey House is illustrated in *Valentine's Manual of Old New York*, Vol. VIII (1924), p. 156. Jefferson Williamson's *The American Hotel, an Anecdotal History*, New York, 1930, is a convenient reference source. As for Stevens House, like the Haight House, it was partially remodeled for use as an apartment hotel. Richardson, unimpressed by its pretentiousness, wrote that, in contrast to the Grosvenor, "its influence on the reform has been hardly favorable" (*Scribner's*, Vol. VIII, p. 69).

[63]In the absence of plans, see Robinson and Pidgeon, *Atlas*, plate 9.

[64]De Forest and Veiller, I, pp. 95-96 and 200.

[65]O.P. Hatfield, "The Elevator as a Substitute for Stairs," *Architects' and Mechanics' Journal*, Vol. I [December 10, 1859], p. 60). Calvert Vaux suggested using two steam-operated elevators simultaneously and envisaged buildings twelve to fifteen stories tall (*ibid.*, Vol. I, p. 15, and his letter to the editor, Vol. I [December 24, 1859], p. 77). The escalator, incidentally, was an invention of this same year. We may safely assume that, had the war years not intervened, the elevator would have made its appearance long before 1870 in commercial buildings (like Gilman, Kendall & Post's Equitable Building, 1868-1871) and in apartments (like Haight House, 1870-1871).

[66]*Scribner's*, Vol. VIII, p. 68.

[67]See description in New York Superintendent of Buildings, "Exhibit A," *Annual Report for 1869*, pp. 571-572.

[68]Alan Burnham kindly sent me this photograph. Brown Brothers, photographers, are at 220 West 42nd Street; their collection is enormous and a source of never-ending surprise.

[69]Portfolio 15, No. 27, consisting of two elevations, two plans, and two working drawings dated March 25, 1871.

[70]New Building Docket #602 of 1871 (for further details, see Appendix II). Lienau also built a stable for Mr. Monson at 156 East 26th Street (New Building Docket #392 of 1876).

[71]A "Forty-niner," Monson had returned east in 1865 after a very successful career in California. For some years, he served as Judge of the District Court; he declined an appointment by California's governor to the State Supreme Court. Monson was one of the founders of the Knickerbocker Club, of which he later became president. Obituary, *The New York Times*, January 1, 1902, p. 7, col. 5.

[72]According to Kennion (p. xxii), this was a $20,000 farmhouse. No drawings or other records of the building are known to have survived. It is quite possible that Richard H. Hunt's mansion for the Belmonts at Hempstead replaced this earlier building.

[73]The Brunswick Hotel, where H.H. Richardson later did a big alteration job (Alternate Docket #25 of 1870), is illustrated in *Valentine's Manual of Old New York*, Vol. VIII (1924), p. 153.

[74]New York (1944), pp. 48-49. This was forwarded to me by Miss Vera Robson, Secretary Office, New York Yacht Club, together with her letter of August 3, 1956.

[75]Attribution based on Kennion, Part II, p. 103.

[76]The notations "Jockey" and "Jacht" [sic] provided the first clues regarding the functions of the building. The New York Yacht Club is listed in the directories at 27th Street and Madison Avenue from 1872 on.

[77]Portfolio 10, No. 18, and photographs, Lienau Collection.

Chapter VIII

[1]See Henry Ward Beecher's comment on how much he loved "the generous old English windows, large as the whole side of a room," where one can converse and "be indoors and out of doors at the same time" (*The Star Papers*, quoted in Cleaveland and Backus, *Village and Farm Cottages*, p. 100).

[2]The extremely pictorial character of the building is seen in Miss Abbott's photograph in Bernice Abbott and Elizabeth McAusland, *Changing New York*, New York, 1939, p. 51. For an earlier example of the Neo-Baroque in New York, a trend that needs study, see reference to Temple Shearith Israel by Robert Mook. For parallel trends elsewhere, see *e.g.*, City Hall (1871-1881) and Post Office (1873-1874), Philadelphia, by John McArthur, Jr. The latter is illustrated in Philadelphia Art Alliance, *Philadelphia Architecture*, plate 59.

The story of the 1867 Post Office competition, for which fifteen architects submitted designs, is interesting for its unconscious revelation of the eclectic attitude of the time. None of the designs, described as generally "wanting in originality and appositeness" in *The New York Times* (cited in Stokes, V, 1928, under date of June 7-9, 1867) were judged worthy of the top $5,000 and $3,000 premiums. Instead, fifteen prizes were awarded, of which $2,000 each went to Hunt, Le Brun, Renwick & Sands, J. Correja, and Schulze & Schoen for their designs. Then, a committee under the chairmanship of Hunt was appointed to draw up a new plan with instructions to combine the best features of the top fifteen designs. The *Times* remarked that "perhaps a result quite as satisfactory would have been reached at less expense, had an architect of standing been employed to select from among the public buildings of several of the most elegant and combine their most excellent points". For further details regarding the competition, see *ibid.*, V, 1929 and 1931 under the dates of December 28, 1867, and February 29, 1868. This whole story calls to mind the editorial comment made some years earlier in *Architects' and Mechanics' Journal* (Vol. II [June 9, 1860], p. 91):

> "formerly, a competition design was selected and the architect left free to execute his design. Now, building committees claim the right to select a little here and a little there—a *hash* suited to their uncultivated palates. The architect from whom they take the largest slice is entrusted with the cooking of the stew."[!]

[3]Meek's essay, "Picturesque Eclecticism" (*Art Bulletin*, Vol. XXXII [September 1950], pp. 226-235), in which he first suggested the use of this all-inclusive term to describe 19th century architecture, has been recently restated in his *Railroad Station* (chapter I, pp. 1-24).

[4]Portfolio XXI, No. 40-A, including seven sheets of drawings for the main house, of which one is stamped June 24, 1875, four sheets of studies for the gardener's cottage, one for the gate lodge, and two for the stables and shed.

[5]Thanks are due to Brother Paul Ambrose, Dean of Marist College, for permission to visit the buildings (May 1953) and to Brother John Malachy for information and photographs (letter of July 7, 1953). I am particularly indebted to Miss Elizabeth Mead, Art Department, Vassar College, who made preliminary enquiries for me (letter of December 7, 1952) and who, with the help of Miss Amy VerNooy, Reference Librarian, Adriance Memorial Library, Poughkeepsie, and Secretary, Dutchess County Historical Society, conducted a search of the records of Christ Church and local newspapers for me. Miss Mead also referred me to Evelyn (Mrs. Alexander G.) Cummins of Poughkeepsie, the widow of the Reverend Cummins, custodian of the Bech vault (letter of January 31, 1953); Mrs. Cummins suggested contacting Alice (Mrs. Arthur T.) Sutcliffe of New York, who knew the Bech family well and from whom I obtained valuable information (letter of May 16, 1953).

[6]New York, Vol. II (December 1875), plate XLVII.

[7]Portfolio XII, No. 21.

[8]Information was derived from various New York directories, Belden's *New York, Past, Present and Future...*, Boyd's *Poughkeepsie and Fishkill Landing Directory, 1864/1865,* and Edmund Platt, *The Eagle's History of Poughkeepsie;*

from the Earliest Settlements, 1683 to 1905, Poughkeepsie: Platt & Platt, 1905, pp. 143 and 158.

[9]Portfolio XXIII, No. 46, consisting of eight sheets of drawings, one dated April 7, 1874.

[10]These color notes are based on the exquisitely rendered watercolor sketch for the gardener's cottage.

[11]Cf., *e.g.,* William A. Potter's design for a country house in *New York Sketch-book,* Vol. I, No. VI (June 1874). Note the extreme verticality, jagged outline, steep gables and turrets, exaggerated stick style, and striped roof.

[12]For the latter, see *The Architectural Sketch-book* (Portfolio Club), Boston, 1873-1876, 4 volumes in 3, *passim.*

[13]*Architecture and Building,* Vol. VII (September 3, 1887), p. 80.

[14]For a thoughtful analysis of both the antiquarian and progressive tendencies of Queen Anne, see *Shingle Style,* p. 12 and especially chapter II, pp. 19-33.

[15]This is the date assigned to the drawings by J. Henry Lienau. We know that the land, originally part of William Lawrence Beach's estate, was purchased in 1879 at a cost of $100,000 (Index of Deeds, County Clerk's Office, Newport). Tax records would make possible a more accurate date.

[16]Interestingly enough, the contract drawings were signed by both husband *and* wife. Walter Herron Lewis (1828-1901) and his wife were both descended from old Puritan stock. Lewis, a Philadelphian, moved to New York, where he and his brother Henry were established in business. He was a Trustee of the New York Life Insurance Company and Chairman of its Auditing Department, a Director of the Home Insurance Company, and a warden of Trinity Church. A quiet, unassuming man, he was active in the affairs of the Republican Party and a liberal contributor to charitable causes, according to his obituary in *Lewisiana, or the Lewis Letter; a Monthly Inter-family Paper,* edited by F.B. Lewis and C.A. Lewis, Guilford, Connecticut, etc., Vol. XI (April 1901), p. 158; see also Vol. I (January 1887), p. 9; Vol. IV (May 1894), p. 168; Vol. V (October 1894), p. 54; Vol. XIII (December 1902), p. 98; Vol. XV (May 1905), p. 196; obituary in *The New York Times,* February 19, 1901, p. 7, col. 6. According to his son's obituary (the New York *Tribune,* January 20, 1899, p. 7, col. 4), Walter Lewis sold his Newport cottage and built one in Tuxedo in the hope that his son's health would improve.

[17]The property was sold for $164,000 to Frederick Pearson, whose descendants hold it today. The chain of title is as follows: from Frederick Pearson to his wife, Leslie J.; after her death in 1928, to her daughter, Josephine (Mrs. Beverly Boget); following her death in 1953, it passed to Mr. Bogert. Information from Index of Deeds, Newport, and Mr. Bogert's attorney, Theodore A. Wick, Esq., of New York (letter of August 26, 1953). I visited the house on August 17, 1953, with the kind permission of Mr. Bogert's daughter, Mrs. Flynn.

[18]Name given in *Newport Plats* (1883), plate 18 (consulted in Tax Collector's Office, City Hall, Newport); corroborated by two views in Bayles, *History of Newport County*, opposite p. 502.

[19]Portfolio XXI, No. 41. Nineteen sheets, including two plot plans, eight studies, eight signed contract drawings (seven for the house and one for the stable), and one working detail.

[20]Although much lower than the fifteen- or sixteen-foot ceilings of some of Lienau's earlier houses, the twelve-foot height is still considerable.

[21]*E.g.*, Bloor & Oakey's Sprague house, Buffalo, New York, *American Architect*, Vol. II (July 14, 1877), No. 81; Holly's Peddar house, Llewellyn Park, Orange, New Jersey, *ibid.*, Vol. X (August 27, 1881), No. 296, and houses in *Holly's Modern Dwellings in Town and Country...*, New York, 1878. Cf. also illustrations in Scully, *Shingle Style, passim.*

[22]For this and Cohasset cottage mentioned below, see *American Architect*, Vol. IX (January 29, 1881), No. 266, and Vol. X (September 3, 1881), No. 297.

[23]Quoting Mr. Wick. The porch was glazed in 1929.

[24]Refers to page in original dissertation.

[25]The house was originally published in *American Architect*, Vol. IV (July 7, 1878), No. 132. See Scully, *Shingle Style*, pp. 79-80, Figs. 42-43.

[26]*Homes in the City and Country*, pp. 75-76.

[27]Pages 5 ff.

[28]Scully's attempt to relate the plan of the Dorsheimer house with a French example in Calliat's *Parallèle* seems rather farfetched (p. 5, n. 12).

[29]Scully, pp. 7-9.

[30]Lewis Mumford stressed this point in "The Regionalism of H.H. Richardson," Dancy Lecture, Alabama College, 1941, published in *The South in Architecture*, New York, 1941, p. 80.

[31]For the reader interested in delving more deeply into this question, see the examples mentioned and illustrated (too numerous to cite here) in the following: Harold Donaldson Eberlein, *The Architecture of Colonial America*, Boston, 1915; John Martin Hammond, *Colonial Mansions of Delaware and Maryland*, Philadelphia, 1914; Thomas Tileston Waterman, *The Mansions of Virginia, 1706-1776*, Chapel Hill, North Carolina, 1945; Edith Tunis Sale, *Interiors of Virginia Homes of Colonial Times*, Richmond, Virginia, 1927; Morrison, *Early American Architecture*; Smith, *White Pillars* (especially the plan of Rosemount, p. 142).

In the North, this type of plan was rare until the advent of central heating. Two little known examples, called to my attention by Talbot Hamlin, are preserved in Portsmouth, New Hampshire. One, the Moffat-Ladd house (1863), built by an English sea captain, is an interesting example of the attempt to integrate the tradition of the English great hall into a relatively small house. See John Mead Howells, *The Architectural Heritage of the Piscataqua*, New York, 1937, p. 31, and Fig. 33.

[32]Cf. Smith, chapter VI, pp. 151 ff.; Morrison, chapter VIII, pp. 253 ff.

[33]For an excellent discussion of this point, see Scully, *Shingle Style*, pp. 22 ff. Walter Knight Sturges, whose interest in Queen Anne was evidenced in "The Long Shadow of Norman Shaw" (*SAH Journal*, Vol. IX [December 1950], pp. 15-20), recently read a paper entitled "The Colonial Revival: A Nineteenth-Century Commentary on an Eighteenth Century Architecture" to a meeting of the Society of Architectural Historians (New York Chapter) on May 15, 1957. He called attention to a review by H.R. Cleveland, Jr., of James Gallier's *American Builder's General Price Book...* (*North American Review*, Vol. XLIII [October 1836], p. 356) as the first favorable mention of Colonial architecture. Perhaps more attention should be given to Arthur Gilman's buildings, not just his theory, particularly his Arlington Street church in Boston, variously dated between the late 1850s and late '60s. Returning to literature, in addition to Allen (1852) and Chamberlain (1858) cited by Scully (*Shingle Style*, p. 23, nn. 8 and 9), one stumbles across many examples of early interest in the Colonial: *e.g.*, Bristed, *Upper Ten Thousand*, p. 249; "Revolutionary Relics," *Ballou's*, Vol. VIII (1855), p. 56; "House Building in America," *Putnam's*, Volume X (July 1857), p. 110. In the latter, a very interesting unsigned article, old Dutch and English type farmhouses are described as "testifying to the worth of simplicity and the beauty of common sense," in contrast to the "pretense and gingerbread work" of current architecture. A tentative attribution is possible to P.B. Wight, who is known to have done considerable writing for *Putnam's* from 1860 on.

[34]Page 6, n. 17.

[35]*Country Houses*, pp. 292, 303, 340, and Figs. 126, 131, and 161; *Village and Farm Cottages*, Design XI. In the references to *Villas and Cottages*, the bracketed numbers refer to the 1864 edition: Nos. 4 (4), 12 (14), 22 (24), 25 (30), 31 (37), 32 (39), and (38).

[36]Design No. 12 (14), p. 189 (201).

[37]Letter of December 8, 1953.

[38]"The Suburban House," *Homes in City and Country*, p. 81.

[39]In describing the plan of Design IX in *Homestead Architecture* (1st edition, 1861; 2nd edition, 1869), Sloan says "we are very partial to this elevation of the character of the hall, which not be used only as a mere thoroughfare" (p. 114). The accelerating trend toward the open plan is strikingly illustrated in *Woodward's Country Homes* (c.1865), Design No. 2, Fig. 5, where a centrally located fireplace in the hall serves to heat parlor, library, and dining room, all of which open onto the hall by means of sliding doors, so that "when the occasion requires, hall, parlor or library, and dining-room may be thrown together" (p. 16).

[40]Designs XI and XII, pp. 75 and 80.

[41]Pages 55-56.

[42]Portfolio XI, No. 19, consisting of thirteen drawings, including two signed contract drawings (including a first-floor plan dated May 6, 1872), eight working drawings (three dated November 25, 1872), and three working details (one dated January 4, 1873).

[43]For information concerning the house, I am indebted to Miss P. Keefer of Cruickston Park, a granddaughter of Matthew Wilks (letter of November 22, 1952). At that time, the house was owned by her brother, Matthew Wilks Keefer, who had inherited the property from his aunt, Katherine Langdon Wilks, who died in 1948.

[44]Spooner, *Historic Families of America*, III, p. 322; *A Standard Dictionary of Canadian Biography*, Toronto, Canada, 1934-1938, II, pp. 469-470.

[45]Illustrated in *History of Real Estate, Building and Architecture*, p. 586, and *King's Handbook*, p. 141. For Lienau's other work for Wilks, see Appendix II.

[46]Mrs. Wilks died recently, leaving an estate of $80,000,000: See obituary, *The New York Times*, February 6, 1951, p. 27.

[47]For photographs and details concerning this house, I am indebted to the Misses Mary M. and Catherine Lienau (interview of November 29, 1956).

[48]The economic filtration downward of the style, at first used only for large resort houses, may be seen in the competition for a $3,000 house run by the *American Architect* in 1883. Nearly all the entries were Queen Anne in style: See Vol. XIII (February 3, 1883); No. 371, March 24, No. 378, April 7, No. 380, April 21, No. 382, etc.

[49]Refers to page in original dissertation.

[50]*E.g.*, William H. Dabney, Jr., "Redcote," York Harbor, Maine, *American Architect*, Vol. XII (September 16, 1882), No. 35, and H.P. Clark and Ion Lewis's Sprague House, Kennebunkport, Maine, *ibid.*, Vol. XIII (November 4, 1882), No. 358, both illustrated also in Scully, *Shingle Style*, Figs. 53 and 54, though without the plan of the Sprague house.

[51]Cf. the contemporary "Sunset Hall" by Lamb & Rich in Lawrence (Long Island), New York, published in *American Architect*, Vol. XV (February 2, 1884), No. 423; also illustrated in Scully, Figs. 69-72.

[52]Refers to page in original dissertation.

[53]Photograph in my possession; Rock Hall is illustrated in Donald C. Mitchell, "The Country House," *Homes in City and Country*, p. 101.

[54]Mosle, who died in 1904, was a well-to-do importer and exporter with interests in the insurance business and sugar industry. He was born in Bremen and is supposed to have migrated in 1849, though he is not listed in the city directories until 1856/1857. He must have been an old friend of Detlef: Both men joined the Deutsche Gesellschaft in the same year, 1854, according to the *Jahrebericht der Deutschen Gesellschaft der Stadt New York für das Jahr 1882*, New York, 1883, p. 7. For further information, see *Directory of Directors of the City of New York*, New York, 1902, p. 515. I am particularly indebted to Miss Marle Moore, former secretary to George Mosle's son, Henry A. Mosle, Esq. (1867-1957), who questioned him on my behalf a few days before his death on May 29, and checked Alexander G. Mosle, *Die Familie Mosle*, Leipzig, 1912, for pertinent data.

[55]Discussed in Jacob Landy, "The Domestic Architecture of the 'Robber Barons' in New York City," *Marsyas*, Vol. V (1947-1949), p. 71, Fig. 8.

⁵⁶Portfolio XXII, No. 42, nineteen drawings, including seven signed contract drawings dated August 24, 1878, one plot plan and eleven studies. According to New Building Docket #532 of 1878, the house was finished late in December 1879. George Mosle occupied it for only a short time, from 1880 to 1885, when he sold it because of financial reverses.

⁵⁷*American Architect*, Vol. II (July 28, 1877), No. 83.

⁵⁸Neo-Grec influence is particularly strong in the interior decoration, *e.g.*, the working detail of the entrance door and the designs for the main staircase.

⁵⁹*American Architect*, Vol. IV (September 7, 1878), No. 141.

⁶⁰Portfolio XIX, No. 36, consisting of five sheets, of which three are working drawings (one elevation and two plans) and two are studies. Five drawings are filed with Miscellaneous Drawings, Series II, all mantels, Louis XV, or Neo-Grec in style.

⁶¹Franklin Howland, *A Brief Genealogical and Biographical History of the Arthur, Henry, and John Howlands and Their Descendants, of the United States and Canada*, New Bedford, Massachusetts, 1885, II, p. 382; Weeks, *Prominent Families of New York*, p. 292.

⁶²See mason's reminiscences of his father's dealings with him in *Architects and Their Environment*, pp. 58-59.

⁶³Lienau Collection, eleven sheets, filed with Miscellaneous Drawings, Series IV.

⁶⁴New Building Docket #1182 of 1881, finished December 1882. Howland is listed at his new address in the directories of 1883/1884.

⁶⁵The Robertson and Bates houses are illustrated in *American Architect*, Vol. IX (March 12, 1881), No. 272, and Vol. VII (May 15, 1880), No. 229. For the latter, cf. Shaw's Hopedene, Surrey, published in *Building News*, May 8, 1874, Fig. 8, and in Scully's *Shingle Style*.

⁶⁶For Price, see *American Architect*, Vol. VI (November 1879), p. 140 and No. 201. Six designs submitted to the Architectural League competition were published in *ibid.*, Vol. IX (April 16, 1881), p. 188 and No. 277.

⁶⁷For the distinctions among the English, French, and American basement types, see "Basement House," Sturgis's *Dictionary of Architecture and Building*, II, cols. 432-434.

⁶⁸Pages 24-26 and plan 11.

⁶⁹The houses are documented by New Building Docket #427 of 1883, listings in Mikkelson, *History of Real Estate, Architecture and Building*, p. 100; "Building Intelligence," *American Architect*, Vol. XIII (April 28, 1883), p. 204. For further details, see Appendix II.

⁷⁰Mikkelson, *ibid.*, pp. 85-105, is the best source of general information; also *American Architect*, Vol. IX (January 4, 1881), p. 23.

⁷¹Vol. V (April 12, 1879), pp. 117-118.

⁷²New York, 1879.

⁷³*Ibid.*, pp. 20-22.

[74]New Building Docket #517-518 of 1879, described and illustrated in Schuyler, *Architectural Record*, Vol. VI, pp. 335-337. Most of these buildings are still standing today (1957).

[75]See Robinson & Pidgeon's *Atlas*, plate 24, for a picture of the West Side in 1885.

[76]See chart in Mikkelson, *History of Real Estate, Building and Architecture*, p. 106.

[77]Schuyler, *Architectural Record*, Vol. VI, p. 352.

[78]*Idem.*, "The Small City House," *ibid.*, Vol. VIII (April-June 1899), p. 376. As an example of how much could be loaded onto an 18-foot, 6-inch, front, see *American Architect*, Vol. VIII (November 11, 1880), No. 257, residence near Fifth Avenue, Harlem, by Kimbell & Wisedell.

[79]New Building Docket #112-115 of 1886, finished in January 1887. The houses were owned as follows: No. 48 by Detlef Lienau, 50 by Elizabeth (Mrs. J. August) Lienau, 52 by Jean M. Williams, and 54 by Mrs. Mary M. Williams. In cost, they ranged from $15,000 for the 16-foot, 8-inch, house to $21,000 for the 22-foot residence. Envelopes referring to Block 1195, Lots 51, 52, 52-1/2, and 53 (Plan Desk, Department of Buildings) contain original specifications, plans, and a letter from Detlef to Albert F. d'Oench, Inspector of Buildings. In 1904, Nos. 48 and 50 were altered by J. August.

[80]Portfolio XXIII, No. 45, consisting of thirty-one sheets of drawings, mostly rendered by J. August, including sixteen studies, eight signed contract drawings, and seven working details.

[81]*American Architect*, Vol. VIII (September 18, 1880), No. 247. Cf. Shaw's New Zealand Chambers, published in *Building News* of 1873, reproduced in Scully, *Shingle Style*, Fig. 7.

[82]New Building Docket #1501 of 1885, begun November 4, 1885, finished September 28, 1886. Original specifications and drawings are in the envelope for Block 1195, Lot 54, Plan Desk.

[83]This committee was constituted by the laws of the State of New York chiefly as a tribunal of appeal from the decision of New York's Inspector of Buildings. In addition, members passed on candidates for inspectorships to the Department for the Survey and Inspection of Buildings and conducted examinations of buildings reported to be unsafe. James MacGregor, New York's Building Superintendent, refers to a survey of the Spingler House at Union Square conducted by Lienau (*Annual Report of 1868*), pp. 390-391. Lienau's obituary in *American Architect* makes special note of his authority in matters of construction (Vol. XXII [September 17, 1887], p. 179).

[84]Only two decades earlier, George Templeton Strong had confided sadly to his *Diary*: "I suppose we must reconcile ourselves to the fact that New York is a grand, commercial, money-making centre of the universe, and that learning and science are exotics which cannot be acclimatized" (III, p. 430, entry of March 18, 1864).

Chapter IX

[1]Refers to page in original dissertation.

[2]This, and the anecdote that follows, are quoted from Hartmann, "A Conversation with Henry Janeway Hardenbergh," *Architectural Record*, Vol. XIX, p. 377.

[3]*E.g.*, his critique of the Noël & Saurel warehouse in *Architectural Record*, Vol. VI, p. 335.

[4]*Ibid.*, p. 337. Cf. the criticism by Daly and Labrouste of Beaux-Arts training mentioned previously. Lienau's letter of May 14, 1868, to Mr. F.O. Matthiessen, President of the New Jersey Sugar Refining Company, is very revealing of his own attitude in this regard. In it, he expresses in no uncertain terms his displeasure at having his advice disregarded. It is a fascinating document, illustrating Lienau's acute awareness of the challenge by a layman—even though he was his client—to the recently acquired professional standing of architects in this country. The letter reads as follows:

"As the time for finishing the building of your new sugar house draws near, I would once more call your attention to the strength of the floor supporting the filter tanks. As I mentioned before to you, there is not sufficient strength in that floor to support the tanks of 4 ft. diameter, having been calculated to support those of only 3 ft. diameter; strength insufficient in the beams, the girders and the columns, which later, as you know, have been refused by me before, not being up to the standard required and contracted for, even for the smaller tanks.

"I reiterate this, which has already been known to you by word of mouth, in order to draw your earnest attention to the importance of the subject, and to advise you once more professionally to have the additional beams and columns put in as proposed by me.

"In order that you may understand the matter perfectly, I repeat that the beams, etc., have been calculated to bear what we call the safe weight, leaving the elasticity of the iron unimpaired, and which in this instance is 1/3 of the weight which would break the same, and that no reliable builder would subject his construction to any greater strain than that produced by this safe weight.

"The difference in the weight between tanks of 3 and 4 ft. diameter: it is like their contents, and the contents of a 3 ft. cylinder is to one of 4 ft. diameter as 10 to 18, now taking the weight of the 3 ft. tank as given to be 10 tons, and present 4 ft. tanks would weigh 18 tons each.

"Such an increase of weight is beyond any prudent risk, and I for my part, therefore, have respectfully to decline the responsibility of this change.

"Please acknowledge receipt of this, and oblige.

Yours respectfully,

D. Lienau"

[5]Hamlin, "Paul Johannes Pelz," *Dictionary of American Biography*, XIV, pp. 411-412; Thieme Becker, XXVI, pp. 371-372. The heartbreaking story of the Pelz-Smithmeyer designs for the Congressional Library was best told by Archibald Hopkins, Chief Clerk, Court of Claims, *Smithmeyer and Pelz v. the United States*, *American Architect*, Vol. XC (July 28, 1906), pp. 27-29. After winning first prize in the competition of 1873, from 1873-1886, the two architects made eight to twelve completely different sets of designs (accounts vary), of which some were modified still further. They gave up

most of their private architectural practice during those years to devote themselves to this project; Smithmeyer even went to Europe in 1882 to visit libraries there, for which he was reimbursed only $800. Finally, in 1886, Congress approved the last design; Smithmeyer was named architect, with Pelz as chief draftsman. In 1888, Smithmeyer was fired, and Brig. Gen. Thomas L. Casey, Chief Engineer of the Army, was brought in. Pelz stayed on until 1892, working out a design based upon the original scheme of 1873; then, he too was dismissed and the building was executed under the supervision of the general's son, E.P. Casey. The final settlement received by Smithmeyer and Pelz for their years of work was $48,000.

⁶Born in Jersey City in 1854, Jacob August Lienau was sent to Germany for study from c.1870 to c.1874. Of the several drawings of this period still in the possession of his daughters, the Misses Mary M. and Catherine Lienau, three deal with city planning (Hiedelberg, Berlin): He must, therefore, have studied at some kind of a technical or architectural school there. A number of drawings post-dating his return to the U.S., particularly two of 1875, shed light on the methods Detlef used to train his draftsmen. These drawings, copies of Detlef's copies of Labrouste's Italian drawings, are proof of Lienau's adherence to the teaching principles of *his* patron. We may assume that Pelz and Hardenbergh went through the same course of instruction. Regarding his work of the 1880s, it should be noted that a great many of his father's commissions of this period were rendered by J. August: See Howland residence and Williams row, Panorama Building, 860 Broadway, Telfair Museum; alterations for First National Bank, Jersey City (1887) and of 62-64 Cedar Street (1890), both completed after Detlef's death (see Appendix II, *passim*). How much of a part he took in designing his father's late work is not known.

According to the list of work kindly furnished to me by Miss Mary M. Lienau, J. August specialized in domestic work, concentrated chiefly in the metropolitan New York area. He would have been far more productive if his career had not been hampered in the last ten years of his life by serious illness. For further information, see his obituary in *American Architect*, Vol. LXXXIX (May 12, 1906), p. 158; article by Hamlin, *Dictionary of American Biography*, XXI, p. 494; an illustration of the work of Lineau [*sic*] & Nash in *Architecture and Building*, Vol. XXIV (May 2, 1896), p. 207, a reference I owe to Julia Sabine; letter of December 1, 1902, to Henry Rutgers Marshall, President, New York Chapter, AIA, on file at the local AIA headquarters; letters and drawings in the possession of the Misses Lienau.

⁷At a meeting of the AIA on June 1, 1858, Charles Babcock severely criticized the eclectic tendencies of the period, stating that "we practice all styles with equal facility, and no style thoroughly well". He went on to say that architects are in "a state of chaos, quite afloat, and at the mercy of every breeze of caprice or gale of prejudice" (*The Crayon*, Vol. V [July 1858], p. 199).

⁸"Creative Eclecticism," *SAH Journal*, Vol. XII, pp. 15-18; "Picturesque Eclecticism," *Art Bulletin*, Vol. XXXII, pp. 226-235, especially p. 231;

Railroad Station, chapter I. See also Hamlin, "The Rise of Eclecticism in New York," *SAH Journal*, Vol. XI, pp. 3-8.

[9]*Early Victorian Architecture*, I, p. xi; see also pp. 216-217.

[10]A point stressed by both Meeks and Hitchcock. For Meeks, see *SAH Journal*, Vol. XII, p. 231, and *Railroad Station*, pp. 16-17; for Hitchcock, "High Victorian Gothic," *Victorian Studies*, I, p. 50.

[11]*The Nature and Function of Art, More Especially of Architecture*, London, 1881, p. 373; see also p. 474.

[12]An anecdote told by Schuyler, "Leopold Eidlitz," *Dictionary of American Biography*, VI, p. 61.

[13]Refers to page in original dissertation.

[14]Reported in full in *The Crayon*, Vol. V (June 1858), pp. 168-169.

[15]"Detlef Lienau," *National Cyclopædia of American Biography*, XIX, p. 16. The critical section of the text here is a reprint of Hamlin's typescript, "The Place of Detlef Lienau in American Architecture" (1948) in Lienau, "Biography, Memorabilia," pp. 5-7.

[16]"Fire-Proof Construction," read for Lienau by William R. Ware and reported in *American Architect*, Vol. III (1878), pp. 5-6.

[17]*E.g.*, gas works in Magdeburg, *Zeitschrift für Bauwesen*, Vol. IV (1854), Heft V-VI, plate 34; sugar refinery in Waghausel, *Allgemeine Bauzeitung*, Vol. XXVI (1861), plates 409-412; a factory by Strack near Berlin, *Architektonisches Skizzenbuch*, Vol. LIX (1862), Heft VI, plate 5.

[18]For Tefft, see Meeks, *Railroad Station*, Fig. 68, or Hitchcock, *Rhode Island Architecture*, Fig. 55; for Hoxie, see *Ballou's*, Vol. VI (January 21, 1854), p. 48, and Withey, p. 304.

[19]This point is stressed in my article in the *SAH Journal*, Vol. XIV, pp. 22-23. For access to the original drawings and information concerning these buildings, I am indebted to Mr. Harry A. Roberts, former Secretary to the Chairman of the Board, American Sugar Company, 120 Wall Street, New York. Three typescripts by J. Henry Lienau on file there were particularly useful: The most informative was the 92-page "History of the Original F.O. Matthiessen Enterprises in Jersey City". For additional information, see Appendix II.

[20]*Railroad Station*, p. 3.

[21]Refers to page in original dissertation.

[22]Meeting of June 1, as reported in *The Crayon*, Vol. V (July 1858), pp. 199-200.

[23]Refers to page in original dissertation.

[24]See Appendix II.

[25]*American Architect*, Vol. II (January 6, 1877), No. 54.

[26]*Ibid.*, Vol. II (September 29, 1877), No. 92. Built on the site of Jauncey Court (see *ante*, p. 67), the description (*ibid.*, p. 313) reveals the extraordinary richness of polychromatic effects so sought in this period.

[27]*Ibid.*, Vol. III (January 26, 1878), p. 31 and No. 109.

[28]Discussed by Hitchcock in "Frank Lloyd Wright and the 'Academic Tradition' of the Early Eighteen-eighties," *Journal of the Warburg and Courtauld Institutes*, Vol. VI (1944), p. 52.

[29]*E.g.*, Hamlin, *The American Spirit in Architecture*, Yale University, 1926, p. 166 (Vol. XIII: *Pageant of America*).

[30]Vol. I (January 15, 1876), p. 18.

[31]This speech was made in response to a toast by Eidlitz to the Committee on Papers, of which Lienau was a member, and is reported in *The Crayon*, Vol. VI (1859), p. 100.

[32]August Belmont's art collection was housed in a special gallery built in the rear of his house and was one of the most famous of the period.

[33]Hamlin, *Greek Revival Architecture*, pp. 334-335.

[34]Russell Sturgis pointed out that eclecticism was always particularly prevalent in periods when the community is comparatively learned, literary, and interested in the work of other epochs (quoted in Mason, *Architects and Their Environment*, p. 99).

[35]See quotation from Hansen, *The Immigrant in American History*, cited previously.

[36]Books by the following authors, listed in the Bibliography, see *post*, p. 316, have been most helpful in clarifying and interpreting the historical background: Charles A. and Mary R. Beard, Henry Steele Commager, Merle Eugene Curti, Albert Bernhardt Faust, Carl Russell Fish, Louis Morton Hacker, Oscar Handlin, Marcus Lee Hansen, Michael Kraus, Francis Otto Matthiessen, Gustavus Myers, Allan Nevins, Ellis Paxton Oberholtzer, Vernon Louis Parrington, Arthur M. Schlessinger, George Soule, and Thorsten Veblen.

[37]It has been pointed out that the large architectural offices from the later 1880s on turned to classical traditions of design partly as a matter of professional expediency, since these offices had to operate quickly, without a hitch, "along clearly understood and well defined lines" ("Review of Architecture. History of Work Done in New York City During the Last Quarter of a Century," *History of Real Estate, Architecture and Building*, p. 606).

[38]Hamlin, *American Spirit in Architecture*, p. 150.

[39]*American Architecture*, p. 121.

[40]*Sticks and Stones, a Study of American Architecture and Civilization*, new edition, New York, 1933, pp. 95-96. Originally published in 1924.

[41]*The Beginnings of Critical Realism in America*, New York, 1930, pp. 48-49.

[42]Pages 20-21.

[43]*American Building: the Forces That Shape It*, Boston, 1948, especially chapter vi, "The Great Victorians," pp. 99 ff.

[44]A rather touching tribute to Lienau is contained in a letter of November 25, 1872, from a certain Mr. Iauch to Lienau, of which a copy is preserved in Lienau, "Biography, Memorabilia," p. 16. After describing the effects of a recent hurricane on the houses at Long Branch, New Jersey, half of which were destroyed, with the rest in pitiable condition, A. Iauch, the owner of a well known French restaurant in New York (see Augustin P.

Mangé, *Directory Français et Guide des Affaires en Amérique*, New York, 1864, p. 134), continued:

> "Ce n'est que ma maison qui, par la grâce de Dieu et par la science de Monsieur Lienau, en est sortie saine et sauve de la terrible lutte des éléments déchaînés! Après la Providence, c'est bien à vous, mon cher Monsieur Lienau, que je dois d'avoir échappé à cette terrible épreuve. C'est pour cela que je ne puis m'empêcher de vous dire combien je vous suis reconaissant pour les soins consciencieux que vous avez donnés à la construction de ma maison qui sans votre zèle et votre habilité serait peut-être maintenant un monceau de ruines."

> *English translation:* "It isn't [just] that my house, which by the grace of God and the science of Mr. Lienau, remained safe and sound after the terrible beating [it took] from the unrestrained elements. Through Providence, it was because [of] you, my dear Mr. Lienau, that I [also] must have escaped from this terrible ordeal. It is for this then that I am inclined to say how much I am grateful for the conscientious care that you gave to the construction of my house, which without your enthusiasm and your ability perhaps would now be a heap of ruins."

[45]The most entertaining account by far is still Thomas E. Tallmadge's *The Story of Architecture in America*, New York [1927], chapter vi, entitled "The Parvenu Period, 1860-1880. The Age of Innocence (or Where Ignorance Was Bliss)," pp. 140 ff.

[46]A phrase quite appropriately borrowed from the title of a book by that great spokesman of the time, Walt Whitman.

Appendix I.
Resume of Detlef Lienau

Catalogue of Student Drawings and
Early European Commissions, 1836-1847

(Revised list by Ellen W. Kramer, 1954)
The following is an outline of the contents of my typescript
(16 pp., 1954) on deposit at the Avery Library

Series I. Architectural Details, 1836-1838
Five large drawings in pen and ink on tracing paper, of which
four are signed and three dated respectively 1836, 1837, and 1838.
All are evidently traced from Vulliamy's *Ornamental Sculpture in
Architecture*, London, 1824.

Series II. Architectural Details, c.1837-c.1846
Seventy-three small drawings on mounted tracing paper. Related
to Lienau's training in Germany (1837-1841) and in the *atelier*
Labrouste in Paris (c.1842-c.1846). Interesting for subject matter and
sources. While most of the German drawings correspond to
illustrations in slightly earlier or contemporary German publications,
several drawings derive from English books, notably Nos. 11-13,
traced from August Pugin's *A Series of Ornamental Timber Gables*, 2nd
edition, London, 1839, and No. 22, from Pugin's *Gothic Ornaments*,
London, 1831.

Most interesting, however, is the direct connection of a number
of the Lienau drawings with drawings by Labrouste, the latter
executed when he was a student at the French Academy in Rome
(Nos. 30[?], 31, 59, 61, 65[?], 66-70). The original Labrouste drawings
are at the Bibliotheque Nationale in Paris: see R.-A. Weigart,
"Inventaire des dessins d'architecture de l'antiquite a l'epoque
moderne executés par Henri Labrouste en Italie (1825-1830)" in
Labrouste, architecte de la Bibliotheque nationale de 1854 a 1875, Paris,
1953, the catalog of an exhibition of Labrouste drawings and
memorabilia held in 1953.

Also noteworthy is a series of studies of *chalets* (Nos. 38, 48-58),
as well as several studies reflecting LaBrouste's interest in structural
iron (Nos. 71-73) and decorative ironwork (Nos. 27, 28, 33, and 34).

Lienau also made copies of the drawings of some of his classmates and of Beaux-Arts competition projects (Nos. 41, 62, and 63).

Series III. Measured Drawings, c.1842–c.1846

Twenty-two large-scale drawings, mostly studies of the orders and executed in ink and wash, are all related to Labrouste's Italian drawings. Undated, but the majority were executed on Whatman paper watermarked 1842, 1843, and 1844, with one drawing on paper watermarked 1846.

Series IV. Watercolors, c.1842–c.1846

Sixty-two drawings, many on tracing paper, chiefly watercolors. Many signed; a number executed in 1842 (Nos. 5, 8, 9, 10, 15, 19, 21, and 52). A remarkably fine collection, of which the majority were copied from Labrouste's Italian drawings. Several of the Lienau drawings acquire added documentary interest because they were most certainly copied from Labrouste originals, which have since disappeared (Nos. 7, 11, 40, 52, etc.).

Series V. Early European Commissions, 1847

Plan of a hospital signed and dated 1842, evidently connected with Lienau's period of study at the Konigliche Baugewerksschule in Munich. Three signed and dated drawings relating to the installation of new machinery at the Chemical Works of Conrad & Waldmann at St.-Denis, Paris, March and April 1847. Sheet of drawings (with public bathing project on verso) and a press clipping related to competition of 1847 for a new municipal hospital for the city of Altona, Germany, in which Lienau won first prize.

Series VI. Miscellaneous Drawings, 1840s

Ten drawings, of which four may be by Lienau and which probably were copied from Labrouste. The other six are drawings given to him by friends (C. Patouelle, Adam, Briffou[?], Langlais, J. Marye, and P. Seyboth), of whom at least five were fellow students in the *atelier* Labrouste. Some evidently were copied from Labrouste's drawings; three are dated May 1847.

Appendix II.
Chronological List of Documented Work
by Detlef Lienau

This compilation, which includes alterations, studies, and unexecuted projects, is based on material known to me [the author] at the present time. It should not be construed as a definitive catalog: There are undoubtedly many omissions, and I would be extremely grateful for additional information. Only basic sources are listed as reference here; others are cited in the text and notes. Dates supplied by means of external evidence are enclosed in brackets, e.g. [c.1849]. An asterisk (*) indicates that the building is still standing today (October 1957).

Student Days, 1835-1846
See student notebooks and drawings, Lienau Collection.

Work in Europe, 1847
Paris-Lyons Railroad, Paris. Employed as draftsman, Architectural Office, 1847. Letter in Lienau, "Biography, Memorabilia," pp. 25-26.

Conrad & Waldmann Chemical Works, St.-Denis, Paris, 1847. Boiler installation. Original drawings dated March 10, April 2 and 10, 1847, Student Drawings, Series V, Lienau Collection.

*Municipal Hospital, Altona. First prize in competition, November 1847. Present structure built by O. Winkler, 1859-1861, enlarged 1888-1889. Original drawings, Student Drawings, Series V, and press clipping, *Altonaer Nachrichten*, April 17, 1855, Lienau Collection.

Study for a swimming pool [c.1847]. Original drawing, Student Drawings, Series V, Lienau Collection.

1849-1860
Michael Lienau. Suburban cottage, 44 Jersey Avenue, Jersey City, NJ, [c.1849], demolished before 1879. Original drawings, Portfolio I, No. 2, Lienau Collection.

Ernest Fielder. Alterations in his store, 32 Broadway, New York [c.1849]. Original drawings, Portfolio I, No. 2, Lienau Collection.

*Grace (Van Vorst) Church, Erie and Second Streets, Jersey City, NJ, 1850-1853, enlarged 1864, rectory 1867 (see below). Church and rectory in fairly good condition. Sunday school building and tower (1912) not by Lienau. Original drawings, Portfolio III, No. 4, old photographs, and illustrated pamphlet, *Historical Sermon... by the Reverend G.S. Bennitt*, New York, 1888, all in the Lienau Collection.

Hart M. Shiff. Town house and stable, 32 Fifth Avenue, New York, 1850-[c.1852], demolished 1923. Original drawings signed May 4, 1850, Portfolio II, No. 3, carpenter's and mason's specifications of May 10 and May 4, 1850, and an old photograph, all in the Lienau Collection; Tax Assessment Records, Manhattan; Demolition Application #13 of 1923, Department of Buildings.

*Hart M. Shiff. Vault, Greenwood Cemetery, Brooklyn, NY [c.1852]. Original drawings, Portfolio XXIII, No. 46.

*Francis Cottenet. "Nuits," villa and gardener's cottage, Dobbs Ferry, NY, 1852, enlarged [c.1858-1859] (see below), minor alterations 1918. In excellent condition. Original drawings, Portfolio IV, No. 6, and old photograph, Lienau Collection; original drawing and material in possession of present owners.

Study for an Italian villa, undated, possibly related to Cottenet villa. Original drawing in envelope containing unidentified, unexecuted projects, Lienau Collection.

*DeLancey Kane. "Beach Cliffe," Newport, RI, 1852. Main house demolished 1939; *gate lodge and *stable altered. Original drawings, Portfolio IV, No. 5, and old photographs, Lienau Collection.

Study for a town house, undated, stylistically related to Cottenet villa and Kane house. Original drawing in envelope containing unidentified, unexecuted projects, Lienau Collection.

J. Dickinson Miller. Suburban house, Henderson and Second Streets, Jersey City, NJ, 1852, demolished. Photostats of original drawings, Portfolio VI, No. 4, Lienau Collection.

Studies for several churches, not executed. Two signed "Lienau & Marcotte," [c.1852-1854]. Original drawings, Portfolio III, No. 4, Lienau Collection.

Ernest Fiedler. Studies and working drawings for unidentified commercial buildings [c.1852-1854]. Original drawings, Portfolio I, No. 2, Lienau Collection.

Mrs. Mayo. Suburban house, Elizabethtown (Elizabeth), NJ [c.1855-1856], demolished. Original drawings, Portfolio VI, No. 9, Lienau Collection.

William C. Schermerhorn. Residence, 49 West 23rd Street, New York [c.1858-1859], demolished 1911. Original drawings, Portfolio V, No. 7, and old photograph, Lienau Collection; Tax Assessment

Records, Manhattan; Demolition Application #149 of 1911, Department of Buildings.

*Francis Cottenet. Villa (see above), additional wing [c.1858-1859]. Original drawings, Portfolio IV, No. 6, and extended plan published in *Villas on the Hudson*, New York, 1860 [plate 9].

Hugh A. Toler. Residence, Belleville Road, Newark, NJ [c.1859], demolished 1924. Original drawings, Portfolio VI, No. 11, Lienau Collection.

Mechanics' and Traders' Bank (after 1864, First National Bank of Jersey City; see below), Jersey City, NJ, 1859. Lienau reported engaged in the "decoration" of the building. *The Crayon*, Vol. VI (September 1859), p. 282.

Langdon Estate. Three-loft building, 577-579-581 Broadway, New York, 1859[-c.1860]. Interior alterations, new storefront on No. 581, in fairly good condition. *Architects' and Mechanics' Journal*, Vol. I (October 1858), p. 23, wherein name is given as Langen [*sic*] Estate; Tax Assessment Records, Manhattan; Department of Buildings.

1860-1870

Mr. Schermerhorn. [Peter?] [William?]. Dwelling and coach house [28?] West 24th Street, New York [c.1861-1862?], demolished. Original drawings, Portfolio V, No. 8A, Lienau Collection; Tax Assessment Records, Manhattan.

F.O. Matthiessen & Weichers. Sugar refinery, South Street, Jersey City, NJ, 1862, demolished c.1925 (see below, New Jersey Sugar Refining Company for later additions). Photostats of original drawings, Portfolio VII, No. 12, and old photograph, Lienau Collection; original drawings, photographs, and manuscripts by J. Henry Lienau at American Sugar Refining Company, 120 Wall Street, New York.

*French & Belgian Plate Glass Company. (Noel & Saurel). Loft building, 22-26 Howard and 5-7 Crosby Streets, New York [c.1863-1864], two-story extension 1871 (see below), sundry modern improvements. In sound condition, but very dirty. Original drawings, Portfolio XIV, No. 26, and old photographs, Lienau Collection; Tax Assessment Records, Manhattan; Department of Buildings.

Grace Church (Van Vorst), Jersey City, NJ. Nave extended, 1863-1864. See above.

First National Bank of Jersey City. Bank building, 1 Exchange Place, Jersey City, NJ [c.1864], enlarged 1876, two-story addition 1887 (see below), replaced by present building 1922. Original drawings, Portfolio XIII, Nos. 24, 24a, and old photograph, Lienau Collection; bank records.

*LeGrand Lockwood. Elm Park, Norwalk, CT, [c.1864-1868], known variously as Elm Park, Veterans Memorial Park and Mathews Park. Main house and other buildings occupied by Lockwood-Mathews Mansion Museum. Original drawings, Portfolio IX, No. 16, old photographs, and descriptive material, Lienau Collection.

New York Life & Trust Company. Bank building, 52 Wall Street, New York [c.1865], demolished 1927. Old photograph, Lienau Collection; bank records; Tax Assessment Records, Manhattan; Demolition Application #150 of 1927, Department of Buildings.

*Grace (Van Vorst) Church, Jersey City, NJ. Rectory, 1867. See above.

New Jersey Sugar Refining Company. Sugar refinery, Washington and Essex Streets, Jersey City, NJ, 1867-1868, demolished c.1925. See above under Matthiessen & Weichers.

L. Marcotte. Factory and warehouse, 160-162-164 West 32nd Street, New York, 1867-1868, demolished 1922. New Building Dockets #1055 of 1867, filed 8/30, value $25,000; Demolition Application #48 of 1922, Department of Buildings.

August Belmont. Farmhouse [Hempstead?], Long Island, before 1868. Kennion, *Architects' and Builders' Guide*, New York, 1868, p. xxi.

Edmund H. Schermerhorn. Double house, 45-47 West 23rd Street, New York, [c.1867-c.1869], replaced by new building 1892. Original drawings, Portfolio V, No. 8, Lienau Collection; Tax Assessment Records, Manhattan; New Building Dockets #619 of 1892, Department of Buildings.

Study for a town house, undated, close in style to above. Original drawing in envelope containing unidentified, unexecuted projects, Lienau Collection.

*St. Mary's Hall, Burlington, NJ. *Odenheimer Hall, cornerstone April 2, 1868, opening in autumn. The first of several building planned (see below). Original drawings, Portfolio XII, No. 21, Lienau Collection; Helen L. Shaw, *The First Hundred Years of St. Mary's Hall on the Delaware*, Yardley, PA, 1936, pp. 33 ff.

Mr. Quackenbush. Alteration of first story, 163 Broadway, New York, 1868. Alternate Docket #34 of 1868, filed 2/18, Department of Buildings.

Rebecca (Mrs. Colford) Jones. Block of eight houses, 705-719 Fifth Avenue, with stable on East 55th Street, New York, 1868-1870, demolished 1911, 1926. Original drawings variously dated between November 21, 1868, and November 6, 1870, Portfolio VIII, Nos. 15,

15a, old photograph, and itemized account of costs, Lienau Collection; New Building Dockets #807 of 1869, filed 7/21, erected 7/15/69 to 7/30/70 and #533 of 1870 for stable, filed 5/18, erected 6/1 to 7/30; Demolition Application #17 of 1911 for No. 715, #241 of 1911 for Nos. 717-719, and #185 of 1926 for Nos. 705-713.

Thomas Storm. Vault for Stephen Storm, St. Jones's Church, 1869. Original drawings dated June 24, 1869, Portfolio XXIII, No. 46, Lienau Collection.

J.R. Broadhead and Cisco. Vault, undated. Original drawings, Portfolio XXIII, No. 46, Lienau Collection.

C.R. Jackson, Burnet & Company. Second-class dwelling with offices, south side 14th Street between Avenues C and D, 1869-1870, demolished. New Building Dockets #760 of 1869, filed 7/10, erected 7/6/69 to 6/30/70, value $8,000, Department of Buildings.

1870-1880

New Jersey Sugar Refining Company. Syrup refinery, Essex Street, Jersey City, 1870. See above under Matthiessen & Weichers.

W.M.L. Cobb. First-class store and warehouse, 179 Greenwich Street, New York, 1870-1871, demolished. New Building Dockets #829 of 1870, filed 8/8, erected 9/7/70 to 1/27/71, value $20,000; Alternate Dockets and other records, Department of Buildings.

Rebecca (Mrs. Colford) Jones. First-class store and loft building, 21 Bowery, New York, 1870-1871, demolished 1954. Original drawings, Portfolio XIII, No. 23, Lienau Collection; New Building Dockets #836 of 1870, filed 8/10, erected 9/10/70 to 5/19/71; Demolition Application #401 of 1954, Department of Buildings.

*Estate of Peter Schermerhorn. Four second-class dwellings [French flats] with ground-floor stores, 1231-1237 Third Avenue, New York, 1870-1871. Extensively modernized, in first-class condition. Original drawings dated May 18 and 21, 1870, Portfolio XVI, No. 30, Lienau Collection; New Building Dockets #837 of 1870, filed 8/10, erected 9/13/70 to 4/29/71; Alternate Dockets and other records, Department of Buildings.

L. Marcotte. Store and showroom, 29 East 17th Street, New York, 1870, demolished 1921. New Building Dockets #879 of 1870, filed 8/22, erected 9/1 to 9/30/70, value $5,000; Demolition Application #125 of 1921, Department of Buildings.

*Mrs. Charles T. Bunting. Store and loft building, 269 Canal Street, New York, 1871. In fair condition. New Building Dockets #140 of 1871, wherein name is listed as Bamberg [*sic*], filed 1/20, erected 2/1 to 4/28/71, value $30,000; Alternate Dockets and other records, Department of Buildings.

A.C. Manson. Clubhouse for American Jockey Club, 56-60 Madison Avenue, New York, 1871, demolished 1909. Original drawings dated March 25, 1871, Portfolio XV, No. 27, Lienau Collection; old photograph, courtesy Brown Brothers; New Building Dockets #602 of 1871, filed 4/18, erected 4/20 to 11/28/71; Demolition Application #89 of 1909, Department of Buildings.

Francis Cottenet. Grosvenor House, 37 Fifth Avenue, New York, 1871-1872, demolished 1925. Old photograph with descriptive text, Lienau Collection; Tax Assessment Records, Manhattan; New Building Dockets #658 of 1871, filed 4/25, erected 5/3/71 to 3/27/72, value $85,000; Demolition Application #276 of 1925, Department of Buildings.

William C. Schermerhorn. Alteration of building for commercial use, 109 Front Street, New York, 1871. Alternate Docket #710 of 1871, filed 5/23, executed 6/1 to 9/25/71, value $3,000, Department of Buildings.

*General Theological Seminary, New Brunswick, NJ. *Suydam Hall, cornerstone September 28, 1871, dedicated June 5, 1873. In good condition. Original drawings dated June 6, 1871, Portfolio X, No. 17, and old photograph, Lienau Collection; *Centennial of the Theological Seminary...*, New York, 1885.

Frederick DeBary. Two stables, north side 52nd Street between Madison and Park Avenues [Nos. 47-49?], New York, 1871, demolished [1908?]. New Building Dockets #972 of 1871, filed 6/27, erected 7/10 to 10/17/71, value $11,000; Demolition Application #351 of 1908, Department of Buildings.

Henry A. Booræm. Row of ten attached single-family houses, Second Street, Jersey City, NJ, 1871, demolished. Original drawings dated August 21, 1871, Portfolio XVI, No. 29, Lienau Collection.

*Michael Lienau. Schloss Düneck, Ütersen, Germany, 1872. Original drawings dated February 3 and 5, 1872, and photostats of originals by Detlef and J. August Lienau, Portfolio XIV, No. 25, and old photograph, Lienau Collection.

*Jacob Lienau. House, Ütersen, undated [c.1872?]. Original drawings, Portfolio XX, No. 38, Lienau Collection.

Edmund H. Schermerhorn. Alteration of attic, 67 Greenwich Street, New York, 1872. Alternate Docket #204 of 1872, filed 3/4, executed 3/10 to 6/3/72, value $10,000, Department of Buildings.

*Matthew Wilks. Extension to country residence, Cruickston Park, Blair, Ontario, Canada, 1872-1873, very little altered. See original drawings variously dated May 6 and November 25, 1872, and January 4, 1873, Portfolio XI, No. 19, and old photograph, Lienau Collection.

A. Iauch. House in Long Branch, NJ, before 1872. Letter of November 25, 1872, Iauch to Lienau in Lienau, "Biography, Memorabilia," p. 17.

Edmund H. Schermerhorn. Alteration at [18] Fulton Street, southeast corner Front Street, New York, 1873. Alternate Docket #137 of 1873, filed 2/27, executed 3/21 to 5/31/73, value $4,000, Department of Buildings.

*DeLancey Kane. Store and loft building, 676 Broadway, New York, 1873-1874, some interior alterations, new storefront. Original drawings, dated March 14, 1873, Portfolio XV, No. 28, and old photograph, Lienau Collection; New Building Dockets #411 of 1873, filed 5/15, erected 6/25/73 to 1/31/74; Alternate Dockets and other records, Department of Buildings.

*General Theological Seminary, New Brunswick, NJ. *Sage Library, cornerstone June 5, 1873, dedicated June 4, 1875. In excellent condition. Original drawings and photostats of originals preserved in the library archives dated July 17, 1873, Portfolio X, No. 18, and old photographs, Lienau Collection; *Centennial of the Theological Seminary*....

Edmund H. Schermerhorn. Alteration of first story, 109 Wall Street, New York, 1873. Alternate Docket #693 of 1873, filed 6/23, executed 6/25 to 9/20/73, value $5,000, Department of Buildings.

*Georgia Historical Society, Savannah, GA. *Hodgson Hall, 1873-1876, dedicated February 14, 1876. Still in fine condition, little altered. Original drawings dated July 31, 1873, Portfolio XII, No. 22, Lienau Collection.

Matthew Wilks. Remodeling of interior, front of new extension to be strengthened, Fourth Avenue, south of Astor Place, 1873 (see below under Brokaw Brothers). Alternate Docket #741 of 1873, filed 7/15, executed 7/18 to 10/4/73, value $15,000, Department of Buildings.

James Ingram. Unspecified alteration at 113 East 26th Street, New York, 1874. Alternate Docket #486 of 1874, filed 4/11, erected 4/16 to 7/31/74, value $7,000, Department of Buildings.

St. Mary's Hall, Burlington, NJ. Studies for new building complex, not executed (see above). Original drawings dated May 16, 1874, Portfolio XII, No. 21, Lienau Collection.

*Mrs. Edward Bech. Roselawn, now occupied by Marist College, Poughkeepsie, NY, 1875. Main house either altered beyond recognition or never built; *gate lodge and *gardener's cottage somewhat altered. Original drawings dated June 24, 1875, Portfolio XXI, No. 40, 40a, 40b; *New-York Sketch-book of Architecture*, II (December 1875), plate XLVII.

First National Bank of Jersey City, Jersey City, NJ (see above). Extension, 1876. Original drawings dated January 14, 1876, Portfolio XIII, No. 24, Lienau Collection.

DeLancey Kane Estate. Office building, 62-64 Cedar Street, New York, 1876-1877, altered by J. August Lienau and Thomas Nash, 1890, demolished 1927. Original drawings of May 4, June 17, and July 18, 1876, Portfolio XI, No. 20, and old photograph, Lienau Collection; New Building Dockets #492 of 1876, filed 7/20, erected 7/15/76 to 5/29/76 [*sic*]; Demolition Application #12 of 1927, Department of Buildings.

A.C. Manson. Stable, 156 East 26th Street, New York, 1876, demolished c.1894. New Building Dockets #392 of 1876, filed 5/31, erected 6/6 to 7/31/76, value $1,260; New Building Dockets #985 of 1894, Department of Buildings.

Brokaw Brothers. Unspecified alteration, 28-34 Fourth Avenue, New York. Alternate Docket #976 of 1876, filed 10/14, executed 10/19 to 11/28/76, Department of Buildings.

Matthew Wilks. Second-class dwelling, Fourth Avenue, New York, 1878-1879. New Building Dockets #516 of 1878, filed 8/9, erected 8/19/78 to 3/25/79, value $4,500.

George Mosle. Townhouse, 5 West 51st Street, New York, 1878-1879, demolished at unknown date. Original drawings dated August 24, 1878, Portfolio XXII, No. 42, Lienau Collection; New Building Dockets #532 of 1878, filed 8/21, erected 9/5/78 to 12/23/79.

Grace Church (Van Vorst), Jersey City, NJ. Studies for proposed Sunday school building 1879, not executed. See above.

C.F. Chrystie. Tenement house, 162 Elm Street, New York, 1879, demolished at unknown date, presumably when Elm Street became Lafayette Street. Original drawings, Portfolio XVII, No. 31, Lienau Collection; New Building Dockets #377 of 1879, erected 5/20 to 11/13/79, Department of Buildings.

1880-1887

Peter Marie. Alterations, 74 Broadway, New York, 1880. Alternate Docket #224 of 1880, filed 3/3, erected 3/27 to 7/31/80, value $12,000, Department of Buildings; report in *American Architect*,

Vol. VII (March 13, 1880), p. 112, indicating additional story and interior alterations.

*William C. Schermerhorn. Store and loft building, 116-118 East 14th Street, New York, 1880-1881; modern storefront, extensively altered. New Building Dockets #336 of 1880, filed 4/23, erected 5/3/80 to 12/29/81; *American Architect*, Vol. VII (May 1, 1880), p. 190; Alternate Dockets and other records, Department of Buildings.

Peter Marie. Alterations, 72 Broadway, New York, 1880. Alternate Docket #608 of 1880, filed 5/7, executed 5/17 to 7/31/80, value $15,000, Department of Buildings; report in *American Architect*, Vol. VIII (May 15, 1880), p. 219, indicating rebuilding of front and rear walls and interior alterations.

*Dr. John C. Barron. Store and loft building, 129-131 Greene Street, New York, 1880-1881, interior somewhat altered. Original drawings, Portfolio XXII, No. 43, Lienau Collection; New Building Dockets #408 of 1880, filed 5/13, erected 6/4/80 to 2/26/81; Alternate Dockets and other records, Department of Buildings.

*Walter H. Lewis. "Anglesea," Newport, RI, c.1880, altered 1917. Original drawings, Portfolio XXI, No. 41, and old photograph, Lienau Collection.

Studies for suburban or resort house, undated. By J. August Lienau? Original drawings in envelope containing unidentified, unexecuted projects, Lienau Collection.

Daniel Parish estate. Office building, 67 Wall Street, New York, 1881-1882, demolished 1920. Original drawings, Portfolio XVII, No. 33, Lienau Collection; *American Architect*, Vol. IX (April 23, 1881), p. 203; New Building Dockets #336 of 1881, filed 4/21, erected 6/13/81 to 7/22/82; Demolition Application #71 of 1920, Department of Buildings.

Matthew and Elizabeth Wilks. Proposed alteration, 28-34 Fourth Avenue, New York (see above under Brokaw Brothers). Alternate Docket #872 of 1881, filed 6/20, Department of Buildings. Lack of further information indicates abandonment of project.

Societé Anonyme des Panoramas de New-York. Panorama building, northeast corner Seventh Avenue at 55th Street, New York, 1881-1882, altered by J. August Lienau for Tattersall, Ltd., 1890, demolished at unknown date. Original drawings, including two dated 1880 by the Societé anonyme de construction et des ateliers de Willebroeck, Brussels, Portfolio XIX, No. 33, and old photograph, Lienau Collection; New Building Dockets #1096 of 1880, filed 11/7, erected 12/8/81 to 11/29/82, wherein architects are listed as Lienau

& Renwick, very little clarified by reference to D. Lienau and F.[?] Renwick in *American Architect*, Vol. X (November 19, 1881), p. 248.

French and Belgian Plate Glass Company (see above). Proposed one-story addition, 1881, disallowed. Alternate Docket #1317 of 1881, filed 11/19, value $4,000, and other records, Department of Buildings.

Samuel S. Howland. Residence, 10 West 18th Street, New York, 1881-1882, demolished at unknown date, possibly after reported damage by fire c.1890-1891. Original drawings, mostly by J. August Lienau, Portfolio XIX, No. 36, and mantel designs (Miscellaneous drawings, Series II), Lienau Collection; New Building Dockets #1182 of 1881, filed 12/12/81, erected 12/27/81 to 12/28/82, Department of Buildings.

August Belmont. Studies for proposed alterations to his residence, Fifth Avenue and 18th Street, New York [c.1881?]. Original drawings, Miscellaneous drawings, Series IV, Lienau Collection.

*Grace Church (Van Vorst), Jersey City, NJ. Proposed alterations to coping and iron fence, 1882. Original drawings, Portfolio III, No. 4, Lienau Collection.

Henry Parish. Alteration to his residence, 1 West 19th Street, New York, 1882. Alternate Docket #873 of 1882, filed 6/12, executed 6/15 to 12/15/82, value $10,000, Department of Buildings. Building of a three-story extension reported in *American Architect*, Vol. XII (July 1, 1882), p. 12.

Lewis H. Williams. Unspecified alteration, 313 East 15th Street, New York, 1882. Alternate Docket #910 of 1882, filed 6/19, executed 7/5 to 7/29/82, value $3,500, Department of Buildings.

Royal Insurance Company. Proposed alterations, 50 Wall Street, New York, 1882. Alternate Docket #1427 of 1882, filed 11/1, value $25,000, Department of Buildings. Lack of further information indicates probable abandonment of project, described as the raising of the building by one story in *American Architect*, Vol. XII (November 11, 1882), p. 236.

M. Morgan & Sons [name unclear]. Unspecified alteration, New York Hotel, Waverly Place, 1883. Alternate Docket #1525 of 1882, filed 11/29, executed 2/1 to 3/28/83, value $7,000.

*William C. Schermerhorn. Repairs, 116-118 East 14th Street, New York, 1883. Alternate Docket #23 of 1883, filed 1/9, executed 1/12 to 2/26/83, value $6,420, Department of Buildings; specified as repairs of fire damage in *American Architect*, Vol. XIII (January 13, 1883, p. 23.

Mary M. (Mrs. John S.) Williams. Row of six one-family dwellings, [37-47] West 82nd Street, New York, 1883-1884, demolished [1911, 1915]. Old photograph, Lienau Collection; New Building Dockets #427 of 1883, filed 4/19, erected 5/1/83 to 5/31/84; Demolition Application #219 of 1911 and #395 of 1915, Department of Buildings.

_____. Row of six one-family dwellings, [46-56] West 83rd Street, New York, 1883-1884, demolished [1910]. New Building Dockets #27 of 1883, filed 4/19, erected 6/5/83 to 5/31/84; Demolition Application #415 of 1910, Department of Buildings.

*_____. Cottage, New Brunswick, NJ, 1883, in collaboration with J. August Lienau. Still standing, condition not known. Old photograph, Lienau Collection; verbal description by the Misses Mary M. and Catherine Lienau.

*Telfair Hospital for Indigent Females, Savannah, GA. "Alternate plan" [elevation], undated. Date of 1883 *ante quam non* established by founding of hospital in that year. Not known if Lienau was architect of present building. Original drawing, Lienau Collection.

*Telfair Academy of Arts and Sciences, Savannah, GA, 1885-1886. Alterations to original mansion, erection of annex, and residence of the director. Original drawings, including plans of Telfair mansion before conversion, some by J. August Lienau, Portfolio XX, No. 37, and old photograph, Lienau Collection; records of Telfair Academy.

*W.W. Gordon. Remodeling of Wayne-Gordon house, Savannah, GA, 1886, originally built by William Jay, now the National Girl Scout Shrine. Photostats of original drawings, Lienau Collection; Stephen P. Bond, letters of October 18 and 23, 1957.

*William Low. Consulted on remodeling of Low house, Savannah, GA, c. 1886. Stephen P. Bond letters.

*Williams and Lienau families. Row of four dwellings for Detlef, Elizabeth (Mrs. J. August) Lienau, Miss Jean M. Williams, and Mrs. Mary M. Williams, 48-54 West 82nd Street, New York, 1886-1887. Now converted to rooming houses. Original drawings, mostly by J. August Lienau, Portfolio XXIII, No. 45, Miscellaneous drawings, Series I, and old photograph, Lienau Collection; New Building Dockets #112-115 of 1886, filed 2/1 and 2/2, erected 4/9/86 to 1/29/87; Alternate Dockets and other records, Department of Buildings.

Estate of Daniel DeRay [name unclear]. Unspecified alterations, 305 First Avenue, New York, 1886. Alternate Docket #188 of 1886, filed 2/13, executed 3/4 to 3/15/86, value $500, Department of Buildings.

New York Life Insurance and Trust Company. Office building, 55-57 Pine Street, New York, 1887-1889, extension to 52 Wall Street executed by J. August Lienau, demolished 1927. Original studies, Lienau Collection; New Building Dockets #928 of 1887, filed 5/3, erected 6/6/87 to 1/31/89; Alternate Application #928 of 1887, filed 5/2, giving some dates of construction; Demolition Application #150 of 1927, Department of Buildings.

First National Bank of Jersey City, Jersey City, NJ. Additional story, 1887 (see above for earlier history) executed by J. August Lienau. Original drawings, Portfolio XIII, No. 24a, Lienau Collection.

Appendix III.
Detlef Lienau: A Bibliographic Catalog

A. Primary Sources

1. Biographical Data

Lienau, Detlef. Testimony, *Hunt v. Parmly*, February 22, 1861, Superior Court of New York. *Architects' and Mechanics' Journal*, Vol. III (March 16, 1861), p. 233.

Lienau, J. Henry. "Detlef Lienau, Architect, 1818-1887; Biography, Memorabilia." [New York? 1942?] On deposit at the Avery Library. Contains copies of the following items of importance:

Personal Documents

Extract from Birth and Christening Registry, Ütersen, folio 40, April 14, 1837 (p. 31).

Certificates from Carpenters' Guild, Berlin, March 30, 1840, Carpenters' Guild, Hamburg, October 4, 1841, and from Konigliche Bausewerksschule, Munich, March 26, 1842 (pp. 22, 23, and 24, respectively).

Letters from A. Jullien and Cendrier, January 22, 1847, notifying Lienau of his appointment as draftsman in the architectural office of the Paris-Lyons railroad; also a list of employees of the railroad who attended the first annual banquet, and the menu, on January 1, 1847 (pp. 25-28).

Letters

Iauch, A., to Lienau, November 25, 1872 (p. 16).

Lienau to R.G. Hatfield, April 4, 1866, regarding his standing in the AIA (p. 28a).

Lienau to F.O. Matthiessen, May 14, 1868 (p. 17).

Van Brunt, Henry to Lienau, March 8, and April 4, 1865, with reference to his proposed translation of Viollet-le-Duc's *Entretiens* (pp. 14-15).

Photographs of Lienau

Photographs of 1864 (see frontispiece) and 1871.

Descriptions and Critiques of Lienau's Work

See *post.*

Obituaries

American Architect, Vol. XXII (September 17, 1887), p. 179.

American Institute of Architects. Resolutions passed by the Board of Trustees. Prepared by Messrs. Congdon and R.M. Upjohn and read by A.J. Bloor at the Twenty-first Annual Convention of the AIA, October 19, 1887. In *Proceedings* (1887), pp. 4-6.

Architecture and Building, Vol. VII (September 3, 1887), p. 80.

The New York Times, August 31, 1887, p. 5, col. 6. Death notice.

2. Lienau's Work

Drawings

Lienau Collection, Avery Library
> Student Drawings and Early European Commissions, 1836-1847. Over 170 drawings, filed in folders, Series I-VI. See ante, Chapter I and Appendix I.
> Drawings for Executed Commissions. Over 550 drawings, filed in 23 portfolios.
> Studies in Unexecuted Projects. Filed in separate folder.
> Miscellaneous Drawings. Mostly interior decoration. 60 sheets, filed in folders, Series I-III.

Private Collections; Public Records
> Ardsley-on-Hudson, NY. Mr. and Mrs. J. Fearon Brown. 1 sketch for Cottenet villa.
> New Brunswick, NJ. Sage Library, General Theological Seminary. 9 working drawings.
> New York, NY. American Sugar Refining Company, 120 Wall Street. 20 drawings for Matthiessen-Weichers and New Jersey Sugar Refining Companies, Jersey City, NJ. Formerly hung in Director's Room, but now stored.
> New York, NY. Department of Buildings, Municipal Building. A number of sketches submitted with building applications. See *ante*, footnotes, and Appendix II, *passim*.
> New York, NY. Mr. J. Henry Lienau. Unknown number.
> Savannah, GA. National Girl Scout Shrine. 8 working drawings for alterations (Wayne-Gordon house).

Photographs

Lienau Collection, Avery Library. 45 photographs of executed work.
Private Collections
> Ardsley-on-Hudson, NY. Mr. and Mrs. J. Fearon Brown. Several photos.
> New York, NY. Wayne Andrews, Architectural Photographs. Photos of Cottenet and Lockwood houses, Series VII, Nos. 879, 245-46.
> New York, NY. Mr. J. Henry Lienau. Unknown number.

Original Manuscripts

Lienau Collection, Avery Library
> "Carpenter's Specifications," Shiff house, May 10, 1850.
> "Mason's Specifications," Shiff house, May 4, 1850.
> "Statement of Cost of Eight Houses Built for Mrs. Jones on Fifth Avenue" [c.1871].
> Three student notebooks, 1835-1837. Described *ante*.

Private Collections; Public Records
> New York, NY. Department of Buildings. A number of applications for building and alteration permits, and several letters. See Appendix II.
> New York, NY. Mr. J. Henry Lienau. Unknown quantity.

3. Lienau and the American Institute of Architects
Official Status: Participation in Activities

Lienau's activities on various committees, particularly the Committee on Examinations (see *ante*), his official posts as Trustee of the national organization (c.1867-c.1871) and Treasurer of the New York Chapter (1868-1869), are fully documented by the following sources:

AIA. Official records at national headquarters, Washington, DC.

AIA. Official records at New York local headquarters, see "Minutes of Trustees' Meetings" and "Minutes" of chapter meetings, Vol. 1867-1877.

AIA. *Proceedings* (1867 ff.), *passim.*

The Crayon, passim.

"Hobart Upjohn Papers" (courtesy Everard Upjohn).

New York, NY Superintendent of Buildings. *Annual Report of 1868-1869*, pp. 389-391.

Published Statements of Opinion and Papers by Lienau

Committee Reports. See *The Crayon, Architects' and Mechanics' Journal,* and *Proceedings, passim,* for reports and recommendations.

Letters protesting proposed changes in design of State Capitol, Albany, NY.

Hunt, Dudley, and Lienau to Fuller, March 14, 1876. *American Architect,* Vol. I (April 1, 1876), p. 107.

Post, Hunt, LeBrun, Dudley, and Lienau to New York newspapers, March 6, 1877. *Ibid.,* Vol. II (March 17, 1877), p. 85.

Papers; Miscellaneous Discussions and Statements

Discussion on "What is the Best Style for a City Hall in New York," AIA meeting, New York, June 1, 1858. *The Crayon,* Vol. V (July 1858), p. 200.

"Fire-Proof Construction." Read for Lienau by William R. Ware at Eleventh Annual Convention, AIA, Boston. *American Architect,* Vol. II (1877), p. 341; full text in *ibid.,* Vol. III (1878), pp. 5-6.

"On Romantic and Classic Architecture." Read at AIA meeting, New York, May 4, 1858. *The Crayon,* Vol. V (June 1858), pp. 168-169.

Response to a toast by Leopold Eidlitz to the Committee on Papers. Second annual dinner, AIA, February 22, 1859. *The Crayon,* Vol. VI (March 1859), p. 100.

B. Secondary Sources

1. Biographical Data

Brault, Elie. *Les architects par leurs oeuvres.* Paris [1893], III, p. 429-430.

Hamlin, Talbot. "Detlef Lienau," *Dictionary of American Biography,* Vol. XXI, p. 493-494.

_____. "Detlef Lienau," *National Cyclopædia of American Biography,* Vol. XXIX, pp. 16-17.

Lienau, J. Henry. "Detlef Lienau, Architect...," pp. 3-4.

Lienau, J. Henry Letters to Talbot Hamlin. Lienau Folder, North Office, Avery Library.

Withy, Henry F., and Withey, Elsie Rathbun. *Biographical Dictionary...*, Los Angeles [1956], pp. 371-372. Inaccurate.

2. Catalogs, Listings, Descriptions, and Critiques of Lienau's Work
General Reference

American Architect, passim. Listings under "Building Intelligence" (see *ante,* Appendix II, *passim*).

Architects' and Mechanics' Journal, passim. Similar listings.

Hamlin, Talbot. "Detlef Lienau." Two articles cited above.

——————. *Greek Revival Architecture in America.* New York, 1944, pp. 132-133.

——————. "Partial List of the Architectural Work of Detlef Lienau, 1848-1886." Typescript, Avery Library, no date.

——————. "The Place of Detlef Lienau in American Architecture." Typescript [1948] in Lienau, "Biography, Memorabilia," pp. 5-7 (substantially the same as text in *National Cyclopædia of American Biography*, Vol. XXIX, p. 17).

——————. "Preliminary Catalog of Students Drawings." Typescript, Avery Library, no date.

——————. "The Rise of Eclecticism in New York," *SAH Journal*, Vol. XI (May 1952), pp. 6-8.

Hartmann, Sadakichi. "A Conversation with Henry Janeway Hardenbergh," *Architectural Record*, Vol. XIX (May 1906), p. 377.

History of Real Estate, Building and Architecture, New York, 1898, *passim.*

Kennion, John W. *Architects' and Buildings' Guide...*, New York, 1868, pp. xxi-xxii.

Kramer, Ellen W. "Detlef Lienau, an Architect of the 'Brown Decades'," *SAH Journal*, Vol. XIV (March 1955), pp. 18-25.

——————. "Detlef Lienau: Catalog of Student Drawings and Early European Commissions, 1836-1847." 16-page typescript, May 1954, on deposit at the Avery Library.

Schuyler, Montgomery. "Works of Henry J. Hardenbergh," *Architectural Record*, Vol. VI (January-March 1897), pp. 335-336.

3. Chronological List of References to Some Lienau Buildings
Individual Buildings

Shiff house, 1850-c.1852

> *The Stranger's Handbook for the City of New York*, New York, 1853/1854,
> p. 89 (better known under the title, *Francis's New Guide to the Cities
> of New-York and Brooklyn...*, New York: C.F. Francis, no date.
>
> "New York Daguerreotyped," *Putnam's*, Vol. III (March 1854), p. 234,
> with illustration, p. 238.
>
> [Clarence Cook?], "The Modern Architecture of New York," *New York
> Quarterly*, Vol. IV (April 1855), pp. 119-120.
>
> Bloor, A.J., "Report on Mansard Roofs," *AIA Proceedings* (1873), p. 45.
>
> Train, Arthur. *His Children's Children*. New York, 1923, *passim*.

Grace Church (Van Vorst), 1850-1853

> Bennitt, the Reverend George Stephen. *Historical Sermon Preached on the
> First Sunday in May 1887, Being the Fortieth Anniversary of the Founding
> of Grace Church (Van Vorst)...*, New York: John Medole & Son,
> 1888. Pamphlet, Lienau Collection.
>
> *Grace Church (Van Vorst) Messenger*, Jersey City, N.J. Whitsunday, 1915.
> Pamphlet, Lienau Collection.
>
> *The Newark Churchman*, Vol. XVI (June 1922), p. 65. Lienau Collection.
>
> McLean, Alexander. *History of Jersey City, New Jersey*. Jersey City [1895],
> II, pp. 278-279.

Cottenet Villa, 1852

> Lossing, Benson J. *The Hudson...* New York, 1866, p. 355.
>
> *Villas on the Hudson...* New York, 1860, 2 plates.

Kane Cottage, 1852

> Mason, George Champlin. *Newport and Its Cottages*. Boston, 1875, pp.
> 47-48.
>
> Scully, Vincent J., Jr. Downing and Scully, *The Architectural Heritage of
> Newport, Rhode Island*, Cambridge, MA, 1952, pp. 139-140.

William C. Schermerhorn Residence, c.1858-1859

> Strong, "Journal," Vol. 1854-1862, entry of May 18, 1859, folio 278.
>
> Kennion, John W. *Architects' and Builders' Guide...*, New York, 1868, p.
> xxi.
>
> Clipping from a New York newspaper, 1908. Lienau, p. 11.

Matthiessen-Weichers and New Jersey Sugar Refining Company, 162 ff.

> Lienau, J. Henry. Three typescripts at American Sugar Refining
> Company, 120 Wall Street, New York, of which the most
> important in "A Description of the F.O. Matthiessen & Weichers
> Sugar Refinery in Jersey City as the Writer Found It in 1893," New
> York, 1950. Bound together with "A History of the Original F.O.
> Matthiessen Enterprises in Jersey City, 1862-1867-1870," New
> York, 1938 and 1944.

French & Belgian Plate Glass Company (Noel & Saurel), c.1864

> "Our Streets, *New-York Weekly Review*, February 4, 1865, p. 3. A very
> favorable description by a critic known for his caustic wit.

M.S. [Montgomery Schuyler]. "Recent Building in New York—II. Commercial Buildings," *American Architect*, Vol. IX (April 16, 1881), p. 183.

——————. "Hardenbergh," *Architectural Record*, Vol. VI (1897), p. 335.

Lockwood Mansion, c.1864-c.1868

The New York Times, August 5, 1867, p. 5, col. 3

Advertisement in a New York newspaper, March 1873. Lienau, p. 18.

Advertisement, source unknown. City Planning Commission (Lockwood-Mathews Mansion), Norwalk, CT.

Bloor, A.J. "Annual Address," *AIA Proceedings* (1876), p. 28.

Selleck, the Reverence Charles M. *Norwalk*, Norwalk, 1895, pp. 213-214.

Danenberg, Elsie Nicholas. *The Romance of Norwalk*. New York, 1929, p. 314.

Recent clippings, the *Norwalk Hour*. Courtesy Mr. Peter Collins; also report of talk given by the writer to the Kiwanis Club of Norwalk, March 4, 1954, *ibid.*, March 5, pp. 1-2.

Editorial, *Mark*, August 18, 1956, p. 12. Courtesy Mr. Robert Koch.

Edmund Schermerhorn Residence, c.1867-1869

Kennion, p. xxi.

Strong Diary, IV, p. 350, entry of April 13, 1871.

"House of the Dead Hermit," *The New York Herald*, October 3, 1891, p. 8, col. 2.

Jones Block, 1868-1870

Redfield's Traveler's Guide to the City of New York. New York, 1871, pp. 71-72.

Appleton's New York Illustrated, New York, 1876, p. 30.

The Grosvenor, 1871-1872

Clipping from a New York newspaper, c.1872. Lienau, "Biography, Memorabilia," pp. 9-10; another copy pasted on back of photograph of building.

Richardson, James H. "The New Homes of New York...," *Scribner's*, Vol. VIII (1874), p. 69.

Kane Office Building, Cedar Street, New York, 1876-1877

M.S. [Montgomery Schuyler]. "Recent Building in New York—II. Commercial Buildings," *American Architect*, Vol. IX (April 16, 1881), p. 183. Described as less successful than Noel-Saurel warehouse.

——————. "Hardenbergh," *Architectural Record*, Vol. VI (1897), p. 336.

4. Exhibitions of Lienau's Work

[Hamlin, Talbot]. Forty Years of New York Architecture. Original Architectural Drawings by Detlef Lienau, FAIA. Avery Library, Columbia University, January 11-31, 1936.

Appendix IV.
Bibliography

Architecture and Arts in the 19th Century
A. General Reference

1. History and Criticism (General)

Giedion, Sigfried. *Space, Time and Architecture; the Growth of a new Tradition.* (The Charles Eliot Norton Lectures for 1938-1939). 3rd edition, revised and enlarged. Cambridge: Harvard University Press, 1954.

Hamlin, Talbot. *Architecture Through the Ages.* Revised edition. New York: G.P. Putnam's Sons, 1953.

Michel, Andre. *Histoire de l'art depuis les premiers temps chretiens, jusqu'à nos jours.* 8 volumes in 17. Paris: A. Colin, 1907-[c.1929].

Propylaen-Kunstgeschichte. 16 volumes. [Berlin: Propylaen-Verlag, 1923-31].

2. Bibliographic Aids

Bibliotheque Nationale, Paris. Departement des Imprimes. *Catalogue générale des livres imprimes...* 183 volumes to date. Paris: Paul Catin, 1924-1955.

Columbia University. Avery Architectural Library. *General Catalog and Periodical Catalog.*

Royal Institute of British Architects, London. *Catalogue of the Royal Institute of British Architects Architectural Library...* 2 volumes. London: The Royal Institute of British Architects, 1937-1938.

Union List of Serials in the Libraries of the United States and Canada (edited by Winifred Gregory). 2nd edition. New York: H.W. Wilson and Company, 1943. Supplement, 1941-1943, published 1945. Supplement, 1944-1949, published 1953.

Victoria and Albert Museum. South Kensington, England. National Art Library. *First Proofs of the Universal Catalogue of Books on Art...* 2 volumes. London: Chapman and Hall, 1870.

3. Biographical Aids and Dictionaries
(European and American Architects)

Bauchal, Charles. *Nouveau dictionnaire biographique et critique des architects français.* Paris: André, Daly fils et cie, 1887.

Brault, Elie. *Les architects par leurs oeuvres.* 3 volumes. Paris: Laurens [1893].

Columbia University, Avery Library. Obituary File.

Delaire, E. *Les architects élèves de l'école des beaux-arts.* 2nd edition. Paris: Chaix, 1907.

Thieme, Ulrich, and Becker, Felix. *Allgemeines Lexikon der bildenden Künstler von der Antike bis zur Gegenwart...* 37 volumes. Leipzig: W. Engelmann, 1907-1950.

Withey, Henry F., and Withey, Elsie Rathbun. *Biographical Dictionary of American Architects (Deceased)*. Los Angeles, CA: New Age Publishing Company [1956].

B. European Architecture

1. Primary Sources: 19th Century Publications
Architectural Magazines:

Allgemeine Bauzeitung. Vienna, 1836-1919.

Architektonisches Album (Architekten-verein zu Berlin). Potsdam, 1838-1862.

Architektonisches Skizzenbuch. Berlin, 1854-1885.

Builder; An Illustrated Weekly Magazine for the Architect, Engineer, Archeologist, Constructor, Sanitary-reformer and Art-lover. London, 1842.

Building News and Engineering Journal. London, 1854-1926. Continuous publication with varying titles.

Encyclopédie d'architecture et des arts qui s'y rattachment. Paris, 1851-1892.

Moniteur des architects; recueil mensuel de monuments pour server à l'étude de l'art architectural & des travaux publics. Paris: 1847-1865; new series 1866-1900.

Paris architects; revue illustrée. Paris, January 1865-May 1869, 3 volumes only.

Revue générale de l'architecture et des travaux publics; journal des architects, des ingenieurs, des archeologues, des industriels et des proprietaires. Paris, 1840-1890.

Zeitschrift für Architektur und Ingenieurwesen (Architekten und Ingenieur-Verein, Hannover). Wiesbaden, Hannover, 1851-1854, new series 1855-1921.

Zeitschrift für Bauwesen. Berlin, 1851-1931.

Books and Articles:

Adams, G. Louis. *Recueil des maisons les plus remarquables...* Paris: Librairie d'architecture de Caudrillier, 1858.

Architekten- und Ingenieur-Verein, Berlin. *Architektonische Entwurfe...* Potsdam: Ferdinand Riegel, 1837-1842.

Architekten- und Ingenieur-Verein, Hamburg. *Hamburg's Privatbauten.* Hamburg: Strumper, 1877.

———, Hamburg. *Hamburg und seine Bauten....* Hamburg: Selbstverlag des Vereins, 1890.

Barqui, F. *L'Architecture moderne en France; maisons les plus remarquables des departments.* Paris: Baudry [1871].

Batissier, Louis. *Histoire de l'art monumentale dans l'antiquité et au moyen âge.* Paris: Furné et compagnie, 1845.

Benoist, Philippe, and Jacottet, Jean. *Nouvelles vues de Paris.* Paris: Gihaut [184?].

Bicknell, W.I. *The Public Buildings of Paris and Its Environs...* London: E.T. Brain Company [1848-1849].

Boisseree, Sulpiz. *Monuments d'architecture du septième au treizième siècle dans les contrées du Rhin inferieur.* Munich: J.G. Cotta, 1842.

Borne, Louis. *Etudes et documents sur la construction des hopitaux.* 2 volumes. Paris: Librairie de la construction moderne [1898].

Brandon, Raphael, and Brandon, J. Arthur. *Paris Churches*. London: George Bell, 1848.

Brooks, Samuel H. *Designs for Cottage and Villa Architecture...* London: T. Kelly [1840].

The Builder. Papers and letters on housing for the middle and lower classes, late 1840s and early '50s. Referenced in footnotes.

The Builder's Practical Directory; or Buildings for All Classes... Leipzig and Dresden: A.H. Payne, 1855-1858.

Burdett, Henry C. *Hospitals and Asylums of the World*. 4 volumes. London: J. & A. Churchill, 1891-1893.

Calliat, Victor. *Hôtel de ville de Paris...* 2volumes in 1. Paris: Chez l'auteur, 1844-[1856].

————. *Parallele des maisons de Paris construites depuis 1830 jusqu'à nos jours*. 2 volumes. Paris: Vol. I, Bance, 1850; Vol. II, A. Morel et cie, 1864. Vol. II entitled *Parallele... depuis 1850 jusqu'à nos jours*.

Castermans, Auguste. *Parallele des maisons de Bruxelles et des principales villes de Belgique construites depuis 1830 jusqu'à nos jours...* [1. serie]. Liege: Noblet [1852-1857].

Chabat, Pierre. *Bâtiments de chemins de fer...* 2 volumes. Paris: Morel, 1862-1866.

Chambers, William. *Improved Dwelling-Houses for the Humbler and Other Classes in Cities Based on the Scottish Dwelling-House System*. London: W. & R. Chambers, 1855.

Chapuy, Nicholas Marie Joseph. *Le moyen-âge monumental et archeologique...* 3 volumes. Paris: A. Hauser, 1843.

————. *Moyen-âge pittoresque; monuments d'architecture, meubles et decors du Xe au XVIIe siècle...* 5 volumes. Paris: Veith, 1837-1840.

————. *Vues pittoresques de la cathédrale de Strasbourg...* Strasbourg: F.G. Levrault, 1827.

Chateauneuf, Alexis de. *Architectural domestica*. London: Ackerman and Company, 1839.

Chevenard, A. *Album de l'ornementiste; recueil d'ornements dans tous les genres et dans tous les styles*. Paris: Leconte, 1836.

Clochar, Pierre. *Monumens et tombeaux, measures et dessines en Italie*. [1.-6. cahiers]. Paris, 1815.

————. *Palais, maisons et vues d'Italie*. Paris [Imprimerie de P. Gueffier], 1809.

Colling, James K. *Gothic Ornaments*. 2 volumes. London: George Bell, 1848-1850.

Daly, Cesar. *Architecture funeraire contemporaine*. Paris: Ducher, 1871.

————. *L'Architecture privée au XIX siècle sous Napoleon III; nouvelles maisons de Paris et des environs*. 2 volumes in 3. Paris: A. Morel et cie, 1864. Editions of 1870, 1872 published under title of *L'Architecture privée au XIX siècle*.

_____. "L'Architecture des chemins de fer," *Revue générale de l'architecture*. Vols. XVII-XVIII (1859-1860). Articles on specific stations referenced in footnotes.

_____. "La bibliothèque Sainte-Geneviève," *ibid*, Vol. X (1852), cols. 380-381.

_____. "Coup d'oeil retrospectif: movement de l'architecture de 1830... [1860]," *ibid.*, Vol. XVIII (1860), cols. 1-8.

_____. "Henri Labrouste," *ibid.*, Vol. XXXIV (1877), cols. 60-63.

_____. Miscellaneous articles on training of architects and related topics, *ibid.*, *passim.* Referenced in footnotes.

_____. *Motifs historiques d'architecture et de sculpture d'ornement, pour la composition et la decoration exterieure des edifices publics et privés.* 2 volumes. Paris: Ducher, 1870.

Degen, Ludwig. *Der Bau der Krankenhauser...* Munchen: Jos. Lindauer, 1862.

Delaborde, Henri. "La vie et les ouvrages de Henri Labrouste," *Encyclopédie d'architecture*, Vol. VII (1878), pp. 82-88.

Desgodetz, Antoine. *Les édifices antiques de Rome...* Carlo Fea, editor of work first published in 1682. Roma: Poggioli, 1822.

Durand, Jean Nicholas Louis. *Précis de leçons d'architecture données à L'Ecole polytechnique.* 3 volumes in 2. Paris, 1801-1805.

_____. *Recueil et parallèle des édifices de tout genre, anciens et modernes...* Paris: Chez l'auteur [1800].

Eastlake, Charles L. *Hints on Household Taste in Furniture, Upholstery, and Other Details...* London: 1868. 1st American edition, 1872.

_____. *A History of the Gothic Revival...* London: Longmans, Green, and Company, 1872.

_____. *Examples of the Architecture of the Victorian Age...* London: Darton & Dodge, 1862.

Egle, Joseph von. *Mittelalterliche Baudenkmale aus Schwaben. Der Munster zu Ulm...* Stuttgart: Ebner, 1872.

Forster, Ernst. *Denkmale deutscher Baukunst. Bildnerei und Malerei...* 12 volumes. Leipzig, 1855-1869.

Gailhabaud, Jule. *Monuments anciens et modernes, collection formant une histoire de l'architecture de differents peoples à toutes les époques.* 4 volumes. Paris, 1846-1850. Edition cited: Paris: Firmin Didof frères, 1865.

Gauthier, Martin Pierre. *Les plus beaux edifices de la ville de Genes et de ses environs.* 2 volumes in 1. Paris: Chez l'auteur, 1830-1832.

Girault de Prangey, Philibert Joseph. *Choix d'ornements moresques de l'Alhambra...* Paris: Hauser [1842].

_____. *Monuments arabes et moresques de Cordoue, Seville et Grenade...* [Paris: Veith et Hauser, 1836-1839].

Gladbach, Ernst Georg. *Die Holzarchitektur der Schweiz.* Zurich: Orell, Fussli & Company, 1876.

Gourlier, Charles Pierre, *et al. Choix d'édifices publics projetés et construites en France depuis le commencement de XIXe siècle.* 3 volumes. Paris: Colas, 1825-1850.

Goury, Jule, and Jones, Owen. *Plans... of the Alhambra...* 2 volumes. London: O. Jones, 1842-1845.

Gaffenreid, Adolf von, and Sturler, Moritz von. *Schweizerische Architecktur...* 2nd edition. Bern: Wagner [1844].

Grandjean de Montigny, Auguste, and Famin, Auguste. *Architecture toscane, ou palais, maisons, églises... et autres edifices...* Paris, Impr. de P. Didot l'aine, 1815.

_____. *Recueil des plus beaux tombeaux executes en Italie dans les XVᵉ et XVIᵉ siècles...* Paris: Didot, l'aines, 1813.

Gravina, Domenico Benedetto. *Il duomo di Monréale...* Palermo: Stab. tip. di F. Lao, 1859-[1870].

Guilmard, Desire. *La connaissance des styles de l'ornementation...* Paris: Guillmard, 1849.

_____. *La decoration du XIX siècle...* Paris: Bureau du Journal de garde-meuble [1888?].

Haghe, Louis. *Sketches in Belgium and Germany.* Series 1. London: Hodgson, 1840.

Hakewill, James. *A Picturesque Tour of Italy.* London: J. Murray, 1820.

Hamburgs Neubau: Sammlung Façaden der Gebaude an den neubebauten Strassen... Hamburg: Charles Fuchs [1844-1848].

Heideloff, Karl von. *Ornamentik des Mittelalters.* 4 volumes. Nurnberg: C. Geiger, [1838-1855].

Hittorff, Jacques Ignace, and Zanth, Karl Ludwig. *Architecture antique de la Sicilé, Recueil des monuments de Segeste et de Selinonte...* Paris [1827?]. Edition cited: Paris: E. Donnaud, 1870.

_____. *Architecture moderne de la Sicilé...* Paris: Paul Renouard, 1835.

Hitzig, Friedrich. *Ausgefuhrte Bauwerke.* 2 volumes plus supplement in 1. Berlin: Ernst & Korn [1855-1862].

Huillard-Breholles, Alphonse. *Recherches sur les monuments et l'histoire des Normands... dessins par Victor Baltard.* Paris: Impr. de C.L.F. Pankouche, 1844.

Hundeshagen, Bernard. *Kaiser Friedrichs I. Barbarossa Palast in der Burg zu Gelnhausen...* 2nd edition. [Mainz: Florian Kupferberg] 1819. 1st edition 1813 destroyed by fire.

Husson, M. Armand. *Etude sur les hopitaux...* Paris: Paul Dupont, 1862.

Kerr, Robert. *The Gentleman's House...* London, 1864. Edition cited: *The English Gentleman's House.* 3rd edition, London: John Murray, 1871.

Knight, Henry Gally. *The Ecclesiastical Architecture of Italy...* 2 volumes. London: H. Bohm, 1843.

_____. *Saracenic & Norman Remains, to Illustrate the Normans in Sicily.* London: John Murray [1840].

Krafft, Johann Karl, and Thiollet, Francois. *Choix des plus jolies maisons de Paris et des environs...* Paris: Morel [1829].

_____. *Maisons de campagne, plans et decorations de parcs et jardins français, anglais, allemands...* Paris: Morel, 1876, for edition cited.

_____. *Plans, coupes, elevations des plus belles maisons et des hotels construites à Paris et dans les environs...* Paris: The Editors [1801-1803?].

_____. *Traites sur l'art de la charpente...* 2nd edition. Paris: Chez l'auteur, 1820. Earliest known edition 1812, in English.

Kugler, Franz. *Kleine Schriften und Studien zur Kunstgeschichte.* 3 volumes. Stuttgart: Ebner & Seubner, 1853-1854.

Labrouste, Henri. Miscellaneous articles on training of architects and related topics, *Revue générale de l'architecture, passim.* Referenced in footnotes.

_____. *Souvenirs d'Henri Labrouste.* Listed under modern criticism.

_____. *Les Temples de Paestum. Restauration execute en 1829...* (Livre III: *Restaurations de monuments antiques par les architects élèves de l'Academie de France a Rome.* [Paris: Firmin-Didot et cie., 1877]).

Lange, Ludwig. *Werke der hoheren Baukunst für die Ausfuhrung...* Darmstadt: Lange, 1856-1860.

Lassus, Jean Baptiste Antoine. *Album de Villard de Honnecourt...* Paris: Imprimerie imperiale, 1858.

Lenoir, Albert. *Statistique monumentale de Paris...* Paris: Imprimerie imperiale, 1867.

Letarouilly, Paul Marie. *Edifices de Rome moderne...* 4 volumes. Paris: Didot, 1840.

Lienard, Michel. *Livre d'ornements par Lienard.* Paris: Liege Berlin: Claesen, 1872.

Loudon, John Claudius. *Encyclopædia of Cottage, Farm, and Villa Architecture and Furniture...* London, 1833. Edition cited: new edition, Longmans, Brown, Green, & Longmans, 1836.

Libke, Wilhelm. *Geschlichte der Architektur von den altesten Zeiten bis zur Gegenwart.* 4th edition, enlarged. Leipzig: E.A. Seemann, 1870.

Magne, Lucien. *L'Architecture française du siècle.* Paris: Imprimerie nationale, 1890.

Mallay, Armand-Gilbert. *Essai sur les églises romens et roman-bysantines* [sic] *du department du Puy-de-Dome.* Moulins: Desrosiers, 1838.

Mazois, Francois. *Les ruines de Pompeii...* 4 volumes. Paris: Firmin Didot, 1824-1838.

Moller, Georg. *Denkmaler der deutschen Baukunst.* 2 parts. Leipzig, 1815-1821, 1820-1825. 2nd edition includes a third part by Ernest Gladbach. See Avery Library copy, 3 parts in 1, Leipzig: Leske [1846?-1851?].

Mollinger, Karl. *Elemente des Rundbogenstiles.* Munchen: Roller, 1845-1847.

Millet, Eugene. "Notice sur la vie et les ouvrages de Labrouste," *Souvenirs d'Henri Labrouste*, pp. 25-26.

Narjoux, Felix. *Paris; monuments élèves par la ville, 1850-1880.* 5 volumes. Paris: Vve A. Morel et cie, 1880-1883.

Norman, Charles. *Le guide de l'ornementiste, ou de l'ornement pour la decoration des bâtimens...* Paris: Chez l'auteur, Pillet aine, 1826.

_____. *Nouveau parallèle des orders d'architecture...* Paris: Firmin Didot, 1819.

_____. *Recueil varie de plans et de façades...* Paris: Chez l'auteur, 1831.

_____. *Le Vignole des ouvriers...* Paris: Chez l'auteur, 1835.

Normand, Louis Marie. *Paris moderne; ou choix de maisons construites dans les nouveaux quartiers de la capitale et dans les environs.* 3 volumes. Liege: Avanzo, no date.

_____. *Monuments funeraires...* Paris: Normand [1847].

Norvins, Jacques Marquet de, Baron de Montbreton, *et al. L'Italie pittoresque...* 2 volumes. Paris: A. Costes, 1835-1836.

Oppert, F. *Hospitals, Infirmaries, and Dispensaries...* London: John Churchill and Sons, 1867.

Paris dans sa splendeur... 3 volumes. Paris: H. Charpentier, 1861.

Paris. Ecole nationale superieure des beaux-arts. *Les grands prix de Rome d'architecture.* Issued at various dates and under different titles. Edition cited: Academie des beaux-arts. *Grands prix d'architecture, 1799-1833...* Liege: D. Avanzo et cie, 1842.

Percier, Charles, *et al. Palais, maisons et autres edifices moderne dessines a Rome...* Paris: Ducamp, 1798; later edition, Chez les auteurs, 1830.

Persius, Friedrich Ludwig. *Architectonische Entwurfe...* Potsdam: F. Riegel, 1843-1845.

Petit, Victor. *Architecture nouvelle; recueil de constructions modernes executés en France, en Angleterre, en Allemagne, en Italie.* Paris: Monrocq freres [1863].

_____. *Chateaux de France des XVe et XVIe siècles.* Paris: Boivin, 1855.

_____. *Habitations champêtres; recueil de maisons, villas, chalets, pavillons, kiosques, parcs et jardins.* Paris: Monrocq freres [1848].

_____. *Habitations cosmopolites; recueil de maisons et habitations françaises, anglaises, italiennes, belges, suisses, espagnoles, mauresques, allemandes, hollandaises, turques, eqyptiennes, arabes, chinoises, indiennes, grecques, americaines, russes, suedoises, etc.* [Paris: Monrocq, 18--].

_____. *Maisons de campagne des environs de Paris.* Paris: Monrocq freres, no date.

_____. *Parcs et jardins des environs de Paris...* Paris: Monrocq freres, [18--?].

_____. *Petites constructions pittoresques pour la decoration des parc, jardins, fermes et basses-cours.* Paris: Monrocq [186-?].

Petites maisons de plaisance et d'habitations choisies aux environs de Paris. Paris: Librairie d'architecture de Bance, editeur, 1857.

Pigeory, Felix. *Les monuments de Paris; histoire de l'architecture civile, politique et religieuse sous le regne du roi Louis-Philippe.* Paris: Hermitte, 1847.

Pugin, Augustus Charles. *Examples of Gothic Architecture...* 3 volumes. London: Augustus Pugin, 1831-1838. Vol. I by A. Pugin, text by Edward James Willson, 1831. Vol. II by A. Pugin and A.W.N. Pugin and J.A. Willson, 1836. Vol. III by A.W.N. Pugin and Thomas Larkins Walker, 1838.

_____. *Gothic Ornaments, Selected from Various Ancient Buildings, Both in England and France...* London: Pugin, 1831.

_____. *Paris and its Environs...* 2 volumes in 1. London: Jennings and Chaplin, 1831.

_____. *A Series of Ornamental Timber Gables, from Existing Examples in England and France of the Sixteenth Century.* 2nd edition. London: H.G. Bohn, 1839.

_____. and E.J. Willson. *Specimens of Gothic Architecture; Selected from Various Ancient Edifices in England...* 2 volumes in 1. London: Taylor, 1823.

Pugin, Augustus Welby Northmore. *Contrasts, or a Parallel Between the Architecture of the Fourteenth and Fifteenth Centuries, and Similar Buildings of the Present Day...* London: Pugin, 1836.

_____. *The True Principles of Pointed or Christian Architecture...* London: John Weale, 1841.

Rellstab, Ludwig. *Berlin und seine nachsten Umgebungen...* Darmstadt: Gustav Georg Lange [1852].

Reichensperger, August. *Georg Gottlob Ungewitter.* Leipzig: T.D. Weigel, 1866.

Reynaud, Leonce. *Traite d'architecture...* 4 volumes. Paris, 1850. Eds. cit., Vol. I, 3rd edition, 1867; Vol. II, 2nd edition, 1863.

Robinson, Peter Frederick. *Domestic Architecture in the Tudor Style...* London: Printed for the author, 1837.

_____. *A New Series of Designs for Ornamental Cottages and Villas...* [New edition] London: Henry G. Bohn, 1853. Earlier edition, 1825-1827.

_____. *Rural Architecture; or a Series of Designs for Ornamental Cottages.* London: Rodwell, 1823.

Rondelet, Jean. *Traite theorique et pratique de l'art de batir.* 9 parts in 7 volumes. Paris: Chez l'auteur, 1802-1817. 8th edition (1835-1855) and ff. issued with a supplement by Guillaume Abel Blouet. Avery Library edition in 5 volumes, Paris: Firmin Didot freres, fils et cie, 1855-1868.

Rosengarten, Albert. "Die Architektur und die Architekten Venedigs," *Allgemeine Bauzeitung,* Vol. XIV (1849), pp. 66-90.

Roargue, Adolphe. *Choix de 26 vues et monuments de Paris actuel...* [Paris] Chamoin [185-?].

Ruhl, Julius Eugen. *Gebaude des Mittelalters in Gelnhausen...* [Frankfurt a.M., Andreaische Buchdruckerey, 1831].

_____. *Denkmaler der Baukunst in Italien.* Hanau [1830].

Runge, Ludwig, and Rosengarten, Albert. *Architektonische Mitteilungen über Italien...* 2 volumes in 1. Berlin: G.W.F. Miller [pref, 1847].

Ruskin, John. *The Seven Lamps of Architecture.* London, 1849. The Avery Library's copy of the 1st American edition (New York: John Wiley, 1849) came from Detlef Lienau's library.

_____. *The Stones of Venice.* 3 volumes. London: Smith, Elder, and Company, 1851-1853.

Sauvageot, Claude. *Palais, chateaux, hotels et maisons de France du XVe au XVIIIe siècle.* 4 volumes. Paris: A. Morel, 1867.

Schinkel, Karl Friedrich. *Aus Schinkel's Nachlass; Reisetagebucher, Briefe Aphorismen...* Edited by Alfred von Wolzogen. 4 volumes. Berlin: R. Decker, 1862-1864.

——————. *Grundlage der praktischen Baukunst...* 2 volumes. Berlin. The Avery Library's copy (Vol. I, 3rd edition, 1841; Vol. II, 2nd edition, 1835) came from Detlef Lienau's library.

Schmidt, Christian Wilhelm. *Die Baudenkmale der romischen Periode und das Mittelalter in Trier und seiner Umgebung.* Trier: J.J. Lintz, 1836-1845.

Schramke. "Einrichtung und Konstruckzion der Waaremagazine, Stadt- und Landhauser in den Vereinigten Staaten von Nord-Amerika, mit besonderer Rucksicht auf die Stadt und Landschaft New-York," *Allgemeine Bauzeitung,* Vol. XI (1846), pp. 73-110.

Seheult, Francois Leonard. *Recueil d'architecture, dessine et mésure en Italie dans les années 1791, [17]92 et [17]93 par F.L. Scheult* [sic]... Paris: Bance aine, 1821.

Semper, Hans. *Gottfried Semper.* Berlin: S. Calvary & Company, 1880.

Seroux d'Agincourt, Jean Baptiste Louis Georges, *Histoire de l'art par les monuments, depuis sa decadence au IVe siècle jusqu'à son renouvellement au XVIe...* 6 volumes. Paris: Treuttel & Wurtz, 1823.

Serradifalco, Domenico Lo Faso Pietresanta, duca di. *Le antichita della Sicilia...* 5 volumes in 3. Palermo: Tipographia del Giornale letterario, 1834-1842.

——————. *Del duomo di Monréale de di alter chiese sicule normanne...* Palermo: Tip. Roberto, 1838.

Shaw, Henry. *The Encyclopedia of Ornament.* London: William Pickering, 1842.

Suys, Tilman Franz, and Haudebourt, Louis Pierre. *Palais Massimi a Rome.* Paris: Normand fils, 1818.

Ungewitter, Georg Gottlob. *Entwurfe zu Stadt- und Landhausern.* Glogau: Carl Flemming, 1858-1864.

——————. *Vorlegeblatter für Holzarbeiten.* Glogau: Flemming [1864?]. The Avery Library's copy of edition cited and of the book immediately following came from Detlef Lienau's library.

——————. *Vorlegeblatter für Ziegel und Steinarbeiten.* 2nd edition. Leipzig: Romberg [1846].

[Vacquer, Theodore]. *Maisons les plus remarquables de Paris construites pendant les trios dernieres années...* Paris: Caudriller [1863].

Varin, Pierre Amedee. *L'Architecture pittoresque en Suisse.* Paris: A. Morel, 1873.

Verdier, Aymar, and Cattois, François. *Architecture civile et domestique au moyen âge et a la renaissance.* 2 volumes. Paris: Librairie archeologique de V^er Didron, 1855-1857.

Viollet-le-Duc, Eugene Emmanuel. *Dictionnaire raisonné de l'architecture du XIe au XVIe siècle.* 10 volumes. Paris: B. Bance [etc.], 1854-1868.

——————. *Entretiens sur l'architecture.* 2 volumes. Paris: A. Morel et cie, 1863-1872.

Vulliamy, Lewis. *Examples of Ornamental Sculpture in Architecture...* London: Lewis Vulliamy *et al.* [1824].

Wagner, Johann Friedrich. *Ansichten von Burgan, Schlossern und Ruinen der Schweiz...* Berlin, 1840.

Weichert, Carl. *Das Stadthaus und die Villa.* 2nd edition. Weimar: Bernhardt Voigt, 1884.

Wiebeking, Karl Friedrich. *Architecture civile theorique et pratique...* 7 volumes. Munich: M. Lindauer, 1827-1831.

Zahn, Cleophea. *Ornamente enthaltend eine reiche Auswahl voin Capitalen, Consolen, Arabesken, Friesen, Borduren, Rosetten... für Architekten, Dekorationsmaler, Stuccateurs...* Hamburg: Charles Fuchs [1848?]. Bound with *Hamburg Neubau.*

2. Late 19th and 20th Century Histories and Criticism

Alaux, Jean-Paul. *Academie de France a Rome, ses directeurs, ses pensionnaires.* 2 volumes. Paris: Editions Ducharte, 1933.

Architekten-Verein zu Berlin. *Berlin und seine Bauten...* 3 volumes in 2. Berlin: W. Ernst & Sohn, 1896.

Bayerischer Architekten- und Ingenieur-Verein, Munchen. *Munchen und seine Bauten.* Munchen: F. Bruckmann A.G., 1912.

Berlin, Deutsche Bauakedemie. *Über Karl Friedrich Schinkel.* Berlin: Henschel, 1951.

Casson, Hugh. *An Introduction to Victorian Architecture.* New York: Pellegrini & Cudahy [1948].

Clark, Sir Kenneth. *The Gothic Revival, an Essay in the History of Taste.* Revised and enlarged edition. London: Constable [1950].

Clarke, Basil F.L. *Church Builders of the Nineteenth Century, a Study of the Gothic Revival in England.* London: Society for Promoting Christian Knowledge, 1938.

Clasen, Karl Heinz. "Schinkel und die Tradition," *Über Karl Friedrich Schinkel,* pp. 31-52.

Clouzot, Henri. *Des Tuileries a Saint-Cloud; l'art decorative du second empire.* Paris: Payot, 1925.

De Zurko, Robert Edward. "Functionalist Trends in Writings Pertaining to Architecture with Special Emphasis on the Period ca. 1700-1850." 2 volumes. Ph.D. dissertation, Institute of Fine Arts, New York University, 1954.

_____. *Origins of Functionalist Theory.* New York: Columbia University Press, 1957.

Dutton, Ralph. *The Victorian Home; Some Aspects of Nineteenth Century Taste and Manners.* London: B.T. Batsford, Ltd. [1954].

Ehmig, Paul. *Das Deutsche Haus...* 3 volumes, Berlin: Ernst Wasmuth, 1914-1922.

Ettlinger, Leopold. *Gottfried Semper und die Antike; Beitrage zur Kunstanschauumg des deutschen Klassizismus.* Dissertation, Halle Wittenberg. Bleicherode am Harz: C. Nieft, 1937.

Finch, James Kip, and Hamlin, Talbot Faulkner. *The William Barclay Parsons Railroad Prints.* [New York:] Columbia University Library, 1935.

Fischer, Friedrich Wilhelm Heinrich. *Norddeutscher Ziegelbau.* Munchen: G.D.W. Callaway, 1944.

Grisebach, August. *Carl Friedrich Schinkel.* Leipzig: Insel-Verlag, 1924.

Goodhart-Rendel, Hary Stuart. *English Architecture since the Regency, an Interpretation.* London: Constable [1953].

Hamlin, Talbot. "The Architecture of Railroads." Exhibition, Avery Library, January 1939.

Hautecoeur, Louis. *Histoire de l'art classique en France.* 7 volumes. Paris: Picard, 1943-1957. The last two volumes were particularly helpful, *viz.*, Vol. VI: *La restauration et le gouvernement de juillet, 1815-1848*; Vol. VII: *La fin de l'architecture classique, 1848-1900.*

Hitchcock, Henry-Russell. *Early Victorian Architecture in Britain.* 2 volumes. New Haven: Yale University Press, 1954. (Yale Historical Publications, edited by George Kubler. History of Art: 9).

_____. "High Victorian Gothic," *Victorian Studies*, Vol. I, No. 1 (September 1957), pp. 47-71.

_____. "Second empire 'avant la letter,'" *Gazette des beaux-arts*, Series 6, Vol. XLII (1953), pp. 115-130.

_____. "Victorian Monuments of Commerce," *Architectural Review*, Vol. CV (February 1949), pp. 61-74.

Joseph, David. *Geshichte der Baukunst des XIX Jahrhunderts.* Bd. III[1]: Geschichte der Baukunst vom Alterthum bis zur Neuzeit. Berlin: B. Hessling [1902-1909].

Keim, Albert. *Le decoration et le mobilier a l'époque romantique et sous le second empire...* 4 volumes in 1. Paris: Editions Nilsson [1929].

Labrouste, architecte de la bibliotheque nationale de 1854 a 1875. Paris: bibliotheque nationale [1953]. Catalog of an exhibition of Labrouste drawings and memorabilia held at the Bibliotheque Nationale from March 10 to April 11, 1953. For contents, see *ante*, pp. 26-27.

Labrouste, Henri. *Souvenirs d'Henri Labrouste. Notes recueillies et classes par ses enfants.* [Fontainebleau: Imprimerie Cuenot] 1928. Negative Photostats on deposit at the Avery Library.

Lapauze, Henri. *Histoire de l'academie de France a Rome.* 2 volumes. Paris: Plon, 1920.

Lichten, Frances. *Decorative Art of Victoria's Era...* New York: Scribner's [1950].

Lorck, Carl von. *Karl Friedrich Schinkel.* Berlin: Rembrandt-Verlag [1939].

Mackowsky, Hans. *Karl Friedrich Schinkel. Briefe, Tagebucher, Gedanken.* Berlin: Propylsen-Verlag [c.1922].

Madsen, Stephan Tschudi. *Sources of Art Nouveau.* Translated by Ragnor Christophersen. New York: George Wittenborn, Inc. [1955].

Meeks, Carroll Louis Vanderslice. "Creative Eclecticism," *Journal of the Society of Architectural Historians,* Vol. XII (December 1953), pp. 15-18.

―――――. "Picturesque Eclecticism," *Art Bulletin,* Vol. XXXII (September 1950), pp. 226-235.

―――――. *The Railroad Station; an Architectural History.* New Haven: Yale University Press, 1956. (Yale Historical Publications. History of Art: 11).

Meier, Burkhard. *Potsdam, Palaces and Gardens...* 4th edition. Berlin: Deutscher Kunstverlag, 1930.

Millech, Knud. *Danske Arkitektursttromninger, 1850-1950...* Kobenhavn: udgivet af Ostifternes Kreditforening, 1951,

Moeller van der Bruch, Arthur. *Der preussische Stil. Neue Aufl.* Munchen: R. Piper & Company, 1922.

Much, Hans. *Norddeutsche Backsteingotik, ein Heimatbuch.* 4 bis 7 Aufl. Braunschweig: G. Westermann, 1923.

Pauli, Gustav. *Die Kunst des Klassizismus und der Romantik.* Berlin: Propylaen-Verlag, 1922. (Vol. XIV: *Propylaen-Kunstgeschichte*).

Priester, Karl. Bremische Wohnhauser um 1800... Bremen: Franz Leuwer, 1912.

Pevsner, Nicolaus. *High Victorian Design, a Study of the Exhibits of 1851.* London: Architectural Press [1951].

―――――. *Pioneers of Modern Design from William Morris to Walter Gropius.* [2nd edition] New York: Museum of Modern Art [1949].

―――――. "Review of C.L.V. Meeks's The Railroad Station," *Victorian Studies,* Vol. I, No. 1 (September 1957), pp. 78-81.

―――――. "Schinkel," *Journal of the Royal Institute of British Architects,* Third Series, Vol. LIX (January 1952), pp. 89-95.

Preussische Akademie des Bauwesens, Berlin. *Schinkel Ausschus, Karl Friedrich Schinkel.* [Edited by Paul Ortwin Rave. Berlin] Akademie des Bauwesens [1939-] 8 volumes have been published to date. The last 4 were issued under a different title: *Karl Friedrich Schinkel: Lebenswerk.* Berlin, Deutscher-Kunstverlag. For individual volumes, see under Gunther Grundsmann, Hans Kania, Paul Ortwin Rave, Johannes Sievers, and Hans Vogel.

Rave, Paul Ortwin. Berlin. *Karl Friedrich Schinkel. Bauten für die Kunst, Kirchen, Denkmalpflege.* Berlin: Deutscher Kunstverlag, 1941.

Richardson, Albert Edward. *Monumental Classic Architecture in Great Britain and Ireland during the Eighteenth and Nineteenth Centuries.* London: B.T. Batsford, Ltd. [1914].

Schellenberg, Carl. *Das alte Hamburg.* Leipzig: Insel-Verlag, 1936.

Schmidt, Joseph. *Karl Friedrich Schinkel, der Vorlaufer neuer deutscher Baugesinnung.* Leipzig: [G. Kummer], 1943.

Schneider, Rene. *Quatremere de Quincy et son intervention dans les arts (1788-1830).* Paris: Hachette, 1910.

Schumacher, Fritz. *Stromungen in der deutschen Baukunst seit 1800.* Leipzig: Seemann [c.1935].

Sturgis, Russell. *A Dictionary of Architecture and Building, Biographical, Historical, and Descriptive...* 3 volumes. New York: The Macmillan Company, 1901-1902.

Summerson, John. *Architecture in Britain, 1530-1830.* Baltimore: Penguin Books [1954].

Taut, Bruno. *Modern Architecture.* London: The Studio, Ltd., [1929].

Turnor, Reginald. *Nineteenth Century Architecture in Britain.* London: B.T. Batsford, Ltd. [1950].

Valdenaire, Arthur. *Heinrich Hubsch; eine Studie zur Baukunst der Romantik.* Karlsruhe: G. Braun, 1926.

Vogel, Hans. *Deutsche Baukunst des Klassizismus.* Berlin: Verlag Gebr. Mann, 1937.

Wasmuth, Ernst. *Lexikon der Baukunst.* 5 volumes. Berlin: E. Wasmuth A.G. [c.1929-c.1937].

Whiffen, Marcus. "The Reform Club: a Barry Triumph," *Country Life,* Vol. CVIII, Part 2 (November 1950), pp. 1498-1501.

Wiebenson, Dora. "City Planning: 1850-1875." Seminar report, Institute of Fine Arts, New York University, April 29, 1957.

Zieler, Otto. *Potsdam, ein Stadtbild des 18. Jahrhunderts.* Bd. I: *Stadtarchitektur.* Berlin: Weise, 1913.

Ziller, Hermann. *Schinkel.* Rielefeld und Leipzig: Velhagen & Klasing, 1897.

Architecture and Culture in the Eastern Part of the United States in the Second Half of the 19th Century

A. America in the 19th Century
1. Bibliographic Aids

Columbia University. Special Collections. Chronological Index.

Handlin, Oscar, *et al. Harvard Guide to American History.* Cambridge: Belknap Press of Harvard University Press [1954].

2. Description, Guides, and Travel Books
Primary Sources

Ampere, Jean Jacques. *Promenade en Amerique...* 2 volumes. Paris: Michel Levy freres, 1855. An interesting study by a friend of de Toqueville; good material on architecture.

Ashworth, Henry. *A Tour of the United States, Cuba, and Canada. A Course of Lectures Delivered before the Members of the Bolton Mechanics Institution.* London: A.W. Bennett [pref. 1861].

Atlantische Studien. Von Deutschen in Amerika. 8 volumes in 4. Gottingen: Georg Heinrich Wigand, 1853-1857. An excellent collection of essays. See also *post,* under New York City.

Baird, Robert. *Impressions and Experiences of the West Indies and North America in 1849.* Philadelphia: Lea & Blanchard, 1850.

Baxter, William Edward (M.P.). *America and the Americans.* London: George Routledge & Company, 1855. A well known book based on a tour made in 1853-1854.

Beauvallet, Léon. *Rachel et le nouveau mondes; promenade aux Etats-Unis et aux Antilles.* Paris: Cadot, 1856. Amusing descriptions by Rachel's leading man; immediately appeared in an English translation (New York: Dix, Edwards & Company, 1856).

[Bishop, Isabella Lucy (Bird)]. *The Englishwoman in America.* London: John Murray, 1856. Excellent. Interesting information on architecture and society.

Bremer, Fredericka. *America in the Fifties: Letters of Frederika Bremer*, selected and edited by Adolph B. Benson. New York: The American Scandinavian Foundation, 1924. First published in English as *Homes of the New World; Impressions of America*, 2 volumes, New York, 1853. Particularly interesting for contacts with A.J. Downing and other famous personalities.

Bromme, Traugott. *Neuesten vollstandigtes Hand- und Reisebuch für Auswanderer... nach den Vereinigten Staaten...* 3rd edition. Bayreuth: Buchner'sche Buchhandlung, 1846.

Bryant, William Cullen. *Letters of a Traveller; or Notes of Things Seen in Europe and America.* New York: G.P. Putnam, 1850.

[Burn, James Dawson]. *Three Years Among the Working-classes in the United States During the War.* London: Smith, Elder and Company, 1865. A classic, but nothing on architecture.

Chambers, William. *Things as They Are in America.* Philadelphia: J.B. Lippincott, Grambo & Company, 1854. Excellent description by a prominent Scottish publisher and writer.

Comettant, Jean Pierre Oscar. *Trois ans aux Etats-Unis, etude des moeurs et coutumes americaines.* Paris: Pagnerre, 1857.

———————. *L'Amerique telle qu'elle est...* Paris: Achille Faure, 1864.

Dana, Charles Anderson (editor). *The United States Illustrated, in Views of City and Country...* 2 volumes. New York: Hermann J. Meyer [pref. 1854]. One of the finest sources for its period, with excellent descriptions of architecture.

Dicey, Edward. *Six Months in the Federal States.* 2 volumes. London: Macmillan and Company, 1863. A classic in its field by the special correspondent of *Macmillans Magazine* and the *Spectator*; nothing on architecture.

Dickens, Charles. *American Notes for General Circulation.* 2 volumes. 3rd edition. London: Chapman and Hall, 1842.

Dixon, William Hepworth. *New America.* Philadelphia: J.B. Lippincott & Company, 1867.

Dizac, F. *Excursion aux Indes occidentals et aux Etats-Unis d'Amerique (1853-1854)...* Brive: Léon Roche, 1855. A very unflattering picture of America.

Duvergier de Hauranne, Ernest. *Huit mois en Amerique. Lettres et notes de voyage, 1864-1865.* 2 volumes. Paris: A. Lacroix, Verboeckhoven & cie, 1866. Extremely critical and unsympathetic.

Dwight, Theodore. *Travels in America.* Glasgow: R. Griffin & Company, 1848. By the editor of *Dwight's American Magazine.*

Ferri Pisani, Camille. *Lettres sur les Etats-Unis d'Amerique.* Paris: L. Hachette et cie, 1862. Letters written by the *aide de camp* of Prince Napoleon, whom he accompanied on a two-month tour of the U.S. in 1861.

Frobel, Julius. *Aus Amerika. Erfahrungen, Reisen und Studien.* 2 volumes. 2nd edition. Leipzig: J.J. Weber, 1857-1858. Interesting sociological study by a German Socialist; nothing on architecture.

Grattan, Thomas Colley. *Civilized America.* 2 volumes. London: Bradbury and Evans, 1859. By the former British consul in Massachusetts; somewhat condescending in tone.

Hubner, Baron Joseph A. *A Ramble Around the World,* 1871. Translated by Lady Herbert. 2 volumes. London: Macmillan and Company, 1874. A classic. Some interesting material on New York.

[Joerg, Eduard]. *Briefe aus des Vereinigten Staaten von Nord-Amerika.* 2 volumes. Leipzig: J.J. Weber, 1853.

Jouve, Eugene. *Voyage en Amerique. Extrait du Courrier de Lyon.* 2 volumes in 1. Lyon: Imprimerie de Mougin-Rusand, 1853.

[Kohler, Karl]. *Briefe aus Amerika für deutsche Auswanderer.* Darmstadt: Gustav Georg Lange, 1852.

Lyell, Sir Charles. *A Second Visit to the United States and North America.* 2 volumes. London: John Murray, 1849. An interesting account by the eminent British geologist based on his trip in 1845-1846.

Mackay, Alexander. *The Western World; or Travels in the United States in 1846-1847...* 3 volumes. 3rd edition. London: Richard Bentley, 1850. Perhaps the best general description of America of the period.

Macrae, David. *The Americans at Home...* 2 volumes. Edinburgh: Edmonston and Douglas, 1870, A classic in its field.

Maury, Sarah Mytton. *An Englishwoman in America.* London: Thomas Richardson and Son, 1848.

Myers, John C. *Sketches on a Tour Through the Northern and Eastern States, the Canadas & Nova Scotia.* Harrisonburg: J.H. Wartmann and Brothers, 1849. Excellent.

Norton, Charles. *Der treue Fuhrer des Auswanderers nach den Vereinigten Staaten...* 2nd edition. Refensburg: Georg Joseph Manz, 1848.

Pairpoint, Alfred. *Uncle Sam and His Country; or Sketches of America in 1854-1855-1856.* London: Simpkin, Marshall and Company, 1857.

Pascal, Cesar. *A travers l'Atlantique et dans le nouveau-monde.* 2nd edition. Paris: Grassart, 1870.

Peto, Sir Samuel Morton. *The Resources and Prospects of America.* London and New York: Alexander Strahan, 1866. A classic study, but nothing on architecture.

Playfair, Robert. *Recollections of a Visit to the United States and the British Provinces of North America in the Years 1847, 1848, and 1849.* Edinburgh: Thomas Constable and Company, 1856.

Prentice, Archibald. *A Tour in the United States, with Two Lectures on Emigration...* 4th edition. London: J. Johnson, 1849. Based on a tour of 1848 by the former editor of *The Manchester Times.*

Pulszky, Francis and Theresa. *White, Red, Black; Sketches of American Society in the United States...* 2 volumes. New York: Redfield, 1853. Very interesting letters by two members of Kossuth's entourage on his visit to the U.S. in 1851-1852.

Quentin, Karl. *Reisebilder und Studien aus dem Norden der Vereinigten Staaten von Amerika.* 2 volumes in 1. Arnsberg: H.F. Grote, 1851. Excellent general study.

Rey, William. *L'Amerique protestante. Notes et observations d'un voyageur.* 2 volumes. Paris: Joel Cherbuliez, 1857. Unusually sympathetic French account by a minister, based on a trip in 1855.

Robertson, James. *A Few Months in America: Containing Remarks on Some of Its Industrial and Commercial Interests.* London: Longman & Company, [1855]. Based on a trip in 1853-1855.

Russell, Sir William Howard. *My Diary North and South.* Boston: T.O.H. Burnham, 1863. One of the best known accounts of America during the Civil War by the war correspondent of the London *Times*, but nothing on architecture.

Sala, George Augustus Henry. *America Revisited: from the Bay of New York to the Gulf of Mexico, and from Lake Michigan to the Pacific.* 2nd edition. London: Vizetelly and Company, 1882. Excellent all-round coverage, including comments on architecture.

Schliemann, Heinrich. *Schleimann's First Visit to America, 1850-1851.* Edited by Shirley H. Weber. Cambridge: Harvard University Press, 1942.

[Smith, T.]. *Rambling Recollections of a Trip to America.* Edinburgh: David S. Stewart, 1875.

Thummel, Dr. A.R. *Die Natur und das Leben in den Vereinigten Staaten von Nord-Amerika...* Erlangen: Palm'sche Verlagsbuchhandlung, 1848. Good general account by a minister, but nothing on architecture.

Treu, Georg. *Das Buch der Auswanderung... Ein zuverlassiger Ratgeber...* Bamberg: Frankischer Merkur, 1848. Perhaps the best German guide book of the period.

Towle, George Makepeace. *American Society.* 2 volumes. London: Chapman and Hall, 1870. Classic work, but nothing on architecture.

Trollope, Anthony. *North America.* Edited by Donald Smalley and Bradford Allen Booth. New York: Alfred A. Knopf, 1951. Originally published 1862. Based on a trip in America in 1861-1862. A classic work containing many interesting descriptions and comments on architecture.

[Trotter, Isabella (Strange)]. *First Impressions of the New World... Autumn of 1858.* London: Longman, Brown, Green, Longmans, & Roberts, 1859.

Wagner, Moritz, and Scherzer, Karl. *Reisen in Nordamerika in den Jahren 1852 und 1853.* 3 volumes. Leipzig: Arnoldische Buchhandlung, 1854.

Weichardt, Karl (Pfarrer zu Nermsdorf, bei Weimar). *Die Vereinigten Staaten von Nord-Amerika nebst einem Blick auf Kanada...* Leipzig: August Weichardt, 1848.

Wortley, Lady Emmeline [Charlotte Elizabeth] Stuart. *Travels in the United States, etc., during 1849 and 1850.* 2 volumes. London: Richard Bentley, 1851. Excellent account by an observant traveler who knew the "best" people.

Ziegler, Alexander. *Skizzen einer Reise durch Nordamerika und Westindien...* 2 volumes. Dresden: Arnoldische Buchhandlung, 1848.

Zirckel, Otto. *Skizzen aus den und über die Vereinigten Staaten. Ein Beitrag zur Beurtheilung der Aussichten für die gebildete deutsche Mittelklasse... für Auswanderer, Politiker und Kapitalisten.* Berlin: G.W.F. Muller, 1850.

Later Compilations:

Commager, Henry Steele (editor). *America in Perspective; the United States through Foreign Eyes.* New York: Random House, 1947.

Handlin, Oscar. *This Was America; True Accounts of People and Places, Manners and Customs, as Recorded by European Travelers to the Western Shore in the Eighteenth, Nineteenth and Twentieth Centuries.* Cambridge: Harvard University Press, 1949.

Nevins, Allan (editor). *America through British Eyes.* New edition, revised and enlarged. New York: Oxford University Press, 1948. Contains a useful annotated bibliography, pp. 503 ff.

Tryon, Warren Stenson (editor). *A Mirror for Americans; Life and Manners in the United States, 1790-1870, as Recorded by American Travellers.* 3 volumes. Chicago: University of Chicago Press, 1952.

Tuckerman, Henry Theodore. *America and Her Commentators...* New York: Charles Scribner, 1864. Contains some materials not available in modern collections.

Memoirs and Letters

Cooper, James Fenimore (editor). *Correspondence of James Fenimore Cooper.* 2 volumes. New Haven: Yale University Press, 1922.

James, Henry. *Notes of a Son and Brother.* New York: Charles Scribner's Sons, 1914.

McAllister, Ward. *Society as I Have Found It.* New York: Cassell Publishing Company, 1890.

Strong, George Templeton. See under New York City, *post.*

Wharton, Edith. *A Backward Glance.* New York: D. Appleton-Century Company, Inc., 1934.

Literature
Some Interesting Essays and Novels:

Bristed, Charles Astor. *The Upper Ten Thousand: Sketches of American Society.* 2nd edition. New York: Stringer & Townsend, 1852. 1st edition also 1852.

Curtis, George William. *Lotus-eating: a Summer Book.* New York: Harper & Brothers [c.1852]. Originally written as letters to the New York *Tribune.*
_____. *The Potiphar Papers.* New York: G.P. Putnam & Company, 1853. Originally published in *Putnam's Magazine* of the same year.

Howells, William Dean. *A Hazard of New Fortunes.* 2 volumes in 1. New York: Boni & Liveright, Inc., 1889.

James, Henry. *The American Scene, together with Three Essays from Portraits of Places.* Edited by W.H. Auden. New York: Charles Scribner's Sons, 1946. Essay on Newport (1870) reprinted from *Portraits of Places* (1884); essays on New York and Newport reprinted from *American Scene* (1907).

Stowe, Mrs. Harriet Elizabeth (Beecher). *House and Home Papers.* By Christopher Crowfield [pseudonym]. Boston: Ticknor and Fields, 1865.

Twain, Mark, and Warner, Charles Dudley. *The Gilded Age, a Tale of Today.* Hartford: American Publishing Company, 1874.

Wharton, Edith. *The Age of Innocence.* New York: D. Appleton and Company, 1920.

Whitman, Walt. See *post*, under New York City.

Willis, N. Parker. *Rural Letters and Other Records of Thoughts at Leisure.* New York: Baker and Scribner, 1849.

Criticism and Interpretation:

Hicks, Granville. *The Great Tradition; an Interpretation of American Literature since the Civil War.* New York: The Macmillan Company, 1933.

Matthiessen, Francis Otto. *American Renaissance; Art and Expression in the Age of Emerson and Whitman.* London: Oxford University Press [c.1941].

Parrington, Vernon Louis. *The Beginnings of Critical Realism in America.* Vol. III: *Main Currents in American Thought; an Interpretation of American Literature...* New York: Harcourt, Brace and Company [c.1930].

History, Historiography, and Interpretation
General Reference:

Beard, Charles A., and Beard, Mary R. *The Rise of American Civilization.* New edition, 2 volumes in 1, revised and enlarged. New York: The Macmillan Company, 1944.

Commager, Henry Steele, and Nevins, Allan. *The Heritage of America.* Boston: Little, Brown and Company [1949].

Curti, Merle, Shyrock, Richard H., Cochran, Thomas R., and Harrington, Fred Harvey. *An American History.* 2 volumes. New York: Harper & Brothers [1950].

Curti, Merle Eugene. *The Growth of American Thought.* 2nd edition. New York: Harper & Brothers, 1951.

Davie, Emily *et al. Profile of America. An Autobiography of the U.S.A.* New York: Thomas Y. Crowell Company [1954].

Fish, Carl Russell. *The Rise of the Common Man.* New York: The Macmillan Company, 1927. (Vol. VI: *A History of American Life*).

Hacker, Louis Morton. *The Shaping of the American Tradition.* Text by Lewis M. Hacker, documents edited by *idem.* and Helene S. Zahler. 2 volumes. New York: Columbia University Press, 1947.

_____. *The Triumph of American Capitalism; the Development of Forces in American History to the End of the Nineteenth Century...* New edition. New York: Columbia University Press, 1946.

_____ and Hendrick, Benjamin B. *The United States since 1865.* 4th edition. New York: Appleton-Century Crofts, Inc., 1949.

A History of American Life (Dixon Ryan Fox and Arthur Meier Schlessinger, editors). New York: The Macmillan Company, 1927-1943. Pertinent individual volumes listed under specific authors in this section.

Jones, Howard Mumford. *America and French Culture, 1750-1848.* Chapel Hill: University of North Carolina Press, 1927.

Kraus, Michael. *The Writing of American History.* 1st edition. Norman: University of Oklahoma Press [1953].

Myers, Gustavus. *History of the Great American Fortunes.* New edition. New York: The Modern Library [c.1937].

Nevins, Allan. *The Emergence of Modern America, 1865-1878.* New York: The Macmillan Company[1927]. (Vol. VIII: *A History of American Life*).

Oberholtzer, Ellis Paxton. *A History of the U.S. since the Civil War.* 5 volumes. New York: The Macmillan Company, 1922.

Schlessinger, Arthur Meier. *The Rise of the City, 1878-1898.* New York: The Macmillan Company, 1933. (Vol. IX: *A History of American Life*).

_____. *Political and Social Growth of the American People, 1865-1940.* 3rd edition. New York: The Macmillan Company [1941].

Soule, George. *Economic Forces in American History.* New York: Sloane Associates, Inc., 1952.

Tarbell, Ida Minerva. *The Nationalization of Business, 1878-1898.* New York: The Macmillan Company, 1936. (Vol. IX: *A History of American Life*).

Van Rensselaer, Mrs. May King, and Vander Water, Frederic. *The Social Ladder.* New York: Henry Holt and Company, 1924.

Veblen, Thorsten. *The Theory of the Leisure Class.* New York: The Modern Library, 1934. First published 1899.

Reference Works on Immigration:

Common, John R. *Races and Immigrants in America.* New edition. New York: The Macmillan Company, 1927.

Ernst, Robert. Listed under New York City.

Faust, Albert Bernhardt. *The German Element in the United States with Special Reference to Its Political, Moral, Social and Educational Influence.* 2 volumes. New edition. New York: The Steuben Society of America, 1927.

Hansen, Marcus Lee. *The Immigrant in American History.* Cambridge: Harvard University Press, 1948.

Klaghorn, Kate H. Listed under New York City.

Mayo-Smith, Richard. *Emigration and Immigration.* New York: Charles Scribner's Sons, 1890.

_____. *The Influence of the Immigrant on the United States...* Rome: Botta, 1888.

New York State. Commissioners on Emigration. *Annual Reports,* 1861-1869.

Ross, Edward Alsworth. *The Old World in the New...* New York: The Century Company, 1914.

U.S. Treasury Department. *Tables Showing Arrivals of Alien Passengers and Immigrants...,* 1820 to 1880. Washington, D.C., 1889.

Biographical Aids and Dictionaries

Bibliographic and Genealogical Aids:

The American Genealogical-Biographical Index... [1st series]. Fremont Rider, editor. 48 volumes. Middleton, CT, 1942-1952. 2nd series. 18 volumes to date, 1952-1957.

Index to American Genealogies... 5th edition. Albany, NY: Joel Munsell's Sons, 1900; Supplement, 1900-1908.

Biographical Dictionaries and General Reference Works:

Appleton's Cyclopaedia of American Biography. Edited by James Grant Wilson and John Fiske. 7 volumes. New York: Appleton and Company, 1888-1889, 1900.

Dictionary of American Biography. Under the Auspices of the American Council of Learned Societies. Edited by Allen Johnson and Dumas Malone. 21 volumes. New York: Charles Scribner's Sons, 1928-1944.

Lamb's Biographical Dictionary of the United States. Edited by John Howard Brown. 7 volumes. Boston: James H. Lamb Company, 1900-1903.

National Cyclopædia of American Biography... 41 volumes to date. New York: J.T. White Company, 1892-.

Spooner, Walter W. (editor). *Historic Families of America.* 3 volumes. New York: Historic Families Publishing Association, 1907-1908.

Local History

Boston, Massachusetts:

Winsor, Justin (editor). *The Memorial History of Boston, Including Suffolk County, Massachusetts, 1830-1880.* 4 volumes. Boston: Ticknor & Company, 1880-1881.

New Jersey (Northern Counties):

Directories

    Boyd's Jersey City and Hoboken Directory, 1859-1910.

    Gopsill's Jersey City and Hoboken Directory, 1855/1856 and ff.

    Dillistin, William H. *Directory of New Jersey Banks, 1804-1942.* New Jersey Bankers Association, no date.

    Industrial Directory of New Jersey. Trenton: William Stainsby, 1901.

History

    Hatfield, the Reverend Edwin F. *History of Elizabeth, New Jersey.* New York: Carlton & Lanahan, 1868.

    Biographical and Genealogical History of the City of Newark and Essex County, New Jersey. 2 volumes. New York: The Lewis Publishing Company, 1898.

    McLean, Alexander. *History of Jersey City, New Jersey.* 2 volumes. Jersey City: Press of the Jersey City Printing Company, 1895.

    Muirhead, Walker G. *Jersey City of Today; Its History, People, Trades, Commerce, Institutions and Industries.* Jersey City, 1909.

New Jersey. A Guide to Its Present and Past... New York: Hastings House, 1946 (*American Guide Series*).

Shaw, William H. *History of Essex and Hudson Counties, New Jersey.* 2 volumes. Philadelphia: Everts & Peck, 1884.

[Urquhart, Frank John *et al.*]. *A History of the City of Newark...*, *1666-1913.* 3 volumes. New York: The Lewis Historical Publishing Company, 1913.

Winfield, Charles H. *History of the County of Hudson, New Jersey, from Its Earliest Settlement to the Present Time.* New York: Kennard & Hay, 1874.

Newport, Rhode Island:
Public Records, etc.

Deeds. Card index file. City Clerk's Office.

Plats. Tax Assessor's Office.

Atlases for years 1870 (earliest), 1883, 1895, 1907, 1921. Tax Assessor's Office.

Map of the City of Newport, RI New York: M. Dripps, 1859. Map Room, New York Public Library.

History

Amory, Cleveland. *The Last Resorts; a Portrait of American Society at Play.* New York: Harper & Brothers, 1952.

Barrett, Richmond Brooks. *Good Old Summer Days: Newport, Narragansett Pier, Saratoga, Long Branch, Bar Harbor.* New York: D. Appleton-Century Company, Inc., 1941.

Bayles, Richard M. (editor). *History of Newport County, Rhode Island, from the Year 1683 to the Year 1887...* New York: L.E. Preston & Company, 1888.

Bridenbaugh, Carl. "Colonial Newport as a Summer Resort," *Rhode Island Historical Society Collections*, Vol. XXVI (January 1933), pp. 1-23.

Browne, H. Junius. "The Queen of Aquidneck," *Harper's Magazine*, Vol. XLIX (August 1874), pp. 305 ff.

Elliott, Maud (Howe). *This Was My Newport.* Cambridge: The Mythology Company, A.M. Jones, 1944.

James, Henry. "Newport" (1870), reprinted in *Portraits of Places.* Boston: James R. Osgood & Company, 1884.

Mason, Georg Champlin, *Newport Illustrated.* Newport: C.E. Hammett, Jr., 1854

_____. *Reminiscences of Newport.* Newport, 1884.

"Newport—Historical and Social," *Harper's Magazine*, Vol. IX (August 1854), pp. 289-317.

Van Rensselaer, May (King). *Newport: Our Social Capital.* Philadelphia and London: J.B. Lippincott Company, 1905.

Norwalk, Connecticut:
Danenberg, Elsie Nicholas. *The Romance of Norwalk*. New York: The States
  History Company, 1929.
Selleck, the Reverend Charles H. *Norwalk*. Norwalk: The author, 1895.

B. Architecture
General Reference
Bibliographic Aids:
Hamlin, Sarah Hill Jenkins Simpson. "Some Articles of Architectural
  Interest in American Periodicals Prior to 1851," Appendix B in Talbot
  Hamlin's *Greek Revival Architecture in America*, pp. 356-382.
Hamlin, Talbot. "Bibliography," *ibid.*, pp. 383-409.
Hitchcock, Henry-Russell. *American Architectural Books: A List of Books,
  Portfolios, and Pamphlets on Architecture and Related Subjects Published in
  America before 1895*. 3rd edition, revised. Minneapolis: University of
  Minnesota Press, 1946.
Roos, Frank John, Jr. *Early American Architecture, an Annotated List of Books
  and Articles on Architecture Constructed before 1860 in the Eastern Half of the
  United States*. Columbus: The Ohio State University Press, 1943.

Pictorial Material:
Important Photographic Collections
  Andrews, Wayne. *Architectural Photographs*. New York, Series I-XIII to
    date [194-].
  Morris, Nathalie Lorillard Bailey. Collection of Photographs of Gothic
    Revival Houses in New York City and the Eastern Part of the
    United States, mainly by Alexander Jackson Davis. Morris
    Memorial Collection, Avery Library.

Collections of 19th Century Drawings, New York City
  Reference has been made, *passim*, to the important collections of
    drawings, and their respective catalogs or inventories, at the Avery
    Library by the following architects: Alexander Jackson Davis,
    Wilson Eyre, Calvin Pollard, John Calvin Stevens, Richard
    Upjohn, and Richard M. Upjohn. See also New-York Historical
    Society and Metropolitan Museum of Art for additional items of
    interest, particularly for Davis, Pollard, and Renwick.

Contemporary Sources

Periodical and Illustrated Weeklies:
*American Architect and Builders' Monthly, a Journal Devoted to Architecture and Art
  Generally*. [Philadelphia], March 1870-January 1871.
American Architect and Building News. Boston and New York, 1876-1908;
  American Architect and Architecture, 1908-1938.

American Builder. Chicago and New York, March 1868-May 1895. Continuous publication under different titles: *American Builder and Journal of Art,* March 1868-June 1873; *American Builder, a Journal of Industrial Art,* July 1873-December 1879; *Builder and Woodworker,* January 1880-March 1893; *Architectural Era,* April-December 1893; *Builder and Woodworker,* January-November 1894.

American Institute of Architects. *Proceedings of the Annual Conventions.* New York, 1867-1891.

Architects' and Mechanics' Journal. New York, 1859-1861. Complete copy at U.S. Patent Office, Washington, D.C.; Vol. I and microfilm of Vols. II-IV, Avery Library.

Architectural Record. New York, 1891-.

Architectural Review. Boston, 1891-1910.

Architectural Review and American Builders' Journal. Philadelphia. Vols. I-III. Separate numbers, July-December 1868, published as *Sloan's Architectural Review and Builder's Journal.*

Architectural Sketch-book (Portfolio Club). 4 volumes in 3. Boston, 1873-1876.

Architecture and Building. Continuous publication under varying titles: *Building, an Architectural Monthly,* 1882-1885; *Building, a Journal of Architecture,* 1886-1887; *Building, an Architectural Weekly,* 1888-1889; *Architecture and Building,* 1890-1899; *Architecture and Building, A Magazine Devoted to Contemporary Architectural Construction,* 1900-.

Ballou's Pictorial Drawing-Room Companion... Boston, 1851-1859. Vols. I-VII published as *Gleason's Pictorial Drawing-room Companion.*

College Art Association of America. *Art Bulletin.* Providence, New York, etc., 1913-.

Century. New York, November 1870-May 1930. Known as *Scribner's Monthly* to October 1881, thereafter as *Century Illustrated Magazine* and *Century.*

The Crayon. New York, January 1855-July 1861.

Gazette des beaux-arts. American edition. New York, 1942-.

Harper's Magazine. New York, 1850-. *Harper's New Monthly Magazine,* 1850-1900. Indexed for Vols. I-LXXXV, 1850-1892.

Harper's Weekly. New York, 1857-May 19, 1916.

Leslie's Illustrated Weekly Newspaper. New York, December 15, 1855-June 17, 1922. Known as *Frank Leslie's Illustrated Newspaper,* 1855-November 1891.

Magazine of Art. Washington, D.C., etc., 1909-1953.

New-York Ecclesiologist. New York, 1848-1853.

New-York Quarterly. Devoted to Science, Philosophy and Literature. New York, March 1852-July 1855.

New-York Weekly Review of Music, Literature, Fine Arts and Society. New York, June 1850-April 12, 1873.

Putnam's Magazine; Original Papers on Literature, Science, Art, and National Interest. New York, 1853-1870. Known as *Putnam's Monthly Magazine,* Vols. I-X, 1853-1857; new series, Vols. I-VI, January 1868-November 1870; merged with *Scribner's Monthly* in 1870.

Scribner's Monthly. See *ante* under *Century.*

Society of Architectural Historians. *Journal.* Troy, NY, etc., 1941-. First 4 volumes as *American Society of Architectural Historians.*

19th Century Books and Articles:

American Architect and Building News. A valuable source for the period 1876 ff. Specific articles referenced in footnotes.

AIA *Proceedings of the Annual Conventions.* The best source for the period between 1867-1876 before publication of the *American Architect.* Specific articles referenced in footnotes, but see Bloor (*post*, under New York Architecture).

Architects' and Mechanics' Journal. Consistently interesting and informative; the best source for its short period of publication (1859-1861). Specific articles referenced in footnotes.

The Crayon. Particularly valuable for the years 1855-1859 before publication of the *Architects' and Mechanics' Journal.*

Eidlitz, Leopold. *The Nature and Function of Art, More Especially of Architecture.* London: Samson Low, Marston, Searle, & Rivington, 1881. An interesting book, now largely forgotten.

[Gilman, Arthur Delevan]. "Architecture in the United States," a review of Edward Shaw's *Rural Architecture, North American Review,* Vol. LVIII (April 1844), pp. 436-480.

Greenough, Horatio. "American Architecture," *United States Magazine and Democratic Review,* Vol. XIII (August 1843), pp. 206 ff. This important article, now justly considered a classic, was reprinted many times within a few years of publication.

Harper's New Monthly Magazine. An excellent source for the point of view of the intelligent layman, e.g., "Our Houses," Vol. XIX (1859), pp. 513-518; Robert Tomes, "The Houses We Live In," Vol. XXX (May 1865), pp. 735-741, and other articles referenced in footnotes.

Owen, Robert Dale. *Hints on Public Architecture, Containing... Views and Plans of the Smithsonian Institution...* New York: George P. Putnam, 1849.

Poe, Edgar Allan. "The Philosophy of Furniture," (1845), reprinted in Poe, *The Complete Tales and Poems.* Introduction by Hervey Allen. New York: The Modern Library, 1938, pp. 462-466.

Putnam's Magazine. See comment on *Harper's.* Contains many interesting articles, e.g. "House Building in America," Vol. X (July 1857), pp. 107-111.

Sheldon, George William (editor). *Artistic Country Seats, Type of Recent American Villa and Cottage Architecture.* 2 volumes. New York: D. Appleton and Company, 1886-1887.

Sturgis, Russell, *et al. Homes in City and Country.* New York: Charles Scribner's Sons, 1893. A collection of essays of varying quality. The two by Sturgis and Bruce Price, both referenced in footnotes, are particularly interesting.

Villas on the Hudson. A Collection of Photo-lithographs of Thirty-one Country Residences. New York: D. Appleton & Company, 1860. Sometimes catalogued under A.A. turner, the photo-lithographer. An extremely handsome collection of views and plans of villas dating largely from the 1850s.

Wight, Peter Bonnet. "Remarks on Fire-proof Construction." A paper read before the New York Chapter of the AIA, April 8, 1869. [New York] Committee on Library and Publications, 1869.

Young, Ammi Burnham (U.S. Supervising Architect of the Treasury Department). *Plans of Public Buildings in Course of Construction...* Washington, D.C., 1855-1856. See also specifications of 1853 and 1856-1859.

Builder's Guides and Plan Books:

Allen, Lewis Falley. *Rural Architecture: Being a Complete Description of Farmhouses, Cottages and Outbuildings...* New York: C.M. Saxton, 1852 (8 issues to 1865).

Bullock, John. *The American Cottage Builder: a Series of Designs, Plans, and Specifications from $200 to $20,000. For Homes for the People.* New York: Stringer & Townsend, 1854 (4 issues to 1873).

Cleaveland, Henry William, William Backus, and Samuel D. Backus. *Village and Farm Cottages...* New York: D. Appleton and Company, 1856 (4 issues to 1869).

Downing, Andrew Jackson. *Additional Notes and Hints to Persons about Building in the Country* in George Wightwick's *Hints to Young Architects.* 1st American edition. New York and London: Wiley and Putnam, 1847 (first published in London, 1846).

_____. *The Architecture of Country Houses; Including Designs for Cottages, Farm Houses and Villas, with Remarks on Interiors, Furniture, and the Best Modes of Warming and Ventilating...* New York: D. Appleton & Company, 1850 (9 issues to 1866).

_____. *Cottage Residences; or a Series of Designs for Rural Cottages and Cottage-villas...* New York and London: Wiley & Putnam, 1842 (13 issues to 1887).

_____. *A Treatise on the Theory and Practice of Landscape Gardening... With Remarks on Rural Architecture...* New York and London: Wiley & Putnam, 1841 (16 issues of 8 editions to 1879).

Field, M. *City Architecture; or Designs for Dwelling Houses, Stores, Hotels, etc...* New York: G. Putnam & Company, 1853 (2nd issue in 1854).

_____. *Rural Architecture; or Designs for Villas, Cottages, etc., in the Italian, Gothic, Elizabethan, Old English, and Swiss Styles... Including a Critique on Ruskin's New Theoretical Principles of Design...* New York: Miller & Company, 1857.

Fowler, Orson Squire. *A Home for All; or The Gravel Wall and Octagon Mode of Building...* Revised and enlarged edition. New York: Fowlers and Wells, 1854 (1st edition, 1848, 8 issues in all).

Hobbs, Isaac, and Son. *Hobbs' Architecture: Containing Designs... for Villas, Cottages and Other Edifices. Both Suburban and Rural...* Philadelphia: J.B. Lippincott & Company, 1873 (2nd edition, revised and enlarged, 1876).

Holly, Henry Hudson. *Church Architecture...* Hartford: M.H. Mallory and Company, 1871.

_____. *Holly's Country Seats: Containing Lithographic Designs for Cottages, Villas, Mansions...; also Country Churches, City Buildings, Railway Stations, etc., etc...* New York: D. Appleton and Company, 1863 (ready for publication in 1861, according to Preface; 2nd edition, 1866).

_____. *Modern Dwellings in Town and Country... With a Treatise on Furniture and Decoration...* New York: Harper & Brothers, 1878.

A Book of Plans for Churches and Parsonages... Comprising Designs by Upjohn, Downing, Renwick, Wheeler, Wells, Austin, Stone, Cleveland, Backus, and Reeve. New York: Daniel Burgess & Company, 1853.

Lafever, Minard. *The Architectural Instructor...* New York: George P. Putnam, 1856.

Loring, Sanford E., and Jenney, William Le Baron. *Principles and Practice of Architecture... Also, an Explanation and Illustration of the French System of Apartments Houses, and Dwellings for the Laboring Classes...* Chicago, Cleveland, etc.: Cobb, Pritchard & Company, 1869.

Ranlett, William H. *The Architect, a Series of Original Designs, for Domestic and Ornamental Cottages and Villas...* New York: DeWitt & Davenport. Edition cited: Vol. I, 1851 edition, Vol. II, 1849 edition (issued in parts, 1846-1848; published in book form for first time by William H. Graham, 1847-1849).

Ritch, John Warren. *The American Architect, Comprising Original Designs of Cheap Country Houses and Village Residences...* New York: C.M. Saxton, 1852 [?] (8 issues from 1847-[1856?]).

Sloan, Samuel. *City and Suburban Architecture; Containing Numerous Designs and Details for Public Edifices, Private Residences, and Mercantile Buildings...* Philadelphia: J.B. Lippincott & Company, 1859 (2nd issue in 1867).

_____. *The Model Architect. A Series of Original Designs for Cottages, Villas, Suburban Residences, etc...* 2 volumes. Philadelphia: E.S. Jones & Company [c.1852]. (5 editions to 1873).

_____. *Sloan's Constructive Architecture; a Guide to the Practical Builder and Mechanic...* Philadelphia: J.B. Lippincott & Company, 1859 (3 issues to 1873).

_____. *Sloan's Homestead Architecture...* Philadelphia: L.B. Lippincott, 1861 (3 editions to 1870).

Vaux, Calvert. *Villas and Cottages...* New York: Harper & Brothers, 1857 (6 issues of 2nd editions to 1874).

Wheeler, Gervase. *Homes for the People in Suburb and Country; the Villa, the Mansion and the Cottage... With Examples Showing How to Alter and Remodel Old Buildings...* New York: Charles Scribner, 1855 (1st edition, 1854, destroyed, 6 issues through 1868).

Wills, Frank. *Ancient English Ecclesiastical Architecture and Its Principles, Applied to the Wants of the Church at the Present Day...* New York: Stanford and Swords, 1850.

Woodward, George Evertson. *Woodward's Country Homes...*New York: George E. Woodward, c.1865 (8 issues to some time after 1870).

—————. *Woodward's Suburban and Country Houses...* New York: The American News Company [c.1873].

20th Century History and Criticism

Andrews, Wayne. *Architecture, Ambition and Americans...* New York: Harper & Brothers [1955].

Bennister, Turpin C. "Bogardus Revisited," *Journal of the Society of Architectural Historians*, Vol. XV (December 1956), pp. 12-22; Vol. XVI (March 1957), pp. 11-19.

Brown, Glenn. *The American Institute of Architects, 1857-1907; Historical Sketch...* Washington, D.C.: Gibson, 1907?.

Buchanan, Agnes Foster. "Some Early Business Buildings in San Francisco," *Architectural Record*, Vol. XX (July 1906), pp. 15-32.

Coolidge, John Phillips. *Mill and Mansion, a Study of Architecture and Society in Lowell, Massachusetts, 1820-1865.* New York: Columbia University Press, 1942.

Creese, Walter. "Fowler and the Domestic Octagon," *Art Bulletin*, Vol. XXVIII (March 1946), pp. 89-102.

Danes, Gibson. "William Morris Hunt and His Newport Circle," *Magazine of Art*, Vol. XLIII (April 1950), pp. 144 ff.

Dow, Joy Wheeler. *American Renaissance; a Review of Domestic Architecture.* New York: W.T. Comstock [1904].

Edgell, George Harold. *The American Architecture of Today.* New York: Charles Scribner's Sons, 1928.

Fitch, James Marston. *American Building; the Forces That Shape It.* Boston: Houghton Mifflin Company, 1948.

Hamlin, Talbot Faulkner. *The American Spirit in Architecture.* New Haven: Yale University Press, 1926. (Vol. XIII: *The Pageant of America*).

—————. *Greek Revival Architecture in America: Being an Account of Important Trends in American Architecture and American Life Prior to the War Between the States.* London: Oxford University Press, 1944.

—————. *Benjamin Henry Latrobe.* New York: Oxford University Press, 1955.

Hartmann, Sadakichi. "A Conversation With Henry Janeway Hardenbergh," *Architectural Record*, Vol. XIX (May 1906), pp. 377-380.

Hitchcock, Henry-Russell, Jr. *The Architecture of H.H. Richardson and His Times.* New York: The Museum of Modern Art, 1936.

—————. "Frank Lloyd Wright and the Academic Tradition of the Early Eighteen-Eighties," *Journal of the Warburg and Courtauld Institutes*, Vol. VII (January-June 1944), pp. 46-63.

_____. *Rhode Island Architecture*. Providence: Rhode Island Museum Press, 1939.

Howland, Richard Hubbard, and Spencer, Eleanor Patterson. *The Architecture of Baltimore, a Pictorial History*. Edited by Wilbur Harvey Hunter, introduction by Richard Hubbard Howland. [1st edition. Baltimore]: Johns Hopkins University, 1953.

Kimball, Sidney Fiske. *American Architecture*. Indianapolis and New York: The Bobbs-Merrill Company [c.1929].

_____. *Domestic Architecture of the American Colonies and of the Early Republic*. New York: Charles Scribner's Sons, 1922.

Kouwenhoven, John Atlee. *Made in America; the Arts in Modern Civilization*. New York: Doubleday & Company, Inc., 1948.

LaFollette, Suzanne. *Art in America; from Colonial Times to the Present Day*. New York: Harper & Brothers, 1929.

Lancaster, Clay. "Ammi B. Young—His Work as First Supervising Architect of the U.S. Treasury Department". Unpublished manuscript [194?].

_____. "Fads in Nineteenth-Century American Architecture," *Antiques*, Vol. LXVIII (August 1955), pp. 144-147.

_____. "Some Octagonal Forms in Southern Architecture," *Art Bulletin*, Vol. XXVIII (March 1946), pp. 103-111.

Larkin, Oliver W. *Art and Life in America*. New York: Rinehart [1949].

Lynes, Russell. *The Tastemakers*. [1st edition. New York]: Harper & Brothers [1954].

Maass, John. *The Gingerbread Age; a View of Victorian America*. New York: Rinehart & Company, Inc. [1957].

Mason, George Champlin [Jr.]. *Architects and Their Environment, 1850-1907, Together with Notes and Reminiscences of the Fathers of the Profession, Their Clients, and Assistants...* Ardmore, PA: 1907.

McKenna, Rosalie Thorne. "James Renwick, Jr., and the Second Empire Style in the United States," *Magazine of Art*, Vol. XLIV (March 1951), pp. 97-101.

_____. *A Study of the Architecture of the Main Building of Vassar College, 1860-1870*. Poughkeepsie, NY: M.A. thesis, Vassar College, 1949.

Meeks, Carroll [Louis Vanderslice]. "Henry Austin and the Italian Villa," *Art Bulletin*, Vol. XXX (June 1948), pp. 145-149.

_____. "Romanesque Before Richardson in the United States," *ibid.*, Vol. XXXV (March 1953), pp. 17-33.

Morrison, Hugh. *Early American Architecture from the First Colonial Settlements to the National Period*. New York: Oxford University Press, 1952.

Mumford, Lewis. *The Brown Decades; a Study of the Arts in America, 1865-1895*. 2nd revised edition. New York: Dover Publications, Inc., 1955. 1st edition [c.1931] based on "The Arts in America since 1870," lectures at Dartmouth College, December 1929.

_____. *Sticks and Stones, a Study of American Architecture and Civilization.* New York: Dover Publications, Inc. [1955]. 1st edition [c.1924].

Newton, Roger Hale. "Our Summer Resort Architecture—An American Phenomenon and Social Document," *Art Quarterly*, Vol. IV (Autumn 1941), pp. 297-322.

_____. *Town & Davis, Architects, Pioneers in American Revivalist Architecture, 1812-1870...* New York: Columbia University Press, 1942.

Philadelphia Art Alliance. *Philadelphia Architecture in the Nineteenth Century.* Thomas B. White, editor. William B. Harbeson *et al.* Philadelphia: University of Pennsylvania Press, 1953.

Saylor, Henry H. "The AIA's First Hundred Years," *Journal of the American Institute of Architects*, Vol. XXVIII (May 1957), Part II.

Schuyler, Montgomery. *American Architecture.* New York: Harper & Brothers, 1892.

_____. "Architectural Essays, 1879-1913". 3 volumes. A collection of Schuyler's essays, specially bound for him. On deposit at the Avery Library.

_____. "A Great American Architect: Leopold Eidlitz," *Architectural Record*, Vol. XXIV (1908), pp. 163-179, 277-292, and 364-378.

_____. "The Romanesque Revival in America," *ibid.*, Vol. I (October-December 1891), pp. 151-198.

_____. "Work of Henry Janeway Hardenbergh," *ibid.*, Vol. VI (January-March 1897), pp. 335-375.

_____. "The Work of N. Le Brun & Sons," *ibid.*, Vol. XXVII (May 1910), pp. 365-381.

_____. "The Work of William Appleton Potter," *ibid.*, Vol. XXVI (July-December 1909), pp. 176 ff.

_____. "The Works of the late Richard Morris Hunt," *ibid.*, Vol. V (October-December 1895), pp. 97-180.

Scully, Vincent, Jr. "American Villas; Inventiveness in the American Suburb from Downing to Wright," *Architectural Review*, Vol. CXV (March 1954), pp. 168-179.

_____. "Nineteenth Century Resort Architecture". Part IV of Antoinette A. Downing and Scully, *The Architectural Heritage of Newport, Rhode Island, 1630-1915.* Cambridge: Harvard University Press, 1952.

_____. "Romantic Rationalism and the Expression of Structure in Wood: Downing, Wheeler, Gardner and the 'Stick Style,'" *Art Bulletin*, Vol. XXXV (June 1953), pp. 121-142.

_____. *The Shingle Style; Architectural Theory and Design from Richardson to the Origins of Wright.* New Haven: Yale University Press, 1955. (Yale Historical Publications. History of Art: 10).

Smith, Robert C. *John Notman and the Atheneum Building.* Philadelphia, 1951.

Sturges, Walter Knight. "The Long Shadow of Norman Shaw," *Journal of the Society of Architectural Historians*, Vol. IX (December 1953), pp. 15-20.

Sturgis, Russell. "Scrapbook of Architectural Clippings". 3 volumes. On deposit at the Avery Library.

Tallmadge, Thomas Eddy. *The Story of Architecture in America.* New, enlarged and revised edition. New York: W.W. Norton & Company [c.1936].

Tatum, George Bishop. "Andrew Jackson Downing: Arbiter of American Taste, 1815-1852". [Ann Arbor, MI, 1950]. Ph.D. dissertation, Princeton University.

Upjohn, Everard Miller. *Richard Upjohn, Architect and Churchman.* New York: Columbia University Press, 1939.

Upjohn, Hobart. Miscellaneous papers on the early years of the American Institute of Architects. Owned by Everard M. Upjohn.

Vogel, F. Rud. *Das Amerikanische Haus....* Berlin: Wasmuth, 1910.

Wight, Peter Bonnett. "Reminiscences of Russell Sturgis," *Architectural Record,* Vol. XXVI (August 1909), pp. 123-131.

Wischnitzer, Rachel. *Synagogue Architecture in the United States, History and Interpretation.* Philadelphia: The Jewish Publication Society of America, 5716-1955.

Wriston, Barbara. "The Architecture of Thomas Tefft," *Bulletin of the Museum of Art, Rhode Island School of Design,* Vol. XXVIII (November 1940), pp. 37-45.

New York City in the Second Half of the 19th Century

General Reference
Primary Sources

Public Records:

New York City. Department of Buildings, Municipal Building.
New Building Dockets, June 4, 1866-. Room 2000.
Alteration Dockets, 1866-. Room 2000.
Index. Room 2012.
Plan Desk. Room 2021. Plans, new building and alteration applications, inspection reports. Filed according to Block and Lot.
_____. Department of Health.
Index of Deaths, 1884-1954. Available at the New York Public Library.
_____. Tax Assessment Records. Municipal Archives and Records Center, New York Public Library, 238 William Street.

New York County. Surrogates Court. Record of Wills.
Bound volumes preserved in Room 402, Hall of Records, 31 Chambers Street. For index, see *post* under Biography and Genealogy.

New York State. Census Records. Preserved in County Clerk's Office of their respective boroughs. For Manhattan: Room 703, Hall of Records, 31 Chambers Street.

Newspapers:
The Evening Post, 1901-.
The New York Times, 1851-. Index available on microfilm.
The New York Tribune, 1841-. Index, 1875 ff.
The World: New York, 1860-1893.

Periodicals:
Listed under U.S.

Directories:

General Directories

New York City directories are most conveniently consulted on microfilm in the Main Reading Room, New York Public Library. Available for 1786-1933/1934 on 77 reels.

Pictorial Directories

In addition to furnishing illustrations, several of the pictorial directories of 1848 and 1850 list each firm and every occupant of a building, often in both numerical and alphabetical order.

Business Directories

Directories such as *The Citizen and Strangers' Pictorial and Business Directory of 1853* (edited by Solyman Brown), G. Danielson Carroll's *New York City Directory* of 1859, Gobright's *Union Sketch-Book* of 1860, and many others, are particularly valuable for their illustrated advertisements. In some cases, directories of special trades or business associations (bankers' almanacs, etc.) are available.

Social Directories

Directories such as *Phillips' Elite Directory*, issued under varying titles in the 1870s, and Maurice Minton's *The List*, 1880 ff., forerunners of the *Social Register*, 1887 ff., are often useful.

Directories of Foreign Nationals

E.g., Augustin P. Mange, *Directory français...*, New-York: Mange, 1864, which has been useful for this study—one of many such directories.

Contemporary Descriptions, Guides, and Travel Books

Andrews & Co.'s Stranger's Guide in the City of New-York, 1852. New York: Andrews & Company, 1852. A catalog of important merchants in New York, well illustrated.

Belden, Ezekiel Porter. *New-York: Past, Present, and Future...* New York: G.P. Putnam, 1849. Bound together with *idem.*, *New-York—as It Is; Being the Counterpart of the Metropolis of America...* New York: John P. Prall, 1849. The best book on New York in the mid-century, illustrated with fine prints.

Browne, Junius Henri. *The Great Metropolis; a Mirror of New York...* Hartford: American Publishing Company, 1869. A very informative book covering all phases of life.

The Citizen and Strangers' Pictorial and Business Directory for the City of New York... 1853. Edited by Solyman Brown. New York: Spalding [1853].

The City of New York: a Complete Guide... New York: Taintor Brothers, 1867 and various dates. Very well illustrated.

A Description of the Cities, Townships, and Principal Villages and Settlements, within Thirty Miles of the City of New-York... New York: Colton & Disturnell, 1839.

[Disturnell, John]. *Guide to the City of New York...* New York: J. Disturnell, 1836 and various dates.

Francis's New Guide to the Cities of New-York and Brooklyn, and the Vicinity... New York: C.S. Francis, various dates 1853 edition issued under title of *The Strangers' Handbook for the City of New York...*

Frei, Joh. *Drei Monate in New York; oder, Die grosse Metropole der neuen Welt...* Zurich: Im Selbstverlag des Verfassers, 1869.

Gobright, John Christopher, and Dawes. *The Union Sketch-book: a Reliable Guide, Exhibiting the History and Business Resources of the Leading Mercantile and Manufacturing Concerns of New York...* New York: Pudney & Russell, 1860.

[Greene, Asa]. *A Glance at New York...* New York: A. Greene, 1837.

Holley, Orville Luther. *A Description of the City of New York: with a Brief Account of the Cities, Towns, Villages, and Places of Resort within Thirty Miles...* New York: Disturnell, 1847.

King, Moses. *King's Handbook of New York City; An Outline History and Description of the American Metropolis, with over one thousand illustration...* 2nd edition. Boston: Moses King [c.1893]. The Avery Library's copy of this valuable book has manuscript notes by Dr. E. Allen Jennings.

[Lester, Charles Edwards]. *Glances at the Metropolis.* New York: Isaac D. Guyer [1854].

Macoy, Robert. *Centennial Illustrated. How to See New York and Its Environs.* New York: Robert Macoy, 1876.

Miller's New York as It Is; or Strangers' Guide-book to the Cities of New York, Brooklyn, and Adjacent Places... New York: James Miller, 1859-1877. 17 volumes, of which no one institution has a complete set.

New York Illustrated. New York: D. Appleton & Company, 1869 and various dates. Very well illustrated; good text.

Phelps' New York City Guide... New York: T.C. Fanning [1850-1870]. A small pocket edition, with clear prints.

Redfield's Traveler's Guide to the City of New York. New York: J.S. Redfield, 1871. Excellent for this period.

Reiss, N., le docteur. *Excursion a New-York, en 1850.* Bruxelles: J.N. Gregoir, 1851. Excellent general description, with comments on architecture.

Ross, Joel H., M.D. *What I Saw in New-York; or A Bird's Eye View of City Life.* Auburn, NY: Debry & Miller, 1851. Entertaining, well written account.

Ruggles, Edward. *A Picture of New-York in 1846...* New York: C.S. Francis & Company, 1846. Same as Homans & Ellis edition.

Saunders, Frederick. *New-York in a Nutshell, or Visitors' Handbook to the City...* New York: T.W. Strong, 1853. An excellent description containing personal reminiscences, etc.

Smith, Matthew Hale. *Sunshine and Shadow in New York.* Hartford: J.B. Burr and Company, 1868. A very long, chatty book covering all phases of life, similar to Brown's *The Great Metropolis;* excellent biographical sketches of city's leading men.

Stranger's Guide around New York and Its Vicinity... New York: W.H. Graham [c.1853].

Suvorov, Knyaginya. *Quarante jours a New-York: impressions de voyage.* Paris: E. Dentu, 1878. Intelligent observations of a Russian princess.

Thehla, Georg. *Drei Jahre in New-York...* Zwickau: Verein zur Verbreitung gutter und wohnfeiler Volksschriften, 1862.

Vetter, Christof. *Zwei Jahre in New-York, Schilderung einer Seereise von Havre nach New-York und Charakteristik des New-Yorker Politischen und Socialen Lebens.* Hof: Im Selbstverlag des Verfassers, 1849.

Viele, Egbert L. *The West End Plateau of the City of New York.* New York: Johnson & Pratt, 1879.

Walling, Henry Francis. *The City of New York: A Complete Guide...* New York: Taintor Brothers & Company, 1867.

Whitman, Walt. *New York Dissected, by Walt Whitman; a Sheaf of Recently Discovered Newspaper Articles by the Author of Leaves of Grass.* Introduction and annotation by Emory Holloway and Ralph Adamari. New York: R.R. Wilson, Inc., 1936.

Wood's Illustrated Hand-book to New York and Its Environs New York: G.W. Carleton & Company, 1873. Excellent guide, well illustrated.

Diaries and Memoirs

Armstrong, David Maitland. *Day before Yesterday; Reminiscences of a Varied Life, by Maitland Armstrong, 1836-1918.* Edited by Margaret Armstrong. New York: Charles Scribner's Sons, 1920.

Chambers, Julius. *The Book of New York; Forty Years' Recollections of an American Metropolis.* New York: The Book of New York Company [1912]. Reminiscences of the former managing editor of *The New York Herald* and *World*; good biographical material on the architects of the later 19th and early 20th centuries.

Clews, Henry. *Twenty-eight Years in Wall Street.* New York: Irving Publishing Company, 1888.

Dayton, Abram Child. *Last Days of Knickerbocker Life in New York.* New York: G.W. Harlan, 1882.

Floyd-Jones, Thomas. *Backward Glances; Reminiscences of an Old New Yorker.* New York, 1914.

Harris, Charles Townsend. *Memories of Manhattan in the Sixties and Seventies.* New York: The Derrydale Press, 1928.

Haswell, Charles H. *Reminiscences of an Octogenarian of the City of New York (1816-1860).* New York: Harper & Brothers, 1896. Interesting memoirs by an important consulting engineer.

Hone, Philip. *The Diary of Philip Hone, 1828-1851.* Edited with an introduction by Allan Nevins. New and enlarged edition. New York: Dodd, Mead & Company, 1936. Original preserved at the New-York Historical Society.

Mines, John Flavel. *A Tour Around New York and My Summer Acre; Being the Recreations of Mr. Felix Oldboy.* New York: Harper & Brothers, 1893.

Strong, George Templeton. *The Diary of George Templeton Strong.* Edited by Allan Nevins and Milton Halsey Thomas. 4 volumes. New York: The

Macmillan Company, 1952. Microfilm copy of original "Journal" at the New York Public Library; microfilm prints at Columbiana, Columbia University.

Biography and Genealogy

Bibliographic Aids:

Bailey, Rosalie Fellows. *Guide to Genealogical and Biographical Sources for New York City (Manhattan), 1783-1898.* New York: Published by the author, 1954. Invaluable guide to sources on New York.

Barber, Gertrude A. "Deaths Taken from *The New York Evening Post,* 1800-1890." 54 volumes. Typescript, Room 328, New York Public Library.

Sawyer, Ray C. "Index of Wills for New York County, New York. From 1851 to 1865, Inclusive." 3 volumes. Typescript, 1950-1951, New York Genealogical and Biographical Society, 122 East 58th Street.

Sources and Reference Works

Armstrong, William. *The Aristocracy of New York: Who They Are, and What They Were; Being a Social and Business of the City... by an Old Resident.* New York: New York Publishing Company, 1848.

[Beach, Moses Yale]. *Wealth and Biography of the Wealthy Citizens of New York City, Comprising an Alphabetical Arrangement of Persons Estimated to be Worth $100,000 and Upwards... and Now Containing Brief Biographical and Genealogical Notices.* 6th edition. New York: The Sun Office, 1845. Published at various dates, 1842 ff.

Fiske, Stephen. *Off-hand Portraits of Prominent New Yorkers.* New York: G.R. Lockwood & Son, 1884.

Hamm, Margherita Arlina. *Famous Families of New York; Historical and Biographical Sketches of Families... Identified with the Development of the Nation.* 2 volumes. New York: G.P. Putnam's Sons [c.1902]. Standard reference work.

[King, Moses]. *Notable New Yorkers of 1896-1899...* New York: M. King [c.1899].

Lemke, Theodor. *Gesschichte des Deutschthums von New York von 1848 bis zur Gegenwart.* New York: T. Lemke, 1891.

Medbury, James K. *Men and Mysteries of Wall Street.* Boston: Fields, Osgood & Company, 1870.

Morris, Charles (editor). *Makers of New York; An Historical Work Giving Portraits and Sketches of the Most Eminent Citizens of New York.* Philadelphia: L.R. Hamersly & Company, 1895. His *Men of Affairs in New York,* 1906, is actually a 2nd edition of the above.

New York Genealogical and Biographical Record. 86 volumes to date. New York: Genealogical & Biographical Society, 1870-.

[Scoville, Joseph A.]. *The Old Merchants of New York City.* By Walter Barrett, clerk [pseudonym]. 2nd series, 2 volumes. New York: Carlton, 1863. Number of volumes and dates of publication of the various series are impossible to ascertain without extensive research, since entries vary from library to library. A 5-volume edition was published by Thomas R. Knox in 1885. An excellent reference source for earlier period.

[Sprague, John Franklin]. *New York, the Metropolis. Its Noted Business and Professional Men...* [New York:] The New York Recorder, 1893. Part II (Biographical) contains a great deal of information on New York architects of the latter part of the century.

Van Rensselaer, May (King). *New Yorkers of the XIXth Century.* New York and London: F.T. Neely, 1897.

Vose, Reuben. *The Rich Men of New York.* Series No. 2. New York: Francis & Loutrel, 1861. Series Nos. 3 and 4 issued 1862.

_____. *Reuben Vose's Wealth of the World Displayed.* New York: Reuben Vose, 1859. Contains a great deal of interesting information.

[Weeks, Lyman Horace (editor)]. *Prominent Families of New York.* Revised edition. New York: The Historical Company [1898]. Classic reference work.

Histories of New York

General

Albion, Robert Greenlalgh, and Pope, Jennie Barnes. *The Rise of New York Port (1815-1860).* New York: Charles Scribner's Sons, 1939. An extremely useful book; excellent bibliography.

Booth, Mary Louise. *History of the City of New York.* 2 volumes. New York: W.R.C. Clark, 1867; also E.P. Dutton & Company, 1880.

Brown, Henry Collins. *Book of Old New-York.* New York: Privately printed [The Lent & Graff Company], 1913.

_____. *Fifth Avenue, Old and New, 1824-1924.* New York: The Fifth Avenue Association, 1924.

_____. *The Story of Old New York...* New York: E.P. Dutton & Company, Inc. [c.1934].

_____ (editor). *Valentine's Manual of Old New York.* New York: Valentine's Manual, Inc., c.1916-c.1928.

Dunshee, Kenneth Holcomb. *As You Pass By.* New York: Hastings House [1952].

Kouwenhoven, John Atlee. *The Columbia Historical Portrait of New York.* Garden City, NY: Doubleday and Company, 1953. An excellent all-round reference work, profusely illustrated.

Fifth Avenue Bank of New York. *Fifth Avenue. Glances at the Vicissitudes and Romance of a World-renowned Thoroughfare.* Boston: [Walton Advertising and Printing Company], 1915.

Lamb, Mrs. Martha Joanna Reade (Nash), and Harrison, Mrs. Burton. *History of the City of New York: Its Origins, Rise and Progress.* 3 volumes. Enlarged edition. New York: A.S. Barnes and Company [c.1877-1896].

Lanier, Henry Wysham. *A Century of Banking in New York, 1822-1922.* The Farmers' Loan and Trust Company edition. New York: The Gilliss Press, 1922.

Leonard, John William. *History of the City of New York, 1609-1909... together with Brief Biographies of Men Representative of the Business Interests of the City.* 2 volumes. New York: Journal of Commerce and Commercial Bulletin, 1910.

Lossing, Benson John. *History of New York City... from 1609 to... 1884.* New York: G.E. Perine [c.1884].

Morris, Lloyd R. *Incredible New York; High Life and Low Life of the Last Hundred Years.* New York: Random House [1951].

New York City, Common Council. *Manual of the Corporation of the City of New York...,* known as Valentine's Manuals. 28 volumes. New York, 1841/1842-1866; 1868-1870. See *Historical Index to the Manuals of the Corporation of the City of New York, 1840 to 1870...* New York: F.P. Harper, 1900.

New-York Historical Society. *New York City, Then and Now, 1626-1924* (Alexander J. Wall, Jr., editor). New York: New-York Historical Society, 1942.

Richmond, John Fletcher. *New York and Its Institutions, 1609-1872...* New York: E.B. Treat, 1872.

Roosevelt, Theodore. *New York.* New edition. New York: Longmans, Green, and Company, 1895. First published c.1891.

"Scrapbook of Newspaper Clippings on Old New York." [New York? 1927?] Available in Room 328, New York Public Library.

Stokes, Isaac Newton Phelps. *New York Past and Present, Its History and Landmarks, 1524-1939...* [New York: Plantin Press, 1939].

——————. *The Iconography of Manhattan Island, 1498-1909.* 6 volumes. New York: Dodd, 1915-1929. The classic reference work, monumental in scope.

Van Pelt, Daniel. *Leslie's History of Greater New York.* 3 volumes. New York: Arkell Publishing Company [c.1898].

Wilson, James Grant (editor). *The Memorial History of the City of New-York, from Its First Settlement to the year 1892.* 4 volumes. New York: New York History Company, 1892-1893.

Immigrant Life

Ernst, Robert. *Immigrant Life in New York City, 1825-1863.* New York: King's Crown Press, Columbia University, 1949. Contains a great deal of useful information; excellent bibliography.

Klaghorn, Kate H. "The Foreign Immigrant in New York City," *U.S. Industrial Commission Reports.* Washington, DC: U.S. Government Printing Office, Vol. XV (1901), pp. 449-492.

Housing Reform (the French Flat and the Tenement Problem):

Atkins, Gordon. *Health, Housing and Poverty in New York City, 1865-1898.* Ph.D. dissertation, Columbia University, 1947. Ann Arbor, MI: Edwards Brothers, Inc., 1947.

De Forest, Robert W., and Veiller, Lawrence (editors). *The Tenement House Problem*. 2 volumes. New York: The Macmillan Company, 1903.

Ford, James, *et al. Slums and Housing*. 2 volumes. Cambridge: Harvard University Press, 1936.

Newspaper Editorials. Various articles in *The New York Times* and *The World: New York*, references in footnotes.

Richardson, James H. "The New Homes of New York—A Study of Flats," *Scribner's Monthly*, Vol. VIII (1874), pp. 63-76.

Riis, Jacob August. *How the Other Half Lives; Studies among the Tenements of New York*. New York, 1890.

Runnion, James B. "Our City Homes—What They Are and What They Should Be," *American Builder*, Vol. I (October 1869), pp. 184-186.

Vaux, Calvert. Paper, later published under the title of "Parisian Dwellings for City Residents," read at a meeting of the AIA, June 2, 1857, *The Crayon*, Vol. IV (July 1857), p. 218.

Whitman, Walt. "Decent Homes for Working Men," and "Wicked Architecture," *Life Illustrated*, April 12, and July 19, 1856. In Whitman, *New York Dissected...; A Sheaf of Recently Discovered Newspaper Articles by the Author of Leaves of Grass*. Introduction and notes by Emory Holloway and Ralph Adamari, New York: R.R. Wilson, Inc., 1936, pp. 98 ff. and 92 ff. respectively.

Architecture

General Pictorial Material:

Contemporary Prints and Views

Since there is considerable duplication and overlapping among the various print collections (Davies, Eno, Pyne, Stokes, etc.), as well as in modern publications (Brown, Stokes, etc.), the following list includes only those items that were most directly useful for this study.

Eno Collection of New York City Views, New York Public Library
  Original prints and photostatic reproductions in 4 volumes, available in the Print Room; rare items in the Reserve Room
  Catalog by F. Weitenkampf, New York: The New York Public Library, 1925, available in most libraries.
Note especially the following for New York c.1850:
  Henry Hoff's *Views of New York*, 1850. *Eno*, No. 230.
  Jones, Newman & Ewbank, *The Illuminated Pictorial Directory of New York*, New York, 1848. *Eno*, No. 222.
  New-York Pictorial Directory of Wall-st., 1850, New York: C. Lowenstrom [1849]. *Eno*, No. 230.
  And other items referenced in footnotes.

New York City, Common Council. *Manual of the Corporation of the City of New York... Valentine's Manuals*. 28 volumes. New York: 1841/1842-1866; 1868-1870. Use with *Index to the Illustrations in the Manuals of the Corporation of the City of New York, 1841-1870*. New

York: Society of Iconophiles, 1906. See also Valentine, David T. [*Illustrations for Valentine's Manual*. New York: 1854-1867].

Maps, Atlases, and Land Books
Maps of Special Interest:
> *Map of the City of New-York Extending Northward to Fiftieth Street.* New York: M. Dripps, 1852.
> *Plan of New York from the Battery to Spuyten Duyvil.* New York: M. Dripps, 1868, 20 plates.

Atlases and Land Books
> *Land Book of the Borough of Manhattan, New York City.* New York: G.W. Bromley, etc., various dates.
> Robinson, E., and Pidgeon, R.H. *Robinson's Atlas of the City of New York.* E. Robinson, 1885.

Photographic Collections and Scrapbooks
Brown Brothers, photographers, 220 West 42nd Street, New York.

Fifth Avenue Association, Empire State Building, New York. "Fifth Avenue from Start to Finish," New York, 1911. Etc.

Municipal Art Society, 119 East 19th Street.

Museum of the City of New York. "Scrapbook," Print Room.

New-York Historical Society. Photographic Collection, Print and Map Room.

New York Public Library.
> American History Division, Room 300.
>> Sperr, P.L. "A Collection of Photographic Views of New York City Streets." Bulk of photographs taken in 1935-1938, with some earlier views.
> Local History and Genealogy Division, Room 328.
>> "Scrapbook of Views of New York City." Bound in volumes according to street numbers.
>> Rosenfeld, J.C. "New York City Scrapbook."
> Picture Collection, Room 73.

Real Estate Board of New York, 12 East 41st Street.

Picture Books (or Books with Special Pictorial Interest)
Abbott, Bernice, and McAusland, Elizabeth. *Changing New York.* New York: E.P. Dutton, Inc., 1939.

Brown, Henry Collins. *Views of Old New-York.* New York: Valentine's Manual, 1928.

_____. *Glimpse of Old New-York.* New York: Privately printed [Lent & Graff Company], 1917.

_____. *Old New York, Yesterday and Today.* New York: Privately printed for Valentine's Manual, 1922. Another edition entitled *Old New York* issued same year.

Feininger, Andreas, and Lyman, Susan E. *The Face of New York, the City as It Was and As It Is.* New York: Crown Publishers, Inc., 1954.
King, Moses. *King's Views of New York.* [New York] King [c.1905]. Later issues in 1906, 1908, etc.
Pelletreau, William Smith. *Early New York Houses, with Historical and Genealogical Notes.* New York: Harper, 1900.
Old Buildings of New York City with Some Notes Regarding Their Origin and Occupants. New York: Brentano's, 1907.

Contemporary Publications and Articles:
Architectural Iron Works of the City of New York, *Illustrations of Iron Architecture...* New York: Baker & Goodwin, 1865. Available at the Avery Library.
American Builder and Journal of Art, 1868-1869. Contains an interesting series, "Our New York Letter," beginning in issue of December 1868 and terminating in November 1869. Probably by Clarence Cook.
[Cook, Clarence Chatham]. "The Modern Architecture of New York," *The New-York Quarterly,* Vol. IV (April 1855), pp. 105-123.
Description, Guide, and Travel Books. References to the many interesting descriptions of New York's architecture in these books are documented in footnotes.
Diaries and Memoirs. See *ante* for references to Haswell, Hone, Strong, Wharton, etc. For Strong, see Ellen W. Kramer, *post.*
A History of Real Estate, Building and Architecture in New York City during the Last Quarter of a Century. New York: Record and Guide [c.1898]. Copies of this unique reference work are at the Avery Library and the New York Public Library. The earlier edition (1894) in the NYPL contains neither the interesting articles on special topics by Montgomery Schuyler and others, nor the informative chronological list of buildings and alphabetical lists of work by prominent New York architects, so useful in the 1898 edition.
Kennion, John W. *The Architects' and Builders' Guide. An Elaborate Description of All the Public, Commercial, Philanthropic, Literary & Ecclesiastical Buildings Already Constructed, and About to be Erected Next Spring in New York and Its Environs, with Their Cost Respectively, and the Names of Their Architects and Builders.* New York: Fitzpatrick & Hunter [c.1898]. Preface dated November 1867. A very useful source.
Nikkelson, Michael A. "A Review of the History of Real Estate on Manhattan Island," *A History of Real Estate, Architecture and Building,* pp. 1-129.
New-York Weekly Review, 1865. Contains the extremely interesting series of articles devoted to New York architecture, "Our Streets," which appeared weekly from January 14 to May 20 and from September 2 to 23, 1865. The caustic tone and stylistic preferences indicate strong possibility of attribution to Clarence Cook.

Newspapers. See footnotes for specific references to articles in the *Evening Post, The Herald, The New York Times,* and *The World.*

Periodicals. See footnotes and *ante* for comments on *The Crayon, Architects' and Mechanics' Journal, Harper's, Putnam's, etc.*

Putnam's New Monthly Magazine, 1853-1854. Contains the anonymous, well informed and charmingly illustrated series, "New York Daguerreotyped," whose tentative attribution to Clarence Cook merits investigation. Seven articles covering all phases of architecture, beginning in Vol. I (February 1853), p. 121 ff. and ending in Vol. III (March 1854), pp. 233 ff.

"Review of Architecture. History of Work Done in New York City during the Last Quarter of a Century," *A History of Real Estate, Architecture and Building,* pp. 553-612.

Schuyler, Montgomery. "Italian Gothic in New York," *Architectural Record,* Vol. XXVI (July 1909), pp. 46-54.

_____. "Recent Building in New York," a series of five articles on public and commercial buildings, and dwellings, in *American Architect,* Vol. IX (April and May 1881), pp. 176-177, 183-184, 196-197, 207-208 and 243-244.

_____. The Small City House in New York," *Architectural Record,* Vol. VIII (April-June 1899), pp. 537-588.

_____. The Romanesque Revival in New York," *Architectural Record,* Vol. I (July-September 1891), pp. [7]-38.

[Thomson, John W.]. *Cast-iron Buildings: Their Construction and Advantages. By James Bogardus, C.E., Architect in Iron...* New York: J.W. Harrison & Company, 1856.

Types of Mercantile Buildings; an Illustrated Review of Thirty Years Work. New York: Record and Guide, 1899.

Whitman, Walt. "Grand Buildings in New York City," *The Brooklyn Daily Times,* June 5, 1857. In Whitman, *I Sit and Look Out, Editorials from the Brooklyn Daily Times.* Edited by Emory Holloway and Vernolian Schwarz. New York: University Press, 1932, pp. 127-130. An important article whose significance was not made clear by Charles Netzger, "Whitman on Architecture," *SAH Journal,* Vol. XVI (March 1957), pp. 25-26.

_____. "Splendid Churches," two articles from *The Brooklyn Daily Times,* March 9 and 30, 1846. In Whitman, *The Gathering of the Forces; Editorials, Essays... Written by Walt Whitman as Editor of the Brooklyn Daily Eagle in 1846 and 1847.* 2 volumes. Edited by Cleveland Rogers and John Black. New York: J.P. Putnam Sons, 1920.

_____. "Tear Down and Build Again," *American Review,* Vol. II (November 1845), pp. 536-538. In Emory Holloway, *The Uncollected Poetry and Prose of Walt Whitman...* Garden City, NY: Doubleday, Page & Company, 1921, I, pp. 92-97.

Recent Papers and Articles:

Burnham, Alan. "The Dwelling in Greater Manhattan, 1850-1895." Unpublished paper. New York, c. 1953.

——————. "Last Look at a Structural Landmark," *Architectural Record*, Vol. CXX (September 1956), pp. 273-279.

——————. "The New York Architecture of Richard M. Hunt," *Journal of the Society of Architectural Historians*, Vol. XI (May 1952), pp. 9-14.

Hamlin, Talbot. "The Rise of Eclecticism in New York," *ibid.*, XI (May 1952), pp. 3-8.

Huxtable, Ada Louise. "Grand Central Depot, 1869-1871, New York, NY," *Progressive Architecture*, Vol. XXXVII (October 1956), pp. 135-138.

——————. "Harper and Brothers Building—1854, New York, NY," *ibid.*, Vol. XXXVIII (February 1957), pp. 153-154.

Landy, Jacob. "The Domestic Architecture of the 'Robber Barons' in New York City," *Marsyas*, Vol. V (1947-1949), pp. [63]-85.

Kramer, Ellen W. "Detlef Lienau, an Architect of the 'Brown Decades'," *Journal of the Society of Architectural Historians*, Vol. XIV (March 1955), pp. 18-25.

——————. "George Templeton Strong: Architectural Historian." Scarsdale, NY, 1953. 14-page typescript of excerpts from the *Diary* and "Journal". On deposit at the Avery Library and the New-York Historical Society.

Sturges, Walter Knight. "Cast-iron in New York," *Architectural Review*, Vol. CXIV (October 1953), pp. 232-237.

Weisman, Winston. "Commercial Palaces of New York: 1835-1875," *Art Bulletin*, Vol. XXXV (December 1954), pp. 285-302.

——————. "New York and the Problem of the First Skyscraper," *Journal of the Society of Architectural Historians*, Vol. XII (March 1953), pp. 13-20.

Editor's Epilogue.

History is a pageant of facts, shreds of facts, inferences, deductions, coincidences, inconsistencies, ironies, and opinions (usually a lot of them). History is also always unfinished. For every question answered, more questions seem to crop up. Here are a few of the questions and answers (and more questions) that came up while I was editing Ellen Kramer's dissertation:

Form follows function. Chicago architect Louis Sullivan has been credited as the author of the philosophy that "form follows function," which Ludwig Mies van der Rohe, another Chicago-based architect, picked up and amended slightly to read, "form *is* function". Even Frank Lloyd Wright, who also practiced in Chicago for many years at the beginning of his long and fruitful career, believed that all architecture should be organic in form—that is, inspired by and derived from nature. Sullivan introduced the phrase in an article he wrote in 1896, entitled "The Tall Office Building Artistically Considered". Yet, as we learned from Ellen Kramer's exploration, it was in fact Henri Labrouste who originated the philosophy in the early 1800s, when he said, "form must be appropriate to function and subordinated to the materials of construction" (see Chapter I).

L'Ecole des Beaux-Arts and architecture. The bubbling cauldron from which this great and pervasive philosophy originated was L'Ecole des Beaux-Arts in Paris, where many prominent European and American architects studied over the years and who, undoubtedly, heard the "fff" philosophy mentioned many times. Looking back at its history, we uncover an interesting irony.

Way back in 1648, a group of young French artists broke off from other artisans (with whom they had been grouped) and formed a union to establish the first French fine arts institution in Paris, modeled after existing institutions in Italy. Free to all students, it was called the Academie Royale de Peinture et de Sculpture, and it had two sections, one for art and one for architecture. The first class was given by 29-year-old Charles LeBrun on February 1, 1648, who told the large assembly of students, artists, and art enthusiasts to study works of art from Greek and Roman antiquity. The prestigious Prix de Rome competition was established in 1663 to encourage the development of classical tastes and to give students access to original classical artworks.

In 1816, the school was moved to its present location in the heart of Paris and, in 1863, it was renamed L'Ecole des Beaux-Arts.

(The official name is actually L'Ecole Nationale Superieure des Beaux-Arts, or ENSBA.) Ironically, architecture is no longer taught at the school. This program was discontinued as an instructional option following the student revolt of May 1968, at which time the 320-year-old tradition of the Prix de Rome competitions was also terminated.

Mansion saved by foresight and dedication. Of all the commissions earned and all the structures designed by Detlef Lienau, his most notable surely is the LeGrand Lockwood Mansion, now called the Lockwood-Mathews Mansion Museum in Norwalk, Connecticut. On many occasions, it came perilously close to being torn down, but somehow it survived. Today, although within a stone's throw of the New England Thruway (Interstate 95), it stands proudly as a symbol of an opulent era in American history. So many inner-city roads of the Interstate Highway System (developed by the Eisenhower administration in the 1950s and 1960s) destroyed thousands of these elegant homes in countless communities around the country—all in the name of "progress". In her dissertation, Kramer said that "even the demolition of some of these structures has a positive aspect: It mirrors faithfully the changing patterns of urban growth..." That it does, but time has also proven over and over again that the promised effect of demolishing these old structures has been a miserable failure, and in the process we have lost a treasure trove of architecture and the decorative arts.

(It is ironic that, while most larger, so-called enlightened cities in the United States have been quick to demolish their great old Victorian structures since the 1920s, many medium to small cities and communities have felt no similar need to replace these grand, and often ornate, edifices. So, happily, today these towns are able to please historic preservationists and often to yield for themselves a steady stream of heritage tourism dollars.)

Lienau family details are still sketchy. From my standpoint, Kramer provided few details about Lienau's death and his survivorships, although she did cite a number of tributes that were given to him after his death. Detlef Lienau was born on February 17, 1818, and died on August 29, 1887. On May 11, 1853, he married the former Catherine Van Giesen Booræm, who was born in 1819 and died on December 19, 1861. It was his first marriage and her second. Previously, she had been married to Francis Diedrichs, who died in 1844. Detlef and Catherine had five children: [Jacob] August, Detlef (Jr.), Catherine Cornelia, Lucy, and Louise. Eldest son J. August, who was born in March 1854 and died on May 6, 1906, followed in his father's footsteps and became an architect, designing mostly residential structures. Second son Detlef apparently didn't survive past childhood, and his burial site is unknown. Likewise, Lucy and Louise died young, and they are interred in Vault 182 at the New York City Marble Cemetery. The cemetery was co-founded in 1830 by Catherine's father Henry (or Hendrik) Booræm. He, his daughter Catherine and his three other children are buried in Vault 182, along with Diedrichs.

At his death, Detlef was survived by only his two sons. His youngest son J. Henry Lienau was born in 1871—10 years after the death of Detlef's wife Catherine—and he died on November 21, 1957, shortly before Kramer finished her dissertation. *The New York Times*, in its obituary on J. Henry Lienau (dated November 22, 1957), reported that he was survived by no direct descendants, but only his widow, the former Mrs. Adelaide B. Connfelt and her two sons by a previous marriage (Harry C. Cushing and Leonard J. Cushing). No mention at all was made of J. Henry's parents. But, we learn that he had graduated from Stevens Institute of Technology in Hoboken, New Jersey, as a mechanical engineer in 1891 and became a draftsman with the Robert Deeley Iron Works, which manufactured machinery for the sugar industry. That same year, he joined the American Sugar Refining Company in Brooklyn, which had earlier absorbed the F.O. Matthiessen & Wiechers Company. This is the firm that commissioned Detlef Lienau to design The Sugar House in Jersey City. In 1901, J. Henry Lienau transferred to the National Sugar Refining Company in New York, where he began writing several books on the sugar industry and articles for trade journals.

He too remained close to his father's profession, not only as an executive in the industry for which his father had done design and construction work, but also as an archivist of his father's architectural memorabilia. Ironically, it was J. Henry—not J. August, the architect—who demonstrated the initiative and dedication to collect, classify and donate his father's professional materials to the Avery Library at Columbia University.

Author lives out her philosophy. The worst example of wanton destruction of architectural monuments was in the early 1960s when the owners of the Penn Central Railroad decided to demolish the McKim, Mead & White-designed Penn Station in New York City. The monumental station had been in use for little more than a half century! Its sad demolition, however, galvanized public opinion to the degree that a new government agency was formed to make sure that building owners and developers would not—and could not—arbitrarily alter or destroy such historic structures. That agency was the New York City Landmarks Preservation Commission, which was established by Mayor Robert Wagner in 1965. A year later, Congress passed the National Historic Preservation Act.

Not surprisingly, Ellen Kramer had been active in the early landmarks preservation movement. She and Henry-Russell Hitchcock, her academic advisor, had helped found the Metropolitan New York Chapter of the Victorian Society in America, one of whose primary missions was (and still is) to ensure that important historic structures like Penn Station won't ever again fall to the dreaded wrecker's ball. And she began to work as a consultant to the New York City Landmarks Preservation Commission soon after it was established, then served as its Deputy Director of Research, with the responsibility for compiling the first edition of its now-popular *Guide to New York City Landmarks*.

At last, the book. Many people, therefore, played parts (big and small) in this long-developing saga, from Labrouste to Michael Lienau and Léon Marcotte, to Detlef Lienau's illustrious clients, to his two sons, to Talbot Hamlin, to Ellen Kramer, to Mimi Findlay, to me and Felix Kramer, and to many others impossible to mention here...

But at last, the book has been published—65 years after the idea for it was conceived by Ellen Kramer, and nearly 70 years after J. Henry Lienau graciously presented his father's professional and personal memorabilia to the Avery Library for all of us to appreciate.

Felix Kramer and I were fully aware that his mother's manuscript had been rendered somewhat imperfect by the passage of time. And most of the three dozen prominent 19th century architectural historians we consulted during the early stages of this project told us that the manuscript would not find a traditional institutional publisher. But we were compelled to have it published anyway. (To the few historians who did offer us encouragement, we are most grateful.)

Perhaps the publication of this book will now uncover new and vital information about other Lienau historic landmarks (both preserved and previously demolished), plus related structures, sites and neighborhoods, and his prominent and lesser patrons. About Lienau, most of the facts are here, and they are very well documented. Ellen Kramer's observations and opinions are also instructive and enlightening, whether you agree with them or not.

In sum, her efforts (and ours) offer a provocative and near-complete portrait of Detlef Lienau. But more than anything else, we are now proud to say—on Ellen Kramer's behalf—that the memory of Detlef Lienau and his work is now public and will most assuredly endure within the mainstream of architectural history.

Dale Chodorow
Chapel Hill, North Carolina

About the Author.

Ellen Weill Kramer grew up in a family of scholars and educators. She was born in New York City on February 2, 1915. Her father, Felix Weill, was chairman of the Department of Romance Languages at the College of the City of New York (now City College of New York). Her mother, Elsa Weill, was chairman of the German Department at Hunter College High School in New York. Because her father was one of nine children, she had a large circle of cousins whom she visited almost every summer during the long academic breaks. As a result, she also became trilingual in English, French, and German.

Her earliest professional training was at the Traphagen School of Fashion in New York from 1931 to 1933. In 1937, she earned a bachelor's degree in art history and French literature from Barnard College in New York. After a number of trips to Europe, including the entire year in 1938-1939, she earned a masters degree in art history from New York University in 1940.

After she earned her master's degree, Kramer worked briefly as a docent in the education department of the Metropolitan Museum of Art, conducting tours for school children and adults. In the 1941-1942 academic year, she served as a lecturer in the Fine Arts Department of Barnard College, where between 1944 and 1946 she also lectured in two introductory courses.

In the mid-'40s, inspired by Talbot F. Hamlin of Columbia University, she embarked on the pioneer inquiry into the life and work of Detlef Lienau, focusing on some 800 original drawings, photographs, and documents that comprise the Lienau Collection in the Avery Library of Columbia University. She researched and wrote her 429-page dissertation under the supervision of Hamlin and Henry-Russell Hitchcock of Smith College (her dissertation advisor), Carroll Meeks of Yale University, and Richard Krautheimer of New York University. She earned her doctoral degree in 1958 and, after some additional research, copyrighted her dissertation in 1961.

Coincidentally, Kramer had relatives named Lienau, as noted in footnote 2, Chapter I, where she expresses gratitude to her cousin, Eva Marie [Frau Werner] Lienau of Goslar, Germany. However, they weren't related to Detlef's part of the family.

During the 1940s and '50s, she wrote a number of articles for various publications on topics that included architectural historian George Templeton Strong; some of the forgotten founders (including Lienau) of the AIA; the *Hunt v. Parmly* case that established the legal rights of architects in the U.S.; the Ward House in Port Chester, NY, a pioneering structure in reinforced concrete; Harriet Beecher Stowe as an architectural and community-planning thinker and client; Walt Whitman as architectural critic; and the development of the apartment house system in New York City in the third quarter of the 19th century.

Kramer was a founding member of the Committee to Preserve Architectural Records (COPAR) and a lecturer at Queens College. She was an active member of the Society of Architectural Historians and, as noted, a founding member of the Metropolitan New York Chapter of the Victorian Society in America, its first.

Beginning in 1966, she was a consultant to the newly established New York City Landmarks Preservation Commission and, from 1972 to 1976, served as Deputy Director of Research with the Commission. As the Commission's purview evolved from designating individual buildings to protecting entire neighborhoods and districts, she became involved in developing the methodology for this expanding role. She was responsible not only for providing the documentary basis for designating Greenwich Village as a historic district, but also for compiling the first edition of the Commission's *Guide to New York City Landmarks* (1979), now a popular book among architects, historians and sightseers. She was also largely responsible for the Commission's first *Pocket Guide to New York City Landmarks*, a popular and free publication. Gerard Wolfe gave "special recognition" to her for her help in preparing his *New*

York: A Guide to the Metropolis, Walking Tours of Architecture and History (New York: McGraw-Hill, 1994).

In 1961, she became a founder and active member of Women Strike for Peace, based in Washington, DC, which began by promoting a ban on the testing of nuclear weapons and became a leading opponent of the war in Vietnam.

In the mid-'40s, she married George Kramer, a salesman and real estate broker, who was a graduate of Columbia University. They had two sons, Stephen Daniel Kramer and Lawrence Felix Kramer, both of whom now live in the San Francisco Bay area. (Felix and his wife Rochelle have a son Joshua, who was born in 1990.) From 1952 to 1988, the Kramer family lived in the northern part of Yonkers, NY (which had a Scarsdale mailing address). Her husband died in 1984, and four years later she moved back to Manhattan on the Upper West Side.

Ellen Kramer died on August 13, 1993. Her family published a brief death notice in the August 17 issue of *The New York Times*. She was cremated, and her ashes were scattered in Central Park, which she loved dearly.

About the Editor.

Dale Chodorow comes from a family that includes a number of writers, essayists, editors, playwrights and other men and women "of letters". He was born in Buffalo, New York, and as a youth spent a great deal of time admiring the large Victorian homes there, especially the half dozen or so that had been designed by Frank Lloyd Wright. (He wasn't aware at the time that one of Wright's most brilliant achievements—the Larkin Company administration building downtown—had been maliciously demolished in 1950.) Inspired by these homes and similar landmark structures, he decided to become an architect, just about the time that Wright died in the spring of 1959 at the age of 92.

In 1961, Chodorow enrolled in the School of Architecture at Carnegie Institute of Technology in Pittsburgh. One of his first assignments was to chair a student committee that was assigned to research and write a comprehensive report for developing a master plan for the borough of Ohiopyle, Pennsylvania. The small town was near Fallingwater, Wright's most famous commission for Pittsburgh department store magnate Edgar Kaufmann. That year, Chodorow also joined the staff of *The Carnegie Tartan*, the university's weekly newspaper and, a few months later, was called upon to write the front-page obituary on architect Henry Hornbostel, who died at the age of 94. Like Lienau, Hornbostel was a graduate of L'Ecole des Beaux-Arts in Paris. He had founded and served as chairman of the architectural school at "Carnegie Tech" and designed the master plan of the campus and many of its original academic and administrative buildings, plus many other noteworthy structures in Pittsburgh.

In the spring of 1964, despite having won an IAESTE fellowship to work at an architectural firm in the United Kingdom over the summer, Chodorow ended his formal architectural studies and transferred to the University of Pittsburgh, where he earned a bachelor's degree in English in 1967. During that time, he also worked as a staff writer with the *Pittsburgh Post-Gazette*. He then moved south to earn a master's degree in journalism from the University of North Carolina at Chapel Hill in 1970.

Later that year, Chodorow moved to New York to begin working as a public relations associate with the City University of New York. From 1972 to 1975, he served as director of public relations with the architectural firm of Gruzen & Partners, whose founder, Barnett Sumner ("Barney") Gruzen, FAIA, had also studied at L'Ecole des Beaux-Arts from 1930 to 1932. In 1973, with the help of Chodorow's promotional efforts, Barney Gruzen earned a Diamond Jubilee Award from the City of New York, which was presented by Mayor John V. Lindsay at the dedication of One Police Plaza downtown, one of about a dozen projects Gruzen & Partners had designed in the Manhattan Civic Center. In 1974, the firm earned the highest award in its history—the Medal of Honor for distinguished achievements in architecture and urban design, and outstanding contributions to the city, presented by the New York City Chapter of the American Institute of Architects. Three months later, Barney Gruzen died, and once again Chodorow had the responsibility of writing an obituary on a renowned architect.

In the late 1970s, Chodorow served as director of public relations with Sleepy Hollow Restorations in Tarrytown, New York (now Historic Hudson Valley, which has a publishing division that focuses on special-interest historical and literary works). While traveling in nearby Norwalk, Connecticut, he discovered and was overwhelmed by the 62-room post-Civil War mansion of LeGrand Lockwood, the largest and most opulent ever built in America to that day, which was designed by Detlef Lienau. Chodorow returned there often to observe its on-going restoration and traveled frequently throughout the northeast to visit other grand Victorian homes. But the name Detlef Lienau and his yet-undiscovered other works remained on his mind.

From the early 1980s through the mid-'90s, Chodorow held management positions with several industrial advertising agencies in New York, Connecticut and Indiana. He also served briefly as an adjunct faculty member in the School of Business at the University of Indianapolis. Throughout his career, he has written countless promotional publications for numerous clients, including several Fortune 500 companies, and has edited more than a dozen corporate and organizational magazines, newsletters and similar periodicals. Since 1997, he has served as publications and Website coordinator with the Chapel Hill/Orange County Visitors Bureau in North Carolina, and his numerous responsibilities have included research and writing about the history of Orange County and the many celebrities who have contributed to its development.

Chodorow and his wife Taffy live in Chatham County, about five miles south of Chapel Hill. Their son Harrison is a student at New York University, where coincidentally Ellen Kramer earned her doctoral degree.

Chodorow's discovery of Ellen Kramer's dissertation was one of those "Eureka!" moments, because he had searched for so many years for something—anything—about Lienau. A search on the Internet finally gave him the key reference he had been seeking. In early December 2003, after acquiring a copy of Kramer's dissertation and reading it during the Christmas holidays, he became increasingly interested in, and excited about, the possibility of seeing it published. So, early in January 2004, he began another search, this time for Kramer or her descendants, and—based only on the brief death notice that her family had placed in *The New York Times*—found one of her sons, Felix Kramer, in Redwood City, California. Once several emails had been exchanged, the two spoke for a long time on the phone and decided with great enthusiasm to embark on this project.

Index to Text Pages.

Production Note.

All of the text in this book was set in Garamond, ranging in size from 9 to 24 points. The typeface was designed by Paris-born Claude Garamond (1480-1561), the first independent designer and maker of printing types.

According to Loyalist College in Belleville, ON: "Because of the soundness of Garamond's designs, his typefaces have historical staying power, and they are likely to remain the day-to-day tools of professional typographers... Reading a well set Garamond text page is almost effortless, a fact that has been well known to book designers for over 450 years."

Our choice of Garamond would no doubt have pleased Mr. Lienau.